T0039153

Get the eBook FREE!

(PDF, ePub, Kindle, and liveBook all included)

We believe that once you buy a book from us, you should be able to read it in any format we have available. To get electronic versions of this book at no additional cost to you, purchase and then register this book at the Manning website.

Go to https://www.manning.com/freebook and follow the instructions to complete your pBook registration.

That's it!
Thanks from Manning!

Praise for the First Edition

A one-stop shop for anyone who wants a guided introduction, not only to React, but to the ecosystem of tools, concepts, and libraries surrounding it.

—Peter Cooper, Editor of *JavaScript Weekly*

Perfect for new React developers and seasoned veterans alike.

—Matthew Heck, TechChange

An absolutely engaging read, where theory meets practice!

—Dane Balia, Entelect

Excellent introduction for getting up to speed on React . . . quickly!

—Art Bergquist, Cognetic Technologies

This book is simple to follow. It uses very basic language that helps you understand each concept step by step.

—Israel Morales, SavvyCard

I finally understand how to utilize React, and it's awesome.

—Peter Hampton, Ulster University

React Quickly *is a great resource for coming up to speed with React. Very thorough and relevant. I'll be using it as a reference for my next app.*

—Nathan Bailey, SpringboardAuto.com

If you're new to React and would like to truly master it, I would look no further than this book.

—Richard Kho, Capital One

React Quickly

Second Edition

Morten Barklund
Azat Mardan

MANNING

Shelter Island

For online information and ordering of this and other Manning books, please visit
www.manning.com. The publisher offers discounts on this book when ordered in quantity.
For more information, please contact

>   Special Sales Department
>   Manning Publications Co.
>   20 Baldwin Road
>   PO Box 761
>   Shelter Island, NY 11964
>   Email: orders@manning.com

Manning Publications Co.	Development editor: Frances Lefkowitz
20 Baldwin Road	Technical development editor: Ninoslav Čerkez
PO Box 761	Review editor: Adriana Sabo
Shelter Island, NY 11964	Production editor: Kathleen Rossland
	Copy editor: Julie McNamee
	Proofreader: Katie Tennant
	Technical proofreader: Chris Villanueva
	Typesetter: Dennis Dalinnik
	Cover designer: Marija Tudor

ISBN: 9781633439290
Printed and bound by CPI Group (UK) Ltd, Croydon, CR0 4YY

To my wife and son, who inspire me to be a better person and writer. "Family is not an important thing, it's everything." (Michael J. Fox)

—Morten Barklund

To my grandfather, Khalit Khamitov. Thank you for being such a kind and just person. You will always stay in my memory, along with the crafts you taught me, the trips we took to the dacha, and the chess games we played.

—Azat Mardan

brief contents

1 ■ Meeting React   1

2 ■ Baby steps with React   23

3 ■ Introduction to JSX   62

4 ■ Functional Components   103

5 ■ Making React interactive with states   136

6 ■ Effects and the React component life cycle   182

7 ■ Hooks to fuel your web applications   214

8 ■ Handling events in React   228

9 ■ Working with forms in React   272

10 ■ Advanced React hooks for scaling   313

11 ■ Project: Website menu   350

12 ■ Project: Timer   379

13 ■ Project: Task manager   401

contents

preface   xv
acknowledgments   xvii
about this book   xix
about the authors   xxiii
about the cover illustration   xxiv

1 *Meeting React   1*

1.1 Benefits of using React   2

Simplicity   3 ▪ Speed and testability   8 ▪ Ecosystem and community   9

1.2 Disadvantages of React   10

1.3 How React can fit into your website   10

Single-page applications and React   12 ▪ The React stack   13

1.4 Your first React app: Hello World   15

The result   16 ▪ Writing the application   16 ▪ Installing and running a web server   19 ▪ Going to the local website   20

1.5 Quiz   21

Quiz answers   22

2   *Baby steps with React   23*

2.1   Creating a new React app   24

*React project commands   27 ▪ File structure   29
Templates   30 ▪ Pros and cons   31*

2.2   A note about the examples in this book   32

2.3   Nesting elements   33

Node hierarchy   35 ▪ Simple nesting   36 ▪ Siblings   38

2.4   Creating custom components   42

2.5   Working with properties   45

*A single property   46 ▪ Multiple properties   48 ▪ The special
property: children   52*

2.6   Application structure   55

2.7   Quiz   60

Quiz answers   60

3   *Introduction to JSX   62*

3.1   Why do we use JSX?   63

*Before and after JSX   63 ▪ Keeping HTML and JavaScript
together   64*

3.2   Understanding JSX   66

*Creating elements with JSX   66 ▪ Using JSX with custom
components   67 ▪ Multiline JSX objects   69 ▪ Outputting
variables in JSX   70 ▪ Working with properties in JSX   72
Branching in JSX   76 ▪ Comments in JSX   83 ▪ Lists of JSX
objects   84 ▪ Fragments in JSX   86*

3.3   How to transpile JSX   89

3.4   React and JSX gotchas   89

*Self-closing elements   90 ▪ Special characters   90 ▪ String
conversion   91 ▪ The style attribute   93 ▪ Reserved names: class
and for   94 ▪ Multiword attributes   94 ▪ Boolean attribute
values   95 ▪ Whitespace   97 ▪ data- attributes   100*

3.5   Quiz   101

Quiz answers   101

4   *Functional Components   103*

4.1   The shorter way to write React components   104

*An example application   105 ▪ Destructuring properties   109
Default values   111 ▪ Pass-through properties   113*

4.2   A comparison of component types   116

*Benefits of functional components   117 ▪ Disadvantages of
functional components   118 ▪ Nonfactors between component
types   118 ▪ Choosing the component type   118*

4.3   When not to use a functional component   119

*Error boundary   119 ▪ Codebase is class-based   120
Library requires class-based components   120 ▪ Snapshot
before updating   121*

4.4   Conversion from a class-based to a functional
       component   121

*Version 1: Render only   122 ▪ Version 2: Class method as
utility   125 ▪ Version 3: Real class method   128 ▪ Version 4:
Constructor   131 ▪ More complexity equals harder
conversion   133*

4.5   Quiz   134
       Quiz answers   134

5   **Making React interactive with states   136**

5.1   Why is React state relevant?   137

*React component state   139 ▪ Where should I put state?   139
What kind of information do you store in component state?   141
What not to store in state   142*

5.2   Adding state to a functional component   143

*Importing and using a hook   146 ▪ Initializing the state   148
Destructuring the state value and setter   154 ▪ Using the state
value   156 ▪ Setting the state   158 ▪ Using multiple states   169
State scope   172*

5.3   Stateful class-based components   176

*Similarities with the useState hook   178 ▪ Differences from the
useState hook   179*

5.4   Quiz   180
       Quiz answers   181

6   **Effects and the React component life cycle   182**

6.1   Running effects in components   183

*Running an effect on mount   185 ▪ Running an effect on mount
and cleanup on unmount   187 ▪ Running cleanup on
unmount   190 ▪ Running an effect on some renders   192*

Running an effect and cleanup on some renders 195
Running an effect synchronously 198

6.2 Understanding rendering 201

Rendering on mount 202 ▪ Rendering on parent render 203
Rendering on state update 205 ▪ Rendering inside functions 207

6.3 The life cycle of a class-based component 210

Life cycle methods 210 ▪ Legacy life cycle methods 211
Converting life cycle methods to hooks 211

6.4 Quiz 212

Quiz answers 213

7 *Hooks to fuel your web applications 214*

7.1 Stateful components 215

Simple state values with useState 216 ▪ Creating complex state
with useReducer 216 ▪ Remembering a value without re-rendering
with useRef 216 ▪ Easier multicomponent state with
useContext 220 ▪ Low-priority state updates with
useDeferredValue and useTransition 221

7.2 Component effects 222

7.3 Optimizing performance by minimizing re-rendering 222

Memoizing any value with useMemo 223 ▪ Memoizing functions
with useCallback 223 ▪ Creating stable DOM identifiers with
useId 223

7.4 Creating complex component libraries 223

Creating component APIs with useImperativeHandle 223
Better debugging of hooks with useDebugValue 224
Synchronizing non-React data with useSyncExternalStore 224
Running effect before rendering with useInsertionEffect 225

7.5 The two key principles of hooks 225

7.6 Quiz 225

Quiz answers 226

8 *Handling events in React 228*

8.1 Handling DOM events in React 230

Basic event handling in React 230

8.2 Event handlers 235

Definition of event handlers 236 ▪ Event objects 237
React event objects 239 ▪ Synthetic event object persistence 241

8.3   Event phases and propagation   243

How phases and propagation work in the browser   247
Handling event phases in React   250 ▪ Unusual event
propagation   250 ▪ Nonbubbling DOM events   251

8.4   Default actions and how to prevent them   251

The default event action   252 ▪ Preventing default   253
Other default events   255

8.5   React event objects in summary   255

8.6   Event handler functions from properties   256

8.7   Event handler generators   259

8.8   Listening to DOM events manually   260

Listening for window and document events   260 ▪ Dealing with
unsupported HTML events   263 ▪ Combining React and DOM
event handling   265

8.9   Quiz   270

Quiz answers   270

9   **Working with forms in React   272**

9.1   Controlled vs. uncontrolled inputs   274

9.2   Managing controlled inputs   275

Filtered input   277 ▪ Masked input   280 ▪ Many similar
inputs   282 ▪ Form submission   289 ▪ Other inputs   295
Other properties   302

9.3   Managing uncontrolled inputs   303

Opportunities   307 ▪ File inputs   310

9.4   Quiz   311

Quiz answers   311

10   **Advanced React hooks for scaling   313**

10.1   Resolving values across components   315

React Context   319 ▪ Context states   323 ▪ React Context
deconstructed   326

10.2   How to handle complex state   333

Interdependent state   335

10.3   Custom hooks   341

When is something a custom hook?   342 ▪ When should I use a
custom hook?   343 ▪ Where can I find custom hooks?   348

10.4   Quiz   348

Quiz answers   349

11   *Project: Website menu*   350

11.1   Scaffolding for the menu   353

HTML output   353 ▪ Component hierarchy   354 ▪ Icons   354
CSS   356 ▪ Template   357 ▪ Source code   358 ▪ In the
browser   359

11.2   Rendering a static menu   360

The goal of this exercise   361 ▪ Desired HTML output   361
Component tree   361 ▪ Source code   363 ▪ In the browser   364

11.3   Homework: A dynamic menu   364

Goal for this step   364 ▪ Hints for solving this step   365
Component hierarchy   365 ▪ What now?   366

11.4   Homework: Retrieving items from context   367

Goal for this step   367 ▪ Hints for solving this step   367
Component hierarchy   368 ▪ What now?   368

11.5   Homework: Optional link   370

Goal for this step   370 ▪ Hints for solving this step   372
Component hierarchy   376 ▪ What now?   376

11.6   Final thoughts   377

12   *Project: Timer*   379

12.1   Scaffolding for the timer   382

HTML output   383 ▪ Component hierarchy   385 ▪ Project
structure   386 ▪ Source code   387 ▪ Running the
application   390

12.2   Adding a simple play/pause timer   390

The goal of this exercise   390 ▪ Component hierarchy   391
Updated project structure   392 ▪ Source code   393
Running the application   396

12.3   Homework: Initializing the timer to a custom time   397

12.4   Homework: Resetting timers   398

12.5   Homework: Multiple timers   398

13   *Project: Task manager   401*

    13.1   Scaffolding for the task manager   405

       Component hierarchy   405 ▪ *Project structure   405*
       Source code   406 ▪ *Running the application   408*

    13.2   A simple list of tasks   408

       The goal of this exercise   408 ▪ *Component hierarchy   409*
       Updated project structure   410 ▪ *Source code   411*
       Running the application   417

    13.3   Homework: Task steps and progress   417

    13.4   Homework: Prioritization of steps   418

    13.5   Homework: Drag and drop   419

    13.6   Conclusion   420

    index   423

preface

Get ready for the ultimate love story! Boy meets library and, oh boy, does the library rock! It's love at first sight and the library is all in. Cue the happy ending because they are going to live happily ever after!

I had been working as a web developer for more than a decade, but I had always felt like there was something missing. I tried my hand at JavaScript, jQuery, and even Angular 1.0, but they just didn't cut it. Honestly, who wants to write spaghetti code that falls apart six months later?

But then, one day, I stumbled upon React, and it was an instant connection, an undeniable attraction that I couldn't ignore. From the moment I laid eyes on the library, I knew we were meant to be.

Suddenly, everything made sense. React's handling of components and data flow was exactly what I'd been searching for. Who knew that coding could be this exciting?

I dove headfirst into learning everything I could about React. I read documentation, watched tutorials, and built projects until my fingers bled. Okay, maybe not literally, but you get the point.

I just couldn't get enough of this new paradigm. I wanted to rewrite everything I had ever done. Once I really started to understand the deeper design philosophy behind this library, the attraction only grew deeper, becoming a lifelong relationship.

As fate would have it, years after my initial foray into the world of React, I stumbled across the charismatic Azat—a kindred spirit with an unbridled passion for this wondrous library. Imagine my delight when I discovered that Azat had even gone so far as to immortalize his love for React in a tome of epic proportions—the first edition of *React Quickly*.

Oh, how that book sang to my soul! With its practical examples, clear organization, and beginner-friendly approach, *React Quickly* was the perfect companion for any React enthusiast. The community showered it with praise and accolades, and rightfully so.

But, like any young prodigy, React continued to evolve and mature with each passing year. Then, on that fateful day in 2019, hooks arrived on the scene with a flurry of excitement and innovation. It was a game changer that completely revolutionized the way applications were coded.

And so it was that Azat and I joined forces to bring *React Quickly* into a new era, while keeping its original essence alive and thriving. With our energies aligned, we set out to craft a second edition that captured all the magic of React as it's used today. The structure and spirit of the first edition remain intact, while we've updated it to keep pace with the times. Oh, what a joy it is to share our love for React with the world!

—MORTEN BARKLUND

acknowledgments

We would like to express our deepest gratitude to the team at the publishing house who helped make this book a reality. At the forefront is our main editor, Frances Lefkowitz, who tirelessly helped us shape and polish the text, making it accessible and useful to readers of all levels. Her invaluable insights and guidance have been critical to producing a book that we are truly proud of.

We also want to extend a special thank you to our acquisition editor, Andy Waldron, who believed in this project from the beginning and helped us navigate the complex world of publishing.

A special thanks goes to our tech editor, Ninoslav Čerkez, who provided meticulous technical feedback and helped ensure that the code examples and explanations are accurate and up to date. We are also indebted to our tech proofer, Chris Villanueva, for his careful technical proofreading, which caught countless errors and inconsistencies.

We also want to give a special shout-out to our copy editor, Julie McNamee, for her stellar work on the manuscript. She's not just a grammar expert, but a linguistic wizard who made sure all our excess adverbs *really* were *actually* removed—leaving the text more concise and punchy. Thanks, Julie!

Thank you, our reviewers: Amit Lamba, Andres Sacoo, Bernard Fuentes, Brendan O'Hara, Brent Boylan, Chris Villanueva, Danilo Zeković, Derick Hitchcock, Fernando Bernardino, Francisco Rivas, Ganesh Swaminathan, Harsh Raval, James Bishop, Jason Hales, Jeff Smith, John Pantoja, Karthikeyarajan Rajendran, Kelum Prabath Senanayake, Kent Spillner, Larry Cai, Matt Deimel, Matteo Battista, Michelle Williamson, Mick Wilson, Miranda Whurr, Nitendra Bhosle, Nouran Mahmoud, Patrice Maldague, Pieter

Gyselinck, Richard Harriman, Richard Tobias, Rodney Weis, Roman Zhuzha, Saioa Picado Fernández, Santosh Joseph, Thefanis Despoudis, and Yves Dorfsman—your suggestions helped make this a better book.

Thank you all for your dedication, hard work, and expertise. We couldn't have done this without you.

about this book

This book aims to take the reader from a React novice to an experienced React practitioner. It's a comprehensive guide to React fundamentals, designed to help both beginners and experienced developers master the core concepts of this popular library, such as JavaScript XML (JSX), components, state, hooks, events, and form elements.

Overall, this book is an essential resource for anyone looking to build React applications, regardless of their experience level. By providing a strong foundation in the core concepts of React, the book can help developers write clean, maintainable code that is easy to understand and extend.

React Quickly, Second Edition, will teach you all the fundamentals you need to design clean, effective, and easy-to-update web applications using React. As you'll see, the React ecosystem of tools and libraries is enormous. After finishing this book and working through the projects, you may decide you want to continue to build on your skills with an eye toward advancing your career. If so, check out *Job-Ready React* by Morten Barklund (Manning, 2024), which builds on the skills and methodologies taught in this book. It will get you *job-ready* by introducing the advanced libraries, techniques, and tools used by professional React developers.

Audience

For beginners, the book provides practical examples and exercises that can help them build their first React applications and gain a solid understanding of how React works. The book offers step-by-step guidance on how to build React applications from scratch, with practical examples and exercises that reinforce the concepts.

For experienced developers, the book serves as a useful reference and refresher on the fundamental concepts of React. This can be particularly helpful for those who may have learned React in a less structured way or who want to deepen their understanding of React best practices.

To make the most of this book, it's helpful to have a bit of experience with HTML, CSS, and JavaScript, but you don't need to be a master of these skills. Importantly, you don't need any prior knowledge of React at all—we'll start at the beginning and guide you all the way through building complex applications with confidence!

Roadmap

The book is structured with 10 subject matter chapters followed by 3 project chapters at the end. The first 10 chapters are designed to build on one another in a natural progression. For those who are new to React, we recommend that you read these chapters in sequence to get the most out of the learning experience.

However, if you already have some experience with React, feel free to skip around. Chapters 1 through 4 introduce React and some core concepts such as component structure, JSX, and functional components. These chapters may be skippable if you're already familiar with these topics.

Chapters 5 through 7 introduce various hooks, starting with the basic state hook in chapter 5, effect hooks in chapter 6, and a brief introduction to all the other hooks in chapter 7. Chapters 8 and 9 cover events and forms, respectively. Understanding events is crucial before diving into form input–handling practices.

Chapter 10 builds further on all the previous concepts by introducing some advanced component and logic patterns that you might encounter in more complex applications.

Finally, chapters 11 through 13 are project chapters, where you can put your newfound knowledge to the test in three guided projects of increasing complexity. You'll build an interactive website menu, a timer, and a feature-rich task manager. If you're already experienced with React, you might want to start with these projects to see where your knowledge gaps lie.

Source code

All the source code used in the book is available on GitHub as well as on the book's accompanying website. The latter includes an online source code browser where you can not only *see* and *download* the source code for every single example but also *run* the resulting application right in the browser without downloading anything. The GitHub repository is available at https://github.com/rq2e/rq2e, and the source code browser can be found at https://reactquickly.dev/browse.

You can get executable snippets of code from the liveBook (online) version of this book at https://livebook.manning.com/book/react-quickly-second-edition. The complete code for the examples in the book is also available for download from the Manning website at www.manning.com/books/react-quickly-second-edition.

This book contains many examples of source code both in numbered listings and in line with normal text. In both cases, source code is formatted in a `fixed-width font like this` to separate it from ordinary text.

In many cases, the original source code has been reformatted; we've added line breaks and reworked indentation to accommodate the available page space in the book. In rare cases, even this wasn't enough, and listings include line-continuation markers (➥). Code annotations accompany many of the listings, highlighting important concepts.

Software requirements

To use and run the examples and projects in this book, you only need two things:

- A command-line environment with a recent version of Node.js and npm installed
- A text editor

That's it! Now, let us show you how to quickly set up your command-line environment and select a text editor, so you'll be ready for the first exercises in chapter 1.

Command-line environment with Node.js and npm

First, you want to check if you already have compatible versions of Node.js and npm installed. You need at least Node.js version 12 to use the examples in this book.

In Windows:

- Open the Command Prompt or PowerShell by pressing the Windows key-R and typing `cmd` or `powershell` in the Run dialog box.
- Type `node -v` in the Command Prompt, and press Enter.
- If you have Node.js installed, it will display the version number.

In macOS and Unix-like systems:

- Open the Terminal app.
- Type `node -v` in the terminal, and press Enter.
- If you have Node.js installed, it will display the version number.

If you don't have Node.js installed or your version is older than 12, go to https://nodejs.org/en/download, download the proper package for your operating system, and follow the installation instructions.

If you're a power user of your operating system, feel free to use any other package manager to install Node.js, as long as you get at least version 12.

Text editor

You probably already possess a text editor or have prior experience using one, given your familiarity with JavaScript, HTML, and CSS, which are crucial to make the most out of this book. However, in case you don't have a text editor installed, here are some widely used options that are compatible with most platforms:

- Sublime Text: www.sublimetext.com/download (free trial)
- Brackets: https://brackets.io/ (open source and free)
- Visual Studio Code: https://code.visualstudio.com/ (free)

liveBook discussion forum software requirements

Purchase of *React Quickly, Second Edition*, includes free access to liveBook, Manning's online reading platform. Using liveBook's exclusive discussion features, you can attach comments to the book globally or to specific sections or paragraphs. It's a snap to make notes for yourself, ask and answer technical questions, and receive help from the authors and other users. To access the forum, go to https://livebook.manning.com/book/react-quickly-second-edition/discussion. You can also learn more about Manning's forums and the rules of conduct at https://livebook.manning.com/discussion.

Manning's commitment to our readers is to provide a venue where a meaningful dialogue between individual readers and between readers and the authors can take place. It's not a commitment to any specific amount of participation on the part of the authors, whose contribution to the forum remains voluntary (and unpaid). We suggest you try asking them some challenging questions lest their interest stray! The forum and the archives of previous discussions will be accessible from the publisher's website as long as the book is in print.

about the authors

MORTEN BARKLUND, an independent software engineer, works as a lead developer in various teams, including an open source React project funded by Google. With a degree in computer science from the Technical University of Denmark, Morten has been actively involved in the web community for more than two decades and has worked on hundreds of projects.

AZAT MARDAN is an author of best-selling books on JavaScript, React, and Node.js, including *React Quickly, First Edition*; *Practical Node.js*, *Pro Express.js*, *Full Stack JavaScript*, and *100 TypeScript Mistakes*. He is a visiting professor at a technology university, startup mentor, and a software engineer/leader with experience in small startups and large corporations, including YouTube, Google, Capital One, Indeed, and DocuSign. Azat has taught many workshops and courses, including a course on edX with more than 40,000 international students. At one point, Azat was awarded Microsoft Most Valuable Professional in Developer Technologies, and was the 239th most active GitHub contributor in the world. He spoke at more than 30 conferences worldwide, keynoted, and shared the stage with prominent technologists such as Douglas Crockford, Jeff Atwood (cocreator of Stack Overflow), Jim Jagielski (creator of Apache), Scott Hanselman, and Danese Cooper.

about the cover illustration

The figure on the cover of *React Quickly, Second Edition*, is "Homme Baschkir," or "Bashkir man," taken from a collection by Jacques Grasset de Saint-Sauveur, published in 1788. Each illustration is finely drawn and colored by hand.

In those days, it was easy to identify where people lived and what their trade or station in life was just by their dress. Manning celebrates the inventiveness and initiative of the computer business with book covers based on the rich diversity of regional culture centuries ago, brought back to life by pictures from collections such as this one.

Meeting React 1

This chapter covers

- Understanding what React is
- Solving problems with React
- Fitting React into your web applications
- Writing your first React web app: Hello World

React is the groundbreaking tool that web developers may not even know they need, but can't let go of once they've tried. This is definitely true for the two authors of this book, as well as for many other enthusiastic web developers out there. React is immensely popular—and for good reason.

If you were doing web development in the early 2000s, all you needed was some HTML and a server-side language such as Perl or PHP. Ah, the good old days of putting in `alert()` boxes just to debug your frontend code. The internet has evolved a lot since then, and the complexity of building websites has increased dramatically. Websites have become web applications with complex user interfaces (UIs), business logic, and data layers that require changes and updates over time—and often in real time.

Many JavaScript template libraries have been written to try to solve the problems of complex UIs. But they still require developers to adhere to the old separation of concerns—which splits style (Cascading Style Sheets [CSS]), data and structure (HTML), and dynamic interactions (JavaScript)—and they don't meet modern-day needs (remember DHTML?).

In contrast, React offers a new approach, which, when used correctly, streamlines frontend web development. React is a powerful UI library offering an alternative that many big firms such as Facebook, Netflix, and Airbnb have adopted and see as the way forward. Instead of defining a one-off template for your UIs, React allows you to create reusable UI components in JavaScript that you can use again and again on your sites.

Do you need a captcha control or date picker? Use React to define a `<Captcha />` or `<DatePicker />` component that you can add to your form: a simple drop-in component with all the functionality and logic to communicate with the backend. Do you need an autocomplete box that asynchronously queries a database once the user has typed four or more letters? Define an `<Autocomplete charNum="4"/>` component to make that asynchronous query. You can choose whether it has a text box UI or has no UI and instead uses another custom form element—perhaps `<Autocomplete textbox="..." />`.

This approach isn't new. Creating composable UIs has been around for a long time, but React is the first to use pure JavaScript without templates to make this possible. And this approach has proven easier to maintain, reuse, and extend.

React is a great library for building UIs, and it should be part of your frontend web toolkit, but it isn't a complete solution for all frontend web development. We'll spend part of this chapter looking at the pros and cons of using React in your applications and how React might fit into your existing web development stack.

In this book, we'll cover the basics of React and no more, providing readers with a solid foundation in the core concepts and principles of the React library without delving into any external or advanced topics. By focusing solely on React, readers will gain a comprehensive understanding of its capabilities and be well equipped to apply their knowledge to a wide range of web development projects.

> **NOTE** The source code for the example in this chapter is available at https://rq2e.com/ch01.

1.1 Benefits of using React

Every new library or framework claims to be better than its predecessors in some respect. In the beginning, we had jQuery, and it was leaps and bounds better for writing cross-browser code in native JavaScript. If you remember JavaScript from the old days, a single server request would take many lines of code, as it had to account for Internet Explorer and WebKit-like browsers. With jQuery, this took only a single line: `$.ajax()`, for example. Back in the day, jQuery was in some respects known as a framework—but not anymore! Now a framework is something bigger and more powerful.

Similarly, with Backbone and then Angular, each new generation of JavaScript frameworks has brought something new to the table. React isn't unique in this. What is new is that React challenges some of the core concepts used by most popular front-end frameworks, for example, the idea that you need to have templates.

The following list highlights some of the benefits of React versus other libraries and frameworks that existed at the time React emerged:

- *Simpler web apps*—React uses a component-based architecture (CBA) with pure JavaScript; a declarative style; and powerful, developer-friendly Document Object Model (DOM) abstractions (and not just DOM, but also iOS, Android, etc.).
- *Fast UIs*—React provides outstanding performance thanks to its virtual DOM and smart reconciliation algorithm, which, as a side benefit, lets you perform testing without spinning up (starting) a headless browser.
- *Less code to write*—React's great community and vast ecosystem of components provide developers with a variety of libraries and components. This is important when you're considering what framework to use for development.

Many features made React simpler to work with than most other frontend frameworks available in its infancy. However, many new frameworks have spawned since React came around. Partially due to the popularity of React, some of these new frameworks have been developed with similar benefits or thoughts, each slightly altered in different ways. Some other frameworks might just be inspired by the overall idea, but work completely differently, whereas others are very similar to React, just with a smaller feature set requiring you to sometimes write more code, but other times end up with a much smaller application codebase.

We'll consider the benefits that make React popular. These are the main selling points of React, and they made the framework unique at its introduction, although other modern frameworks have similar benefits today. Let's start to unpack these benefits one by one, starting with how wonderfully simple React is to use.

1.1.1 Simplicity

The concept of simplicity in computer science is highly valued by developers and users, but it doesn't equate to ease of use. Something simple can be hard to implement, but in the end, it will be more elegant and efficient. And often, an easy thing will end up being complex. Simplicity is closely related to the KISS principle (keep it simple, stupid). The gist is that simpler systems work better.

React's approach allows for simpler solutions via a dramatically better web development experience for software engineers. When we began working with React, it was a considerable shift in a positive direction that reminded us of switching from using plain, no-framework JavaScript to jQuery.

In React, this simplicity is achieved with the following features:

- *Declarative over imperative style*—React embraces declarative style over imperative by updating views automatically.

- *CBA using pure JavaScript*—React doesn't use domain-specific languages (DSLs) for its components, just pure JavaScript. And there's no separation when working on the same functionality.
- *Powerful abstractions*—React has a simplified way of interacting with the DOM, allowing you to normalize event handling and other interfaces that work similarly across browsers.

Let's cover these features one by one.

DECLARATIVE OVER IMPERATIVE STYLE

Declarative style means developers write *how it should be*, not *what to do*, step by step (imperative). But why is the declarative style a better choice? The benefit is that the declarative style reduces complexity and makes your code easier to read and understand.

The distinction between imperative and declarative coding styles can quickly become academic to some extent. When taken to the extreme, declarative programming can become really complex to read unless you understand some fairly complex concepts well, such as monads and functors. Here are a few different ways to describe the difference between the two styles:

- *Statements versus expressions*—Imperative-style programming often works with independent statements that individually advance the program state, while declarative programming uses expressions that build upon each other to progress the flow of logic.
- *Reserved word usage*—Imperative-style programming often uses many reserved words such as for, while, switch, if, and else, while declarative-style programming uses array methods, arrow functions, object access, Boolean expressions, and ternary operators to achieve the same results.
- *Function composition*—Imperative-style programming often uses independent function calls and method invocations, while declarative-style programming uses function composition to build upon the previous expression and make small generalized pieces of logic that, when composed, achieve the desired result.
- *Mutability*—Imperative-style programming often uses mutable objects and manipulates existing structures, while declarative-style programming uses immutable data and creates new structures from old ones rather than editing existing ones.

Let's create a simple example to illustrate these different points. The goal of this task is to create a function, countGoodPasswords, that, given a list of passwords, will return how many of the passwords are *good*. Here, we'll define a *good* password as any password at least nine characters long.

This is a great simple task that can be solved in any programming language in a multitude of ways. Some programming languages inherently make one style more natural to reach for, but JavaScript is a bit special, as it's a member of both worlds. You can solve this task either imperatively or declaratively.

Let's start with a (very) naive imperative solution:

```
function countGoodPasswords(passwords) {
  const goodPasswords = [];
  for (let i = 0; i < passwords.length; i++) {
    const password = passwords[i];
    if (password.length < 9) {
      continue;
    }
    goodPasswords.push(password);
  }
  return goodPasswords.length;
}
```

New statement changes the program state (pointing to `const goodPasswords = [];`, `const password = passwords[i];`, and `goodPasswords.push(password);`)

Reserved word controls program flow (pointing to the `for` loop and `if` block)

Mutates an existing object (pointing to `goodPasswords.push(password);`)

This is, of course, partially taken to an extreme, and even under a fully imperative programming paradigm, this could be much shorter.

Let's implement this same example using a declarative programming mindset:

```
function countGoodPasswords(passwords) {
  return passwords.filter(p => p.length >= 9).length;
}
```

We arrive directly at the goal in a single statement by manipulating an object in several steps, using function composition to arrive at the target. We filter the original array to arrive at a temporary value, which is the array of only good passwords. However, we never store this array anywhere; we go directly to the next step of taking the length of that array.

That was just some generic JavaScript code. How does this relate to React? React takes the same declarative approach when you compose UIs. First, React developers describe UI elements in a declarative style. Then, when there are changes to views generated by those UI elements, React takes care of the updates. Yay!

The convenience of React's declarative style fully shines when you need to make changes to the view. Those are called changes of the *internal state*. When the state changes, React updates the view accordingly.

NOTE We'll cover how states work in chapter 5.

COMPONENT-BASED ARCHITECTURE USING PURE JAVASCRIPT

CBA existed before React came on the scene. Separation of concerns, loose coupling, and code reuse are at the heart of this approach because it provides many benefits; software engineers, including web developers, love CBA. A building block of CBA in React is the component class. As with other CBAs, it has many benefits, with code reuse being the main one (you can write less code!).

What was lacking before React was a pure JavaScript implementation of this architecture. When you're working with Angular, Backbone, Ember, or most of the other Model-View-Controller (MVC)-like frontend frameworks, you have one file for JavaScript and another for the template. (Angular uses the term *directives* for components.)

There are a few problems with having two languages (and two or more files) for a single component. The HTML and JavaScript separation worked well when you had to render HTML on the server, and JavaScript was only used to make your text blink. Now, *single-page applications* (SPAs) handle complex user input and perform rendering on the browser. This means HTML and JavaScript are closely coupled functionally. For developers, it makes more sense not to require separation of HTML and Java-Script when working on a piece of a project (component).

Under the hood, React uses a *virtual DOM* to find differences (the delta) between what's already in the browser and the new view. This process is called *DOM diffing* or *reconciliation of state and view* (bringing them back to similarity). This means developers don't need to worry about explicitly changing the view; all they need to do is update the state, and the view will be updated automatically as needed. You'll see us implicitly using this concept over and over in the book. We never do DOM manipulation directly; we let React do that work for us.

Conversely, with jQuery, you'd need to implement updates imperatively. By manipulating the DOM, developers can programmatically modify parts of the web page without re-rendering the entire page. DOM manipulation is what you do when you invoke jQuery methods.

Think of the help provided by the underlying framework on a scale as shown in figure 1.1. At one end of the scale, you have a "framework" that doesn't actually help you at all. If you built your application in plain JavaScript, you would be at this extreme. Using jQuery would make it easier to manipulate the DOM, but you would still have no help from the framework when things update. You would have to manually make sure that your jQuery views update when your jQuery data updates.

Figure 1.1   How much does the framework help you? jQuery does nothing; Angular does it all. For some, React hits the sweet spot in between.

At the other end of the scale, we have frameworks such as Angular, which is another very popular framework and comparable to React in every way. However, Angular works in a fundamentally different way with a lot more "magic" happening behind the scenes. You often merely described how your components fit together, and Angular will try to connect things correctly behind the scenes. The problem with Angular is that you often lose the desired fine-grained control if things don't work correctly. Many things are hidden from you, which makes things unnecessarily complex.

React strikes that happy medium, where the framework helps you with a lot of the tedious work of connecting various things behind the scenes, but without locking you out of the fine-grained control required to make complex web applications. This is obviously a subjective opinion, but we're not alone in feeling that way.

POWERFUL ABSTRACTIONS

React comes with the following great abstractions that make life as a React developer easier:

- Synthetic events abstracting out browser differences in native events
- JavaScript XML (JSX) abstracting out the JS DOM
- Browser independence allowing rendering in nonbrowser environments (e.g., on the server)

React has a powerful abstraction of the browser event model. In other words, it hides the underlying interfaces and provides normalized/synthesized methods and properties. For example, when you create an onClick event in React, instead of the event handler receiving a native browser–specific event object, it receives a synthetic event object that's a wrapper around native event objects. You can expect the same behavior from synthetic events regardless of the browser in which you run the code. React also has a set of synthetic events for touch events, which are great for building web apps for mobile devices.

Then there's JSX, which is one of the more controversial elements of React. For some, the abstraction of JSX is a strong argument *for* using React, while JSX has been a stumbling block or even a deterrent for others.

If you're familiar with Angular, then you've already had to write a lot of JavaScript in your template code because, in modern web development, plain HTML is too static and is hardly any use by itself. Our advice is to give React the benefit of the doubt and give JSX a fair run.

JSX is a bit of *syntactic sugar* on top of JavaScript for writing React elements in JavaScript using HTML-like notation with <>. React pairs nicely with JSX because developers can better implement and read the code. Think of JSX as a mini-language that's compiled into native JavaScript. So, JSX isn't run on the browser but is used as the source code for compilation. Here's a compact snippet written in JSX:

```
if (user.session) {
  return <a href="/logout">Logout</a>;
} else {
  return <a href="/login">Login</a>;
}
```

Even if you load a JSX file in your browser with the runtime transformer library that compiles JSX into native JavaScript on the run, you still don't run the JSX; you run JavaScript instead. In this sense, JSX is akin to CoffeeScript. You compile these languages into native JavaScript to get better syntax and features than that provided by regular JavaScript.

We know that to some of you, it looks bizarre to have HTML interspersed within JavaScript code. It takes every new React developer (including us) a while to adjust because we're expecting an avalanche of syntax error messages. And yes, using JSX is optional. For these two reasons, we aren't covering JSX until chapter 3. Trust us, though—it's very powerful and even addictive once you get familiar with it.

Another example of React's DOM abstraction is that you can render React elements on the server. This can be handy for better search engine optimization (SEO) and improving performance.

There are many options when it comes to rendering React components in both DOM and HTML strings on the server. You can even use hybrid approaches where your templates are rendered with some content on the server and later rehydrated with live data in the browser. We'll talk a lot more about this in section 1.3. And, speaking of the DOM, one of the most sought-after benefits of React is its splendid performance.

1.1.2   *Speed and testability*

In addition to the necessary DOM updates, your framework may perform unnecessary updates, which makes the performance of complex UIs even worse. This becomes especially noticeable and painful for users when you have a lot of dynamic UI elements on your web page.

On the other hand, React's virtual DOM exists only in the JavaScript memory. Every time there's a data change, React first compares the differences using its virtual DOM; only when the library knows there has been a change in the rendering will it update the actual DOM. Figure 1.2 shows a high-level overview of how React's virtual DOM works when there are data changes.

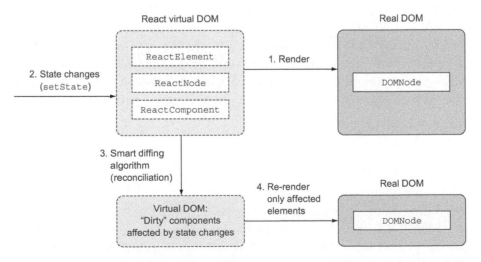

Figure 1.2   Once a component has been rendered, if its state changes, it's compared to the in-memory virtual DOM and re-rendered if necessary.

Ultimately, React updates only those parts that are necessary so that the internal state (virtual DOM) and the view (real DOM) are the same. For example, if there's a <p> element, and you augment the text via the state of the component, only the text will be updated (i.e., innerHTML), not the element itself. This results in increased performance compared to re-rendering entire sets of elements or, even more so, entire pages (server-side rendering).

The geeky details of reconciliation

If you like to geek out on algorithms and Big O notation, these two articles do a great job of explaining how the React team managed to turn an $O(n^3)$ problem into an $O(n)$ one:

- "Reconciliation," on the React website (http://mng.bz/PQ9X)
- "React's Diff Algorithm" by Christopher Chedeau (http://mng.bz/68L4)

The added benefit of the virtual DOM is that you can do unit testing without headless browsers such as PhantomJS (http://phantomjs.org). There are several libraries out there, including Jest and React Testing Library, that allow you to test your components directly from the command line. We'll obsess quite a bit more on unit testing React components and hooks in later chapters.

1.1.3 Ecosystem and community

Last, but not least, React is supported by the developers of the juggernaut web application called Facebook, as well as by their peers at Instagram. As with Angular and some other libraries, having a big company behind the technology provides a sound testing ground (it's deployed to millions of browsers), reassurance about the future, and an increase in contribution velocity. This is, of course, also a risk because if Facebook suddenly wants to take React in a new direction, you might get stranded if you don't like that direction, so weigh your options carefully.

A lot of great content already exists that has been created for React by the community. You'll find that when you need some kind of component or interface, you can just search the web for "react [name-of-component]", and more than 95% of the time, you'll find something worthwhile.

The history of open source software clearly shows that the marketing of open source projects is as important to its wide adoption and success as the code itself. By that, we mean that if a project has a poor website, lacks documentation and examples, or has an ugly logo, most developers won't take it seriously—especially now, when there are so many JavaScript libraries. Developers are picky, and they won't use an ugly duckling library.

As the saying goes, "Don't judge a book by its cover." This might sound controversial, but, sadly, most people, including software engineers, are prone to biases such as good branding. Luckily, React has a great engineering reputation backing it. And, speaking of book covers, we hope you didn't buy this book just for its cover!

1.2   Disadvantages of React

Of course, almost everything has its drawbacks. This is true with React, but the full list of cons depends on whom you ask. Some of the differences, such as declarative versus imperative, are highly subjective. They can be both pros and cons depending on your personal preference. Here's our list of React's disadvantages (as with any such list, it may be biased):

- *React isn't a full-blown, Swiss Army knife–type of framework.* Developers need to pair it with a library such as Redux or XState to achieve functionality comparable to Angular or Ember. This can also be an advantage if you need a minimalistic UI library to integrate with your existing stack.
- *React stacks require maintenance and continuous package management.* Because you never use React only on its own, but almost always combine it with several other packages, you need to constantly maintain your dependencies and make sure you're using the correct versions of various packages. In larger projects, this can become a significant source of extraneous tasks.
- *React uses a somewhat new approach to web development, and JSX and functional programming can be intimidating to beginners.* Especially in the early days, there was a lack of best practices, good books, courses, and resources available for mastering React and similar frameworks. We'll discuss JSX in much more detail in chapter 3.
- *React only has a one-way binding.* Although one-way binding is better for complex web apps and removes a lot of complexity, some developers (especially Angular developers) who got used to a two-way binding will find themselves writing a bit more code. We'll explain how React's one-way binding works compared to Angular's two-way binding in chapter 9, which covers working with form data.
- *React isn't reactive (as in reactive programming and architecture, which are more event-driven, resilient, and responsive) out of the box.* Developers need to use other libraries, such as the React Query library, to make their applications integrate with external content seamlessly and responsively. This also requires developers to use a different mindset when developing React applications, or terribly coded applications will result from attempting to force a round React into a square architecture.

To continue with this introduction to React, let's look at how it fits into a web application.

1.3   How React can fit into your website

Websites come in many variants, and React can be used to create interactive content in many types of websites, either as a replacement for other technologies or as a way to add new functionality to your website. React can be used on both "classic" websites that are mostly rendered by a server as well as client-side web applications, also known as single-page applications (SPAs), as mentioned earlier.

The React core library is a UI library first and foremost. The core library alone is comparable to other UI libraries, but not directly comparable to more full-fledged web application frameworks such as Angular. However, combined with other libraries, either developed by the React team or other parties (e.g., React Router and Redux), React can be a full competitor to any web application framework.

If you're using another SPA framework (e.g., Angular, Vue, Ember, Backbone, etc.) to render your web application today, you'll probably need to replace the entire thing with a React-based stack. It's very difficult and bordering on impossible to create a hybrid SPA with some parts rendered by, for example, Angular, and others by React.

You can use React for just part of your UI if you have a website with smaller interactive UI elements (or *widgets*). In such a case, you can replace your widgets one by one with small React applications, without changing everything else. These existing widgets might be written in plain JavaScript, jQuery, or even Angular or similar frameworks. As you go along converting widgets to React, you can evaluate the best fit for your organization.

React is backend agnostic for frontend development. In other words, you don't have to rely on a JavaScript-based backend (Node or Deno) to use React. It's fine to use React with any other backend technology, such as Java, Ruby, Go, or Python. React is a UI library, after all. You can integrate it with any backend and any frontend data library (Backbone, Angular, Meteor, etc.).

Another popular use case for React is for static site generators. In such a setup, React is used to define your website locally on your environment, but when deployed to the live server, it's rendered "down" to a plain HTML website with JavaScript only doing a minimal bit of work to add interactivity. All your templates, and so on, will have been resolved. Initially, this was mostly popular for smaller websites, such as blogs, which don't update too frequently.

Recent advances in server-side React rendering have made this pre-rendered approach more and more popular even for larger SPAs that update often. You can do this with popular frameworks built on top of React, such as Next.js or Remix. These are considered *partially server-rendered web applications*, where your React code runs on both the server and in the client. You might, for example, pre-render a list on the server and add interactive filtering and sorting options in the client. This can sound a bit daunting, but newer frameworks such as Next.js and Remix make it relatively easy.

To summarize how React fits into a website, it's most often used in these scenarios:

- As a UI library in an SPA, such as React+React Router+Redux
- As a drop-in widget in any frontend stack, such as a React autocomplete input component in a website built using any other combination of technologies
- As a static website rendered on deployment to serve infrequently updated content

- As a partially server-side-rendered website or SPA built on top of a more powerful framework potentially fed content by an external CMS, such as WordPress or Contentful
- As a UI library in mobile apps using React Native, or desktop apps using Electron

React works nicely with some frontend technologies, but it's mostly used as a part of SPAs. We cover how React fits into an SPA in the next section.

1.3.1   *Single-page applications and React*

SPAs are a subset of websites in general. A website is considered an SPA if it has a lot of functionality directly available in the browser and not just information. Examples include Facebook, Google Docs, Gmail, and so on.

SPAs are built using a multitude of technologies, of which React is only one potential part in the stack. You can't even use React alone; at least a few other technologies are needed for React to be usable as a standalone application. In this section, we'll establish what an SPA is in general and then point out how React fits into this structure.

SPAs are also known as *thick clients* because the browser, being a client, holds more logic and performs functions such as rendering of the HTML, validation, UI changes, and so on. Contrast this with a thin client, where the browser client is only used to display information that has been pre-rendered by a server. In a thin client, the browser does very little work.

Figure 1.3 is a very high-level example of a generic SPA regardless of the technology used. It shows a bird's-eye view of a typical architecture with a user, a browser, and a server. The figure depicts a user making a request, and the input actions of clicking a button, dragging and dropping, mouse hovering, and so on.

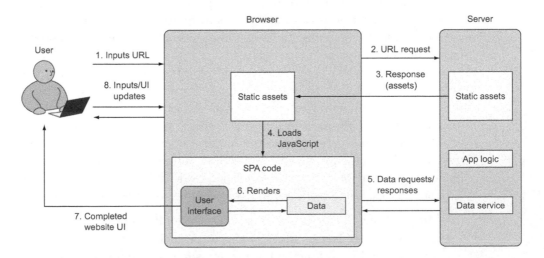

Figure 1.3   A generic SPA architecture

Let's walk through this typical end-to-end process, following the numbered steps in figure 1.3:

1. The user types a URL in the browser to open a new page.
2. The browser sends a URL request to the server.
3. The server responds with static assets such as HTML, CSS, and JavaScript. In most cases, the HTML is bare-bones; that is, it has only a skeleton of the web page. Usually, there's a "Loading . . . " message and/or rotating spinner GIF.
4. The static assets include the JavaScript code for the application. When loaded, this code makes additional requests for data.
5. The data comes back in JSON, XML, or any other format.
6. Once the application receives the data, it can render missing HTML (the User Interface block in the figure). To put it differently, the process of rendering the UI occurs within the browser as the application injects data into pre-rendered templates, also known as *hydration*.
7. Once the browser rendering is finished, the browser updates the displayed content, and the user can work with the application.
8. The user sees a beautiful web page. The user may interact with the page (Inputs in the figure), triggering new requests from the application to the server, and the cycle of steps 2–6 continues. At this stage, browser routing may happen if the application implements it, meaning navigation to a new URL will trigger not a new page reload from the server, but rather an application re-render in the browser.

To summarize, in an SPA, most rendering for UIs happens in the browser. Only data travels to and from the browser. Contrast that with a "classic" website, which is not an SPA, where all the rendering happens on the server. React fits into this SPA architecture in steps 6 and 8 by rendering content based on data as well as handling user input and updating the content based on the updated data that results from these inputs.

1.3.2 The React stack

React isn't a full-blown, frontend JavaScript SPA framework. React is minimalistic in the sense that it only does a single job (rendering reactive UIs) and tries to do that very well. It doesn't enforce a particular way of doing things such as data modeling, styling, or routing (it's non-opinionated). Because of that, developers often need to pair React with a routing and/or data library.

While you can use React as a smaller part of your stack, developers most often opt to use a React-centric stack, which consists of the React core itself as well as data, routing, and styling libraries created to be used specifically with React, such as the following:

- *Data model libraries and backends*—Examples include TanStack Query (https://tanstack.com/query/latest), Redux (http://redux.js.org), Recoil.js (https://recoiljs.org/), XState (https://xstate.js.org/), and Apollo (www.apollographql.com/)

- *Routing library*—Often React Router (https://github.com/remix-run/react-router) or a similar router implemented in many frameworks
- *Styling libraries*—Either a predefined set of styled components such as Material UI (https://mui.com/) or Bootstrap (https://react-bootstrap.github.io/) or a library to easily work with CSS inside React components, such as Styled-Components (https://styled-components.com/), Vanilla Extract (https://vanilla-extract.style/), or even Tailwind CSS (https://tailwindcss.com/)

The ecosystem of libraries for React is growing every day. In addition, React's ability to describe composable components (self-contained chunks of the UI) enables code reuse. Many components are packaged as npm modules.

A great (curated) list of a lot of various React components for many purposes can be found here: https://github.com/brillout/awesome-react-components. This list has everything from UI components (including tons of form elements) to complete UI frameworks to development utilities and testing tools.

React website frameworks

Another category of React frameworks is the full-blown server-side framework, which takes care of everything for you. Such frameworks come in two variants, but sometimes a framework can work in either way:

- Static site generators (SSGs)
- Dynamic server-rendered React (SSR)

SSGs are just that—frameworks that will generate a completely static website for you fully ready to deploy to any static website host, which requires very little work on your part and no expensive hosting. This is particularly popular for smaller personal websites such as blogs, but can also be used for smaller businesses and even e-commerce websites (that don't require updates too often).

SSR frameworks are more complex and will take care of pre-rendering your React application on the server before serving the HTML over the wire to your visitors' browsers. This means it's good for SEO, embraces shareability, and has many other benefits.

We'll list three such frameworks here:

- *Gatsby*—This very popular blogging framework is also useful for many other types of static websites.
- *Next.js*—As probably the most popular React website framework out there, this is useful for both small static websites and huge dynamic behemoths.
- *Remix*—This fairly new kid on the block is gaining traction and popularity very quickly in serving super-fast dynamic React websites.

All of these frameworks—and many, many more—are different extensions of React, each functioning by its own paradigms. They all add extra functionality on top of React and sometimes also come with a set of React components that helps you create your website to utilize the framework to its fullest.

By now, you should have an understanding of what React is, its stack, its place in higher-level web applications, and how you can use tools built on top of React to generate complex websites. It's time to get your hands dirty and write your first React application.

1.4   *Your first React app: Hello World*

Let's explore your first React application by implementing a Hello World application—the quintessential example used for learning programming languages (see figure 1.4). If we don't, the gods of programming might punish us.

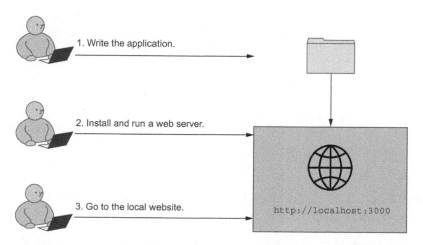

Figure 1.4   The process to create your first React application has just three simple steps.

You'll need a few things before you can get going. Fortunately, because we're developing an application that runs in the browser, you don't need all sorts of compilers or libraries. Here's the short list of things you do need before you can get started:

- A text editor.
- Knowledge of how to use the terminal on your system.
- Have npm version 5.2 or newer installed (given that version 5.2 has been around since July 2017, odds are strong that your npm version is good enough if you have one).
- Have a modern browser installed (any recent version of Edge, Firefox, Chrome, or Safari will work).

And that's about it. If you can check off this list, you're good to go for this first example. When we get to other examples in future chapters, you won't need a lot more than what's on this list.

1.4.1   *The result*

The project will print a "Hello world!!!" heading (<h1>) on a web page. Figure 1.5 shows what it will look like when you're finished (unless you're not quite that enthusiastic and prefer just a single exclamation point).

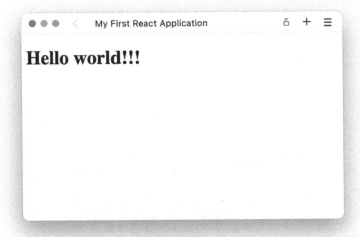

Figure 1.5   Hello World application

You won't be using JSX yet, just plain JavaScript (we actually won't start using JSX until chapter 3 and onward).

> **Learning React first without JSX**
>
> Although all React developers write React using JSX, browsers will only run standard JavaScript and not understand JSX directly. That's why it's beneficial to be able to understand React code in pure JavaScript. Another reason we're starting with plain JavaScript is to show that JSX is optional, albeit the de facto standard template language for React. Finally, preprocessing JSX requires a bit more tooling, but it will make the whole setup simpler because you'll see less of how the sausage is made and do more of the fun stuff—writing awesome React components.
>
> We want to get you started with React as soon as possible without spending too much time on setups in this chapter. You'll be introduced to how to start a new application in chapter 2, and we'll add JSX to the mix in chapter 3.

1.4.2   *Writing the application*

This project is so simple, it'll only consist of a single HTML file. This file will include links to the most recent versions of React 18 (the most stable version at the time of writing) of the React Core and ReactDOM libraries. It will also, of course, include a tiny bit of JavaScript code required to render the very simple application that we're building.

The code for the HTML file is simple and starts with the inclusion of the libraries in <head>. In the <body> element, you'll create a <div> container with the ID root and a <script> element (that's where the app's code will go later), as shown in the following listing.

> **Listing 1.1   Loading React libraries and code**

```
<!DOCTYPE html>
<html>
  <head>
    <title>My First React Application</title>
    <script
      src="//unpkg.com/react@18/umd/react.development.js">          Imports the
    </script>                                                        React library
    <script src="//unpkg.com/react-dom@18/umd
    /react-dom.development.js"></script>          Imports the ReactDOM library
  </head>
  <body>
    <div id="root"></div>            ◁────────      Defines an empty
    <script type="text/javascript">  ◁─────         <div> element to
      ...    ◁──────                                 mount the React UI
    </script>      The actual                        Creates a script
  </body>          JavaScript code                   node that will hold
</html>            will go in here.                  our JavaScript
```

Just type this code using your text editor and save it as a file named index.html in some folder on your machine.

You might be wondering why we have to create a <div> node to render the content into instead of rendering the React element directly in the <body> element. The answer is that doing so can lead to conflict with other libraries and browser extensions that manipulate the document body. If you try attaching an element directly to the body, you'll get this console error:

```
Warning: createRoot(): Creating roots directly with document.body is
  discouraged, ....
```

This is another good thing about React: it has great warnings and error messages!

> **NOTE**   React warning and error messages aren't part of the production build to reduce noise, increase security, and minimize the distribution size. The production build is the minified file from the React Core library, that is, react.min.js. The development version with the warnings and error messages is the unminified version, react.development.js, as you see us using in this example.

By including the libraries in the HTML file, you get access to the React and React-DOM global objects: window.React and window.ReactDOM. You'll need two methods from those objects: one to create an element (React) and another to render it in the <div> container (ReactDOM), as shown in listing 1.2. To create a React element, all you need to do is call `React.createElement(elementName, data, children)` with three arguments that have the following meanings:

- `elementName`—HTML tag as a string (e.g., `'h1'`) or a custom component class as an object. We don't have any custom components just yet, but we'll start creating those in chapter 2.
- `data`—A data object containing attributes and properties for the element. We don't need any properties now, so we just pass `null`. We'll get back to using properties in chapter 2.
- `children`—Child elements or inner HTML/text content. In this example, it's just "`Hello world!!!`".

Listing 1.2   Creating and rendering an `h1` element

```
const reactElement = React.createElement(
  'h1',
  null,
  'Hello world!!!'
);
const domNode = document.getElementById('root');
const root = ReactDOM.createRoot(domNode);
root.render(reactElement);
```

Creates an h1 React element with the text "Hello world!!!"

Grabs a reference to the DOM element on the page with ID "root"

Creates a root holder for the React application connected to the specific DOM element

Renders the h1 element into the root holder

The code in listing 1.2 goes into the `<script>` tag in the HTML file, which you created before, in place of the . . . that we originally put there as a placeholder. This listing gets a React element and stores the reference to this object in the `reactElement` variable. The `reactElement` variable isn't an actual DOM node; rather, it's an instantiation of the React `h1` component (element). You can name it any way you want, for example, `helloWorldHeading`. In other words, React provides an abstraction over the DOM.

Once the element is created and stored in the variable, you then create a React application holder (called *root*) from the DOM element using the `ReactDOM.createRoot()` method. Finally, you render the React element into the root with the `root.render()` method, shown in listing 1.2.

If you prefer, you can move all steps into a single call. The result is the same, except you don't use the three extra variables, as we've done in the next listing.

Listing 1.3   Single statement

```
ReactDOM
  .createRoot(document.getElementById('root'))
  .render(React.createElement('h1', null, 'Hello world!'));
```

We'll be using the more explicit version in listing 1.2, so the full HTML file should now look like the following listing.

Listing 1.4   Creating and rendering an `h1` element

```
<!DOCTYPE html>
<html>
  <head>
    <title>My First React Application</title>
    <script src="//unpkg.com/react@18/umd/react.development.js"></script>
    <script src="//unpkg.com/react-dom@18/umd/react-
    dom.development.js"></script>
  </head>
  <body>
    <div id="root"></div>
    <script type="text/javascript">
      const reactElement = React.createElement(
        "h1",
        null,
        "Hello world!!!"
      );
      const domNode = document.getElementById("root");
      const root = ReactDOM.createRoot(domNode);
      root.render(reactElement);
    </script>
  </body>
</html>
```

The inserted JavaScript is located in its proper place.

With the HTML file completed, we now need to see this in action by serving the content to our browser.

1.4.3   Installing and running a web server

Now comes the next step, serving the HTML page to a browser. Why do we need to serve the content? Can't we just open the HTML file directly in the browser? Due to cross-origin restrictions, you can't open a file located on your local hard drive in the browser and have it access content on other domains (such as the React libraries loaded from https://unpkg.com). Browsers simply don't allow this. You can try to open the file in your browser directly by double-clicking it, but it will just show an empty white page. So that's no good.

Instead, we need to serve the content using a local development web server. That might sound terribly complex, but it's surprisingly simple to do today.

If you have node set up as recommended in the introduction, this will be enough to get you going. Just type the following command in the folder where you saved your `index.html` file:

```
$ npx serve
```

That's it. You might be asked to install a package (if you haven't used this command before, simply press Enter to confirm), but after a few seconds, once the tool reports that everything is rolling, your web server is running.

Local development web server

Unfortunately, in this very first example, you have to worry about setting up your own local web server. Although the task is very simple, it's a bit annoying to do here.

If for some reason the given command doesn't work for you, there are a couple of other ways to easily serve the current folder as a local web server.

If you have Node, you can try this command:

```
$ npx http-server -p 3000
```

Alternatively, if you have a working Python 2 installation on your computer, you can just do the following:

```
$ python -m SimpleHTTPServer 3000
```

Or, if you have a working Python 3 installation, you can do this (you might have to type `python3` rather than `python` in the following depending on your setup):

```
$ python -m http.server 3000
```

Finally, if you have a PHP setup working locally, you can do this:

```
$ php -S localhost:3000
```

Any of those commands will run a local web server on your computer in the folder where you run the command serving your HTML file to http://localhost:3000.

1.4.4   *Going to the local website*

With the web server running, you can now use your browser and go to this site:

```
http://localhost:3000
```

Here, you should be able to see your application in action, and it should look pretty much like figure 1.5 at the start of this section.

Figure 1.6 shows the Elements tab in the browser developer tools with the <h1> element selected. You know that React must have done something here because, in your source HTML file, there's no <h1> element inside the root node—it was empty.

Congratulations! You've just implemented your first React application!

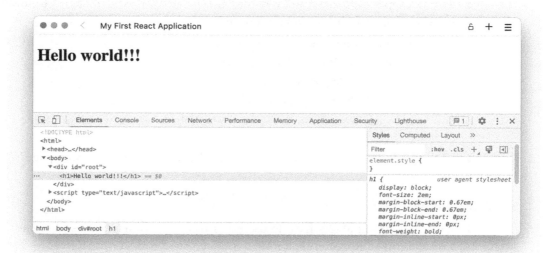

Figure 1.6   Inspecting the Hello World web app as rendered by React

---

Separate JavaScript file

You can abstract the JavaScript code into a separate file instead of including the script directly in the HTML file (refer to listing 1.1). For example, you can create a file named `script.js` and copy and paste the entire snippet from either listing 1.2 or listing 1.3 into that file. Then, in the HTML file, you need to link to your `script.js` file after the `<div id="root">` rather than include the script itself, like this:

```
<div id="root"></div>
<script src="script.js"></script>
```

From the next chapter going forward, we won't be creating our React applications like this. We'll be using a small tool to quickly generate and set up our React application basics for us, which will make this entire process much smoother. It will take care of serving our content as well, so you don't have to worry about web servers anymore.

1.5   *Quiz*

1   React is a complete framework in and of itself, and you can create many applications using nothing but React. *True* or *false*?

2   What is the primary problem that React solves?

   a   Fetching data from the server
   b   Creating beautiful HTML widgets
   c   Rendering dynamic data in a UI layer

3   React components are rendered into the DOM with which of the following methods? (Beware, it's a tricky question!)

    a   `ReactDOM.appendRoot(...).render()`

    b   `ReactDOM.renderRoot(...).render()`

    c   `ReactDOM.createRoot(...).render()`

    d   `ReactDOM.launchRoot(...).render()`

4   You have to use Node.js on the server to be able to use React in your SPA. *True or false?*

5   You must include `react-dom.js` to render React elements on a web page. *True or false?*

Quiz answers

1   *False.* You almost always have to use other frameworks or libraries to create the vast majority of React applications.

2   While you can create beautiful HTML widgets in React, the primary problem that React solves is to *render dynamic data in a UI layer* (answer *c*).

3   `ReactDOM.createRoot(...).render()`.

4   *False.* You can use any backend technology.

5   *True.* You need the ReactDOM library.

Summary

- React for the web consists of the React Core and ReactDOM libraries. React Core is a library geared toward building and sharing composable UI components using JavaScript and (optionally) JSX in a universal manner. On the other hand, to work with React in the browser, you can use the ReactDOM library, which has methods for DOM rendering as well as for server-side rendering.

- React is declarative; it's only a view or UI layer.

- React uses components that you bring into existence with `ReactDOM.create-Root()`.

- You use pure JavaScript to develop and compose UIs in React.

- Although optional, you don't need to use JSX (an HTML-like syntax for React objects) when developing with React, but everyone does.

- React can fit into your web stack in many ways, from just a small widget on some page to the foundation of your entire website.

- React is not a Swiss Army knife, but rather the UI layer of a web application that also consists of many other parts. React is often used together with data libraries such as Redux or XState.

Baby steps with React

2

This chapter covers

- Creating a new React project
- Nesting elements
- Creating a component class
- Working with properties

This chapter will teach you how to create a new React project and how to create custom components to render HTML. Both of these concepts will serve as the basis for all future chapters.

First, we'll examine how to create a new React project. While doing so, we'll teach you both how to start your own React projects and how to utilize the React template system to quickly instantiate the examples and projects that we'll work on in this book. It's quite magical how in a single line you can get the code downloaded and ready to go with everything set up for you!

As we start our first React project, we'll introduce several fundamental React concepts that you'll use frequently, including elements, components, and properties. In a nutshell, elements are instances of components that can be passed properties. What are their use cases, and why do you use them? Hang tight for this information until section 2.3 because, right now, we're going to discuss how to create a new React web application.

NOTE The source code for the examples in this chapter is available at https://rq2e.com/ch02. In section 2.2, however, you'll learn that you don't have to download anything manually. You can instantiate all the examples from this and subsequent chapters directly from the command line using a single command.

2.1   Creating a new React app

In this section, we'll introduce you to a magical command-line program that will make all your React setups go smoothly. In just three short commands and a couple of minutes, you'll download a fully functioning dummy React web app, compile it, run it through a web server, and see it in your browser (see the overview in figure 2.1).

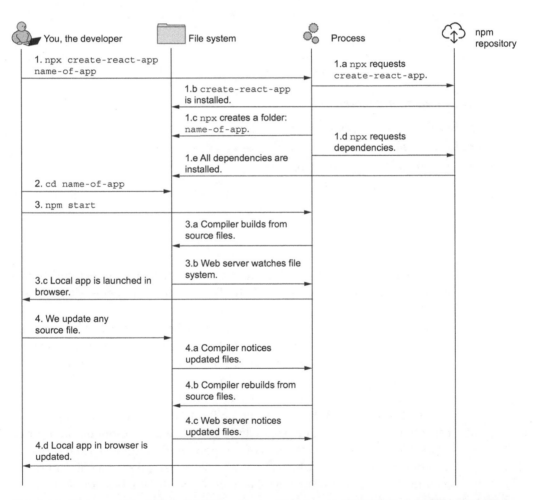

Figure 2.1   Three commands that will take you from nothing to a working React application. From there, you can update the source files, and the system will automatically recompile and update your application in the browser.

If you have a modern version of Node (and npm) installed as advised in the introduction, you should be able to write the following command in your terminal:

```
$ npx create-react-app name-of-app
```

> **NOTE** npx isn't a typo. npx is a package runner tool that comes with npm. It allows us to run commands using packages only present inside this project folder and/or run commands that will be downloaded dynamically when needed.

Run this command, and a new React application is set up for you! The first time you run this command, npm will ask for confirmation to download the create-react-app utility (just press Enter to confirm that). This refers to steps 1.a and 1.b in figure 2.1. Every time you use the command after that, no questions will be asked.

> **NOTE** We'll refer to the create-react-app tool as *CRA* in the following sections.

The command will create a new folder with the passed name, which is name-of-app in the preceding case. Inside this folder, the utility will initialize a new Git project, download the required resources for the application, and then download and locally install all the dependencies required by the project.

The command will run for a short while, probably around 1–3 minutes depending on the project complexity and network conditions. Once the command is complete, you'll see something like this:

```
Success! Created name-of-app at <folder>
Inside that directory, you can run several commands:

  npm start
    Starts the development server.

  npm run build
    Bundles the app into static files for production.

  npm test
    Starts the test runner.

  npm run eject
    Removes this tool and copies build dependencies, configuration
    files and scripts into the app directory. If you do this, you
    can't go back!

We suggest that you begin by typing:

  cd name-of-app
  npm start

Happy hacking!
```

name-of-app and <folder> will be replaced by the actual name and folder location of your project.

This is the first of four commands that you can run in your application (we'll discuss what it does next).

These three other commands will be discussed in the next subsection.

This command changes the folder to the newly created project.

Why, thank you—and may your hacking be forever white hat!

Uh, exciting. Note that if your output mentions a command called `yarn` rather than npm, don't worry. See the sidebar for an explanation.

---

npm alternatives

There are several popular package managers for JavaScript projects that work on the same package repository and structure, but with slightly different commands. The most used manager is npm by far, but alternatives include Yarn and pnpm. The popular choice, npm, comes preinstalled with Node and is the default manager that many people use.

However, you can opt to install a different manager, which will have a slightly simpler command structure. For the purposes of this book, there's no difference between using npm or an alternative, other than some slightly different syntax when typing commands. If you have Yarn or pnpm, you probably also have npm installed, so that will most likely always work for you.

If you want to use one of these package managers, please check the documentation on how to run commands:

- Yarn: https://classic.yarnpkg.com/lang/en/docs/cli/run/
- pnpm: https://pnpm.io/cli/run

Now, let's follow the suggestion in the preceding code snippet and run those two commands:

```
$ cd name-of-app
$ npm start
```

Now the third part of the magic happens. A React development server starts up, compiling all the files and resources used (action 3.a in figure 2.1) and spins up a local development web server (action 3.b in figure 2.1). After a few seconds, the command line will say something like this:

```
Compiled successfully!
You can now view name-of-app in the browser.
  Local:            http://localhost:3000
```

Moreover, the application will already have been launched in your browser, as the command also launches a browser window at the proper URL (action 3.c in figure 2.1). If not, simply open `localhost:3000` in your browser to see the application. This browser window will display a React application (as shown in figure 2.2) that's been created for you by a template. This is the default template used for new React applications that don't specify a specific template to use. We'll discuss templates a bit later in section 2.1.3.

Note that this last command, `npm start`, is a continuously running command that stays active in the terminal. It will watch your source files, recompile the whole

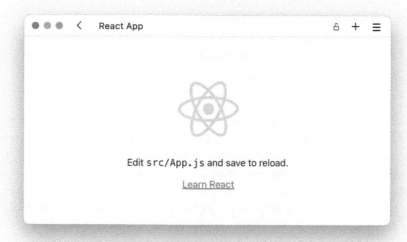

Figure 2.2 The default React application launched by a new React project. Your application will most likely be in *dark mode* with white text on a dark background color. The brightness in this screenshot has been inverted for better print results.

application when any source file changes, and even reload the browser with the updated application (actions 4–4.d in figure 2.1)! Now that is pure magic.

If and when you want to abort this command, simply press Ctrl-C in your terminal, and you'll be back to your regular terminal prompt. However, your application no longer works because you also stopped the local development web server.

You might have noticed that the previous output from creating our application listed not only the start command that we just used but also three other commands: build, test, and eject. We'll go over all four of these commands in more detail in the next subsection.

2.1.1 React project commands

Now that you have this React application source code available on your system, you probably want to interact with it in several ways. The two primary things you want are to see what you're developing as you're developing it and to deploy your application to a web server. You also might want to run all tests in your application to verify that everything is still working as designed. Finally, you might want to escape the confines of CRA to tinker with the engine underneath. CRA abstracts some things away that you don't need to worry about at first, but when applications get more advanced, you might want to access the innards of your application configuration. For these four purposes, a new React application created with CRA comes with these four commands:

- start—Launch a local development web server and continuously compile the project as it changes, serving it to any local browser.

- `build`—Compile all resources into a production-ready package deployable to the right web host.
- `test`—Launch a test runner that will run all unit tests defined in your project.
- `eject`—Reveal the inner workings of the project and make it fully configurable.

Let's go over these one by one and discuss how and when to use them.

START

The `start` command is your primary command, the one you use every time you start a new project or pick up an old project to start work on it again. At the beginning of your coding session, you'll run the `start` command in a terminal, and then you'll be ready to code in your editor while automatically being served the updated content in your browser.

The `start` command will build your project in the background continuously using the development version of React and its utility libraries. This is distinct from the production version of React used in the `build` command. The development version of React includes much better error messages and warnings as well as options for debugging the application as it's running in the browser. However, the development version of React is, for those reasons, also much larger in terms of sheer file size, so you don't want to publish your application using this version. It will make your application unnecessarily large and hinder users trying to access it.

The `start` command will also reload the application in the browser as it's running, but in a much smarter way than just reloading the whole browser window. React will try to reload only the relevant bits of logic that have changed and otherwise leave the application as is. For instance, if you've clicked a button to collapse a section that would otherwise be open by default when the application launches, React will be able to inject updated code while keeping the state in the browser, so this section remains collapsed while the logic is otherwise updated.

BUILD

This is the command to run when you're ready to see your application deployed to a real web server and have users try it out. When you run the `build` command, you'll be using the production version of React, which is much leaner and optimized for deployment. The result of the build will be put in the `/build` folder.

By default, nothing else really happens, but you can set up direct deployment to your cloud web hosting solution in the `build` command as well if you want to. Check your cloud web hosting provider's documentation for help on how to do this. We won't be using this command in this book, as we'll be using another template for deploying applications in the project where deployment to the cloud will be an option.

TEST

If you want to run all unit tests defined in your project, run this command. You can do that on the empty default template as well because the default template even comes with a default test file.

EJECT

This command can be a bit dangerous because it's irreversible. If you eject your application, you'll have access to a lot more configurable options inside the React setup than you do otherwise, but you also lose the option of automatically updating to newer versions of all the tools involved. We won't cover ejecting your application in this book, but we'll discuss it again briefly in section 2.1.4 when examining the pros and cons.

2.1.2   *File structure*

When you create a project with CRA, it almost always follows the same file structure. Custom templates can do things differently, but they rarely do. The structure includes these important elements:

```
/
  public/
    index.html
  src/
    index.js
    App.js
  package.json
```

With these two folders and four files, you're good to go.

The public folder is for files that will be served directly via the web server. This includes the `index.html` file that serves your entire application as well as binary files that you don't want to bundle inside your application, such as content required by the `index.html` file directly (e.g., favicon, Cascading Style Sheets [CSS], fonts, or images for sharing) and large files (e.g., videos and images).

The source (`src`) folder is where all your bundled JavaScript will go as well as any other content that you want to bundle as a single package. This is mostly just JavaScript, but could potentially also include CSS, icons, small images, JSON files, and more. The bundling starts at the `index.js` file inside the source folder. It's commonplace to have the main application reside in a file named `App.js` or `app.js`, depending on personal preference, but otherwise, you are free to be flexible here. Some templates structure the content inside the `src` folder in subfolders, which is necessary to structure larger projects.

The main configuration file for your project is `package.json`, as required by npm and Yarn. This is the starting file for your project and defines the dependencies as well as the commands that you can run, as covered in section 2.1.1.

The root folder will often contain a ton of other configuration files required for various libraries included in the project. It isn't uncommon to see custom templates with 20+ other configuration files at the root of the project. Now let's move on to cover what custom templates are and how they help you.

2.1.3   *Templates*

While the default application that we saw in figure 2.2 is pretty nice, it's not always helpful. The default application sets you up to create a simple web app in the same style as that web app is created, but that might not be what you're looking for. If you want to create a web app using a specific technology stack or using React in a particular way, you probably want to use a different starting template to set you up correctly.

When you use CRA, you can specify a template to use. The default template is the one you saw previously with the (spinning) React logo. If you want to specify another template, you can do so as an argument:

```
$ npx create-react-app name-of-app --template name-of-template
```

You can only use the name of a template that already exists; if it doesn't exist, the application will abort. Often, people don't bother with choosing a template at all and just work with the default one. But if you know that you want a specific setup or want to start your codebase at a certain state, you can use a template that sets you up for exactly that. Some commonly used templates include the following:

- Minimal templates with even fewer features than the default one, for example, `--template minimal`. This one comes without images, CSS, tests, web vitals, and other minor niceness used in the default template.
- Variants of the default or the minimal template using TypeScript, for example, `--template typescript` or `--template minimal-typescript`. This is useful for starting a new project using TypeScript.
- Complex boilerplate setups created by other developers where you have a stack of certain dependencies already baked into your new application, for example, `--template redux-typescript`, which comes prepackaged with Redux and TypeScript, or `--template rb`, which is a popular React boilerplate (hence the *rb*), that comes prepackaged with a ton of reputable libraries, including Redux with Redux-Saga, styled components, ESLint, husky, and many more.

One of the very useful things about the template system for CRA is that it's fully decentralized. Anyone can publish a package to npm and structure it in a way that allows you to use it as a base for your own applications. That is, of course, also one of the downsides. If you find a template on npm, there's no saying whether it's any good or even does what it says. Here, you should probably trust the wisdom of the crowd—if it's popular, it's probably good.

One of the benefits of allowing just about any random developer to publish a template on npm is that this includes *us*, the authors of this book. We'll be using custom React templates for all examples and projects in this book. We'll get back to that in a second. First, we'll discuss the advantages and drawbacks of using CRA.

2.1.4   Pros and cons

There are a lot of advantages to using CRA to create a new React application, but, as always, such advantages have consequences. We've already discussed many advantages, but let's list them here anyway:

- *Simplicity*—You have less to worry about when setting up a new application. You get JavaScript XML (JSX) transpiling, bundling, testing, automatic reloading, and more for free, without dealing with all the interdependencies.
- *Upgradability*—You can easily upgrade to newer versions of React and all the other libraries used. We haven't discussed how to do that, but it's surprisingly simple. Just run `npm install --exact react-scripts@VERSION` to upgrade your entire project to the specific version of React scripts. Check the changelog for `react-scripts` for details.
- *Community*—With the deluge of available CRA templates and the easy path to making more, you can likely always find a premade template with just the right combination of tools so that you don't have to deal with mixing them correctly.
- *Customization*—On top of a variety of templates, you still have the option of adding all the other plugins and libraries that you need for your project. Does your project interface with, for example, both Google Maps and Amazon Web Services (AWS)? Just add their libraries, and you should be good to go.

However, there are also some drawbacks. Some of them can be ignored or glossed over, but, in some situations, you have to seek out other setups besides what CRA can provide. We'll cover some of these situations here as well:

- *Understanding*—Without setting the whole project up from scratch, you won't know all that goes into such an endeavor. If you find yourself in a position where you need a unique setup but have always relied on CRA, you might find yourself stranded quickly because you never really paid attention to it. But that's the duality of all abstractions: you gain the benefit of not worrying at the cost of not knowing what's going on underneath.
- *Control*—You do lose control over which libraries are used. CRA currently uses webpack and BabelJS for JSX bundling and transpiling, but they're by no means the only players around. Recently, tools such as esbuild, Bun, SWC, and Rome have emerged that partially cover the same ground, but you can't easily switch to one of those. You're stuck with the technology stack that CRA currently has chosen for you. On the other hand, that's also an advantage because when another tool becomes standard and maybe even superior to Babel, CRA will adapt and use that instead—without you having to worry about it. For the instances where you insist on using a specific stack, you do have to set your project up from scratch. Another option is to eject your application as described in section 2.1.1, which gives you extra configurability and control at the cost of losing upgradability.

- *Integration*—If you want to integrate your application in a server-side setup, CRA currently can't help you. For projects based on website frameworks as described in the first chapter, you have to use the setups provided by those frameworks rather than CRA.

After weighing the pros and cons just listed, we arrived at the conclusion that CRA is perfect for new developers. You get a lot of simplicity and fewer worries. Once you get more experience, you can start to experiment outside of CRA. That's why we've used CRA for the examples and projects in this book.

2.2   *A note about the examples in this book*

As mentioned, we'll be using CRA for all projects and almost all examples in this book. The only exception is the first example you completed in the first chapter.

All the templates that we've created for this book will be named according to this structure:

```
rqXX-NAME
```

Of course, `rq` refers to *React Quickly*. The XX will be replaced with the chapter number, and the last bit will be a custom short name for each example. For every example and project using CRA, you'll see the template name and how to use it in a sidebar like the following.

Repository: rq02-nesting

This example can be seen in repository `rq02-nesting`. You can use that repository by creating a new web app based on the associated template:

```
$ npx create-react-app rq02-nesting --template rq02-nesting
```

Alternatively, you can go to this website to browse the code, see the application in action directly in your browser, or download the source code as a zip file:

https://rq2e.com/rq02-nesting

Sometimes, examples will contain multiple variants of the source code, and, in such cases, each variant will come with its own template as just shown. There are also examples that come with suggestions for extra homework. In those instances, a template will be specified as the starting point for that extra homework, and another template will contain *one* possible solution. You can use the solution template as either inspiration or to compare with your own solution. All such homework can have infinite solutions, so just because your work doesn't match the template, that doesn't mean it's wrong—it's just different.

For ease of use, you can often use the template name as your application name as well. So, let's say you want to start working on the next example in this book. The template name is `rq02-nesting`, so let's use that as the web app name as well:

```
$ npx create-react-app rq02-nesting --template rq02-nesting
```

Just type that in your console, and you're already up and running and ready to tackle the example to work on the problem along with us if you so desire. You can also just read the chapter and view the code in the listings in the book. If you find some things odd or need to get your fingers into the code to try some things out, you can then instantiate the templates and see the examples in action. Now let's get on with this example, which seems to be about nesting something.

2.3   Nesting elements

Getting back to creating React applications, which is what we've set out to do in this book, let's start making things slightly more complex than that instructive but over-simplified example we looked at in chapter 1. In that chapter, you learned how to create a single React element. As a reminder, the method you use is `React.create-Element()`. For example, you can create a link element like this:

```
const reactLinkElement = React.createElement("a",
  { href: "http://react.dev" },
  "React Website"
)
```

This is fine as long as we're creating just a single element. The problem is that every website has more than one element; otherwise, how would you have any other information than just a single paragraph?

The solution to creating multi-element structures in a hierarchical manner is nesting elements. In the previous chapter, you implemented your first React code by creating a single React element and rendering it in the DOM with `ReactDOM.createRoot().render()`:

```
const title = React.createElement("h1", null, "Hello world!");
const domElement = document.getElementById("root");
ReactDOM.createRoot(domElement).render(title);
```

It's important to note that `ReactDOM.createRoot().render()` can only take a single (root) React element as an argument, which is `reactElement` in this example. The resulting application is shown in figure 2.3.

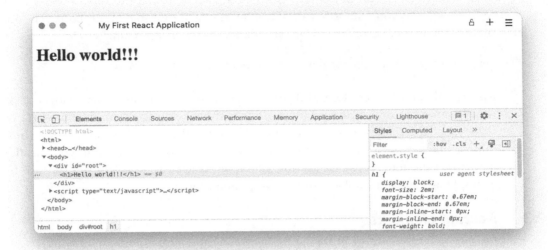

Figure 2.3   Your browser rendering a single heading element. We've opened the developer tools here to show you the underlying HTML structure. Refer to your browser of choice for how to open developer tools, but it's likely that Ctrl-Alt-I/Cmd-Opt-I might do the trick.

> ## Repository: rq02-nesting
>
> This example can be seen in repository `rq02-nesting`. You can use that repository by creating a new web app based on the associated template:
>
> ```
> $ npx create-react-app rq02-nesting --template rq02-nesting
> ```
>
> Alternatively, you can go to this website to browse the code, see the application in action directly in your browser, or download the source code as a zip file:
>
> https://rq2e.com/rq02-nesting

When you check out template `rq02-nesting`, you'll have the preceding application, but this time using CRA instead of manually adding libraries and writing HTML as we did in chapter 1.

Remember that when you use `createElement`, the third argument is the child of the element. In this case, we just supply simple text as the child. But that text is actually another element—at least in the resulting DOM. In React, it doesn't have a specific element type, but it still functions as an element to some extent. We can show this relationship in a very simple diagram, as shown in figure 2.4.

Figure 2.4   The gray node is a real React element, whereas the white element is just a text element.

2.3.1 *Node hierarchy*

Before we look at how we can create complex HTML structures, we need a bit of basic terminology in place first. The HTML document is often represented as an upside-down tree, as shown in figure 2.5. Nodes in a tree are commonly described in a family-like fashion (parent, child, etc.).

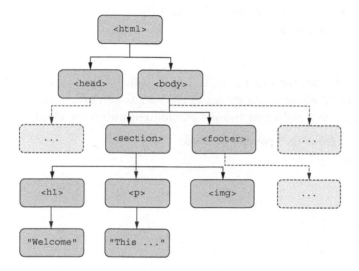

Figure 2.5   The upside-down tree structure of an HTML document, with each node related to the others in a family role, such as parent, child, and sibling

The following terminology relates to the tree structure:

- *Node*—Any member in the tree is a node, including both HTML elements and text nodes. All the boxes in figure 2.5 are nodes. The two bottommost boxes are text nodes, and all the others are element nodes.
- *Root*—The first (topmost) node is the root of the tree. In figure 2.5, the `<html>` node is the root node.
- *Parent*—The node directly above a given node is its parent. Every node in a tree has only one parent. The node above that can be called the grandparent, and so on. In figure 2.5, the parent node of the `<body>` is the `<html>` node. The root node doesn't have a parent, and it's the only node in the tree without a parent.
- *Child*—Any node directly below a given node is a child of that node. A node can have multiple children. The `<section>` node's children are the `<h1>`, `<p>`, and `<img>` nodes. Not all nodes have children. The `<img>` element doesn't have children. Text nodes never have children.
- *Sibling*—Two nodes that have the same parent are considered sibling nodes. The `<p>` node has two sibling nodes: the `<h1>` and `<img>` nodes.
- *Ascendants*—The parent of a node, its parent, its parent's parent, and so on—all the way up to the root—are called the ascendants of a node. The `<h1>` node has three ascendants: the `<section>`, `<body>`, and `<html>` nodes.

- *Descendants*—The children of a node, all their children, all their children's children, and so on are called the descendants of a node. The <section> node has five descendants: its three direct children as well as the two text nodes that are the grandchildren of the first two children.

- *Nesting*—Nesting is the process of organizing nodes in a tree and deciding which nodes will be the children of which other nodes, thus creating the document tree. In figure 2.5, we've decided to nest the <h1>, <p>, and <img> nodes inside the <section> node.

2.3.2 *Simple nesting*

Let's say you want to render the word *world* in italics in the string "Hello world!" but still put all of it in an h1 element. As shown in figure 2.6, you create an em element with the string "world" as a child and another h1 element with three children:

- String "Hello " (note the space at the end)
- em element from before
- String "!"

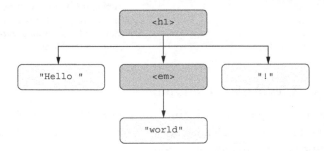

Figure 2.6   The two React elements and three text elements needed to render our slightly emphasized welcome message

Using React.createElement, this becomes the following:

```
const world = React.createElement("em", null, "world");    ⟵——  createElement with
const title = React.createElement(                                three arguments
  "h1", null, "Hello ", world, "!"         createElement with five arguments,
)                                          the last three being its children
```

As you can see here, we're passing five arguments to createElement now: first, the element type, then the properties, and finally the children of the element. You can pass as many arguments as children to an element as you need. You can also pass the child elements as an array:

```
const title = React.createElement("h1", null, ["Hello ", world, "!"])
```

In this case, it doesn't make sense to put the elements into an array before passing them as an argument, but if we already had an array of elements, we could just pass that as an argument by itself. Putting this all together (without using an array), the whole script becomes the following listing.

> **Listing 2.1   Emphatically greeting the world**

```
import React from "react";
import ReactDOM from "react-dom/client";
const world = React.createElement("em", null, "world");
const title = React.createElement("h1", null, "Hello ", world, "!");
const domElement = document.getElementById("root");
ReactDOM.createRoot(domElement).render(title);
```

If we put this into action, we end up with our application looking like figure 2.7 in the browser.

Figure 2.7   Emphasized greeting in the browser. Notice the underlying HTML structure in the developer tools.

Repository: rq02-nesting-italic

This example can be seen in repository `rq02-nesting-italic`. You can use that repository by creating a new web app based on the associated template:

```
$ npx create-react-app rq02-nesting-italic --template rq02-nesting-italic
```

Alternatively, you can go to this website to browse the code, see the application in action directly in your browser, or download the source code as a zip file:

https://rq2e.com/rq02-nesting-italic

But what if you wanted to put an element *after* the h1 and not just *inside* it? We'll cover sibling elements in the next section.

2.3.3   Siblings

In many instances, you can only use a single React element at the top level. This goes for the `ReactDOM.createRoot().render()` method—only a single element can be rendered into the DOM as the root element. You'll also see how custom components can only return a single element a bit later.

But what if you wanted to show a headline *and* then a link after it in our example from before (see figure 2.8)? That would be two different elements next to each other, and you can't render that directly using `ReactDOM.createRoot().render()`.

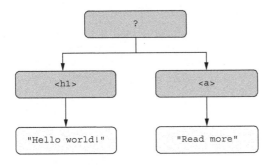

Figure 2.8   Two sibling React elements to be rendered in the root

Instead, you have to wrap them in another element (something in place of the ? in figure 2.8). You have two different options here. One option is to use a neutral DOM element, which is easy, but would add a "physical" element to the output HTML. The alternative is to use a React `Fragment` element, which works like any other element, but doesn't result in any output HTML itself. See the difference between these approaches in figure 2.9.

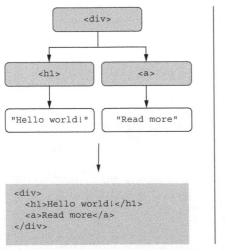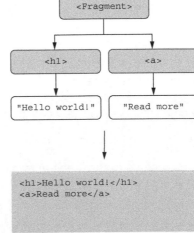

Figure 2.9   Two different approaches to sibling elements with different outputs

If you want to use a neutral DOM element, you can, for instance, use a `<div>` to group them as shown in the next listing. This results in the HTML you see in figure 2.10.

Listing 2.2   Two elements in a grouping container

```
import React from "react";
import ReactDOM from "react-dom/client";
const title = React.createElement("h1", null, "Hello world!");
const link = React.createElement("a", { href: "//react.dev" }, "Read more");
const group = React.createElement("div", null, title, link);
const domElement = document.getElementById("root");
ReactDOM.createRoot(domElement).render(group);
```

Figure 2.10   Title and link in a grouping element

Repository: rq02-siblings-div

This example can be seen in repository `rq02-siblings-div`. You can use that repository by creating a new web app based on the associated template:

```
$ npx create-react-app rq02-siblings-div --template rq02-siblings-div
```

Alternatively, you can go to this website to browse the code, see the application in action directly in your browser, or download the source code as a zip file:

https://rq2e.com/rq02-siblings-div

The `<div>` container is usually a good choice for block-level content, and `<span>` is used for inline-level content. But you don't have to use a "real" element. You can also create an empty React element, whose only purpose is to group multiple other elements and doesn't output itself into the HTML on the page. This can be done with the magical component called `React.Fragment`, and it can be used as the grouping element type. Let's do that in the next listing.

Listing 2.3   Two elements in a fragment

```
import React from "react";
import ReactDOM from "react-dom/client";
const title = React.createElement("h1", null, "Hello world!");
const link = React.createElement("a", { href: "//react.dev" }, "Read more");
const group = React.createElement(
  React.Fragment, null, title, link
);
const domElement = document.getElementById("root");
ReactDOM.createRoot(domElement).render(group);
```

> Notice the use of
> React.Fragment as the first
> argument to createElement.

Repository: rq02-siblings-fragment

This example can be seen in repository `rq02-siblings-fragment`. You can use that repository by creating a new web app based on the associated template:

```
$ npx create-react-app rq02-siblings-frag --template rq02-siblings-fragment
```

Alternatively, you can go to this website to browse the code, see the application in action directly in your browser, or download the source code as a zip file:

https://rq2e.com/rq02-siblings-fragment

The output of this is shown in figure 2.11 in the browser.

You can also render the whole element in a single statement as follows:

```
const group = React.createElement(
  React.Fragment,
  null,
  React.createElement(
    "h1",
    null,
    "Hello world!",
  ),
  React.createElement(
    "a",
    { href: "//react.dev" },
    "Read more",
  ),
);
```

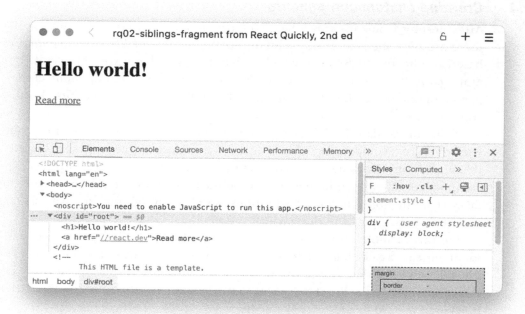

Figure 2.11   Title and link without a grouping element

This is functionally equivalent to the previous code; it just uses less variables. Some would argue it becomes more obvious, whereas others would say that it becomes less readable.

So far, you've mostly provided string values as the first parameter of `create-Element()`. But the first parameter can have two types of input, as we just saw with the fragments:

- Standard HTML tag as a string, for example, `"h1"`, `"div"`, or `"p"` (without the angle brackets). The name is in lowercase.
- React component as a reference (not a string). The name is normally capitalized.

The first approach renders standard HTML elements. You can use any string as an HTML tag name, regardless of whether it has a meaning in the browser by default. So, while you'll mostly be using normal HTML elements, such as `div`, `main`, `section`, and so on, there is nothing stopping you from creating a `tiny-horse` element, which would render as `<tiny-horse>` in the browser. It has no meaning and no default styling, but it would work.

In the second approach just listed, we can supply a React component as a reference. By this, we don't mean the name of a React component as a string, but a direct reference to the component in question. You already saw one instance of that by using `React.Fragment`. Now let's look at how we can create our own custom components in the next section.

2.4   *Creating custom components*

After nesting elements with React, you'll soon stumble across the next problem: there are a lot of elements with a lot of repetition. You need to use the component-based architecture (CBA) described in chapter 1, which lets you reuse code by separating the functionality into loosely coupled parts: meet component classes, or just components, as they're often called for brevity (not to be confused with web components).

Think of standard HTML tags as building blocks. You can use them to compose your own React components, which you can use to create custom elements (instances of components). By using custom elements, you can encapsulate and abstract logic in composable, reusable components. This abstraction allows teams to reuse user interfaces (UIs) in large, complex applications as well as in different projects. Examples include panels, inputs, buttons, menus, and so on.

For this example, we want to create three identical links. It doesn't make a whole lot of sense to create identical links, but, for now, we can't customize them, so let's just go with this scenario. We want to create three links, that all say "Read more about React" and link to the React website at www.react.dev. We also want to wrap each link in a paragraph, so they go on separate lines.

There are two different approaches to this. We can do it the naive way by having three identical copies of elements, or we can do it the smart way by creating a reusable link component and then instantiating it three times, as illustrated in figure 2.12.

Let's first look at the former approach, where we only use a single component with the copies manually duplicated. We want three independent links inside independent paragraphs, and we can do that in a fairly verbose way as in the following listing.

Listing 2.4   Three links, one time each

```
import React from "react";
import ReactDOM from "react-dom/client";
const link1 = React.createElement(
  "a", { href: "//react.dev" }, "Read more about React"
);
const p1 = React.createElement("p", null, link1);
const link2 = React.createElement(
  "a", { href: "//react.dev" }, "Read more about React"
);
const p2 = React.createElement("p", null, link2);
const link3 = React.createElement(
  "a", { href: "//react.dev" }, "Read more about React"
);
const p3 = React.createElement("p", null, link3);
const group = React.createElement(React.Fragment, null, p1, p2, p3);
const domElement = document.getElementById("root");
ReactDOM.createRoot(domElement).render(group);
```

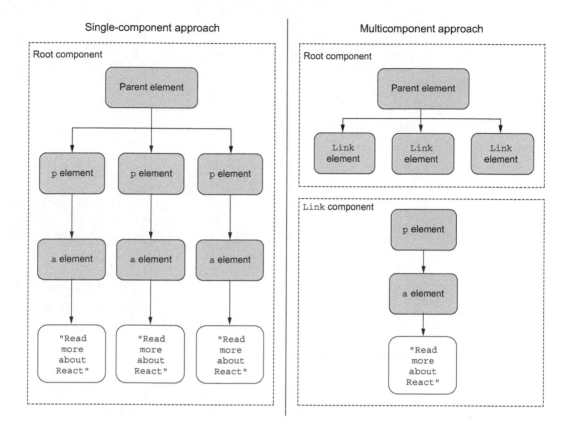

Figure 2.12   Two approaches to creating duplicate elements

If we open this in the browser, we have the result shown in figure 2.13, which is exactly what we wanted.

But we're repeating ourselves a lot in listing 2.4, which, of course, isn't desirable. The whole point of React and similar frameworks is to stop repeating ourselves at all. This calls for a custom component!

A custom component is a named object that contains other elements and component instances. So, in this case, we could create a single Link component that would render the link that we need in the correct way, and then we would include three instances of the Link component rather than the "raw" <p> and <a> elements with all their properties.

You create a React component class by extending the React.Component class with class CHILD extends PARENT ES6 syntax. Let's create a custom Link component class using class Link extends React.Component.

The one mandatory thing you must implement for this new class is the render() method. This method must return a single root element created using createElement(),

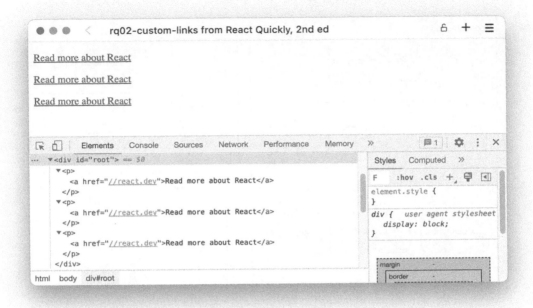

Figure 2.13   Three identical links in our application

which is created from another custom component class or an HTML tag. Either can have nested elements if you so desire as long as there is only one root element.

Listing 2.5   Creating and rendering a React component class

```
import React from "react";
import ReactDOM from "react-dom/client";
class Link extends React.Component {
  render() {
    return React.createElement(
      "p",
      null,
      React.createElement(
        "a",
        { href: "//react.dev" },
        "Read more about React"
      )
    );
  }
}
const link1 = React.createElement(Link);
const link2 = React.createElement(Link);
const link3 = React.createElement(Link);
const group = React.createElement(
  React.Fragment, null, link1, link2, link3
);
```

Defines a React component class with the capitalized name Link

Creates a render() method as an expression (function returning a single element)

Returns a new element with whatever we need for this component

Creates an instance of the new Link component

```
const domElement = document.getElementById("root");
ReactDOM.createRoot(domElement).render(group);
```

Repository: rq02-custom-links

This example can be seen in repository rq02-custom-links. You can use that repository by creating a new web app based on the associated template:

```
$ npx create-react-app rq02-custom-links --template rq02-custom-links
```

Alternatively, you can go to this website to browse the code, see the application in action directly in your browser, or download the source code as a zip file:

https://rq2e.com/rq02-custom-links

By convention, the names of variables containing React components are capitalized. This isn't required in regular JavaScript. You could use the lowercase class name some-Link in the preceding code instead of Link, and it would still work. But because it's necessary for JSX (which we'll cover in the next chapter), we apply this convention here as well.

Analogous to ReactDOM.createRoot().render(), the render() method in a class component can only return a single element. If you need to return multiple same-level elements, wrap them in a container component—either an HTML element or a React fragment. If we now run this code in the browser, we get the exact same HTML as before (refer to figure 2.13).

This new code is much more compact. Unnecessary repetition is removed, and we've compartmentalized a part of the code that can be reused as much as we want. This is the power of component reusability! It leads to faster development and fewer bugs. Components also have properties, life cycle events, states, DOM events, and other features that let you make them interactive and self-contained; these topics are all covered in the following chapters.

Right now, the links are all the same. Wouldn't it be awesome if you could set element attributes and modify their content and/or behavior individually? You can do just that with properties, as we'll discuss next.

2.5 *Working with properties*

Properties are a cornerstone of the declarative style that React uses. Think of properties as unchangeable values within an element. They allow elements to have different variations if used in a view, such as changing a link URL by passing a new value for a property:

```
React.createElement("a", { href: "//react.dev" }, "React");
```

One thing to remember is that properties are immutable within their components. A parent assigns properties to its children upon their creation. The child element isn't supposed to modify its properties. For instance, you can pass property PROPERTY_NAME with value VALUE to a component of type Link, like this:

```
React.createElement(Link, { PROPERTY_NAME: VALUE });
```

Properties closely resemble HTML attributes (as shown with the href in the link of the snippet at the beginning of this section). This is one of their purposes, but they also have another—you can use the properties of an element in your code as you wish for the following:

- To render standard HTML attributes of an element: href, title, style, class, and so on
- As custom instructions for components to make them render individually

The object of properties can be accessed inside a component using this.props. This object is a frozen (immutable) object, from which you can only read values, not set them.

Frozen objects in JavaScript

Internally, React uses Object.freeze(), which is a built-in function in JavaScript to make the this.props object immutable. To check whether an object is frozen, you can use the Object.isFrozen() method. For example, you can determine whether this statement will return true:

```
class Test extends React.Component {
  render() {
    console.log(Object.isFrozen(this.props))
    return React.createElement("div")
  }
}
```

The details of this are pretty complex, but for now, just know that you should never try to edit or add properties inside a component itself. That is something you do in the parent context.

2.5.1   A single property

Let's start with a very simple example. We want the name of the framework in the links we created before to be customized. So, we can say "Read more about React" in one link, "Read more about Vue" in the second, and "Read more about Angular" in the third, as shown in figure 2.14.

To do this, we need to do two things:

1 Pass a property to our component instances.
2 Use the property inside the component.

First, we need to pass a new property to the link instances. So, rather than just using

```
const link1 = React.createElement(Link);
```

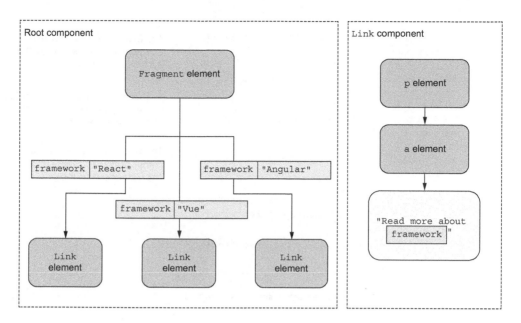

Figure 2.14   Passing a property to components and using the property inside the component

we'll instead be supplying an object as the second argument with a single property:

```
const link1 = React.createElement(Link, { framework: "React" });
```

We used the variable name `framework` here. That is an arbitrary choice that we get to make as the component creator. We just need to make sure to use the same variable name in the second step.

We now need to use this passed property inside our class. Given that we called the variable `framework`, we'll access it through `this.props.framework`. The following listing shows the overall code result.

Listing 2.6   `Link` instances with different text

```
import React from "react";
import ReactDOM from "react-dom/client";
class Link extends React.Component {
  render() {
    return React.createElement(
      "p",
      null,
      React.createElement(
        "a",
        { href: "//react.dev" },
        `Read more about ${this.props.framework}`,
      ),
    );
  }
}
```

> We render the text content of the link by combining this.props.framework with some static content. Note how backticks are used to compose a string with a variable. This is a feature of JavaScript, not React in particular.

```
}
const link1 = React.createElement(Link, {
  framework: "React"
});
const link2 = React.createElement(Link, {
  framework: "Vue"
});
const link3 = React.createElement(Link, {
  framework: "Angular"
});
const group = React.createElement(
  React.Fragment, null, link1, link2, link3
);
const domElement = document.getElementById("root");
ReactDOM.createRoot(domElement).render(group);
```

The first instance of our link component uses "React" as the framework property.

The second instance of our link component uses "Vue" as the framework property.

The third instance of our link component uses "Angular" as the framework property.

You can see this in action in the browser in figure 2.15.

Figure 2.15   Three links with different text, each inside a paragraph

2.5.2   *Multiple properties*

You may have noticed that all the links still point to the same URL, which is the React website. That's no good, of course, because we need the URLs to be different. Using the same approach, we simply invent a new property, `url`, and use it inside the component as well as in the component instances. You can see that illustrated in the diagram in figure 2.16 and implemented in the code in listing 2.7.

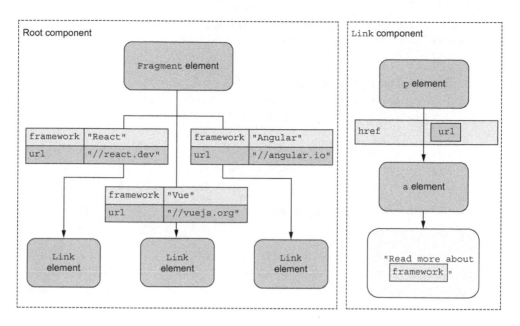

Figure 2.16   Two different properties are passed to our components.

Listing 2.7   `Link` instances with different text and URLs

```
import React from "react";
import ReactDOM from "react-dom/client";
class Link extends React.Component {
  render() {
    const link = React.createElement(
      "a",
      { href: this.props.url },                    ⟵  Using the url property to
      `Read more about ${this.props.framework}`         set the href property on
    );                                                    the <a> element
    return React.createElement("p", null, link);
  }
}
const link1 = React.createElement(Link, {
  framework: "React",
  url: "//react.dev",         ⟵  The URL for React is
});                               https://react.dev.
const link2 = React.createElement(Link, {
  framework: "Vue",
  url: "//vuejs.org",         ⟵  The URL for Vue is
});                               https://vuejs.org.
const link3 = React.createElement(Link, {
  framework: "Angular",
  url: "//angular.io",        ⟵  The URL for Angular
});                               is https://angular.io.
const group = React.createElement(
  React.Fragment, null, link1, link2, link3
);
```

```
const domElement = document.getElementById("root");
ReactDOM.createRoot(domElement).render(group);
```

> **Repository: rq02-link-props**
>
> This example can be seen in repository rq02-link-props. You can use that reposi-tory by creating a new web app based on the associated template:
>
> ```
> $ npx create-react-app rq02-link-props --template rq02-link-props
> ```
>
> Alternatively, you can go to this website to browse the code, see the application in action directly in your browser, or download the source code as a zip file:
>
> https://rq2e.com/rq02-link-props

You can see this in action in the browser in figure 2.17. As you can see, we can use properties on both custom components (which are used inside the component to cus-tomize the returned structure) and HTML elements (which set HTML attributes).

Figure 2.17   Three links with different text *and* different URLs

What happens if you mess up and set a custom property on an HTML element? React will render it anyway. Before React 16, invalid properties would be filtered out, but because modern web applications often use other third-party libraries that might rely on some custom properties, React 16 and onward will allow you to use whichever properties you choose.

You can completely modify the rendered elements based on the value of a property. For example, we can examine the `framework` property and return a huge title with a link in case the framework name is `"React"`:

```
class Link extends React.Component {
  render() {
    const link = React.createElement(                Creates a link
      "a",                                           element and stores
      { href: this.props.url },                      it in a variable
      `Read more about ${this.props.framework}`,
    );                                               Checks if the
    if (this.props.framework === "React") {          framework
      return React.createElement("h1", null, link);  matches "React"
    }
    return React.createElement("p", null, link);     If it matches,
  }                                                  returns an h1
}                                                    element with the
              Otherwise, returns a paragraph         link inside
              element with the link inside
```

This is also a great example of React elements being just plain old JavaScript. We can create an element and store it in a variable, and then later use that variable as we see fit. We can also create branching using regular JavaScript functionality. If we render this new component in the browser, suddenly the links aren't identical anymore, as you can see in figure 2.18.

We've now covered several permutations of some very simple HTML that's almost useless by itself. But by starting small, we're building a solid foundation for future,

Figure 2.18 Three links are shown, but React stands out as a lot more important.

more advanced topics. The truth is that you can achieve a lot of great things with custom components.

It's very important to know how React works in regular JavaScript if you (like many React developers) plan to use JSX. This is because, in the end, browsers will still run regular JavaScript, and you'll need to understand the results of the JSX-to-JS transpiling from time to time. Going forward, we'll be using JSX, which is covered in the next chapter. But before we get to that, we need to discuss a bit about the structure of a React application.

2.5.3   *The special property: children*

React elements take a special property, `children`. This isn't a property you specify in the normal way, but you do use it as any other property.

Let's change our example a little bit and instead create a list of links where the text is just the framework name without the text "Read more about" before it, as shown in figure 2.19.

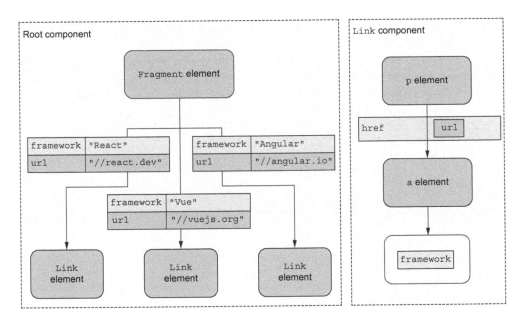

Figure 2.19   Our new structure with the links only containing the framework name

Now let's take this one step further. Let's say we want the framework for React to be displayed in bold. We already know how to make a bold element—just wrap it in an element as follows:

```
React.createElement("strong", null, "React");
```

But how are we going to pass that in as a property? We can do this by creating the node for the React framework like this:

```
const boldReact = React.createElement("strong", null, "React");
const link1 = React.createElement(
  Link,
  { framework: boldReact, url: "//react.dev" }
);
```

Creates a React element in the variable named boldReact

Passes that variable in as the property framework on the Link element

That's a bit weird, though. We're now creating elements, but passing them in as properties, which isn't what we normally do. What if we instead could create an element and pass it in as a child element?

Remember how argument three and onward to `React.createElement` are the children of the element? We haven't used that for custom components, but we can. All the nodes passed as the children to a custom element are accessible through `this.props.children`. That property is either a single node (if only passed one child element) or an array of nodes (if passed multiple child elements).

So, let's change our root component to contain three links, where link text isn't passed in as a property named `framework`, but rather as a child node. For the first link, we still want to make the text bold, as shown in figure 2.20 and then implemented in listing 2.8.

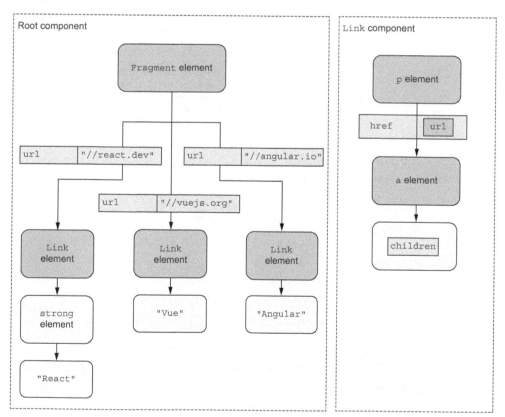

Figure 2.20 The component tree when we pass the link text as a child node rather than as a regular property

Listing 2.8   Links with text as child nodes

```
import React from "react";
import ReactDOM from "react-dom/client";
class Link extends React.Component {
  render() {
    return React.createElement(
      "p",
      null,
      React.createElement(
        "a",
        { href: this.props.url },
        this.props.children
      )
    );
  }
}
const boldReact = React.createElement("strong", null, "React");
const link1 = React.createElement(
  Link,
  { url: "//react.dev" },
  boldReact
);
const link2 = React.createElement(
  Link,
  { url: "//vuejs.org" },
  "Vue"
);
const link3 = React.createElement(
  Link,
  { url: "//angular.io" },
  "Angular"
);
const group = React.createElement(
  React.Fragment, null, link1, link2, link3
);
const domElement = document.getElementById("root");
ReactDOM.createRoot(domElement).render(group);
```

Note how we use the property named children just as if it was any other property.

We now only pass a single named property to each custom component, the url property. But now we also pass a child node, which will become the children property. For React, it's a nested element.

We now only pass a single named property to each custom component, the url property. For Vue and Angular, the child node is just a regular text node.

Repository: rq02-links-children

This example can be seen in repository `rq02-links-children`. You can use that repository by creating a new web app based on the associated template:

```
$ npx create-react-app rq02-links-children --template rq02-links-children
```

Alternatively, you can go to this website to browse the code, see the application in action directly in your browser, or download the source code as a zip file:

https://rq2e.com/rq02-links-children

If you run this in the browser, you get the output displayed in figure 2.21. The distinction between using a normal property and the `children` property might seem insignificant at this point, but in the next chapter, when we start using JSX, you'll see how it starts to make a lot of sense when used correctly.

Figure 2.21   Our link components using children properties where the first link is set in bold

2.6   *Application structure*

From the next chapter on, we're going to structure our applications in the same organized way with similar patterns for easy recognition. We'll also follow the standard structure that the default CRA template provides.

In the previous examples in this chapter, we put our application directly into the `index.js` file inside the source folder. From now on, we're going to use a custom `App` component as the root element of our applications, and we'll render that as the single child to the browser. This means that we won't have to touch `src/index.js` again at all. It will remain the same file for all future applications going forward that use CRA.

For this purpose, we'll rewrite our application with three links from before as two new components. One is the root `App` and the other is the `Link` component. We'll use the latter three times in the former. Finally, we'll destructure some properties from the `React` namespace to shorten our component definition slightly. We'll place all this in `src/App.js`. See figure 2.22 and listing 2.9.

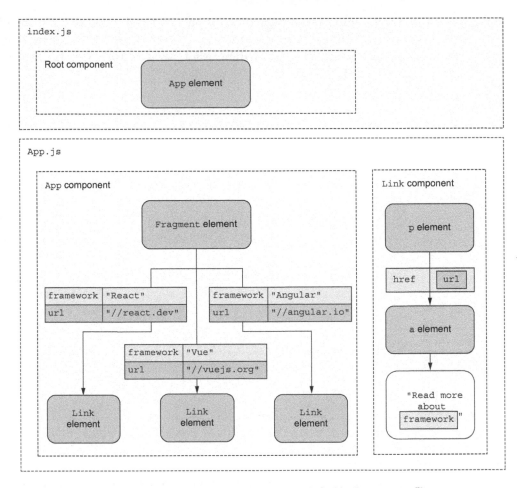

Figure 2.22   Our new file structure with our two components inside the App.js file

Listing 2.9   Application that goes in `src/App.js`

```
import React, { Fragment, Component } from "react";
class Link extends Component {
  render() {
    return React.createElement(
      "p",
      null,
      React.createElement(
        "a",
        { href: this.props.url },
        `Read more about ${this.props.framework}`
      )
    );
  }
}
```

Destructures the import of React to directly reference Fragment and Component

The Link component exactly as in the previous listing

```
class App extends Component {
  render() {
    const link1 = React.createElement(Link, {
      framework: "React",
      url: "//react.dev",
    });
    const link2 = React.createElement(Link, {
      framework: "Vue",
      url: "//vuejs.org",
    });
    const link3 = React.createElement(Link, {
      framework: "Angular",
      url: "//angular.io",
    });
    return React.createElement(
      Fragment, null, link1, link2, link3
    );
  }
}
export default App;
```

A new App component that renders the root of our application

The App component returns a single element as all components must.

In App.js, we export the App component as the single accessible asset inside this file.

We then change `src/index.js` to import our App from `App.js` and render that into the root DOM element, as shown in listing 2.10.

Listing 2.10 `src/index.js`

```
import React from "react";
import { createRoot } from "react-dom/client";
import App from "./App";
createRoot(document.getElementById("root"))
  .render(React.createElement(App));
```

Imports our application from App.js and stores it in the local variable App

Creates a single root element from the HTML element with id="root"

Renders the App component in that root

This new `src/index.js` file is now basically complete. We don't ever need to edit it again; we only edit `src/App.js` to customize our future applications.

Repository: rq02-links-app

This example can be seen in repository `rq02-links-app`. You can use that repository by creating a new web app based on the associated template:

```
$ npx create-react-app rq02-links-app --template rq02-links-app
```

Alternatively, you can go to this website to browse the code, see the application in action directly in your browser, or download the source code as a zip file:

https://rq2e.com/rq02-links-app

As our apps grow larger, we'll grow out of including everything inside a single file in `src/App.js`. When we need to grow, we can just create new files and import those as needed. Although it's customary to create a single file per component and name the file after the component (including the uppercase first letter), it isn't a strict rule. If a component needs several other small components to function, you can freely decide whether you want to put it all in one file, as we did with Link and App in listing 2.10, or split it up into multiple files.

Let's see how we would create the same example with the App and Link components in separate files. Please refer to the diagram in figure 2.23. We would also need to update src/App.js to import the Link component from src/Link.js, as shown in listing 2.11.

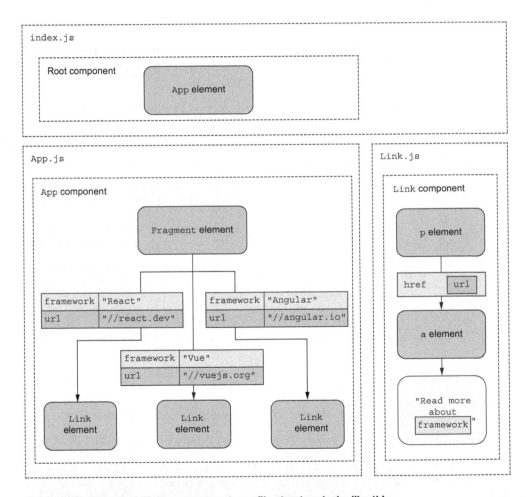

Figure 2.23   Using one file per component, our file structure looks like this.

Listing 2.11   One component per file: `src/App.js`

```
import React, { Fragment, Component } from "react";
import Link from "./Link";
```

Imports the Link component from another file

```
class App extends Component {
  render() {
    const link1 = React.createElement(Link, {
      framework: "React",
      url: "//react.dev",
    });
    const link2 = React.createElement(Link, {
      framework: "Vue",
      url: "//vuejs.org",
    });
    const link3 = React.createElement(Link, {
      framework: "Angular",
      url: "//angular.io",
    });
    return React.createElement(Fragment, null, link1, link2, link3);
  }
}
export default App;
```

Then, we must create the new `src/Link.js` with only the `Link` component and remember to export that at the end.

Listing 2.12   One component per file: `src/Link.js`

```
import React, { Component } from "react";
class Link extends Component {          ⟵┐  The Link component
  render() {                               │  definition is now
    return React.createElement(            │  alone in this file.
      "p",
      null,
      React.createElement(
        "a",
        { href: this.props.url },
        `Read more about ${this.props.framework}`
      )
    );
  }
}                                       ┌─ Remember to export
export default Link;                 ⟵─┘  the component at
                                           the end.
```

Repository: rq02-links-app-alt

This example can be seen in repository `rq02-links-app-alt`. You can use that repository by creating a new web app based on the associated template:

```
$ npx create-react-app rq02-links-app-alt --template rq02-links-app-alt
```

Alternatively, you can go to this website to browse the code, see the application in action directly in your browser, or download the source code as a zip file:

https://rq2e.com/rq02-links-app-alt

We'll be using both approaches throughout the book. In many of the upcoming chapters, our applications will be small and compact, so we'll put everything inside `src/App.js`. But in later chapters, our applications grow larger, and we'll outgrow a single file. We'll also be creating files for other things than components. It could be files for commonly used functions or other shared functionality that we want to use in many files. We'll also be using separate files for custom hooks when we get to that topic in chapter 10.

When projects grow even larger, folder structures are introduced. There are no defined standards for how to use folders to structure a React project, so teams often come up with their own best practices.

2.7 Quiz

1 A custom React component can be created with which of the following statements?

  a `const Name = React.createComponent()`
  b `class Name extends React.Component`
  c `const Name = React.createElement()`
  d `class Name extends React.Class`

2 The only mandatory member of a React component is which of the following?

  a `function`
  b `return`
  c `name`
  d `render`
  e `class`

3 To access the `url` property inside a component, you use which of the following?

  a `this.properties.url`
  b `this.data.url`
  c `this.props.url`
  d `url`

4 React properties are immutable inside the component itself. *True* or *false?*

5 React components allow developers to create reusable UIs. *True* or *false?*

Quiz answers

1 `class Name extends React.Component`. In addition, there's no `React.Class` nor `React.createComponent`, and `React.createElement` is used for creating component instances, not component definitions.

2 `render()` is the only required method. In addition, `function`, `return`, and `class` aren't valid method names.

3 `this.props.url` is correct because only `this.props` returns the properties object.

4   *True.* It's impossible to change a property inside the component itself.

5   *True.* Developers use components to create reusable UIs.

Summary

- You can create new React projects using the command-line program `create-react-app`. This allows you to get up and running with a great starter pack of valuable libraries in no time.

- New React projects can be created from a specified template, and all examples in this book come with a template to allow you to see the example locally in three short commands without having to locate or download anything directly. We'll also provide links to download the examples instead.

- You can nest React elements by putting nested `createElement()` calls inside each other. You can compose sibling nodes by using third, fourth, and so on arguments in `createElement()`.

- You can create elements based on regular HTML node names by using the HTML node name as the first argument to `createElement()`.

- If you want to modify the resulting elements using properties, you can pass these in as an object as the second argument to `createElement()`.

- To use a CBA (one of the features of React), you create custom components. Custom components can use properties internally through the `this.props` variable. Child nodes are received as the specially named `children` property.

- Examples in this book will all follow a very simple file structure.

Introduction to JSX

This chapter covers
- Understanding JSX and its benefits
- Using JSX to implement custom components faster and easier
- React and JSX gotchas

JavaScript XML (JSX) is a syntax extension to JavaScript. It's one of the things that make React great, but it was also one of the more controversial elements of React when it was introduced back in the day.

This is an example of using JSX in JavaScript:

```
const link = <a href="//react.dev">React</a>;
```

JSX is the element that appears between the angle brackets: `<a href="//react.dev">React</a>`. It's not a string, not a template literal, and not HTML. It's a JavaScript object that is created with the syntax extension called JSX. It makes creating React elements much faster and more compact and makes reading React elements much easier. The latter advantage is at least as important as the former.

JSX is made for developers only. By itself, it doesn't do anything to make better or faster web applications. JSX is converted to the same code you get when not using JSX.

Although JSX isn't a requirement, it's universally accepted as the only way to write React components. You may find a few teams out there not using JSX, but they are by far the minority.

In this chapter, we'll dive a bit more into the reasons for using JSX in the first place, then discuss all the different parts of applying JSX in practice, and, finally, cover some tricks that you need to pay attention to when using JSX. Along the way, we'll also briefly discuss converting JSX to JavaScript, called *transpiling*, which you may remember from chapter 2. Luckily, transpiling isn't something you have to worry too much about.

> **NOTE** The source code for the examples in this chapter is available at https://rq2e.com/ch03. But as you learned in chapter 2, you can instantiate all the examples directly from the command line using a single command.

3.1 Why do we use JSX?

JSX is a JavaScript extension that provides syntactic sugar (i.e., making it easier to type, but otherwise functionally equivalent) for function calls and object construction, particularly a replacement for `React.createElement()`. It may look like a template engine or HTML, but it isn't. JSX produces React elements while allowing you to harness the full power of JavaScript. JSX is a great way to write React components and includes the following benefits:

- *Improved developer experience*—Code is easier to read because it's more eloquent, thanks to an XML-like syntax that's better at representing nested declarative structures.
- *Better error messages*—React assumes that you use JSX and reports helpful error messages as if you are. If you're not, the error messages will be somewhat misleading by referring to a different syntax than you actually use.
- *Faster code*—When converting JSX to JavaScript, the transpiler optimizes the code on the fly, making the resulting JavaScript execute faster than you could normally type by hand.
- *More productive team members*—Casual developers (e.g., designers) can modify code more easily because JSX looks like HTML, which is already familiar to them.
- *Fewer syntax errors*—Developers have less code to type, which means they make fewer mistakes.

Although JSX isn't required for React, it fits in nicely, and we highly recommended it, as do React's creators. You'll have a hard time finding any team in the real world that uses React without JSX. While we can't say that *all* recent React projects in the world use JSX, we're pretty confident that *almost all* do.

3.1.1 Before and after JSX

To demonstrate the eloquence of JSX, this is the snippet required to create an element with a few custom components followed by a link:

```
const element = <main>
  <Title>Welcome</Title>
  <Carousel images={6} />
  <a href="/blog">Go to the blog</a>
</main>;
```

That's identical to the following snippet implemented without the benefit of JSX:

```
const element = React.createElement(
  'main',
  null,
  React.createElement(Title, null, 'Welcome'),
  React.createElement(Carousel, {images: 6}),
  React.createElement('a', {href: "/blog"}, 'Go to the blog'),
);
```

We can probably all agree that the JSX version is much easier to understand at a glance. It looks like HTML, which is very easy to read, and it's partially identical to the HTML output that will be rendered, except for the custom components, of course.

3.1.2 *Keeping HTML and JavaScript together*

In essence, JSX is a small language with an XML-like syntax. It has changed the way people write user interface (UI) components. Previously, developers wrote HTML—and JavaScript code for controllers and views—in an MVC-like manner, jumping between various files. That stemmed from the separation of concerns in the early days. This approach served the web well when it consisted of static HTML, a little CSS, and a tiny bit of JavaScript to make text blink.

This is no longer the case; today, we build highly interactive UIs, and JavaScript and HTML are tightly coupled to implement various pieces of functionality. This violates the principle of separation of concerns, which is a fundamental principle sought after in most software development. This principle is about separating unrelated items, but keeping related items together. If you seek to obey this principle, you should break your code down in such a way that every bit in isolation performs one and only one concern, and these "bits" can then be used in different connections. If you split your template and your view logic, but they only work if combined, then you have needlessly separated two items that belong together.

React fixes this invalidated principle by bringing together the description of the UI and the JavaScript logic; and with JSX, the code looks like HTML and is easier to read and write. If for no other reason, we would use React and JSX for this new approach to writing UIs.

JSX is compiled by various transformers (tools) into standard ECMAScript (see figure 3.1). You probably know that JavaScript is ECMAScript too, but JSX isn't part of the specification and doesn't have any defined semantics. That means that if you try to compile JavaScript with embedded JSX in a normal JavaScript compiler without transpiling the JSX first, you'll get errors. JSX isn't valid JavaScript on its own and can't be compiled directly by a JavaScript compiler.

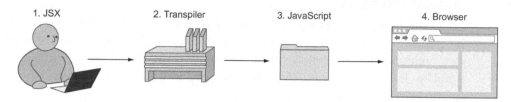

Figure 3.1 JSX is transpiled into regular JavaScript.

NOTE We call it *transpiling* rather than *compiling* because we translate it from one source language (JSX) into another source language (JavaScript). The resulting JavaScript will then, in turn, be interpreted by a "real" compiler that runs the code. Transpiling is merely converting syntax rather than interpreting the code.

When your browser executes your React application, your browser will only see the `React.createElement` statements required to generate the structure that you need. It's only in the editor that the JSX exists. The transpiler converts your files with JSX in them to pure JavaScript with `React.createElement()`s all over the place to save you the trouble.

You may wonder why you should bother with JSX at all. Considering how counterintuitive JSX code looks to begin with for new developers, it's no surprise that a few developers are turned off by this amazing technology. As an example, this bit of JavaScript has JSX in the middle of it, mixing in angle brackets where they normally would never exist:

```
const title = <h1>Hello</h1>;
```

But what makes JSX amazing are the shortcuts to `React.createElement(NAME, ...)`. Instead of writing that function call over and over, you can instead use `<NAME />`. And as mentioned earlier, the less you type, the fewer mistakes you make. With JSX, developer experience is the primary concern, that is, making it easier for developers to create components and applications faster and with fewer errors.

The main reason to use JSX is that many people find code with angle brackets (`<>`) easier to read than code with a lot of `React.createElement()` statements. Once you get into the habit of thinking about `<NAME />` not as XML but as an alias to JavaScript code, you'll get over the perceived weirdness of JSX syntax. Knowing and using JSX can make a big difference when you're developing React components and, subsequently, React-powered applications.

As mentioned earlier, JSX needs to be transpiled into regular JavaScript before browsers can execute the code. In most setups, you'll never have to worry about this, but we'll discuss some transpilers in section 3.3 if you need to do it on your own. For now, we'll dig in to fully understand JSX.

3.2   Understanding JSX

Let's explore how to work with JSX. You can read this section and keep it bookmarked for your reference, or (if you prefer to have some of the code examples running on your computer) start working on the examples using the `create-react-app` (CRA) templates listed throughout. With CRA, you get JSX transpiling "for free," so you don't have to worry about setting it up yourself.

3.2.1   Creating elements with JSX

Creating React elements with JSX is straightforward. See table 3.1 for some examples of the JavaScript that you've previously used and its JSX equivalent.

Table 3.1   JavaScript code versus JSX

JavaScript	JSX equivalent
`React.createElement('h1')`	`<h1 />`

`React.createElement(`
`  'h1',`
`  null,`
`  'Welcome',`
`);`
	`<h1>`
	`  Welcome`
	`</h1>`

`React.createElement(`
`  Title,`
`  null,`
`  'Welcome',`
`);`
	`<Title>`
	`  Welcome`
	`</Title>`

`React.createElement(`
`  Title,`
`  {size: 6},`
`  'Welcome'`
`);`
	`<Title size="6">`
	`  Welcome`
	`</Title>`

`React.createElement(`
`  Title,`
`  {size: 6},`
`  'Welcome to ',`
`  React.createElement(`
`    'strong',`
`    null,`
`    'Narnia',`
`  ),`
`);`
	`<Title size="6">`
	`  Welcome to`
	`  <strong>Narnia</strong>`
	`</Title>`

In the JSX code, the attributes and their values (e.g., `size={6}`) come from the second argument of `createElement()`. We'll focus on working with properties later in this chapter.

For now, let's look at an example of JSX elements without properties. Here is one of our early examples from the previous chapter, upgraded to the recommended structure using a custom App component. It's just an h1 element with the text "Hello world!" where the word "world" is set as italic, as shown next.

Listing 3.1   Emphasized greeting without JSX

```
import React, { Component } from 'react';
class App extends Component {
  render() {
    return React.createElement(
      'h1',
      null,
      'Hello ',
      React.createElement('em', null, 'world'),
      '!',
      );
  }
}
export default App;
```

Implementing this with JSX is so much simpler.

Listing 3.2   Emphasized greeting with JSX

```
import React, { Component } from 'react';
class App extends Component {
  render() {
    return <h1>Hello <em>World</em>!</h1>;
  }
}
export default App;
```

You can even store objects created with JSX syntax in variables because JSX is just a syntactic improvement of React.createElement(). This example stores the reference to the generated element in a variable before returning it:

```
const title = <h1>Hello <em>World</em>!</h1>;
return title;
```

This is completely identical to line 4 in listing 3.2; it just uses an extra variable before returning.

3.2.2   *Using JSX with custom components*

The previous example used the <h1> JSX tag, which is also a standard HTML tag name. When working with custom components, you apply the same syntax. The only difference is that the component class name must start with a capital letter, as in <Title />.

Listing 3.3 shows a more advanced iteration of our three-link application from chapter 2, rewritten in JSX. In this case, you create a new component class and use

JSX to create an element from it. Remember our `Link` example from the previous chapter? The code looked like the following without JSX (converted to the recommended App structure).

Listing 3.3   Three identical links without JSX

```
import React, { Component, Fragment } from 'react';
class Link extends Component {
  render() {
    return React.createElement(
      'p',
      null,
      React.createElement(
        'a',
        {href: '//react.dev'},
        'Read more about React',
      ),
    );
  }
}
class App extends Component {
  render() {
    const link1 = React.createElement(Link);
    const link2 = React.createElement(Link);
    const link3 = React.createElement(Link);
    const group = React.createElement(Fragment, null, link1, link2, link3);
    return group;
  }
}
export default App;
```

Using JSX, this now becomes listing 3.4. If you run this in the browser, you get the exact same result as we did in figure 2.13 in chapter 2, which we show again in figure 3.2.

Listing 3.4   Three identical links with JSX

```
import { Component, Fragment } from 'react';
class Link extends Component {          ◁──┐  Creates a component named Link
  render() {                                that can later be instantiated by
    return (                                using the JSX notation <Link />
      <p>
        <a href="//react.dev">Read more about React</a>
      </p>
    );
  }
}
class App extends Component {
  render() {
    return (                ◁─────┐  Opening parenthesis that starts the
      <Fragment>            ◁──┐     returned multiline JSX expression
        <Link />
        <Link />               React fragments are elements just like
        <Link />               any other and can be rendered using JSX.
```

Three identical instances of the Link component

```
        </Fragment>
    );
    }
}
export default App;
```

Closing parenthesis that
completes the returned
multiline JSX expression

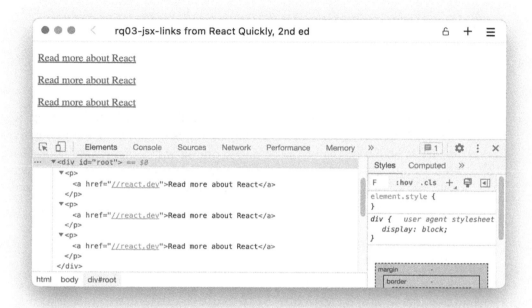

Figure 3.2   Three identical links in our application but now written using JSX

3.2.3   *Multiline JSX objects*

You might have noticed the parentheses around the returned multiline JSX object in
listing 3.4. You have to include these parentheses if you start a multiline JSX object on
a separate line after, for example, a `return`. This is the way to create multiline JSX
objects when not starting on the same line:

```
return (
  <main>
    <h1>Hello world</h1>
  </main>
);
```

Alternatively, you can start your root element on the same line as `return` and avoid the parentheses. For example, this is valid as well:

```
return <main>
  <h1>Hello world</h1>
</main>;
```

A downside of this second approach is the reduced visibility of the opening `<main>` tag. It may be easy to miss in the code. The choice is up to you. We'll exclusively use the former style of using parentheses around multiline JSX content for consistency.

Note that the exact same thing goes for any other use of multiline JSX objects, for example, when you save them in a variable. We'll also be using parentheses there:

```
const message = (
  <main>
    <h1>Hello world</h1>
  </main>
);
```

3.2.4   *Outputting variables in JSX*

When you compose components, you want them to be smart enough to change the view based on some code. For example, it would be useful if a date component uses the current date and time, and not just a hardcoded value.

When working with JavaScript-only React, you have to use string template literals (i.e., backticks) to mix strings with variables—or, even worse, concatenation. For example, to use a variable in a string context in a `DateTimeNow` component without JSX, you would write this code:

```
class DateTimeNow extends React.Component {
  render() {
    const dateTimeNow = new Date().toLocaleString()
    return React.createElement(
      'span',
      null,
      `Current date and time is ${dateTimeNow}.`
    )
  }
}
```

In JSX, you can use curly brace {} notation to output variables dynamically, which reduces code complexity substantially:

```
class DateTimeNow extends React.Component {
  render() {
    const dateTimeNow = new Date().toLocaleString()
    return <span>Current date and time is {dateTimeNow}.</span>
  }
}
```

If you reference a variable that is a React element (optionally created using JSX), you can directly insert that other bit of JSX in the current context:

```
const now = <date>{dateTimeNow}</date>;
const message = <p>Today is {now}</p>;
```

This is equivalent to directly inserting the element:

```
const message = <p>Today is <date>{dateTimeNow}</date></p>;
```

The inserted variables can also be properties, not just locally defined variables:

```
<p>Hello {this.props.userName}, today is {dateTimeNow}.</p>
```

You can also invoke methods of your component that you create yourself. That is a common practice to isolate bits of functionality, as shown in the next listing.

Listing 3.5 `ButtonList` **using a method**

```
import { Component } from 'react';
class ButtonList extends Component {
  getButton(text) {                          ◁── Defines the getButton method that
    return (                                      takes an argument text, which will
      <button disabled={this.props.disabled}>{text}</button>   ◁──  be the label on the button
    );
  }                                                    Our button depends on
  render() {                                           another property passed
    return (                                           to our component.
      <aside>
        {this.getButton('Up')}              │  Invokes our method to get a button
        {this.getButton('Down')}            │  inserted with the proper text
      </aside>
    );
  }
}
```

The example in listing 3.5 is overly simplified, of course, as most of the time, you would probably be using an extra component for such a use case. However, there are situations where component methods do come in handy. The purpose of this example is to show that you can invoke component methods directly in JSX. For example, you can execute arbitrary JavaScript expressions inside the curly braces, such as formatting a date directly:

```
<p>Today is {new Date(Date.now()).toLocaleTimeString()}.</p>
```

Now let's rewrite our emphasized greeting to store the italicized word in a variable first, before outputting it, in the next listing. Then, we'll move on to discuss how you work with properties in JSX in the next section.

Listing 3.6   Emphasized greeting using JSX and a variable

```
import { Component } from 'react';
class App extends Component {
  render() {
    const world = <em>World</em>;
    return <h1>Hello {world}!</h1>;
  }
}
export default App;
```

3.2.5   *Working with properties in JSX*

We touched on this topic earlier, when we introduced JSX. Element properties are defined using attribute syntax. That is, you use `key1=value1 key2=value2...` notation inside the JSX tag to define both HTML attributes and React component properties. This is similar to attribute syntax in HTML/XML.

In other words, if you need to pass properties, write them in JSX as you would in normal HTML. You render standard HTML attributes by setting element properties (discussed in section 2.3) on a React element with an HTML tag. For example, this code sets a standard HTML attribute `href` for anchor element `<a>`:

```
return <a href="//react.dev">Let's do React!</a>;
```

You use the exact same method to set properties on custom components. If we had our `Link` component from the previous chapter, we could use it in JSX as follows:

```
return <Link url="//react.dev" framework="React" />;
```

Using hardcoded values for attributes isn't all that flexible, of course. If you want to reuse the `Link` component, then the `href` must change to reflect a different address each time. This is called dynamically setting values versus hardcoding them. So, next, we'll go a step further and consider a component that can use dynamically generated values for attributes. Those values can come from component properties (`this.props`). After that, everything's easy. All you need to do is use curly braces (`{}`) inside angle braces (`<>`) to pass dynamic values of properties to elements.

For example, suppose you're building a component that will be used to link to user accounts. You need some attributes on your `<a>` tag, but `href` and `title` must be different for each component and not hardcoded. Let's create a dynamic component `ProfileLink` that renders a link with properties `url` and `label` for `href` and `title`, respectively. You pass the properties to `<a>` using `{}`:

```
class ProfileLink extends React.Component {
  render() {
```

```
    return (
      <a
        href={this.props.url}
        title={this.props.label}
        target="_blank">Profile
      </a>
    );
  }
}
```

Where do the property values come from? They're defined when `ProfileLink` is created—that is, in the component that creates `ProfileLink`, aka its parent. For example, this is how the values for `url` and `label` are passed when a `ProfileLink` instance is created, which results in rendering the `<a>` tag with those values:

```
<ProfileLink url="/users/johnny" label="Profile for Johnny" />
```

From the previous chapter, you'll remember that when rendering standard elements (`<h>`, `<p>`, `<div>`, `<a>`, etc.), React will render any and all properties even if they don't have any semantic meaning in HTML. That's not specific for JSX, that's just default React behavior.

   If you have an object with properties that you want to render on an element, you can render each of them one by one as follows:

```
return (
  <Post
    id={post.id}
    title={post.title}
    content={post.content}
  />
);
```

This works great and is a safe solution. However, if you have an object with values, and you want to render *all of them*, you can do so using the spread operator as follows:

```
return <Post {...post} />;
```

Note that this will render *every* property of the post object, regardless of whether that makes sense or not. Only use this process when you're sure that the object only has the properties that you need or at least sure that any excess properties are ignored.

   This will even allow you to render all the properties passed to a component to another element inside that component by spreading `this.props`:

```
return <input value={this.value} {...this.props} />;
```

This is a bit dangerous though, as it allows the parent component to pass in arbitrary values that would supersede any values that you passed to it. If `this.props` contained a `value` property, it would override the `value` property that you set in the component before the spread. Be extra careful when spreading objects and in particular when spreading all props passed to a component. We'll get back to the spreading operator in the next chapter and cover some other common examples of its use.

THE SPECIAL PROPERTY: CHILDREN

If you think back to the previous chapter, we introduced the special property `children`, which only looks like a property inside a custom component, not from the outside. When using JSX, the `children` property becomes a lot neater to use. In the example with child nodes in chapter 2, it looked like the tree structure shown in figure 3.3.

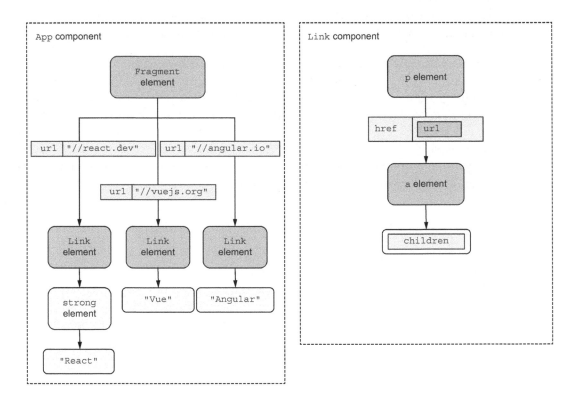

Figure 3.3   The component tree when we use child nodes as link content

Let's reimplement this one in JSX. We know all the things we need to do, so let's go ahead and do them.

Listing 3.7   Link list with child nodes in JSX

```
import { Fragment, Component } from "react";
class Link extends Component {
  render() {
    return (
```

```
        <p>
          <a href={this.props.url}>
            {this.props.children}
          </a>
        </p>
      );
    }
  }
class App extends Component {
  render() {
    return (
      <Fragment>
        <Link url="//react.dev">
          <strong>React</strong>
        </Link>
        <Link url="//vuejs.org">Vue</Link>
        <Link url="//angular.io">Angular</Link>
      </Fragment>
    );
  }
}
export default App;
```

We still use the url property as we did before and also just use this.props.children as if it was any other property.

Note how elegantly these child nodes are added in JSX. It looks just like the rest of the code.

The difference between using properties and child nodes suddenly becomes a lot more obvious. We could have passed the link content in as a property, but it would have looked pretty bad. If we used the regular property approach, it would have looked like this:

```
<Link
  url="//react.dev"
  content={<strong>React</strong>}
/>
```

But when we use the children approach, it becomes

```
<Link url="//react.dev">
  <strong>React</strong>
</Link>
```

We definitely know what we prefer—the latter approach.

3.2.6   *Branching in JSX*

Branching is always important in coding. For example, if the user is logged in, show their account information; otherwise, show a login form. Because JSX is just JavaScript, we can basically use the exact same constructs that we do in regular coding to create branching in our components. That being said, some patterns have emerged that most developers follow about how to use branching in React components using JSX:

- Use early return for rendering nothing.
- Use the ternary operator for rendering alternative elements.
- Use the logical AND operator (&&) for rendering optional elements.
- Use object maps for rendering between many different elements.
- Use extra components for more complex branching.

We'll go through each of these in the next subsections to explain how we use branching in JSX and custom React components.

USING EARLY RETURN FOR RENDERING NOTHING

Imagine you have a component that renders something relevant only when a certain condition is true. For example, imagine a countdown component that renders a value only when the number of remaining seconds is larger than 0.

If a component doesn't render anything, we can simply return `null` from the component. However, to optimize our components, we try to do this as early as possible to short-circuit the execution. The purpose is to branch out to the easiest case as quickly as we can to avoid doing extra calculations or creating JSX objects where we don't need them.

We could create our `Countdown` component like this:

```
class Countdown extends Component {
  render() {
    const seconds = this.props.remaining % 60;
    const minutes = Math.floor(this.props.remaining / 60);
    const message = <p>{minutes}:{seconds}</p>;
    if (seconds > 0 || minutes > 0) {
      return message;
    } else {
      return null;
    }
  }
}
```

There's nothing inherently wrong with this—it works and it's fully functional. But you'll see many developers use the approach of aborting early if the component renders nothing. We can detect this case of rendering nothing before calculating the number of seconds and minutes and before creating the JSX object:

```
class Countdown extends Component {
  render() {
    if (this.props.remaining === 0) {
```

```
        return null;
    }
    const seconds = this.props.remaining % 60;
    const minutes = Math.floor(this.props.remaining / 60);
    return <p>{minutes}:{seconds}</p>;
  }
}
```

Here, we also use the fact that when we return from inside an `if` block, we don't need an `else` block. The `else` is implicit in that anything after the `if` block is only visited if the condition failed.

USING TERNARY FOR ALTERNATIVES

Another very common case in React components is to render different elements based on whether some condition is true or false. For instance, let's imagine a shopping cart in which we want to display the items if there are any items, but display a message saying there are no items when no items are in the cart.

We could do this in JSX by using a variable and assigning it different values via a regular if/else statement block. However, that's a bit lengthy, and it's a lot more common in React to use the ternary operator. Where the if/else construct is a statement, the ternary operator is an expression and can thus be used inline directly in JSX:

```
<p>User is {this.props.isOnline ? 'Online' : 'Offline'}</p>
```

Using this, we can create our shopping cart component from before:

```
class ShoppingCart extends Component {
  render() {
    return (
      <aside>
        <h1>Shopping cart</h1>
        {this.props.items.length === 0 ? (
          <p>Your cart is empty. Go buy something!</p>
        ) : (
          <CartItems items={this.props.items} />
        )}
      </aside>
    );
  }
}
```

USING LOGICAL OPERATORS FOR OPTIONAL RENDERING

Another common pattern is the need to optionally render an element if a condition is true, but render nothing if not true. As an example, we want to display a little checkmark next to a username if the user is a verified user, but nothing for the unverified plebeians. We can do this using logical AND and the fact that logical operators short-circuit by returning as soon as the truthiness of the entire expression is known. So, when doing a `&&` b, JavaScript returns a if a is *falsy* or b if a is *truthy*. If a is truthy, it doesn't matter what b is; it will be returned regardless. Combine this with the fact that React renders `false` as the empty string (more on that later).

> **Truthiness**
>
> In JavaScript, a *truthy* value translates to true when evaluated as a Boolean. For example, in an if statement
>
> ```
> if (someVariable) {
>   // this happens if and only if someVariable is truthy.
> }
> ```
>
> the value is truthy if it's not falsy. That is literally the official definition, not kidding. There are only six falsy values:
>
> - `false`
> - `0`
> - `""` (empty string)
> - `null`
> - `Undefined`
> - `NaN` (not a number)

We can use this to render conditional elements, by making our logical AND operator return `false` if the user isn't verified, and a React element if the user is verified:

```
class UserName extends Component {
  render() {
    return (
      <p>
        {this.props.username}
        {this.props.isVerified && <Checkmark />}
      </p>
    );
  }
}
```

You'll encounter this pattern often in React components, so it's a good one to know.

USING OBJECTS FOR SWITCHING

So far, we've dealt with the case of rendering either an element or nothing, or rendering one element or another, but what if we want to render more than two types of elements based on a condition? For this scenario, we want to render an icon based on some blog post status. If the post is in the draft state, we render a draft icon. If the post is in the published state, we render a published icon. And, if the post is in any other state (which we happen to know to be just the deleted state), we render a trash icon.

Well, we could nest ternaries in order to first check if status === "draft"; then, if not, check if status === "published"; and, if not, assume that it must be deleted:

```
class PostStatus extends Component {
  render() {
    return this.props.status === "draft" ?
      <DraftIcon /> :
      this.props.status === "published" ?
      <PublishedIcon /> :
      <TrashIcon />;
  }
}
```

This would work, but it's not very pretty. Another alternative is to use a switch statement and simply return the different values in each case. But a more declarative approach here is to use an object with properties for the different cases resolving the different outcomes:

```
const status2icon = {
  draft: <DraftIcon />,
  published: <PublishedIcon />,
  deleted: <TrashIcon />,
};
class PostStatus extends Component {
  render() {
    return status2icon[this.props.status];
  }
}
```

That's rather short and neat, no? However, note that this doesn't handle the situation in which the status is none of those things. Before, the component would render the trash icon if the status was neither draft nor published, but now, it will only render the trash icon if the status is deleted.

To handle the case when the status is any other unexpected value, we need to add a logical OR at the end so that if the object indexing resolves to nothing, we still render an alternative. Let's say we just render the trash icon in any unknown case:

```
class PostStatus extends Component {
  render() {
    return status2icon[this.props.status] || status2icon.deleted;
  }
}
```

This pattern is probably less common in React, but you'll still see it for simple cases like those we've discussed.

USING EXTRA COMPONENTS FOR COMPLEX BRANCHING

The preceding scenarios only cover some simple branching cases. What do you do if your component has more complicated logic than that?

Let's say we have a shopping cart component like before with some buttons at the bottom. We have to implement the following business logic as dictated by a customer:

- If the user is logged in, there will be just a Checkout button.
- If the user isn't logged in, there will be a Login button as well as a Checkout as Guest button.
- If any item is out of stock or if the cart is empty, the Checkout or the Checkout as Guest button will be disabled.
- If the user is logged in but hasn't added a credit card yet, show an Add Credit Card button instead.
- If the user is logged in, has a credit card on file, and has entered an address, show a One-Click Buy button next to the Checkout button. This button will be disabled according to the same logic as the Checkout button.

Now, let's implement all of this with the tricks that you've learned so far.

Listing 3.8   Complex shopping cart

```
import { Component, Fragment } from "react";
class ShoppingCart extends Component {
  render() {
    const hasItems = this.props.items.length > 0;
    const isLoggedIn = this.props.user !== null;
    const hasCreditCard = isLoggedIn && this.props.user.creditcard !== null;
    const hasAddress = isLoggedIn && this.props.user.address !== null;
    const isAvailable = this.props.items.every((item) => !item.outOfStock);
    return isLoggedIn ? (
      hasCreditCard ? (
        <Fragment>
          <button disabled={!hasItems || !isAvailable}>
            Checkout
          </button>
          {hasAddress && (
            <button
              disabled={!hasItems || !isAvailable}
            >
              One-click buy
            </button>
          )}
        </Fragment>
      ) : (
        <button>Add credit card</button>
      )
    ) : (
      <Fragment>
        <button>Login</button>
        <button disabled={!hasItems || !isAvailable}>
          Checkout as guest
        </button>
      </Fragment>
```

First ternary operator

Second ternary operator

Logical AND to optionally render a button

Repeated logic for disabled button

```
      );
    }
  }
class App extends Component {
  render() {
    const items = [1, 2, 3];
    const user = { creditcard: null, address: true };
    return <ShoppingCart items={items} user={user} />;
  }
}
export default App;
```

Okay, that seems to cover everything. However, this is getting a bit complicated with the nested conditionals and duplicated attributes. For such a complex case, it's often a good idea to split things into multiple components that deal with each of the different cases one by one.

Here, we can create new components `<UserButtons />` and `<GuestButtons />`. At the top level, we can select which of these components to use and then add the necessary extra checks and conditionals inside each of these.

Listing 3.9   Simplified multicomponent shopping cart

```
import { Component, Fragment } from "react";
class UserButtons extends Component {
  render() {
    const hasCreditCard = this.props.user.creditcard !== null;
    const hasAddress = this.props.user.address !== null;
    const disabled = !this.props.canCheckout;
    return hasCreditCard ? (
      <Fragment>
        <button disabled={disabled}>Checkout</button>
        {hasAddress && (
          <button disabled={disabled}>One-click buy</button>
        )}
      </Fragment>
    ) : (
      <button>Add credit card</button>
    );
```

Ternary operators (annotation pointing to `const disabled = !this.props.canCheckout;` and `return hasCreditCard ? (`)

Logical AND for optional rendering (annotation pointing to `{hasAddress && (`)

```
      }
    }
    class GuestButtons extends Component {
      render() {
        return (
          <Fragment>
            <button>Login</button>
            <button disabled={!this.props.canCheckout}>
              Checkout as guest
            </button>
          </Fragment>
        );
      }
    }
    class ShoppingCart extends Component {
      render() {
        const hasItems = this.props.items.length > 0;
        const isLoggedIn = this.props.user !== null;
        const isAvailable = this.props.items.every((item) => !item.outOfStock);
        const canCheckout = hasItems && isAvailable;
        return isLoggedIn ? (
          <UserButtons user={this.props.user} canCheckout={canCheckout} />
        ) : (
          <GuestButtons canCheckout={canCheckout} />
        );
      }
    }
    class App extends Component {
      render() {
        const items = [1, 2, 3];
        const user = { creditcard: null, address: true };
        return <ShoppingCart items={items} user={user} />;
      }
    }
    export default App;
```

Ternary operators → (pointing to `return isLoggedIn ? (`)

> ### Repository: rq03-cart-multi
>
> This example can be seen in repository `rq03-cart-multi`. You can use that repository by creating a new app based on the associated template:
>
> ```
> $ npx create-react-app rq03-cart-multi --template rq03-cart-multi
> ```
>
> Alternatively, you can go to this website to browse the code, see the application in action directly in your browser, or download the source code as a zip file:
>
> https://rq2e.com/rq03-cart-multi

This works the same as before with exactly the same complexity, but each component is much simpler, and you can easily understand each component on its own by reading through the code. You could even take it an extra step and split the <User-Buttons> component into two for the "has credit card" and "doesn't have credit card" situations.

We must, of course, acknowledge that more components means more code, and more code means more memory and CPU usage (in general), so this latter example is slightly more resource intensive than the former. In most applications, this difference is negligible though, and code quality often trumps such minor optimizations.

3.2.7   *Comments in JSX*

Because JSX is written inside of JavaScript, you can use regular JavaScript comments outside the JSX elements as normal:

```
// This is the page title
const title = <h1>Hello world!</h1>;
```

However, if you have very long segments of JSX code, you might want to add comments inline inside the JSX. If you want to do that, you can't always use a regular Java-Script comment directly.

To add JSX comments between tags, you can wrap standard JavaScript comments using /**/ or // in {}, like this:

```
const content = (
  <div>
    {/* Just like a JS comment */}
    {/* It can also span
        multiple lines */}
    {// Single line comments are possible too
    }
  </div>
);
```

You can also use JavaScript comments directly using either /**/ or // inside tags:

```
const content = (
  <div>
    <input
      /* This element is
         rendered because... */
      name={this.props.name} // Some important comment here
    />
  </div>
);
```

Note that when you use a regular single-line comment between tags inside curly brackets, you need to have a newline character before you end the curly brackets. The following code would fail:

```
const content = (
  <div>
    {// This does NOT work! }
  </div>
);
```

This would result in a compiler error because the ending curly bracket is considered part of the comment, so the opening curly bracket doesn't have a matching ending bracket, which causes a parser error.

3.2.8   *Lists of JSX objects*

A common tactic in React elements is to map an array of elements to an array of JSX objects to be returned in a component. Let's say we want to create a component to render a drop-down list. We want to pass the list of options in the drop-down as an array of strings to a new <Select /> component. We want to be able to do the following in our application:

```
class App extends Component {
  render() {
    const items = ['apples', 'pears', 'playstations'];
    return <Select items={items} />;
  }
}
```

Then our `Select` component should correctly render a `<select>` with `<option>` elements in HTML. How would we go about doing that? The naive way is to simply map the elements from strings to JSX objects using declarative programming, as shown in the next listing.

Listing 3.10   Naive implementation of `select`

```
import { Component } from "react";
class App extends Component {
  render() {
    const items = ["apples", "pears", "playstations"];
    return <Select items={items} />;
  }
}
class Select extends Component {
  render() {
    return (
      <select>
        {this.props.items.map((item) => (     ◁──── For every
          <option>{item}</option>    ◁────            element in the
        ))}                              Returns a JSX      items array
      </select>                         element
    );
  }
}
export default App;
```

This is a pretty decent attempt at solving this. However, if we run this in the browser, we'll get a warning:

```
Warning: Each child in a list should have a unique "key" prop.
```

The application works, but we get this warning about a missing `key` property. The usage of the `key` property is a bit advanced at this stage in our React learning, but it's used by React to track if the same element moves around in the rendered DOM. If the same element moves around, React will reuse the same element, but if React doesn't know whether it's the same element or not, React will delete all the old elements and recreate completely new elements every time the list renders.

For the purposes of this example, we can just use the `item` value as the `key` property on the root element returned inside the mapped array. This results in the code shown in the next listing.

Listing 3.11 Correct implementation of `select`

```
import { Component } from "react";
class App extends Component {
  render() {
    const items = ["apples", "pears", "playstations"];
    return <Select items={items} />;
  }
}
class Select extends Component {
  render() {
    return (
      <select>
        {this.props.items.map((item) => (
          <option key={item}>{item}</option>      ⟵── We've added a
        ))}                                           key property to the
      </select>                                       <option> element.
    );
  }
}
export default App;
```

Repository: rq03-correct-select

This example can be seen in repository `rq03-correct-select`. You can use that repository by creating a new app based on the associated template:

```
$ npx create-react-app rq03-correct-select --template rq03-correct-select
```

Alternatively, you can go to this website to browse the code, see the application in action directly in your browser, or download the source code as a zip file:

https://rq2e.com/rq03-correct-select

This `key` property is an internal React property that will never be rendered to the DOM. It's recommended that the `key` property is some unique identifier for the element in question and not just the index of the element in the array (if elements move around in the array, the indexes change even though the elements don't, so proper element reuse is circumvented).

Keys must be unique. If you render a list with non-unique keys, you'll get a different warning in the console about duplicate keys.

NOTE Keys are local to the individual array, so they only have to be unique within each array, not between all arrays in your application or even your component. Different arrays of JSX objects can have duplicate keys between them as long as no single array has duplicate keys inside it.

As mentioned, this is a fairly complicated feature of React to understand at this point, so, for now, just be aware that if you get a warning in the console about a missing `key` property or duplicate keys, this is the reason.

3.2.9   *Fragments in JSX*

We've already covered JSX fragments a few times. They're used to export multiple elements at the same level in a situation where only a single element is allowed. We've previously done something like this to include both a heading and a link:

```
import { Fragment } from 'react';
...
return (
  <Fragment>
    <h1>Hello and welcome</h1>
    <a href="/blog">Go to the blog</a>
  </Fragment>
);
```

However, from React 16.2 (and Babel 7) forward, a shorter syntax is also allowed. Now you don't even have to import the `Fragment` component:

```
return (
  <>
```

```
    <h1>Hello and welcome</h1>
    <a href="/blog">Go to the blog</a>
  </>
);
```

This new shorthand syntax uses a seemingly empty tag to render fragments. This syntax with <></> can't take any attributes or properties, however. The only property you might want to apply to this would be key because you're rendering a list of elements, where each element has more than a single JSX element at the root.

A classic scenario for this is a definition list. It's defined in HTML like this:

```
<dl>
  <dt>Term A</dt>
  <dd>Description of Term A.</dd>
  <dt>Term B</dt>
  <dd>Description of Term B.</dd>
</dl>
```

As you can see, each entry requires two sibling elements in the list to render (<dt> and <dd>).

For example, if we create an application to render three dog breeds with a little description about each, we need to map our dog breed names and definitions to two elements. We do that by wrapping them in a fragment, but because we need the fragment to have a key property, we have to use the literal Fragment component and, unfortunately, can't use the shorthand syntax mentioned previously. Let's implement this in the following listing.

Listing 3.12 Definition list of dog breeds

```
import { Component, Fragment } from "react";
class App extends Component {
  render() {
    const list = [
      { breed: "Chihuahua", description: "Small breed of dog." },
      { breed: "Corgi", description: "Cute breed of dog." },
      { breed: "Cumberland Sheepdog", description: "Extinct breed of dog."},
    ];
    return <Breeds list={list} />;
  }
}
class Breeds extends Component {
  render() {
    return (
      <dl>
        {this.props.list.map(
          ({ breed, description }) => (           ◄── Uses destructuring to easily
            <Fragment key={breed}>      ◄──           access the properties of
              <dt>{breed}</dt>                          the list item
              <dd>{description}</dd>
            </Fragment>                   Because we need a key property, we have
          )                              to use the proper Fragment component.
                                         Note that we just use the breed as the
                                         key, as that uniquely identifies each
                                         element in the array.
```

```
        )}
      </dl>
    );
  }
}
export default App;
```

Repository: rq03-dog-breeds

This example can be seen in repository `rq03-dog-breeds`. You can use that repository by creating a new app based on the associated template:

```
$ npx create-react-app rq03-dog-breeds --template rq03-dog-breeds
```

Alternatively, you can go to this website to browse the code, see the application in action directly in your browser, or download the source code as a zip file:

https://rq2e.com/rq03-dog-breeds

If we run this in the browser, we get a nice definition list exactly as we wanted to, as you can see in figure 3.4. Using fragments with keys isn't as much of an edge case as it might seem, so this is very useful to know already at this stage.

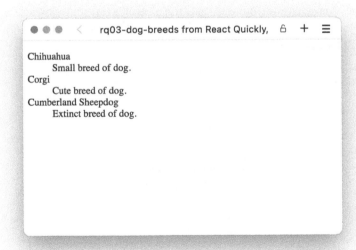

Figure 3.4   A definition list of a curated subset of dog breeds and their primary description

You've now had a taste of JSX and its benefits. The rest of this chapter is dedicated to JSX tools and potential traps to avoid—that's right: tools and gotchas.

Before we can continue, you must understand that for any JSX project to function properly, JSX needs to be compiled. Browsers can't run JSX directly—they can run only JavaScript—so you need to take the JSX and transpile it to normal JavaScript (refer to figure 3.1). Fortunately, that task is a lot less complicated than it sounds.

3.3   *How to transpile JSX*

For all the projects and examples in this book, you don't need to set up your own transpiler (or most other things in your technology stack). The same is true for most projects you'll encounter out in the wild, because existing projects already have a working pipeline, and new projects can be based on the best practice documentation provided by whatever framework you desire to work with.

However, if you want to set up a React project from scratch, you can, and that would include setting up a JSX transpiler. The most popular tool out there to do JSX transpiling is Babel, but there are alternatives you might want to look at as well. Some of the alternatives can be part of a larger package of build tools that make your whole setup easier to maintain or simply be drop-in replacements for Babel. Alternatives include SWC, Sucrase, and esbuild. Please consult their various documentation for details on how to use them:

- Babel: https://babeljs.io/
- SWC: https://swc.rs/
- Sucrase: https://sucrase.io/
- esbuild: https://esbuild.github.io/

We strongly recommend that you don't spend too much time creating a JSX transpiler setup yourself. The good folks at React have created CRA for us, which will serve almost all our needs in this book. You might want to look into custom setups in your own projects, but for this book, you'll be covered by the setups provided by our selection of great tools.

3.4   *React and JSX gotchas*

This section covers some edge cases and oddities that you should be aware of when you use JSX:

- Self-closing tags are required for leaf nodes.
- Special characters are written literally.
- String conversion is a bit peculiar.
- The style attribute is an object.
- Some attributes have reserved names and must be renamed.
- Multiword attributes are in camelCase.
- Boolean attributes are handled differently than in HTML.
- Some whitespace is collapsed (but not all).
- You can add `data-` attributes where desired.

3.4.1   *Self-closing elements*

JSX requires you to have a closing slash (/) either in the closing tag or, if you don't have any children, at the end of that single tag. For example, this is correct:

```
<a href="//react.dev">React</a>
<img src="/logo.png" alt="Logo" />
```

The following is *not* correct, because both nodes are missing an end tag:

```
<a href="//react.dev">React
<img src="/logo.png" alt="Logo">
```

You might know that HTML is more fault tolerant. Browsers will ignore the missing slash or end element and render the element just fine without it. Go ahead: try to create an HTML file with just `<button>Press me` and see for yourself that this renders the button just fine!

3.4.2   *Special characters*

HTML entities are codes that display special characters such as copyright symbols, em dashes, quotation marks, and so on. Here are some examples:

```
&copy;
&mdash;
&ldquo;
```

You can render those codes as any string in text content inside a node or as an attribute to a node. For example, this is static JSX (text defined in code without variables or properties):

```
<span>&copy;&mdash;&ldquo;</span>
<input value="&copy;&mdash;&ldquo;"/>
```

But if you want to dynamically output HTML entities (from a variable or a property), all you'll get is the direct output (i.e., `&copy;&mdash;&ldquo;`), not the special characters. Thus, the following code won't work:

```
// Anti-pattern. Will NOT work!
const specialChars = '&copy;&mdash;&ldquo;'
<span>{specialChars}</span>
<input value={specialChars}/>
```

React/JSX will auto-escape the dangerous HTML, which is convenient in terms of security (security by default rocks!). To output special characters, you need to use one of these approaches:

- Copy the special character directly into your source code. Just make sure you use a UTF-8 character set. This is the recommended method to deal with special characters.

- Escape the special character with \u, and use its Unicode number (use a website such as fileformat.info to look it up).
- Convert from a character code to a character number with `String.fromChar-Code(charCodeNumber)`.
- Use the special property `dangerouslySetInnerHTML` to set the inner HTML (this is dangerous and not recommended).

To illustrate the last approach (as a last resort—when all else fails on the Titanic, run for the boats!), look at this code:

```
const specialChars = '&copy;&mdash;&ldquo;';
<span dangerouslySetInnerHTML={{__html: specialChars}}/>
```

Obviously, the React team has a sense of humor to name a property `dangerouslySet-InnerHTML`.

3.4.3　String conversion

When React outputs the value of your variable (or your expression in general), what is it rendered as? It can only render as one of two things: either a string, which becomes the string content between elements, or an element, which then just becomes an element as if it was rendered directly. But how are "things" converted to a string, if they're not an element? Well, React is a bit peculiar here as it depends on the type of the expression that you're rendering. Take a look at table 3.2 to understand the possibilities for the different primitive values in JavaScript.

Table 3.2　React rendering different types

Type	Output
`"string"`	`"string"`
`" "`	`" "`
`3.4`	`"3.4"`
`0`	`"0"`
`NaN`	`"NaN"`
`Number.POSITIVE_INFINITY`	`"Infinity"`
`Number.NEGATIVE_INFINITY`	`"-Infinity"`
`true`	`"true"`
`false`	`" "`
`undefined`	`" "`
`null`	`" "`

There are a few surprises there. Most importantly, `false` becomes the empty string, but `true` becomes `"true"`. So, four of the falsy values (empty string, `false`, `null`, and `undefined`) all become the empty string.

But what about `0`, which is also falsy? Well, it becomes `0`. It would be weird if you couldn't render a `0` in your components, so that's kind of necessary. Finally, `NaN` is also just `"NaN"`, and not the empty string. This is generally to help you debug your calculations better—if you see a *NaN*, you know you made an error somewhere, but if you just see nothing, you might not find it as quickly.

This fact—that `false` renders nothing, but `0` renders something—especially matters when using logical AND to render optional elements as we discussed earlier. You might be used to doing things like this in JavaScript:

```
if (items.length) {
  hasItems = true;
}
```

Here, we just use `items.length` as the condition for our if statement because we know that 0 is falsy anyway, so we don't have to say `items.length > 0`—the truthiness of the statement is the same.

You shouldn't do that in JSX though. Let's say you want to render a Checkout button in your shopping cart if it contains at least one item, but you want to render nothing when there are no items in the cart:

```
class ShoppingCart extends Component {
  render() {
    return (
      <aside>
        <h1>Shopping cart</h1>
        <CartItems items={this.props.items} />
        {this.props.items.length && (        ◁─┐  Don't do this because
          <button>Checkout</button>              using array length as a
        )}                                       condition directly in a
      </aside>                                    logical AND expression
    );                                           leads to problems.
  }
}
```

This works as long as there are more than 0 items in the cart. But what happens when there are 0 items? The logical AND expression highlighted in the annotation short-circuits and returns the first falsy value as it is. In addition, because the length of the array is 0, the resulting value of the expression is suddenly `0`, which renders as `"0"` in the document, as shown previously in table 3.2. So, if you used the code just shown, your empty shopping cart would suddenly display a `"0"` in the bottom of the component, to the utter confusion of everyone.

To implement this correctly, always compare the length of the array to be greater than 0 to ensure the type is Boolean. Even better, you can store that comparison in another variable, making the code even simpler to read:

```
class ShoppingCart extends Component {
  render() {
    const hasItems = this.props.items.length > 0;
    return (
      <aside>
        <h1>Shopping cart</h1>
        <CartItems items={this.props.items} />
        {hasItems && <button>Checkout</button>}
      </aside>
    );
  }
}
```

◁─┐ **Stores the comparison
    in a variable guaranteed
    to be of type Boolean**

◁─ **Uses that variable to
    conditionally render
    your optional element**

It's not that uncommon to forget this when you're developing, so spotting rogue 0's throughout your application is definitely possible. They are almost always the result of this type of expression.

3.4.4 The style attribute

The style attribute in JSX works differently than in plain HTML. With JSX, instead of a string, you need to pass a JavaScript object, and CSS properties need to be in camel-Case. For example:

- `background-image` becomes `backgroundImage`.
- `font-size` becomes `fontSize`.
- `font-family` becomes `fontFamily`.

You can save the JavaScript object in a variable or render it inline with double curly braces (`{{...}}`). The double braces are needed because one set is for JSX, and the other is for the JavaScript object literal.

Suppose you have an object with this font size:

```
const smallFontSize = { fontSize: '10pt' };
```

In your JSX, you can use the `smallFontSize` object as

```
<input style={smallFontSize} />
```

or settle for a larger font (30 point) by passing the values directly without an extra variable:

```
<input style={{ fontSize: '30pt' }} />
```

Let's look at another example of passing styles directly. This time, you're setting a red border on a `<span>`:

```
<span style={{
  borderWidth: '1px',
  borderStyle: 'solid',
  borderColor: 'red',
}}>Red velvet cake is delicious</span>
```

Alternatively, the following border value will also work and do the same thing:

```
<span style={{border: '1px red solid'}}>Hey</span>
```

The main reason styles aren't CSS strings but JavaScript objects is so that React can work with them more quickly when it applies changes to views.

3.4.5   *Reserved names: class and for*

React (and JSX) accepts any attribute that is a standard HTML attribute, except `class` and `for`. Those names are reserved words in JavaScript/ECMAScript (for creating classes and for loops, respectively), and JSX is converted into regular JavaScript. So, just like you can't create a variable named `for` or any other reserved word, you can't create attributes with these names (not directly, anyway).

Instead, you can use `className` and `htmlFor`, respectively. For example, if you want to apply a class name of `"hidden"` to an element, you have to use the `class-Name` attribute:

```
<p className="hidden">...</p>
```

If you need to create a label for a form element, use `htmlFor`:

```
<input type="checkbox" id={this.props.id} value="hasCorgi" />
<label htmlFor={this.props.id}>Corgi?</label>
```

Both of these are pretty easy to remember because you'll get compiler errors if you forget.

3.4.6   *Multiword attributes*

In the same vein as the two reserved names mentioned in the previous section, other HTML attributes are renamed in React as well. Some of them make sense, but others less so.

Any attribute made up of more than one English word is renamed to camelCase-style naming. This makes sense for scalable vector graphics (SVG) attributes using a hyphen such as `clip-path` or `fill-opacity`. We can't use hyphenated attributes directly in JSX, so these are renamed to `clipPath` and `fillOpacity`, respectively.

However, the same goes for HTML attributes that don't use a hyphen but are all lowercase normally, which can be quite confusing. If you enter

```
return <video autoplay>...</video>;
```

in JSX, it doesn't work because, while the attribute is called `autoplay` (and can be all lowercase in HTML), you have to use camelCase and call it `autoPlay` in React. This can be a bit frustrating. This goes for a huge number of properties that you often use in HTML.

Instead of warning you about skipping these properties, React merely filters them out silently. So, you might never know that you typed it wrong until you realize that your video isn't autoplaying (because of `autoPlay` rather than `autoplay`), your iframe doesn't allow full screen (because of `allowFullscreen` rather than `allowfullscreen`), or your input field doesn't have a maximum of characters allowed (because of `max-Length` rather than `maxlength`).

3.4.7   Boolean attribute values

Some attributes (e.g., `disabled`, `required`, `checked`, `autoFocus`, and `readOnly`) are specific only to form elements. The most important thing to remember here is that the attribute value must be set as a JavaScript expression (i.e., inside {}) and not set as a string. For example, use {false} to enable the input:

```
<input disabled={false} />
```

But don't use a `"false"` value because it'll pass the truthy check (a non-empty string is truthy in JavaScript, as you hopefully remember from section 3.2.6). This is because the string `"false"` isn't any of the six falsy values; it's actually a non-empty string, which is truthy and results in the value `true`. React will render the input as disabled (`disabled` will be set to `true`):

```
<input disabled="false" /> // Don't do this!
```

If you omit a value after a property, React will set the value to `true`:

```
<input required />
```

This is equivalent to manually setting the value to `true`, so just use the preceding code rather than using `required={true}`.

For many of these attributes in HTML, completely excluding the value means setting the value to `false`, so if you want to set a value specifically to `true` or `false`, simply include it without a value or omit it. If you want to set a value based on the contents of a variable, use an expression:

```
<input readOnly={!isEditable} />
```

> **NOTE** Notice the multiword problem mentioned before. This Boolean attribute in React is called `readOnly` and not `readonly` as you know it from HTML.

CUSTOM COMPONENT WITH BOOLEAN PROPERTIES

The same thing is true when you create your own components. If you have a custom component and want to accept a Boolean property, you can just use a property from `this.props` as if it was a Boolean, and React will make sure to set it to `true`, if specified when used.

For example, we can create an alert component that will display an alert message to the user. This message is either an error or a warning. To control the level of the alert, we add a Boolean flag, `isError`, and if true, we include a warning-sign emoji around the message. We'll then use this component to display two different alerts in our application—one as an error and the other as a warning, as shown in listing 3.13. If we run this in the browser, we see how the two messages are correctly displayed (see figure 3.5).

Listing 3.13   Passing and accepting Boolean properties in JSX

```
import { Component } from 'react';
class Alert extends Component {
  render() {
    return (
      <p>
        {this.props.isError && '⚠'}
        {this.props.children}
        {this.props.isError && '⚠'}
      </p>
    );
  }
}
class App extends Component {
  render() {
    return (
      <main>
        <Alert>We are almost out of cookies</Alert>
        <Alert isError>                              ⟵──┐ Sets the isError
          We are completely out of ice cream            │ property to true simply
        </Alert>                                         │ by including it in the JSX
      </main>                                            │ without a value
    );
  }
}
export default App;
```

Repository: rq03-alert

This example can be seen in repository `rq03-alert`. You can use that repository by creating a new app based on the associated template:

```
$ npx create-react-app rq03-alert --template rq03-alert
```

Alternatively, you can go to this website to browse the code, see the application in action directly in your browser, or download the source code as a zip file:

https://rq2e.com/rq03-alert

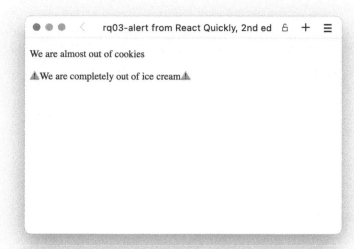

Figure 3.5 The first message is just a warning, but the second is definitely an error.

3.4.8 Whitespace

If you want to add whitespace between components—for example, if you're adding a bold word inside a sentence—you have to be very careful about how you place your newline characters. Let's say you want to write a headline with an emphasized word in the middle, for example, `"All corgis are awesome"` but `"corgis"` must be in italics. You could do this in JSX as shown in the next listing.

Listing 3.14 Naive implementation of a partially emphasized message

```
import { Component } from 'react';
class App extends Component {
  render() {
    return (
      <h1>                         Some
        All                        plain text
        <em>corgis</em>
        are awesome                Then some
      </h1>                        more plain
    );                             text
  }
}
export default App;
```

Then a JSX node

Repository: rq03-bad-whitespace

This example can be seen in repository `rq03-bad-whitespace`. You can use that repository by creating a new app based on the associated template:

```
$ npx create-react-app rq03-bad-whitespace --template rq03-bad-whitespace
```

(continued)

Alternatively, you can go to this website to browse the code, see the application in action directly in your browser, or download the source code as a zip file:

https://rq2e.com/rq03-bad-whitespace

This seems pretty reasonable, no? Let's run this app with CRA and watch it in the browser. You can see the result in figure 3.6.

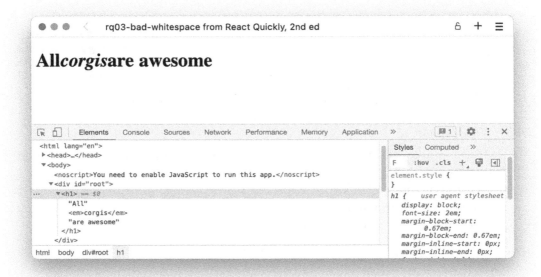

Figure 3.6   Emphasized message with improper whitespace

That's clearly wrong. The space around the word *"corgis"* just collapsed. What happened? Normally, newline characters and tabs are ignored as whitespace in JSX. When we had JSX as

```
return (
  <main>
    <h1>Hello world</h1>
  </main>
);
```

earlier in the chapter, we didn't actually want spaces between the elements <main> and <h1>. We just formatted it on multiple lines because it looks pretty—not because we want a lot of extra whitespace rendered in the browser. So, if there is whitespace between elements in JSX that include newline characters, all the whitespace is collapsed. It doesn't matter if you have an extra normal space at the end of the plain-text line in listing 3.14. If there is a newline character between the elements, all whitespace is collapsed.

So, how could we do this correctly? There are two ways to make sure spaces are rendered:

- Don't use newline characters at all between the elements.
- Add spaces as expressions in the code.

The latter sounds a bit complex and doesn't look all that good, but can be necessary. Let's see the first solution—no newline characters—in practice.

Listing 3.15   Partially emphasized message without newline characters

```
import { Component } from 'react';
class App extends Component {
  render() {
    return (
      <h1>
        All <em>corgis</em> are awesome
      </h1>
    );
  }
}
export default App;
```

Newlines appear before and after the heading.

No newline characters appear inside the heading.

Note that we can have newline characters before and after the message (because the whitespace here can be collapsed—we don't care about it). We just don't want newline characters in places where we want actual space characters to be inserted. Now let's look at space expressions in the next listing.

Listing 3.16   Partially emphasized message with space expressions

```
import { Component } from 'react';
class App extends Component {
  render() {
    return (
      <h1>
        All
        {" "}
        <em>corgis</em>
        {" "}
        are awesome
      </h1>
    );
  }
}
export default App;
```

Spaces inserted as expressions

Here, we add spaces using curly brackets. This will force the JSX engine to include the spaces as actual elements and not treat them as part of the negligible whitespace that normally exists between elements. You'll often see developers append such space-as-expressions at the end of the line before the newline character, as shown next.

Listing 3.17   Partially emphasized message with fewer lines

```
import { Component } from 'react';
class App extends Component {
  render() {
    return (
      <h1>
        All{" "}                          Space expressions appended
        <em>corgis</em>{" "}              at the end of the lines
        are awesome
      </h1>
    );
  }
}
export default App;
```

> ### Repository: rq03-good-whitespace
> This example can be seen in repository `rq03-good-whitespace`. You can use that repository by creating a new app based on the associated template:
>
> `$ npx create-react-app rq03-good-whitespace --template rq03-good-whitespace`
>
> Alternatively, you can go to this website to browse the code, see the application in action directly in your browser, or download the source code as a zip file:
>
> https://rq2e.com/rq03-good-whitespace

Both of the preceding listings will render our message correctly in the browser—a message that no one can contest, as shown in figure 3.7.

3.4.9   *data- attributes*

Sometimes, you want to pass additional data using DOM nodes. While you shouldn't use your DOM as a database or local storage, sometimes that's necessary when you want to pass variables to third-party libraries. If you need to create custom attributes and get them rendered, use the `data-` prefix.

For example, this is a valid custom `data-object-id` attribute that React will render in the view (HTML will be the same as this JSX):

```
<li data-object-id={object.id}>...</li>
```

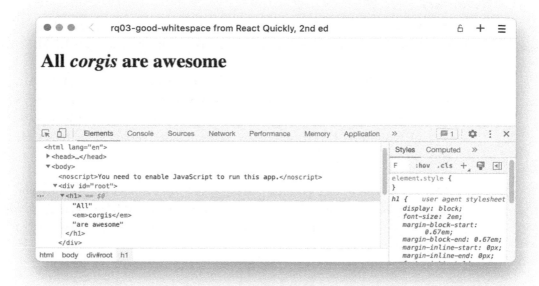

Figure 3.7 All corgis are now correctly rendered as awesome.

3.5 Quiz

1 To output a JavaScript variable in JSX, which of the following do you use? =, <%= %>, {}, or <?= ?>

2 The class attribute isn't allowed in JSX. *True* or *false?*

3 The default value for an attribute without a value is false. *True* or *false?*

4 The inline style attribute in JSX is a JavaScript object and not a string like other attributes. *True* or *false?*

5 If you need to have if/else logic in JSX, you can use it inside {}. For example, class={if (!this.props.isAdmin) return 'hide'} is valid JSX code. *True* or *false?*

Quiz answers

1 You use {} for variables and expressions.

2 *True.* class is a reserved JavaScript statement. For this reason, you use class-Name in JSX.

3 *False.* The default value for a property with no value specified is true.

4 *True.* style is an object for performance reasons.

5 *False.* First, class isn't the proper attribute name; it's className. Then, instead of if return (which isn't valid JavaScript anyway in this context), you should use a ternary operator or logical expressions. You could do it like this: class-Name={this.props.isAdmin || 'hide'}.

Summary

- JSX is just syntactic sugar for React methods such as `React.createElement`.
- You should use `className` and `htmlFor` instead of the standard HTML `class` and `for` attributes.
- The style attribute takes a JavaScript object, not a string like normal HTML.
- Ternary and logical operators are the best ways to implement if/else statements.
- Outputting variables, comments, and HTML entities is easy and straightforward.
- Several multiword HTML and SVG attributes are renamed in React, so pay attention to these special attributes, and remember to verify whether your attributes correctly make it into the HTML document.
- JSX needs to be transpiled into JavaScript before it can run in the browser, but you rarely have to worry about that. However, if you find it necessary, a number of tools are available, including Babel, which is the most popular tool at the time of writing.

Functional Components

React was based on class-based components for a long time in the early years, but an alternative came along for the simplest of components at some point. Functional components are a more succinct and, in some regards, simpler way of writing React components, and they now have the same feature set as their class-based cousins.

The term *functional component* isn't meant as a contrast to a nonfunctional component—no one has any use for those. Rather, the functional part refers to the component definition itself being a JavaScript function rather than a JavaScript class.

In the beginning, functional components were less powerful than class-based components, but when React hooks came about in React 16.8, functional components were suddenly as powerful, if not more, than their class-based siblings. Today, many React developers exclusively use functional components, as they are the primary method recommended by the React team.

Class-based components are still fully supported in React and probably not going anywhere anytime soon. You'll also find them very common "in the wild," for several reasons:

- Not all older codebases have been refactored away from class-based components and must still be maintained.
- Some older libraries still only document how they interface with class-based components and thus require your code to use them to interface with the library correctly.
- Some long-time React developers started using class-based components and feel more comfortable with them, so they prefer to stick to them when possible.
- The mental model of a component life cycle changed quite a bit when going from class-based to functional components, and, in some instances, the re-render life cycle can be easier to maintain when using the old class-based approach.
- A tiny subset of the core functionality in React is only possible using class-based components (error boundary, in particular).

Not only are functional components here to stay, but they're also going to take over the world—at least the React world. All indicators point to functional components being the main way to write React going forward. Writing functional components makes your life as a developer significantly easier with (almost) no downsides.

In this chapter, we'll go over what functional components are, how they differ (and how they don't) from class-based components, how to choose which component type to use in your projects, and how you can convert a class-based component to a functional one.

> **NOTE** The source code for the examples in this chapter is available at https://rq2e.com/ch04. But, as you learned in chapter 2, you can instantiate all the examples directly from the command line using a single command.

4.1   *The shorter way to write React components*

In this section, we'll introduce functional components and slowly add some extra utilities on top of them. These utilities are merely syntactic sugar, often enabled by modern JavaScript features rather than React-specific functionality. However, we'll introduce these techniques in this chapter because we'll be using all of them in later chapters. They are all standard in the industry, so you'll see them in React codebases all the time. These utilities are all about simplifying how you write and interact with components:

- Simplifying access to properties using destructuring
- Simplifying the component interface with default values
- Simplifying the component interface using pass-through properties

Together, these utilities will give you a good foundation to write simple, presentational React components using concise component definitions.

4.1.1   An example application

Let's create a simple React application: a menu with a list of links all built with plain HTML. This is a very simple HTML fragment with a website menu, but it's one of the building blocks of every web application.

We'll use this example to illustrate that when components get even a tiny bit complex, the three utilities mentioned previously will help us keep our components simple both on the outside and the inside. See the component tree in figure 4.1.

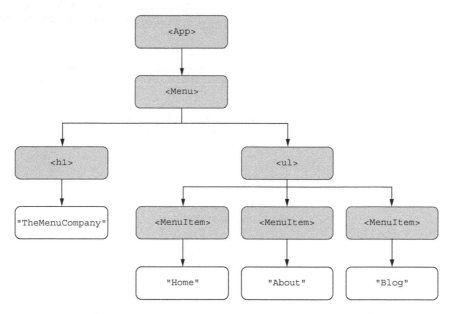

Figure 4.1   A tree diagram of our menu application showing the overall structure of components from the `<App>` at the top to the text nodes at the bottom

The output of this application will look like figure 4.2 in the browser.

First, we'll create it as we've seen previously using class-based components, and then secondly, we'll create those same components using functions. When we get there, we'll have a short discussion about which way is better. Note that this is a subjective discussion—there is no right answer—and you should feel free to use whatever method you feel works best for you.

IMPLEMENTATION USING CLASSES

This application includes three components: `<App/>`, `<Menu />` inside `<App/>`, and `<MenuItem />`s in `<Menu />`. For now, let's just put everything in the same file, that is, the `App.js` file, as shown in listing 4.1.

Figure 4.2   Our menu application as seen in the browser. It's simple HTML with a tiny bit of styling.

Listing 4.1   Menu application using classes

```
import { Component } from "react";
import "./App.css";
class App extends Component {
  render() {
    return (
      <main>
        <Menu />
      </main>
    );
  }
}
class Menu extends Component {
  render() {
    return (
      <nav className="navbar">
        <h1 className="title">TheMenuCompany</h1>
        <ul className="menu">
          <MenuItem label="Home" href="/" />
          <MenuItem label="About" href="/about/" />
          <MenuItem label="Blog" href="/blog" />
        </ul>
      </nav>
    );
  }
}
class MenuItem extends Component {
  render() {
    return (
      <li className="menu-item">
        <a
          className="menu-link"
          href={this.props.href}
        >
          {this.props.label}
```

Imports a CSS file to style the application

Defines a new component

Makes an instance of another custom component without passing properties

Passes properties to a custom component

Uses a standard HTML tag

Uses properties passed to a custom component

```
        </a>
      </li>
    );
  }
}
export default App;
```

This application only uses things we already know. For example, we can nest components, use both built-in HTML components and our own custom components, pass properties to child components, and access properties passed to our custom components.

Yes, we do also import a CSS file in this application. This is supported by CRA out of the box, and you can also see this in the default template when you create a new `create-react-app` (CRA) app as we showed previously in chapter 2.

IMPLEMENTATION USING FUNCTIONS

For this example, we're just going to throw ourselves in at the deep end. Let's see what this same application looks like using functional components.

Listing 4.2 Menu application using functions

```
import "./App.css";
function App() {
  return (
    <main>
      <Menu />
    </main>
  );
}
function Menu() {
  return (
    <nav className="navbar">
      <h1 className="title">TheMenuCompany</h1>
      <ul className="menu">
        <MenuItem label="Home" href="/" />
        <MenuItem label="About" href="/about/" />
        <MenuItem label="Blog" href="/blog" />
      </ul>
```

These two functional components do not take any arguments.

```
      </nav>
    );
  }
function MenuItem(props) {
    return (
      <li className="menu-item">
        <a className="menu-link" href={props.href}>
          {props.label}
        </a>
      </li>
    );
  }
export default App;
```

This functional
component does take
a (single) argument.

Repository: rq04-menu-function

This example can be seen in repository `rq04-menu-function`. You can use that repository by creating a new app based on the associated template:

```
$ npx create-react-app rq04-menu-function --template rq04-menu-function
```

Alternatively, you can go to this website to browse the code, see the application in action directly in your browser, or download the source code as a zip file:

https://rq2e.com/rq04-menu-function

This almost looks too good to be true. To create a functional component, we simply create a function and return JavaScript XML (JSX)—that's it.

If we need to access properties passed to the component, we can do that through the single argument passed to the function, which is a frozen object of properties. This works similarly to `this.props` in a class-based component.

Any function will do

As you saw in listing 4.2 in the annotations, some functional components accept a props argument, but some do not. In addition, we used the statement version (i.e., `function name() {}`) of the function definition, but we didn't have to. Any value that can be executed as a function, that returns JSX, can be used as a component.

You can even define them inline in another component. This isn't generally considered a good practice, but sometimes it might be useful.

```
const App = function() {
  const EmptyMenu = () => { return <nav /> };
  return (
    <main>
      <EmptyMenu />
    </main>
  );
}
```

Functional
expression using
the "function"
keyword

Functional
expression using
arrow notation

Here, we define one component, `App`, using a function expression, and another component, `EmptyMenu`, right in the function body using arrow notation. This is an empty list for now (so it doesn't display any menu items), but it shows just how easy creating a component is.

The latter function can even be shortened further using implicit return:

```
const EmptyMenu = () => <nav />;
```

Yes, this is a fully valid React component. It's a very simple component, for sure, and it doesn't do much (yet), but this *is* a React component.

We'll get back to how this feature of "any function can be a component" can be useful in later chapters. For now, just remember that we write our components in a certain way out of convention rather than framework constraints.

4.1.2 *Destructuring properties*

In the previous `MenuItem` example, we received our properties in the functional component as a `props` object and accessed the properties on the object later using, for example, `props.label`. A more common approach used by many React developers is to *destructure* the properties directly in the function signature. Destructuring is the process of extracting parts of a complex value in a compact way. In JavaScript, destructuring an object generally takes this form:

```
const someObject = { a: 1, b: 2, c: 3 };
const { a, b } = someObject;
```

Destructures "someObject" into parts "a" and "b"

This expression assigns the value of `someObject.a` to the variable a. Similarly, the value of `someObject.b` is assigned to the variable b. The value of `someObject.c` is ignored, as we don't destructure that in our expression.

We can also use destructuring when accepting object arguments to a function:

```
function log({ message, level }) {
  console.log(level.toUpperCase(), "Message:", message);
}
log({ message: "Unknown product", level: "error" });
```

This would result in the following console output:

```
ERROR Message: Unknown product
```

For such a simple example, you might question why we don't make it two different arguments instead, such as the following:

```
function log(message, level) { ...
```

But as functions get more complex and more arguments are added, using just a single object makes it a lot easier to call the function with a variable number of arguments instead of having to remember that `level` is the fifth argument, and so on.

In a functional React component, properties are always given as the first (and only) argument to our defining functions. We can use the method of destructuring the argument object to make the component definition even cleaner in the next listing. Note that this is only an excerpt of the file `App.js` in this example.

Listing 4.3 `MenuItem` **with argument destructuring**

```
...
function MenuItem({ href, label }) {          ◄───┤  Destructs the argument
  return (                                         in the function definition
    <li className="menu-item">
      <a className="menu-link" href={href}>    ┤│  Allows us to use the
        {label}                                     properties without
      </a>                                           going through the
    </li>                                           props object
  );
}
...
```

Repository: rq04-menu-destruct

This example can be seen in repository `rq04-menu-destruct`. You can use that repository by creating a new app based on the associated template:

```
$ npx create-react-app rq04-menu-destruct --template rq04-menu-destruct
```

Alternatively, you can go to this website to browse the code, see the application in action directly in your browser, or download the source code as a zip file:

https://rq2e.com/rq04-menu-destruct

This is, of course, completely identical to doing destructuring in a line of its own inside the function definition in the next listing.

Listing 4.4 `MenuItem` **with explicit destructuring**

```
...
function MenuItem(props) {                    ◄───┤  Here, we still accept a
  const { href, label } = props;         ◄─────┐    props argument without
  return (                                     │    destructuring it.
    <li className="menu-item">
      <a className="menu-link" href={href}>    ┤  However, we destruct it
        {label}                                   as a separate statement
      </a>                                         in the very first line in
    </li>              We can then proceed        the component.
  );                   to use the properties
}                      as separate variables
...                    as before.
```

In this book, we'll use the approach shown in listing 4.3 with argument destructuring directly in the component definition. You'll also often see this in the wild, as many React developers use this convention. As mentioned earlier, however, it's merely a convention; other variants are also possible.

4.1.3 Default values

An added benefit of using destructured properties is that we can also introduce default values. Let's say that our menu link to the blog should be opened in a new browser window (or tab), but the other links should just open regularly in the same session. We can do that by adding a new property, `target`, that the menu has to specify. Note again that this is only an excerpt of `App.js`.

> **Listing 4.5 Menu items with targets**

```
...
function Menu() {
  return (
    <nav className="navbar">
      <h1 className="title">TheMenuCompany</h1>
      <ul className="menu">
        <MenuItem
          label="Home" href="/" target="_self"
        />                                              ⊲─┐
        <MenuItem                                         │  Adds a new property
          label="About" href="/about/" target="_self"  ⊲──┤  to every instance of
        />                                                │  the menu item
        <MenuItem                                         │  component
          label="Blog" href="/blog" target="_blank"   ⊲──┘
        />
      </ul>
    </nav>
  );
}
function MenuItem({ label, href, target }) {    ⊲─┐ Accepts the new
  return (                                         │ property in the
    <li className="menu-item">                     │ destructuring inside
      <a                                           │ the component
        className="menu-link"
        href={href}
        target={target}    ⊲─┐ Assigns the property
      >                      │ to the relevant JSX
        {label}              │ element as an
      </a>                   │ attribute
    </li>
  );
}
...
```

However, one could argue that it makes sense that opening a link in the same session is the default behavior, and the menu shouldn't have to specify that. We can implement this using default values in the function definition. Note that this isn't React-specific functionality, but just normal JavaScript functionality.

Listing 4.6   Menu items with a default target

```
...
function Menu() {
  return (
    <nav className="navbar">
      <h1 className="title">TheMenuCompany</h1>
      <ul className="menu">
        <MenuItem label="Home" href="/" />
        <MenuItem label="About" href="/about/" />
        <MenuItem
          label="Blog" href="/blog" target="_blank"
        />
      </ul>
    </nav>
  );
}
function MenuItem({ label, href, target = "_self" }) {
  return (
    <li className="menu-item">
      <a
        className="menu-link"
        href={href}
        target={target}
      >
        {label}
      </a>
    </li>
  );
}
...
```

We don't have to specify the target property if we don't need to override the default.

But when we do need to override the default, we can do so easily.

Defines the default using built-in JavaScript notation for defaults while destructuring

---

Repository: rq04-menu-default

This example can be seen in repository `rq04-menu-default`. You can use that repository by creating a new app based on the associated template:

```
$ npx create-react-app rq04-menu-default --template rq04-menu-default
```

Alternatively, you can go to this website to browse the code, see the application in action directly in your browser, or download the source code as a zip file:

https://rq2e.com/rq04-menu-default

ORDERING PROPERTIES

You can specify your component properties in any order you like. Although common JavaScript practice is to specify properties with defaults at the end of the definition, nothing prevents you from doing it differently.

This means that the following line is generally not recommended, but still completely valid:

```
function MenuItem({ label, target="_self", href }) {
```

And, this is the recommended order:

```
function MenuItem({ label, href, target="_self" }) {
```

This only refers to the order of nondefault properties versus default properties—the internal order of either list of properties has no general ordering, so it's up to you or your team to set any such recommendations if desired.

4.1.4   Pass-through properties

Let's make our example even more hypothetical and say that we need various extra properties on the different elements:

- The home link doesn't need any extra properties.
- The about link needs an ID of `"about-link"`.
- The blog link needs an ID of `"blog-link"`.

Let's implement this using what we know so far using default values for unspecified values.

Listing 4.7   Menu items with multiple default values

```
...
function Menu() {
  return (
    <nav className="navbar">
      <h1 className="title">TheMenuCompany</h1>
      <ul className="menu">
        <MenuItem label="Home" href="/" />
        <MenuItem label="About" href="/about/" id="about-link" />
        <MenuItem
          label="Blog" href="/blog" target="_blank" id="blog-link"
        />
      </ul>
    </nav>
  );
}
function MenuItem({ label, href, target = "_self", id=null }) {
  return (
    <li className="menu-item">
      <a className="menu-link" href={href} target={target} id={id}>
        {label}
      </a>
    </li>
  );
}
...
```

This is beginning to look a bit repetitive. We're accepting a bunch of arguments only to pass them straight through to a single element—even with the same name and everything else intact.

THE REST SYNTAX

You can indicate that you want some arguments to be handled in a special way and all other arguments to be passed straight through to the target element by using another modern JavaScript concept known as the *rest syntax*. When destructuring an object, you can use the rest syntax, denoted by three periods, to specify an object that will be assigned all the leftover properties not already assigned:

```
const someObject = { a: 1, b: 2, c: 3, d: 4 };
const { a, b, ...otherAttrs } = someObject;
```

The two properties, c and d, which we didn't already reference in the destructuring statement, are transferred as properties to a new object named otherAttrs. Therefore, the preceding code snippet is equivalent to the following code snippet:

```
const a = 1;
const b = 2
const otherAttrs = { c: 3, d: 4 };
```

We can use this in a component function definition like this:

```
function MyComponent({ a, b, ...rest }) {
  // a = 1, b = 2, rest = { c: 3 }
}
// Later:
<MyComponent a="1" b="2" c="3" />
```

We can capture all the remaining properties in an object, often called rest. Now we just need to use this object and apply all the properties inside it to an element in the output.

You've already seen how to assign properties to a JSX element from an object, but to reiterate, we do this using the spread operator:

```
const extraProps = { target: "_blank", id: "link" }
return <a href="/blog/" {...extraProps} />
```

Remember to wrap the spread inside brackets, or it won't work.

REST IN PRACTICE

Let's go back to our example. We want to capture the label and href properties passed to our <MenuItem /> component, but we don't care about the rest. If any other properties are passed to the component, we want to pass them straight through to our target element. Putting this all together, our component becomes the next listing.

Listing 4.8   Menu items with rest and spread

```
...
function MenuItem({ label, href, ...rest }) {          ◄──┤ In this line, "..." is
  return (                                                  the rest syntax.
    <li className="menu-item">
      <a className="menu-link" href={href} {...rest}>   ◄──┐ In this line, "..."
        {label}                                             is the spread
      </a>                                                  operator.
    </li>
  );
}
...
```

Repository: rq04-menu-rest

This example can be seen in repository `rq04-menu-rest`. You can use that repository by creating a new app based on the associated template:

```
$ npx create-react-app rq04-menu-rest --template rq04-menu-rest
```

Alternatively, you can go to this website to browse the code, see the application in action directly in your browser, or download the source code as a zip file:

https://rq2e.com/rq04-menu-rest

This looks a lot nicer now. We don't have to specify all those extra properties that we don't really care about. Any other component can pass whatever it wants except for a few properties—here, `label` and `href`—that will receive special treatment. Note that we could even skip listing `href` as a property now, as it would be included in the `rest` variable, but we still list it because it's a mandatory property that consumers of this component should always specify. Note that this is purely convention, not something enforced by React.

A few things to note here: As you can see, the rest syntax and the spread operator are identical. Both are three periods before a variable name. However, they are used very differently, as one is used for destructuring and the other for assigning. They have a similar nature, which is why they look the same, but they are different operators altogether.

Using the variable name `rest` for the extra parameters is a common convention, but is by no means a requirement anywhere. You'll see many developers use it, but feel free to change it to something that makes sense to you.

In addition, this isn't React-specific functionality, but merely a useful artifact of the JavaScript language that you'll see many React developers use. We'll be using it in future chapters as well.

REST AND PROPERTY ORDERING

The rest syntax has to be the very last element of the object destructuring, so you have to specify it at the end of the property list. When combined with default properties, which, of course, is still possible, the common ordering is as follows:

1 Properties without defaults
2 Properties with defaults
3 Rest

An example of all three types of properties is

```
function MenuItem({ label, href, target="_self", ...rest }) {
```

4.2   *A comparison of component types*

At this stage in your React edification, the differences between functional components and class-based components might seem small or even insignificant. Boiled down to its bare minimum, it's the difference between writing the following as a class-based component:

```
class Menu extends Component {
  render() {
    return <nav />;
  }
}
```

versus writing the following as a functional component:

```
function Menu() {
  return <nav />;
}
```

When we get to more complex components in later chapters, especially when using callbacks and state, things get more complicated, and the differences between functional components and their class-based siblings become larger and larger. When we get to the composition of components and reuse of generalized functionality, very different patterns emerge in the two worlds—almost completely different.

The choice between component types is fundamental in your React journey, but quite frankly, it's not really a choice anymore. You'll probably be using functional components unless there's a strong reason not to for your particular project or development team. Nevertheless, in this section, we'll go over the benefits and disadvantages of functional components, as well as some factors that are actually *not* factors in this choice.

4.2.1 Benefits of functional components

The following is a non-exhaustive list of some subjective benefits of using functional components:

- *Compactness*—Functional components are most often more compact in terms of lines of code and pure template code overhead than class-based components. You simply have to type fewer characters when implementing functional components.
- *Readability*—It can be much harder to track down the origin of some property in a class-based component going through layers of composed higher-order components than to do the same thing in a functional component using hooks (new in React 16.8, which we'll cover in the next couple of chapters). Generally, functional components are much easier to read and understand even at a glance.
- *Purity*—The *purity* of a function (a pure function has no side effects and doesn't depend on any other information than its arguments) is easier to determine, and the side effects of impure functions are easier to deduce due to the existence of hooks. The purity or lack thereof of a class-based component is generally harder to deduce, which can make debugging and understanding a lot harder.
- *Simplicity*—Functions are a fundamental part of any programming language and even mathematics. The theoretical tools used to describe, work with, compose, and explain functions are far greater than those for doing the same for classes. Classes are also fundamental in many programming languages, but they are still a significantly higher-level abstraction than simple functions.
- *Testability*—Due to the ability to break off bits of functionality into independent hooks, functional components are often much easier to unit test, as you can break them down into smaller composable units and easily test each independently.
- *Popularity*—The preference for functional components is a benefit in and of itself. Most other React developers will by now be more at home using functional components; most new development happens in the ecosystem of functional components; and the vast majority of new content about React (videos, tutorials, books, etc.) refers exclusively to functional components.

Note that all of these benefits are about developer experience. The actual end product—the final web application available to end users—isn't improved or degraded by the choice of component type. It's almost exclusively about making it easier for developers to write, maintain, and debug components, where the syntax of functional components really shines.

In general, using functional components is more elegant, more succinct, and—most importantly—far easier to understand. Of course, this is partially a subjective opinion on behalf of the authors, but it's a common opinion found among React developers as can be seen in public codebases on GitHub and similar repositories.

4.2.2   *Disadvantages of functional components*

There are no direct disadvantages to using functional components. For any feature that you can create in both a functional component and a class-based component, there are never any disadvantages to creating said feature in a functional one.

4.2.3   *Nonfactors between component types*

Some factors that are important to developers, development teams, and business units alike are not actually factors at all in the choice of component types. These nonfactors include the following:

- *Speed*—There is no inherent speed difference in running a simple component as a functional one versus a class-based one. The tools to make every component, and thus your entire application, speedy and responsive are slightly different in the two types of components. Most would probably argue that the tools are a bit more transparent and easier to understand in functional components, but similar tools exist for class-based components, so any component can be made fast if optimized properly or can behave sluggishly if not optimized properly.
- *Composability*—Albeit the design patterns used are very different, code reuse and composability of functionality are just as good and well supported in both types of components.
- *Usability*—For the end user visiting your web application, the experience is no different whether you're using one type or the other. User experience does not affect this decision.
- *Accessibility*—Making React components accessible is a skill of its own, but that applies regardless of whether you're writing them one way or the other.
- *Reliability*—Components are just as easy or difficult to make reliable or correct regardless of the choice of component type. Reliability is a property of good software development, not the choice of tooling.
- *Maintainability*—At least for now, there are no indications that class-based components are being deprecated, so both component types are expected to be fully supported by React in all future versions.

While all of these are important aspects of software development, they're not directly influenced by the choice of component types; rather, they are influenced by the competence and vision of the developer or development team wielding the keyboard.

4.2.4   *Choosing the component type*

The short answer to "What component type should I choose for my project?" is simple: *use functional components*. The slightly longer answer adds the following postfix: *unless there's a very strong reason not to.*

In our most informed opinion, you should always use the latest stable version of any technology, and for React, that is most definitely functional components over class-based components. Functional components have been around for quite a while

by now, most new development happens in functional components and their environment (hooks in particular), and most other developers will be using functional components as well. However, there might be scenarios where we would consider using
class-based components, and we'll cover those in the next section.

4.3 When not to use a functional component

As mentioned previously, almost anything you can do with a class-based component,
you can do with a functional component, except for error boundaries. There are a few
other instances where you might want to choose to use a class-based component anyway, even if you don't have to for technical reasons.

In this section, we'll discuss the following cases where you might want to avoid
using functional components:

- You want to set up an error boundary to handle errors occurring further down
  the render tree.
- You're working in a codebase primarily composed of class-based components
  and want to make something that fits in.
- You're using a library that is tailored to class-based components only.
- You're specifically tasked to use the built-in React functionality of `getSnapshot-`
  `BeforeUpdate`.

The preceding items are written in prioritized order of their likeliness to occur in
your everyday work. Given that the first item in the list is a rather specialized case necessary in only the largest and most complex codebases, you're not likely to come
across any of these exceptions at all. We'll cover each of the exceptions in the following subsections.

4.3.1 Error boundary

Establishing an error boundary is a valid concern for a mature React codebase once it
gets to a certain complexity level, so this is something you're likely to come across if
you're working on a large codebase. Currently, at the time of writing, there is still no
way to solve this without using a class-based component. There aren't even any plans
to convert the error boundary functionality to a hook or similar, which would allow it
to be possible in a functional component.

An error boundary is a way of establishing a fallback in case a child component
throws a JavaScript error. You should always strive to never have unhandled errors, of
course, but as things get complex, input changes, APIs evolve, and your codebase gets
more complex and harder to properly cover by tests, errors will occur. An error
boundary is your way of making sure that when such an error does occur, at least the
end user is presented with a nicely formatted error message along with your sincere
apologies. You should probably also log the error to your analytics tool of choice.

Two methods in the React API deal with errors occurring in child components.
One is `getDerivedStateFromError`, where you can set an internal flag that this

component should render differently because an error occurred somewhere. The other is `componentDidCatch`, where you get the actual error that occurred along with its stack trace and other information. This latter part allows you to log it for debugging purposes. We won't go into detail about how these work, as it's outside the scope of this book, but if you need them, the React documentation on both methods is pretty substantial.

If you find yourself needing to catch errors in a component tree, you have to use a class-based component for at least this one component. You can still keep 99% of your components functional, despite having a single class-based error boundary or two.

4.3.2   *Codebase is class-based*

Imagine that you're hired to a development position in a company that has an old React codebase that they're still actively working on. It's a huge application, maybe with hundreds or even thousands of components, and an extensive set of complex functionalities.

You're asked to add some new functionality to just a tiny part of this application. While there is no problem mixing class-based and functional components, it might seem very odd to other developers that some components are written in one style while others are written in a different style.

Refactoring the entire codebase to functional components would be a huge undertaking, but it's hopefully the goal for the engineering team in the long term. However, there will likely be a transition period where only certain parts of the codebase have been converted and you'll be asked to keep using classes in some parts while using functional components in others.

As React ages and the ghost of class-based components is a relic of a further and further past, this scenario becomes less and less likely. If you find yourself in such a scenario, we recommend using the wisdom of the team and going with the flow. Don't force a conversion before the team is ready as a whole, and don't go against the agreed-upon coding conventions of your team.

4.3.3   *Library requires class-based components*

This scenario is somewhat hypothetical, as we can't find a library requiring a class-based component, but that's not to say that it doesn't exist. There might be a circumstance where you're interacting with third-party functionality that requires you to use class-based components.

The most likely case is that you want to use an old library that hasn't been updated since before React hooks came out, and their examples and guides still use class-based components. That doesn't mean that you can't use the library with hooks; it just means that you're on your own and can't use the library documentation to help you out if things don't work. While outdated documentation is the most likely culprit of the library instructing you to use class-based components, we can't rule out that there might be a library that doesn't work with hooks at all.

If either of the preceding scenarios occurs, your best bet is to look around for a more modern library. Many things have changed in the four years since hooks came out—not just notation—and you'll probably find that the library in question is behind the curve on many things if it's been unmaintained for that long.

4.3.4 Snapshot before updating

There is another built-in function in the React API that doesn't exist in a hooks-only React world: `getSnapshotBeforeUpdate`. This is an extremely specific piece of functionality that has the narrowest use case, the details of which we won't go over here. You'll be able to work around it easily with hooks if you just structure your components slightly differently.

However, if you're specifically tasked to use this functionality, there's no way around it (also, who gave you this weird task?). If you're just tasked with solving a problem, where `getSnapshotBeforeUpdate` will be a solution in a class-based component, you can find a similar solution using functional components.

This method is only mentioned here for completion, not because it's a method frequently used at all. A quick search of GitHub reveals only seven repositories mentioning the method. Two are lists of React functions, two are examples of how to use this specific method, and three are old unmaintained demos. So, this whole method is a candidate for functionality that will likely disappear from the React API completely rather than be upgraded to a functional equivalent.

4.4 Conversion from a class-based to a functional component

You've already seen a simple class-based component converted to a functional one between code listings 4.1 and 4.2. In this section, we'll dig more into this conversion, iron out some gotchas, and prepare you for the journey ahead, as we'll keep coming back to this conversion as we add more and more complicated functionality to our components in the next chapters.

For this conversion exercise, we'll create another simple web application: a gallery with images and titles for each. This is a simple visual application that has no interaction (as we've not yet learned how to add that) but highlights different features of component internals, so we have to use some different tricks to convert the components. The output of this application will look like figure 4.3 in the browser.

We'll create four versions of this component, which iterate as follows:

- Version 1, using only the render method
- Version 2, using a secondary method as utility only
- Version 3, using a secondary method with class access
- Version 4, using the constructor to initialize a calculation

The reason we go through these iterations is to see how to convert class-based components to functional components when the classes use more and more advanced patterns that require slightly different solutions in a functional equivalent. Finally, we'll discuss

Figure 4.3   The gallery application as seen in the browser with simple figures and captions

how one-to-one conversion gets more complex—bordering on impossible—as components get more complicated.

4.4.1   *Version 1: Render only*

We'll implement our first iteration with classes completely similar to our menu earlier in this chapter.

ORIGINAL

We use three components, and each uses its render method to return JavaScript.

Listing 4.9   Gallery v1 using classes

```
import { Component } from "react";
class App extends Component {
  render() {                          ◁─┐
    return (                           │
      <main>                           │   Our three class
        <h1>Animals</h1>               │   components only
        <Gallery />                    │   have a render
      </main>                          │   function and no
    );                                 │   other methods.
  }                                    │
}                                      │
class Gallery extends Component {      │
  render() {                        ◁──┘
    return (
      <section style={{ display: "flex" }}>
        <Image index="1003" title="Deer" />
```

```
        <Image index="1020" title="Bear" />
        <Image index="1024" title="Vulture" />
        <Image index="1084" title="Walrus" />
      </section>
    );
  }
}
class Image extends Component {
  render() {
    return (
      <figure style={{ margin: "5px" }}>
        <img
          src={`//picsum.photos/id/${this.props.index}/150/150/`}
          alt={this.props.title}
        />
        <figcaption>
          <h3>Species: {this.props.title}</h3>
        </figcaption>
      </figure>
    );
  }
}
export default App;
```

> **Our three class components only have a render function and no other methods.**

CONVERSION

When converting such a simple component to a functional component, we directly convert the render method of the class to a function with the same name as the class. Thus, it follows this simple template. If you have the class as

```
class MyComponent extends Component {
  render() {
    ...
  }
}
```

you end up with this:

```
function MyComponent() {
  ..
}
```

The only other thing we also have to do is ensure that we directly destructure the props in the component definition rather than access them through this.props as we've seen before. This leads us to the result shown in the following listing.

Listing 4.10   Gallery v1 using functions

```
function App() {                        ◁
  return (
    <main>
      <h1>Animals</h1>                     Component
      <Gallery />                          definition changed
    </main>                                to a function
  );
}
function Gallery() {          ◁
  return (
    <section style={{ display: "flex" }}>
      <Image index="1003" title="Deer" />
      <Image index="1020" title="Bear" />
      <Image index="1024" title="Vulture" />
      <Image index="1084" title="Walrus" />
    </section>
  );                                 This component
}                                    definition also takes
function Image({ index, title }) {   ◁  destructured properties.
  return (
    <figure style={{ margin: "5px" }}>
      <img
        src={`//picsum.photos/id/${index}/150/150/`}   Property reference
        alt={title}                                     changed to a direct
      />                                                 variable rather than
      <figcaption>                                       an object property
        <h3>Species: {title}</h3>
      </figcaption>
    </figure>
  );
}
export default App;
```

Repository: rq04-gallery-function-v1

This example can be seen in repository rq04-gallery-function-v1. You can use that repository by creating a new app based on the associated template:

```
$ npx create-react-app rq04-f1 --template rq04-gallery-function-v1
```

Alternatively, you can go to this website to browse the code, see the application in action directly in your browser, or download the source code as a zip file:

https://rq2e.com/rq04-gallery-function-v1

There's nothing surprising here. We used all the tricks we've learned so far in this chapter:

- A functional component is simply a function returning JSX.
- If we need to accept properties, we destructure them in the function definition.
- When we need to access properties, we can do so directly using the destructured variables.

In the next couple of subsections, we'll iterate the definition of the image component, so you'll see different versions of only that component. For brevity, only the image component will be shown in the sample code listings.

4.4.2   Version 2: Class method as utility

In this version of the implementation, we examine what we would do if the image class had another method that served as a utility function aiding the rendering. The argument is that the src property of the <img /> element is a bit long and windy, and the JSX would look a lot simpler if we had a utility method to render this URL.

ORIGINAL

Let's expand the class-based implementation of the image gallery with some code improvements. In this iteration, we'll imagine that the developer of the gallery wants to reduce the visual clutter of these lines in the original component from listing 4.9

```
<img
  src={`//lorempixel.com/200/100/animals/${this.props.index}/`}
  alt={this.props.title}
/>
```

to something that looks simpler, like this:

```
<img
  src={this.getImageSource(this.props.index)}
  alt={this.props.title}
/>
```

This requires us to define a class method, getImageSource, which takes an argument, index, and returns a string with the URL:

```
getImageSource(index) {
  return `//lorempixel.com/200/100/animals/${index}/`;
}
```

Putting all this together, the resulting image component looks like the next listing.

Listing 4.11   Gallery v2 using classes (excerpt)

```
...
class Image extends Component {        Defines a new
  getImageSource(index) {          ◄── method in the class
```

```
    return `//picsum.photos/id/${index}/150/150/`;
  }
  render() {
    return (
      <figure style={{ margin: "5px" }}>
        <img
          src={this.getImageSource(this.props.index)}
          alt={this.props.title}
        />
        <figcaption>
          <h3>Species: {this.props.title}</h3>
        </figcaption>
      </figure>
    );
  }
}
...
```

Invokes the new method with a property as the argument

Repository: rq04-gallery-class-v2

This example can be seen in repository `rq04-gallery-class-v2`. You can use that repository by creating a new app based on the associated template:

```
$ npx create-react-app rq04-c2 --template rq04-gallery-class-v2
```

Alternatively, you can go to this website to browse the code, see the application in action directly in your browser, or download the source code as a zip file:

https://rq2e.com/rq04-gallery-class-v2

Note that this listing only shows the image component. The app and gallery components are the same as before. We won't bother repeating these in listing 4.11 nor in the conversion that follows. The task now becomes to convert this new class-based component, using multiple methods, to a functional component.

CONVERSION

The key to converting this function is to recognize that the class method isn't, in the object-oriented sense of the word, a method of the class, but merely a utility function. In fact, you could move the function completely outside the class and get the same result.

Imagine that listing 4.11, shown earlier, instead looked like listing 4.12.

Listing 4.12   Gallery v2 using classes and a function (excerpt)

```
...
function getImageSource(index) {
  return `//picsum.photos/id/${index}/150/150/`;
}
class Image extends Component {
  render() {
    return (
```

We've moved the method out as a separate and independent function outside the class.

```
    <figure style={{ margin: "5px" }}>
      <img
        src={getImageSource(this.props.index)}        ⟵┐  Invokes the function
        alt={this.props.title}                           │  as any other function,
      />                                                  │  and not as a method
      <figcaption>                                        │  of the class
        <h3>Species: {this.props.title}</h3>
      </figcaption>
    </figure>
  );
  }
}
...
```

This works in the same way because the `getImageSource` method didn't use any knowledge that was only available inside the class. In other words, the function was pure and only relied on its input and no other outside information, nor did it have any outside consequences.

Converting this new class-based component using a utility function now becomes just as simple as before. We leave the utility function as is and just convert the component itself.

Listing 4.13   Gallery v2 using functions (excerpt)

```
...
function getImageSource(index) {                      ⟵┐  Maintains the utility
  return `//picsum.photos/200/100/animals/${index}/`;    │  function outside the
}                                                         │  component definition
function Image({ index, title }) {
  return (
    <figure style={{ margin: "5px" }}>
      <img src={getImageSource(index)} alt={title} />  ⟵┐  Invokes this
      <figcaption>                                        │  function as any
        Species: {title}                                  │  other function
      </figcaption>
    </figure>
  );
}
...
```

Repository: rq04-gallery-function-v2

This example can be seen in repository `rq04-gallery-function-v2`. You can use that repository by creating a new app based on the associated template:

```
$ npx create-react-app rq04-f2 --template rq04-gallery-function-v2
```

Alternatively, you can go to this website to browse the code, see the application in action directly in your browser, or download the source code as a zip file:

https://rq2e.com/rq04-gallery-function-v2

This does seem a lot simpler and more compact than the previous iteration in listing 4.10. The `<img />` tag is much simpler to read, and the details of the actual URL generation have been moved to a function dedicated to that task only.

Here, we used the knowledge that the method was pure; that is, the method didn't use any outside information but relied on its arguments only. What if this wasn't the case? We'll get to that in the next subsection.

4.4.3   *Version 3: Real class method*

Now let's take a new look at the class method we had in the previous example. Let's instead imagine that the developer implementing this component wanted to use the fact that the method is part of the class and thus has direct access to the properties of the component.

ORIGINAL

Using this information, the method doesn't need to rely on an argument delivering the index but can retrieve the index directly from the component properties using `this.props`:

```
getImageSource() {
  return `//lorempixel.com/200/100/animals/${this.props.index}/`;
}
```

Now, when we use this method, we don't have to provide an argument; we can just call the method. This results in the component definition in the following listing.

Listing 4.14   Gallery v3 using classes (excerpt)

```
...
class Image extends Component {
  getImageSource() {
    return `//picsum.photos/id/${
      this.props.index              ⟵  This time, the class
    }/150/150/`;                         method uses the props
  }                                      object directly.
  render() {
    return (
      <figure style={{ margin: "5px" }}>
        <img
          src={this.getImageSource()}   ⟵  We can now call the
          alt={this.props.title}            method without passing
        />                                  an argument to it.
        <figcaption>
          <h3>Species: {this.props.title}</h3>
        </figcaption>
      </figure>
    );
  }
}
...
```

Now the class method is indeed a method of the class and relies on outside information. What do we do now? The short answer is that there is no direct equivalent of this in a functional component; however, there are similar ways to achieve the same result.

There are two primary approaches to converting this class-based component to a functional component, each with its advantages and drawbacks:

- Convert the method to a pure function and move it outside the component.
- Create a local function inside the component.

We'll cover both of those approaches and compare them in the following subsections.

CONVERSION USING A PURE FUNCTION

Option 1 is to remember the previous version of the gallery image and try to reverse this advancement of complexity and interconnectedness. For this method, it's quite simple: the goal is to remove any direct access to component properties or other component-local information and instead pass it as arguments to the function. This would lead us to the same version of `getImageSource` that we saw in version 2, where it took an argument and returned a string.

Implementing this would look exactly like listing 4.13 earlier. However, imagine that the method was more complex and used a lot of properties:

```
getImageSource() {
  const { width, height, index } = this.props;
  return `//picsum.photos/id/${index}/${width}/${height}/`;
}
```

When we use this method in our class-based component render, it looks quite nice:

```
return (
  ...
  <img src={this.getImageSource()} alt={this.props.title} />
  ...
);
```

The usage of this function is quite compact, and all the complexity of accessing the different properties is moved to the method only.

If we convert it to a pure function, we suddenly have to pass a ton of arguments to it, increasing the complexity. In our functional component with a pure function, we would have to pass all the properties to the function, and it would suddenly look like this:

```
return (
  ...
  <img
    src={getImageSource(width, height, index)}
    alt={title}
  />
  ...
);
```

This isn't as nice and isolated as before, but it would work and would be a valid conversion.

CONVERSION USING A LOCAL FUNCTION

Option 2 is to convert the class method to a local function inside our functional component, which would look like the next listing.

Listing 4.15   Gallery v3 using functions (excerpt)

```
...
function Image({ index, title }) {            Defines a local function
  const getImageSource = () =>                inside the component that
    `//picsum.photos/id/${index}/150/150/`;  has access to properties
  return (
    <figure style={{ margin: "5px" }}>
      <img src={getImageSource()} alt={title}/>   ◁──┐ Invokes this
      <figcaption>                                     function as any
        <h3>Species: {title}</h3>                      other function
      </figcaption>
    </figure>
  );
}
...
```

Repository: rq04-gallery-function-v3

This example can be seen in repository `rq04-gallery-function-v3`. You can use that repository by creating a new app based on the associated template:

```
$ npx create-react-app rq04-f3 --template rq04-gallery-function-v3
```

Alternatively, you can go to this website to browse the code, see the application in action directly in your browser, or download the source code as a zip file:

https://rq2e.com/rq04-gallery-function-v3

Now because this definition of getImageSource is a local function inside our component, it has access to the properties passed to the component, and we don't have to pass all the properties to the helper function. The downside to this approach is that every time we create a new component, we create a new local function. This doesn't matter much in this example with only four components, but imagine a huge, complex application with thousands or even millions of instances of some components. If we had millions of instances of our original class-based component as defined in listing 4.14, we would still only have a single definition of the getImageSource method, which wouldn't occupy a lot of memory.

However, with our functional component as defined in listing 4.15, every instance of our component would have a locally defined function, and each would occupy a slot in the program memory. This isn't normally a worry, but it's a slight difference between the two implementations.

When you're converting a class-based component with extra class methods, you can use either option as outlined previously. Just be aware of the advantages and disadvantages of both. In the concrete example, both options are fully valid solutions, but sometimes one option will be more appropriate than the other, depending on the exact circumstances.

4.4.4 *Version 4: Constructor*

As we've mentioned previously, you can also add a constructor method to your class-based component. Generally, the constructor is used for initializing attributes that will remain the same in the component's entire lifetime, regardless of the properties passed. This is because the constructor is only executed once, the first time the component is created, and not every time the component properties update or the component re-renders for other reasons.

We'll get into a lot more details about component re-rendering in future chapters. For now, just know that the constructor is only called once in the component's lifetime, so you shouldn't put any functionality there that depends on properties that might change in the future.

In this example, we'll add a constructor to our image component that generates a random ID to be applied to our element. Reasons for doing this might include to attach it to some external library or to reference the element using Accessible Rich Internet Applications (ARIA) properties for accessibility.

If we created an ID in the render method, the ID would regenerate every time the component renders. Instead, we create the ID in the constructor to make sure that it stays the same in the component's lifetime.

Listing 4.16 Gallery v4 using classes (excerpt)

```
...
class Image extends Component {
  constructor(props) {
    super(props);
```

Calling super(props) is required in the constructor of a class-based component; otherwise, your component won't work.

```
    this.id =
      `image-${Math.floor(Math.random() * 1000000)}`;    ◁─┐   We create a class
  }                                                           │   variable with the
  render() {                                                  │   generated unique ID.
    return (
      <figure style={{ margin: "5px" }} id={this.id}>
        <img
          src={`//picsum.photos/id/${this.props.index}/150/150/`}
          alt={this.props.title}
        />
        <figcaption>
          <h3>Species: {this.props.title}</h3>
        </figcaption>
      </figure>
    );
  }
}
...
```

We then use this ID in the render method by retrieving it from the class.

Repository: rq04-gallery-class-v4

This example can be seen in repository `rq04-gallery-class-v4`. You can use that repository by creating a new app based on the associated template:

```
$ npx create-react-app rq04-c4 --template rq04-gallery-class-v4
```

Alternatively, you can go to this website to browse the code, see the application in action directly in your browser, or download the source code as a zip file:

https://rq2e.com/rq04-gallery-class-v4

Note that we simply store the ID as a property directly on the class instance itself using `this.id`. We don't put it in `this.props` for two reasons: (1) because we can't (it's a frozen object), and (2) because it's not a property passed to our component—it's something we calculated ourselves. So, how do we convert this to a functional component with the knowledge we have so far? We can't! You'll learn the tools to do this later in chapter 7, using hooks (`useMemo` in particular); for now, however, we don't have the features to do this.

The problem is that unlike class-based components, which have a constructor that runs only once when the component is created the first time, and a separate render method, which runs every time the component renders (and re-renders), a functional component only has a single method that runs every time the component renders, including the first time. In a functional component, there is no real difference between the first render and subsequent renders.

We haven't seen a component yet that re-renders, but, for now, just trust us that almost all components you'll be writing in React will need to render more than once. If a component only ever renders once, it's most likely a very simple component with no internal logic or state. For example, your web application logo might be defined in a simple component that never changes. We'll talk a lot more about component life cycles and rendering in chapter 6.

To give you a sneak peek of what this ID generation would look like using functional components, check out listing 4.17. Here, we use the hook, useMemo, to generate a unique ID the first time the component renders, and then reuse this same calculated result on every subsequent render.

Listing 4.17 Gallery v4 using functions (excerpt)

```
import { useMemo } from 'react';          ◁——┐  Imports the hook
...                                            from the React
function Image({ index, title }) {             package
  const id = useMemo(() =>
    `image-${Math.floor(Math.random() * 1000000)}`,
  []);
  return (
    <figure style={{ margin: "5px" }} id={id}>
      <img src={`//picsum.photos/id/${index}/150/150/`} alt={title} />
      <figcaption>
        <h3>Species: {title}</h3>
      </figcaption>
    </figure>
  );
}
...
```

Applies the hook and adds the magic—an empty array—that makes the hook run only once. This is called a dependency array, which is discussed in chapter 6.

Repository: rq04-gallery-function-v4

This example can be seen in repository `rq04-gallery-function-v4`. You can use that repository by creating a new app based on the associated template:

```
$ npx create-react-app rq04-f4 --template rq04-gallery-function-v4
```

Alternatively, you can go to this website to browse the code, see the application in action directly in your browser, or download the source code as a zip file:

https://rq2e.com/rq04-gallery-function-v4

We won't go into more detail on how this works right now, but this is the logical equivalent of initializing a variable in the constructor. You'll learn more about hooks, rendering, and memoization in chapter 7. This technique does require some rewriting of the component, and you have to think a bit differently, but all the examples seen so far can be converted to functional components without too much work.

4.4.5   *More complexity equals harder conversion*

All the examples shown so far are very simple. We don't have any interaction or any state. Features such as filtering which animals you want to see and clicking to expand the information about each animal require more complex React components, which in turn require more complex logic to convert to a functional component, if that's the task you have.

When we introduce more complex features of functional React components in future chapters, we'll also briefly discuss what this would look like in a class-based component. In addition, we'll cover how you would handle the conversion of a component using these features to the equivalent features in a functional component.

For now, just know that while all functionality (barring the very few exceptions we saw earlier in section 4.3) can be converted from a class-based component to a functional one, it might not always be simple. Just as we had to make judgment calls when converting components using class methods, other degrees of complexity will introduce several different approaches, some of which are more applicable to a given situation than others. On top of that, as the original developer starts to combine all these features, you might end up with a very complex component that needs to be completely reworked to make sense in a functional world.

4.5   *Quiz*

1 Are functional components *less powerful, as powerful,* or *more powerful* than class-based components in terms of React functionality and which applications you can build?

2 How many arguments are passed to a functional component?

3 Which one of these statements is *not* a benefit of using functional components?

   a *Functional components are more compact than class-based components.*

   b *Functional components are faster than class-based components.*

   c *Functional components are easier to understand than class-based components.*

4 If you're starting a brand-new React application, should you use *functional components* or *class-based components*, all else being equal?

5 Converting a class-based component to a functional component is always trivial; *true* or *false?*

Quiz answers

1 Functional components are exactly *as powerful* as class-based components. Any application you can build using one type can also be built using the other.

2 Functional components receive *one* argument: a frozen object of properties.

3 *Functional components are not faster than class-based components.* While there might be a slight difference in speed for any naive implementation, both types of components can be lightning-fast when optimized properly, or, when ill-composed, can drag your whole application down. The choice of component type isn't in itself an indicator of application speed.

4 All else being equal, you should start any new project using *functional components*.

5 *False.* Converting a simple class-based component to a functional one can often be trivial initially, but as component complexity grows, the conversion gets more and more complex.

Summary

- Functional components are another way to write React components as an alternative to class-based components.
- Any JavaScript function returning JSX is a functional component, but for the sake of convention, we tend to write functional components in a certain style.
- Certain JavaScript tricks are often used to aid the definition of functional components, including destructuring, default values, the rest syntax, and the object spread operator.
- Functional components are at least as capable as class-based components in every respect.
- In certain aspects, functional components are more beneficial to the developer experience, but these benefits do not extend to the final product, which is independent of the choice of component type.
- If given the choice, using functional components is the recommended way to write React components.
- Class-based components can generally be converted to functional components, but it might require a lot of work and refactoring of existing functionality.

Making React interactive with states

This chapter covers

- The role of state in a component
- Using state in functional components
- Converting stateful class-based components to functional components

All the components we've created so far take some properties and render some HTML based on those properties. We can pass a label property to a button, so the button is displayed with that exact button text, for instance. But we can't make the button text change when something happens, such as changing between Turn On and Turn Off when toggled. That's because we lack both the ability to react to something that happens and the ability to store the single piece of information that something has changed dynamically.

The output of the components we've created so far depends on nothing but their properties. In other words, the components are "pure" in functional programming terms. The components have no other inputs and no side effects. If you give the same component the same properties, you'll always get the same result and nothing but that result.

That's all good, and it's exactly what we want—but it's also kind of boring. Such components are vital for presenting data but are useless if we want to create an interactive application. If we want to update something when a button is clicked or an input is filled, we need to store that somewhere and pass that information to some other component to react to it. Imagine a login form. When users enter their email and password, we need to store that information somewhere to display error messages if filled incorrectly. When users click the Send button, we need to send the data to a remote server.

Components that depend only on their properties and have no internal logic beyond that are also called *stateless* components. The alternative is a *stateful* component. In this context, *state* refers to the ability to change over time by using internal variables. The same component can have one internal state that results in one Java-Script XML (JSX) output at one point, and later have a different state that results in a different output. Imagine a push button that can toggle between being clicked and not clicked. Whether it's clicked or not is the state of the button, and a component that holds state is *stateful*.

In this chapter, we'll cover exactly what a stateful application is and what a stateful component does in such an application. We'll then make this more concrete by seeing how you set, update, and use component state inside a functional component. Despite the very simple API, which consists of a single function, `useState`, there's a lot of information to cover.

At the end of this chapter, we'll briefly discuss how setting, updating, and using state in a class-based component works. This is done in a related but different way, so there are some important things to be aware of.

When discussing class-based components, we'll also introduce how to convert stateful class-based components to stateful functional components. This will come in handy if you're tasked with working on an older codebase that is still using class-based components, but you want to upgrade it to a functional codebase so you can use the latest and greatest technology available. This knowledge can also help if you find examples and guides online that teach you how to do something in a class-based component. There are still thousands of older and useful tutorials out there, but to use the advice presented in a modern codebase, you have to convert some of the concepts.

> **NOTE** The source code for the examples in this chapter is available at https://rq2e.com/ch05. But as you learned in chapter 2, you can instantiate all the examples directly from the command line using a single command.

5.1 Why is React state relevant?

State is essential for making any kind of interactive application. If your application doesn't have any state, it means that your application is completely static—it can't change at all once opened in the browser. This might be fine for a blog post or a recipe, but if you want users to log in, update, click, or in any other way interact with your application to influence what is being shown, you need your application to be stateful.

React components are *individually stateful*. Keeping state in a component is what makes your React application as a whole stateful.

Note that while almost all React *applications* are stateful, not all *components* are stateful. You might have only a few stateful components in your application, but those few components can control state for your entire application and will update all the stateless components when necessary. While it's extremely hard to generalize about this, a rough estimate is that probably no more than a third of your components are stateful in your final application, and as applications grow larger and more complex, that ratio will likely decrease. Imagine a fictional component tree for a fictional application, as shown in figure 5.1. Only the dark components are *stateful*, whereas the light ones are *stateless*.

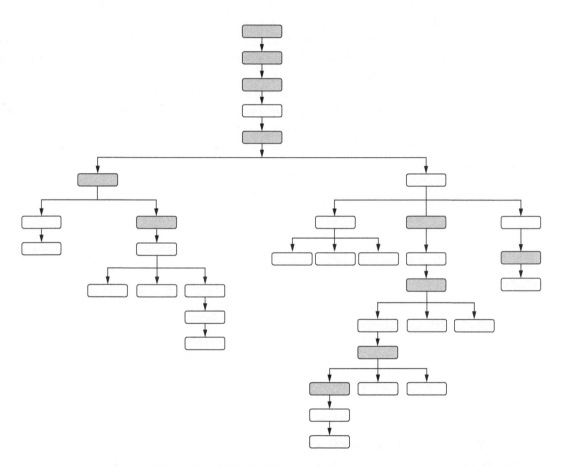

Figure 5.1   The dark components are stateful; the light ones are stateless. Note how stateful components often reside toward the top of your component tree, whereas stateless components are more prevalent toward the leaves.

React doesn't have tools to make your application as a whole stateful. A React application is only defined as the sum of its components, so to make your application stateful, you have to make some of your components stateful.

5.1.1 React component state

Component state is what makes a component stateful rather than stateless:

- *Stateful component*—A stateful component is independent of its context and has the ability to update itself based on internal triggers.
- *Stateless component*—A stateless component can only change or update when its parent component provides it with new properties.

React component state is the mechanism that allows you to store values inside your component that can change over time. Imagine the difference between a clock component that can display some time of day based on a property passed to it, versus a clock component that is able to update itself every second and continually display the current time. To do the latter, the component needs to have a way to store the current time of day (as well as a way to advance that value).

Figure 5.2 illustrates the difference between these two approaches.

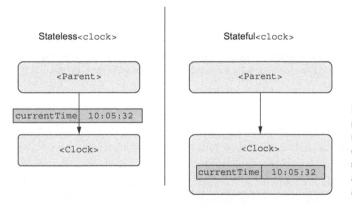

Figure 5.2   The stateless clock needs its parent component to update it every second to display the time, whereas the stateful clock can update itself, and the parent need not worry about it.

Note that for the stateless clock in figure 5.2 to actually work, the parent has to be stateful because we still need to keep the current time in a state *somewhere*. Of course, we could make the parent component stateless as well, but then we would have to push the state higher up the tree.

5.1.2 Where should I put state?

Okay, so we want our application to be stateful. Now where do we put the state? Normally, you would try to put the state as close as possible to the components that need it.

Let's say you have an application that contains a top menu with a (live and functional) clock in it, a main section with many different pages that can update as you navigate around the page, and a footer with some static links. You need the state for the clock to exist somewhere either inside the clock component itself or in any component above it in the tree. If you design your application as in figure 5.3, you have a choice of components for where to put your clock state.

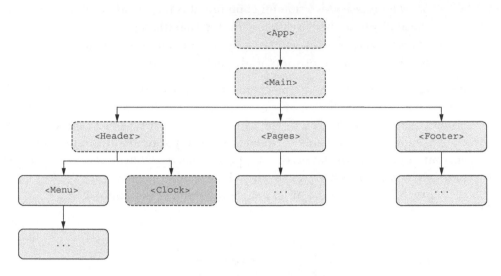

Figure 5.3   Clock state is only required in the component marked in a darker gray. You can put your clock state in any of the components with a dashed border. These represent the clock component and its ancestors.

In this example, it makes sense to put the clock state inside the clock component itself. No other component has a need to know about the current time, so we just have the state localized to the component that needs it.

On the other hand, let's say we also need to keep the state of which page is currently displayed in the application. This information is required both in the Pages component because it actually needs to display the active page, as well as in the Menu component because it needs to display the link to the current page with a highlighted background.

Examining the document tree in figure 5.4 shows that we can put the information in either Main or App, as those are the only two components that contain both of the components that require the state we care about.

Whether you actually decide to put your current page state in Main or App is up to you, as it's probably a matter of taste or personal preference. While there is a practical argument to keep state as "low" in the document tree as possible (i.e., put it in Main), that component might already have a ton of other responsibilities. Therefore, it might make sense to put this information in the parent App for organizational purposes.

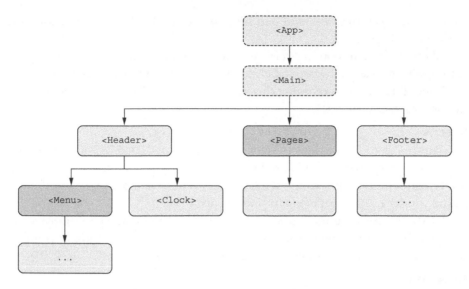

Figure 5.4   Current page state is required in the two components marked in a darker gray. You can then put your current page state in the two components marked with a dashed border. These are the common ancestors of the two target components.

5.1.3   What kind of information do you store in component state?

In general, any state used in a web application belongs to one of three categories:

- Application data
- UI state
- Form data

This isn't a rule or an artifact of React in particular, but it's a consequence of how stateful applications operate.

Different types of data are stored in different ways. We'll cover each of these to talk about how to store and use the data appropriately. There might be other categories of component state, but most of them fall within one of the preceding three categories.

APPLICATION DATA

Application data is the data the user is working on, updating, or reading. If you're building a web application where users can log in, the information about the user is application data. If the user can log in and see available classes in the gym, book a class, and so on, all of that data is application data as well.

Application data is most often stored on a global level in your application. If you have a component that displays gym classes, then it would be possible to store the list of available classes locally in this component, but that would also mean that all the information about the available classes would be lost when the component unmounts, and they would have to be reloaded from the server when the component mounts again later. These two terms, *mounting* and *unmounting*, will be discussed in a lot more detail in the next chapter.

A better solution is often to create a data store in a component that is persistent in your application so that when data is loaded once, it remains through the application. We'll see different ways of doing this in the future involving built-in React functionality (using React Context).

UI STATE

UI state refers to the current state of UI components, such as which tab is currently active, whether a panel is collapsed or not, whether the menu is open or not, and so on. In general, this is intermittent data that isn't persisted but just helps the web application render the correct elements in the correct way.

UI state values are most often kept as local as possible. The information about whether the menu is open or not is only of relevance inside the menu component, so you can easily store this as local state inside this component only.

FORM DATA

As you'll see in chapter 9, form data is another very common use case for component state. While the user is interacting with a form, entering data, moving from one form field to the next, the current state of the form is often kept in local state in the component that covers all the form fields.

5.1.4   *What not to store in state*

A number of things should never be stored in state, including the following:

- *Values that don't change*—This isn't just constants like magic numbers but also configuration values loaded in at application start. If it can't change, don't make it variable.
- *Copies of other state values*—You should try to keep a single source of truth. If you have some data in a global state in your application, it will get messy if you also keep it in a local state in a different component (unless you're locally allowing the user to update the data there in a form).
- *Duplicates of the same data*—If you have two versions of the same data in state, you might want to consolidate that data. For instance, if you have both first name, last name, and full name in state, you'll have to update at least two of these values every time one of the values change. It would be a lot better to only keep the source values, first name and last name, in the state and calculate the full name as needed based on the state.

Of course, there are many more things you should never put in state (e.g., your car keys), but that list is too long to write out. The preceding list shows the common pitfalls that you might think about doing, but probably shouldn't.

5.2 Adding state to a functional component

So far, we've discussed why, where, and what to keep in component state, but we still don't know how to actually do it. Keeping state in a functional component has a surprisingly simple API that is both a main attraction and sometimes also a headache. Because it's a very low-level API, you might have to add some functionality to get a smooth developer experience; however, it allows you to make simple cases of stateful components very, *very*, easily.

Let's jump right in and see the API in action by creating the simplest possible stateful component, a click counter. We need a way to initialize our counter, display the current value, and increment the counter every time we click a button. However, there is one very important last step. We can't simply update any old variable and hope that the component renders correctly. We need to let React know that a value has been updated, which means we need to go through the React-specific API. Refer to figure 5.5 for a simple flowchart.

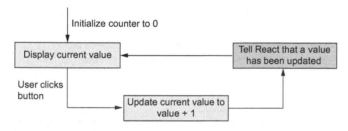

Figure 5.5 The flow of state in our counter component. We initialize the variable and display it, and, on button click, we increment the value and make sure React knows to update the component to display the new value.

To do this in a functional component, we need to use a function from the React package named useState. It takes an initial value and returns the current state and an update function. Let's add in the required relevant bits of the React-specific API, as shown in figure 5.6.

Let's see the code in its entirety in listing 5.1. Note that we cover all the details of the values passed to and returned from the useState hook later, so don't be too confused at this point about the setCounter function. It will be explained in due time.

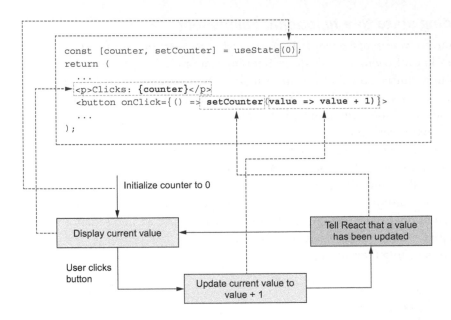

Figure 5.6   The flow of state and the lines of code that refer to each action in the chart. The dashes and arrows translate the concept to the actual piece of code implementing the given goal.

Listing 5.1   A fully functional counter

```
import { useState } from "react";          ⟵─┤  Imports the function useState
function Counter() {                             from the React package
  const [counter, setCounter] = useState(0);  ⟵    Initializes a new state with
  return (                                            an initial value and gets the
    <main>                                             current value and a setter
      <p>Clicks: {counter}</p>         ⟵┐               function back
      <button                 Displays
        onClick={() => setCounter((value) => value + 1)}  ⟵┐  Updates the
      >                                                         value through
        Increment                                              the setter
      </button>                                                function
    </main>
  );
}
function App() {
  return <Counter />;
}
export default App;
```

Displays the value through the current state

Let's go ahead and run this in the browser right away and get clicking, as we have in figure 5.7.

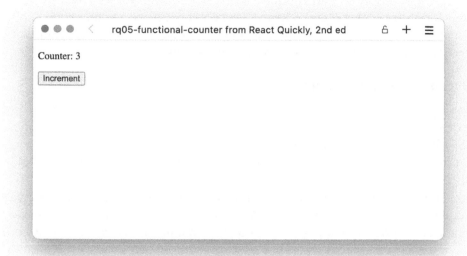

Figure 5.7   The counter in action after only three clicks, but feel free to keep going. The sky's the limit—or actually 9,007,199,254,740,991 is the limit—but you probably won't get that far.

Repository: rq05-functional-counter
This example can be seen in repository `rq05-functional-counter`. You can use that repository by creating a new app based on the associated template:

```
$ npx create-react-app rq05-functional-counter --template rq05-functional-
    counter
```

Alternatively, you can go to this website to browse the code, see the application in action directly in your browser, or download the source code as a zip file:

https://rq2e.com/rq05-functional-counter

There's a lot to cover here, so let's go over these steps one by one:

- Import the function `useState` from the React package.
- Call `useState` in the functional component and supply an initial value.
- Destructure the response from calling `useState` as two array elements:
  - The first element is the current value.
  - The second element is a setter function.
- Use the current value however you see fit.
- When you want to update the state, call the setter with either a function or a plain value.

We'll cover each of these steps one at a time in the next subsections. We'll also discover how you can use multiple `useState`s to create more complex components.

Oh, and did we mention, useState is a hook? This is the first and simplest of the new React hooks that came in React 16.8 and changed everything. Hooks are special functions that you can't treat like any other function. We'll cover some of that in this section, but will go even deeper into the topic of hooks in chapter 6.

5.2.1 *Importing and using a hook*

useState is a hook. *Hook* is an umbrella term for a new kind of special function that exists in React 16.8 and forward. React comes with a number of built-in hooks, and they are hooks because React says so. They don't do the same things nor provide overlapping functionality, but are all "hooks" into the React core functionality and require special attention to work correctly.

The fact that useState is a hook is actually very easy to see because the function starts with the word use*. In modern React, it's now a convention that any function starting with the word use* is a hook, and non-hooks should never start with that word.

So, what's so special about hooks? Hooks are named like that because they are hooks *from* your component *to* the "insides" of the React machinery. You can do some magic things that aren't possible without having this extra access. A functional component is just a function, so it can't really do much beyond controlling a single render if we don't have this deeper access.

React comes with 15 hooks (as of React 18), which are low-level units that can be combined to create all sorts of advanced components. New built-in hooks can be added to the React API over time, so by the time you're reading this, there might be more than 15.

You can create your own custom hooks on top of the React hooks. If you do, you should name your custom hooks use* as well. For example, we could have created a useCounter hook for the preceding component. We'll cover custom hooks in chapter 10.

RULES OF HOOKS

When you use a hook in a component, you must always use that hook. In addition, you must use the exact same hooks in the exact same order every time you render the component. This might seem weird, but it's required by React to make your function work correctly.

By "always use," we mean that the same hook must always be called every time the component renders, that is, every time the component definition function runs. This means that you can't conditionally run a hook, for example, by putting it inside an if block or include it after an optional return statement.

Imagine a variant of the counter component where we pass a property to the component to indicate whether it should be visible at all. You might think that we would be able to do something like figure 5.8.

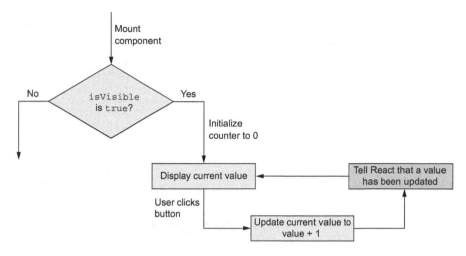

Figure 5.8 Can we check the property first, and, if false, simply ignore initializing the state altogether?

We can implement this as follows:

```
function Counter({ isVisible }) {            If isVisible is false, we
  if (!isVisible) {                          just return null from
   return null;                              the very start.
  }
  const [counter, setCounter] = useState(0);   Only if isVisible isn't false do
  return (                                      we actually initialize the state
   ...                                          using the useState hook. This
  );                                            is wrong!
}
```

Well, that's not allowed! What's wrong here? The hook function, `useState`, isn't called every time, only sometimes. If the `isVisible` property is set to `true` in one render, the hook *will* be called, but if it's set to `false` in the next render, the hook *won't* be called. And, that's not just bad, it will completely break your React application. React will throw an error message similar to this:

```
React Hook "useState" is called conditionally. React Hooks must be called
in the exact same order in every component render. Did you accidentally
call a React Hook after an early return?
```

For this reason, you'll need to sometimes make what looks like suboptimal code. You need to put all your hooks before any attempt to return anything in the component, as shown in figure 5.9.

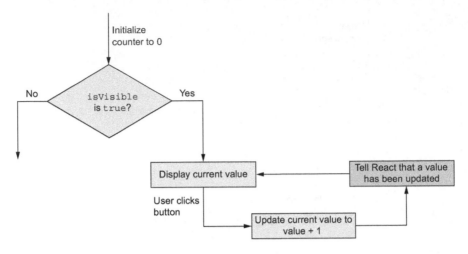

Figure 5.9   We have to initialize the state before optionally aborting rendering even if we don't need the state at all.

Let's implement this as follows:

```
function Counter({ isVisible }) {
  const [counter, setCounter] = useState(0);          Initializes two variables
  if (!isVisible) {                                    that might never be
   return null;          Only returns something        needed
  }                      after all our hooks have
  return (               been executed
    ...
  );
}
```

This also means that you can never conditionally run a hook (e.g., inside an `if` block), you can never run a hook in a loop (because that would mean you might have a varying number of hook calls), and you can never call a hook inside a callback or event handler (it has to run directly in the component body when called). You'll see some examples of some of these restrictions in the next sections and how you can work around those restrictions to still achieve the desired goal.

We'll also cover much more about hooks in the next chapter, where we go deeper under the hood of hooks and how they must be used.

5.2.2   Initializing the state

When you call `useState`, you must pass an initial value; if not, the initial value is assumed to be `undefined`. Only the value that you pass to `useState` the first time around for each component instance matters. When your hook re-renders for whatever reason, the initial value is ignored.

The most obvious use case for this is setting up a baseline in your component. When it mounts the first time, what should the state be? If it should be some dynamic value passed in as a property, use that property. If it should be any static value, write that. In 99% of cases, you'll set your initial value to either a static value (including null very often) or a property. We'll cover some examples of initialization in the rest of this section.

INITIAL VALUE

Every state has an initial value. Our counter had an initial value of 0, but it didn't need to be 0, of course. We could have initialized it to 10, 100, or even some dynamic value.

Let's say we want to create a variant of the counter, where we can initialize the value to some property that we pass in. We'll then create an application with three different instances of this counter initialized with different starting values. The resulting component tree will look like figure 5.10.

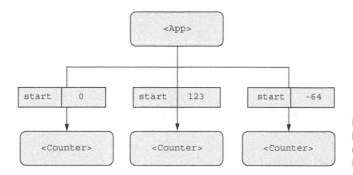

Figure 5.10 **We now want to have three counters initialized to different starting values because it looks cool.**

We can implement this as shown in the following listing. The result in a browser will look like figure 5.11.

Listing 5.2 Triple counters

```
import { useState } from "react";
function Counter({ start }) {                         The property passed to this
  const [counter, setCounter] = useState(start);      component is named start.
  return (                                            We use that property
    <main>                                            to initialize our state.
      <p>Counter: {counter}</p>
      <button onClick={() => setCounter(value => value + 1)}>
        Increment
      </button>
    </main>
  );
}
function App() {
  return (
    <>
      <Counter start={0} />       Three instances of
      <Counter start={123} />     the counter with three
      <Counter start={-64} />     different start values
    </>
```

```
    );
}
export default App;
```

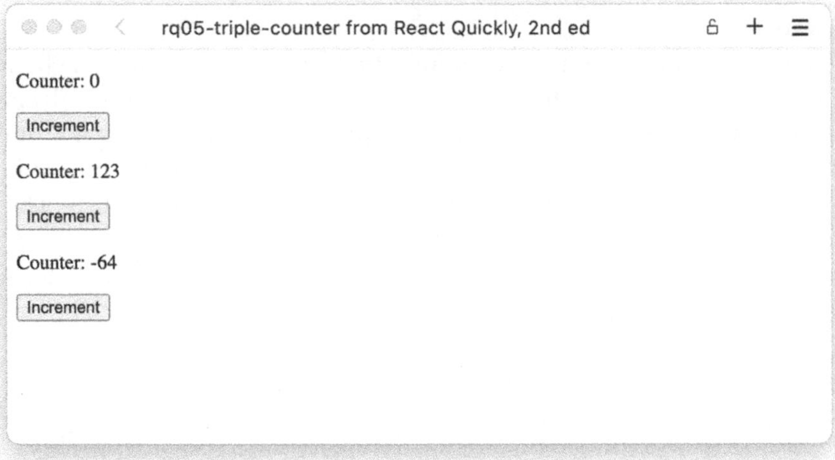

Figure 5.11   **Our three counters before we start clicking any of them**

Repository: rq05-triple-counter

This example can be seen in repository `rq05-triple-counter`. You can use that repository by creating a new app based on the associated template:

```
$ npx create-react-app rq05-triple-counter --template rq05-triple-counter
```

Alternatively, you can go to this website to browse the code, see the application in action directly in your browser, or download the source code as a zip file:

https://rq2e.com/rq05-triple-counter

The following are other common static initial values besides numbers:

- `true` *or* `false` *for Booleans*—If your menu is hidden until a button is clicked, the `isMenuVisible` state is initialized to `false`.
- *Empty string*, `""`—If you have an input for a login email address, you'll initialize your state to the empty value so the input is empty until the user starts typing.
- `null`—If you have a complex value that hasn't been set to anything yet, `null` is the perfect placeholder value for indicating that no value exists yet.

The most common dynamic initial value is to use a property. We did that with the previous counter. Similarly, you would use a property if you had a component to change your name. You would pass in the current name as a property and initialize your state based on that.

You could also initialize your state to a value from a cookie or similar local storage. For a login form, you could initialize the email address state with the last known email address used in this same form as stored in a cookie.

ONLY THE FIRST INITIAL VALUE MATTERS

Let's make a new variant of the counter with a variable start value. This time, we want to add a new button outside the counter that will change the start value of the counter. So, instead of initializing the value to 0 every time, we have a button that, if clicked, will lower the start value of the counter by 10, as illustrated in a flowchart in figure 5.12. We're actually creating a stateful component on top of our stateful component.

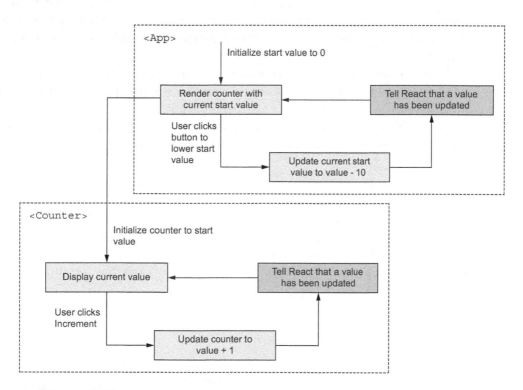

Figure 5.12   We now have state in both the app and the counter, and we want to use the app state to initialize the counter state.

Rather than blindly implementing this, let's think through some scenarios. What happens in this scenario?

1 At first, the counter will be initialized with a start value of 0.
2 We then click the button to lower the start value, so the start value should now be –10.
3 Does the counter then update to –10?

Let's expand with another scenario:

1 At first, the counter will be initialized with a start value of 0.

2 We then click Increment in the counter to increase the counter value to 1.

3 We then click the button to lower the start value (which was 0), so the start value should now be –10.

4 Does the counter then update to -10? Or does it update to –9?

In fact, both of these scenarios are meaningless because, as we've briefly mentioned, only the first value passed to useState is used as the value for the state. If the initial value changes in a subsequent render, the state never updates. This is both good and bad. It's good because otherwise our counter would always be the same value, as we keep passing the same value in every render. The bad thing is that if we actually want the value to change based on some passed parameter, we can't do that (not in this way, at least).

In this instance, it wasn't actually clear what we wanted to happen if we started lowering the start value after we had begun counting. It's important to figure out exactly what we want to happen before we try to implement it in code.

It's possible to have a state value update based on a property, but that requires other hooks—in particular, the useEffect hook—that we'll introduce in the next chapter.

INITIALIZER FUNCTION

There are times when you want to set the initial value to the result of some calculation. Let's say you have a password input that you want to initialize to a good, strong password, but once the user starts typing, you just use whatever the user types. We have an expensive function somewhere else in our codebase, generatePassword, that we'll use to create this initial password. Let's go ahead and diagram this as earlier, in figure 5.13.

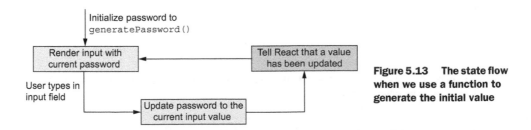

Figure 5.13   The state flow when we use a function to generate the initial value

If we implement this using the initial value, we get something like this:

```
function Password() {
  const [password, setPassword] = useState(generatePassword());
  ...
}
```

However, this `generatePassword()` function will actually be called on every render (because it's executed on every render), while the return value will be ignored on every render except the first, as just explained. It might be a complex function that runs a lot of expensive algorithms, so we should avoid running it if we don't need the returned value.

For this purpose, the initial value can instead be a function that returns the initial value. In such a setup, the initial value function will only be invoked the first time around and will be ignored for future renders, as shown in figure 5.14.

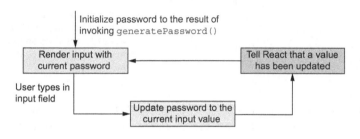

Figure 5.14 We don't actually call `generatePassword` **in this instance. We rather instruct the hook to call the function itself only when it needs to (which is only the first time around).**

We can do that generally as

```
const [password, setPassword] = useState(() => generatePassword());
```

or, in this instance, much simpler:

```
const [password, setPassword] = useState(generatePassword);
```

Because `generatePassword` is already a function, we can pass it as is. However, if the function took an argument, perhaps the length of the generated password, we would have to use the former form:

```
const [password, setPassword] = useState(() => generatePassword(12));
```

INITIALIZING TO A FUNCTION

What if your state is a function? If we pass a function to the initial value, it will be called, so how can we store a function as the initial value? We make another function that returns the first one. It sounds a bit weird, but it actually can make sense.

Let's say that we have a calculator component with which we can do some mathematical operation (e.g., addition, subtraction, and multiplication) on two values entered in two input fields. This calculation is a function that takes two values and returns a single response. We can implement this as an enum-like type as follows:

```
const OPERATORS = {
  ADDITION: (a, b) => a + b,
  SUBTRACTION: (a, b) => a - b,
  PRODUCT: (a, b) => a * b,
};
```

```
function Calculator() {
  const [operator, setOperator] = useState(OPERATORS.ADDITION);
  ...
}
```

This looks pretty good, but it doesn't work. What we've done is shown in figure 5.15.

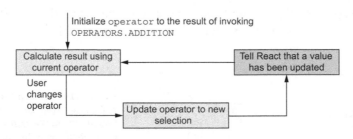

Figure 5.15   Because we pass in a function as the initial value, React treats it as an initializer function and invokes it—just like before.

If you type the preceding code snippet into a component, the operator will initialize to the value NaN. That's, of course, because useState is invoked with a function as initializer, so it calls the function, but that function doesn't know what to do without arguments, so it just returns NaN. What we need is a function that returns the operator, as shown in figure 5.16.

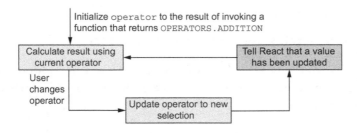

Figure 5.16   This time, we'll still pass in a function as the initializer value, but that function will then return our desired value (which happens to be a function).

We can implement that as

```
function Calculator() {
  const [operator, setOperator] = useState(() => OPERATORS.ADDITION);
  ...
}
```

This works and is a perfectly fine construction. You'll see this construction repeated when we talk about the setter function in a bit.

5.2.3   *Destructuring the state value and setter*

When we need a stateful component, we use the useState hook. This hook returns a value, which we've destructured into a state value and a setter function like this:

```
const [value, setter] = useState(initial);
```

This is as close to mandatory as it gets. There are other ways to do it, but everyone uses the useState hook in this manner. If you do the same thing, your code will make sense to other developers. This is simply a necessary convention when using this hook. Other hooks work in similar ways, and you just have to get used to this notation.

THE useState RETURN VALUE

The useState hook return value is a bit cryptic. The hook returns an array with two elements. The first element is the current value of the state, and the second element is the setter function. There are many ways we could "accept" this return value and change it to our use. We could store the returned array in a variable and address the two items as value[0] and value[1], respectively, or we could copy those elements to two other variables. But the recommended and most common way is to destructure the array directly in the assignment of the return value to a variable and name the two returned values as we see fit:

```
const [counter, setCounter] = useState(0);
```

At this point, for most React developers, this is just instinctive. Because this is how you use the useState hook, after a while, you don't really think about it. The only thing to think about here is the naming of the two destructured variables. The common approach is to name the state value after what we store in it, and name the setter function the same, but with a set* prefix. This is what we did earlier with counter and setCounter, respectively.

Teams will often come up with their own naming standards or apply those from others, but what we've suggested here is a safe default. The only potential deviation is when it comes to Boolean state values. You might have a state value called isCollapsed. The setter function would then be called setIsCollapsed, which just sounds like terrible English, so some might just call it setCollapsed and skip the prefix of is* or has* that Boolean variables often have.

Why useState returns an array

Okay, you understand that useState returns an array and that's just how it is. But, why does useState return an array with two unrelated values? It's clearly not a list of something!

Imagine that you're a React core developer creating the useState hook. The useState function needs to return two values. One value is the current state, which can be any type. The second value is the setter function, and it's a function that can take any value or even an update function.

JavaScript doesn't have tuples or structures, where you can structurally combine different types in a "nice" way. You might think we could return an object with the two properties and just have to agree on their naming, for example, obj.value and obj.set. These would also destructure well as simply

```
const { value, set } = useState(0); // This doesn't actually work!
```

(continued)

But as you're inclined to have multiple states in the same component, you would have to rename them often. Even if you only have a single state, you might still want to have a more descriptive name, and destructuring the named properties in an object to different local variables is more verbose than doing it for an array:

```
const {
  value: counter,
  set: setCounter,
} = useState(0); // This still doesn't work
```

That's a lot of extra typing and unnecessary overhead. So, rather than returning a more well-defined object with the two named properties, the React developers chose the array for ease of use.

Because React developers know this `useState` function so well, and it's used so many times in their daily workflow, the unusual syntax just becomes muscle memory, and they don't really think about it. But we agree that it's actually a bit weird.

5.2.4 *Using the state value*

Imagine our counter from earlier. What would happen if we changed the Increment button from incrementing the value to setting the value to the string "hi there"? So, it's not a number anymore, but a string. This would look like figure 5.17.

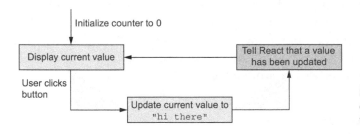

Figure 5.17 We set the counter value to a string when we click the button.

Let's try to implement that:

```
import { useState } from "react";
function Counter() {
  const [counter, setCounter] = useState(0);       // Initializes the
                                                    // counter to a
                                                    // number
  return (
    <main>
      <p>Counter: {counter}</p>                     // Displays whatever the
                                                    // counter currently is
      <button onClick={() => setCounter("hi there")}>   // On click, changes
        Increment                                        // the value of the
      </button>                                          // counter to a
    </main>                                              // string
  );
}
```

This actually works. If we click the button, the result will look like figure 5.18.

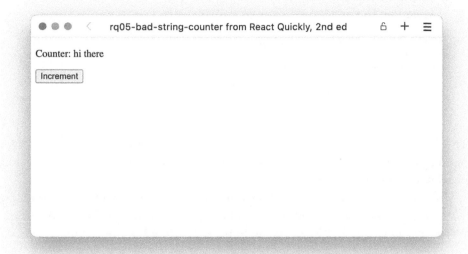

Figure 5.18   Our "counter" value is now a string, and it's still displayed because we don't actually check if it's a number.

It's pretty nonsensical to change the type of a state, just like it's nonsensical to change the type of any other variable.

The state value returned by the useState hook is whatever you set it to. You can change the type, complexity, and so on. You have full control over the value. The value will start at whatever you pass in as the initial value, and from then on, it will be whatever you pass to the setter function.

Most of the time, your state type should not change, however. Just as any other variable in your codebase, keeping the type consistent is a huge help, even though JavaScript doesn't put any such constraints on you. For instance, you can initialize a value to null and later set it to a number, where null would represent that you don't know what the number would be yet, so initializing to 0 would be misleading. This could be the case with an age input, for example. Just because you haven't typed your age yet, doesn't mean that it's 0. This would be a change of type, where the type is initially null but later changes to a number.

You can, of course, have object literals in the state, which might make sense for related values that you either always update together or use together. You might, for instance, have a loader component that displays the loading progress of a file in both a percentage and in text with loaded bytes out of total bytes:

```
function Loader() {
  const [progress, setProgress] = useState(null);
  const someCallback = () => {
    ...
```

```
    setProgress({ loaded, total });
  };
  if (!progress) {
    return null;
  }
  const { loaded, total } = progress;
  return (
    <h2>{Math.floor(100 * loaded / total)}%</h2>
    <p>Loaded { loaded } out of {total}.</p>
  );
}
```

This is a partial example only, as we don't actually load anything here, so we would need more logic to actually fetch something and check the values. But it is an example of related values stored in a single state value.

In later sections, we'll discuss how you can use multiple states rather than cram all your states into a single value. You should only put multiple values into a single state when the values are tightly related, as in the preceding `Loader` example.

5.2.5   *Setting the state*

Setting the state is fairly straightforward in that it works exactly like setting the initial value, with all the same quirks and workarounds. We can update the state either by setting it to a static value or by using an update function that returns the new value to be set.

SETTING TO A STATIC VALUE

Let's create a simple accordion component where you can expand and collapse the contents. The headline contains two buttons with a plus and minus, respectively. Clicking the Plus button will expand the accordion and show the contents, and clicking the Minus button will collapse the accordion and hide the contents. This is illustrated as a diagram in figure 5.19 and implemented in listing 5.3.

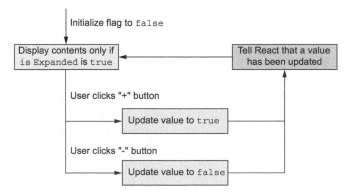

Figure 5.19   The flowchart for an accordion. The Boolean is set to `true` or `false` depending on which button is clicked.

Listing 5.3 A simple accordion

```
import { useState } from "react";
function Accordion() {
  const [isExpanded, setExpanded] = useState(false);
  return (
    <main>
      <h2 style={{ display: "flex", gap: "6px" }}>
        Secret password
        <button onClick={() => setExpanded(false)}>
          -
        </button>
        <button onClick={() => setExpanded(true)}>
          +
        </button>
      </h2>
      {isExpanded && (
        <p>
          Password: <code>hunter2</code>.
        </p>
      )}
    </main>
  );
}
function App() {
  return <Accordion />;
}
export default App;
```

◁── **Initializes the state to false**

◁── **Invokes the setter with either true or false when a button is clicked**

Displays the secret accordion contents if the Boolean is true

Repository: rq05-accordion

This example can be seen in repository `rq05-accordion`. You can use that repository by creating a new app based on the associated template:

```
$ npx create-react-app rq05-accordion --template rq05-accordion
```

Alternatively, you can go to this website to browse the code, see the application in action directly in your browser, or download the source code as a zip file:

https://rq2e.com/rq05-accordion

The result in a browser will look like figure 5.20. This component is an example of using the setter with a static value. The minus button always sets the state value to `false` no matter how many times you click it. Because we set it to a fixed value, we don't need to look at the current value.

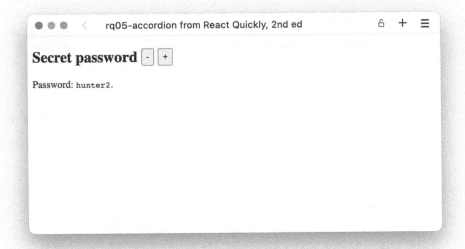

Figure 5.20   After clicking the Plus button, the secret accordion contents are revealed.

SETTING USING AN UPDATE FUNCTION

You can set the value as either a direct value as we've just done or with an update function that returns the new value. If you use an update function, it will be passed the current state as an argument.

We've already seen an example of using an update function:

```
const [counter, setCounter] = useState(0);
...
<button onClick={() => setCounter((value) => value + 1)}>
```

This updates the value in the state by using a simple increment function that takes an argument and returns the argument + 1.

SETTING TO A FUNCTION

To set the state value to a function, we have to use the same workaround as with the initial value. We need a function that returns our operator function.

So, if we expand our calculator example from earlier with buttons to change the operator, we would be implementing a full application. Let's first look at the diagram of the state flow in figure 5.21 and then see its implementation in listing 5.4.

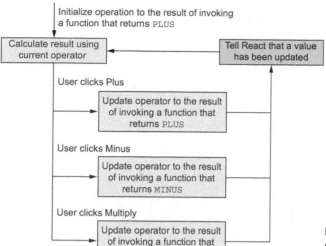

Initialize operation to the result of invoking
a function that returns PLUS

Calculate result using current operator

Tell React that a value has been updated

User clicks Plus

Update operator to the result of invoking a function that returns PLUS

User clicks Minus

Update operator to the result of invoking a function that returns MINUS

User clicks Multiply

Update operator to the result of invoking a function that returns MULTIPLY

Figure 5.21 The expanded calculator example now has three buttons to change the operator.

Listing 5.4 Simple calculator

```
import { useState } from "react";
const PLUS = (a, b) => a + b;
const MINUS = (a, b) => a - b;
const MULTIPLY = (a, b) => a * b;
function Calculator({ a, b }) {
  const [operator, setOperator] = useState(() => PLUS);
  return (
    <main>
      <h1>Calculator</h1>
      <button
        onClick={() => setOperator(() => PLUS)}
      >
        Plus
      </button>
      <button
        onClick={() => setOperator(() => MINUS)}
      >
        Minus
      </button>
      <button
        onClick={() => setOperator(() => MULTIPLY)}
      >
        Multiply
      </button>
      <p>
        Result of applying operator to {a} and {b}:
        <code> {operator(a, b)}</code>
      </p>
    </main>
  );
}
```

Initializes the state with a function returning the default operator function

Updates the state with a function returning the clicked operator function

We can now call the state value as a function because we've made sure it's always a function.

```
function App() {
  return <Calculator a={7} b={4} />;
}
export default App;
```

> ### Repository: rq05-calculator
> This example can be seen in repository `rq05-calculator`. You can use that repository by creating a new app based on the associated template:
>
> `$ npx create-react-app rq05-calculator --template rq05-calculator`
>
> Alternatively, you can go to this website to browse the code, see the application in action directly in your browser, or download the source code as a zip file:
>
> https://rq2e.com/rq05-calculator

See this fancy (but a bit simple) calculator in action in figure 5.22.

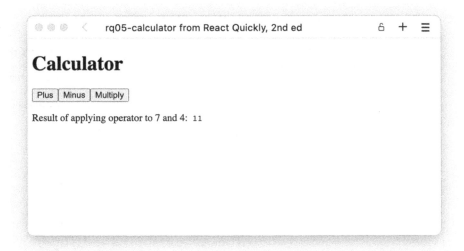

Figure 5.22   Our calculator with the default operator, PLUS. We don't actually display anywhere what the operator is, we just display the result of the calculation of applying that operator to the two operands.

SETTING AND RENDERING

What happens if we keep clicking the Plus button in the calculator? Does the component re-render every time, doing the calculation every time? We set the state to the exact same value every time, so why should it?

Actually, the component won't re-render. React includes built-in optimization, so `useState` will wait until the end of the current cycle to update the component. It checks whether the value actually changed and then only re-renders the component if it has changed. Because of this, there can be situations where you call the state setter function, but no re-render happens (because no re-render should be necessary as nothing has changed).

Let's expand our counter from earlier and add a Reset button that resets the counter to 0. The state flowchart now looks like figure 5.23.

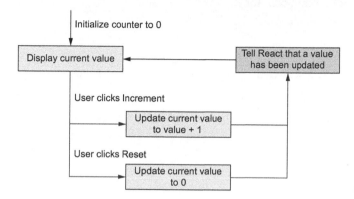

Figure 5.23 The new Reset button sets the counter to 0 regardless of the old value.

If we implement this, we get the following listing. You can see this new resettable counter in figure 5.24.

Listing 5.5 A resettable counter

```
import { useState } from "react";
function Counter() {
  const [counter, setCounter] = useState(0);
  return (
    <main>
      <p>Counter: {counter}</p>
      <button onClick={() => setCounter((val) => val + 1)}>
        Increment
      </button>
      <button onClick={() => setCounter(0)}>        ⟵  When you click
        Reset                                            Reset, the counter
      </button>                                          is set to 0.
    </main>
  );
}
function App() {
  return <Counter />;
}
export default App;
```

Repository: rq05-reset-counter

This example can be seen in repository `rq05-reset-counter`. You can use that repository by creating a new app based on the associated template:

```
$ npx create-react-app rq05-reset-counter --template rq05-reset-counter
```

(continued)

Alternatively, you can go to this website to browse the code, see the application in action directly in your browser, or download the source code as a zip file:

https://rq2e.com/rq05-reset-counter

Figure 5.24   A resettable counter that we've just set back to 0

Clicking Reset works by resetting the value to 0. If we click the button again, nothing happens. But how can you tell if the component re-rendered or not? The answer is a very useful plugin available for Chrome, Firefox, and modern versions of Edge, called *React Developer Tools*. It's available for download from their respective stores:

- Chrome and Edge: http://mng.bz/wvoq
- Firefox: http://mng.bz/qrYw

With this plugin, we're able to see when any component renders. React Developer Tools instructions are shown in figure 5.25.

When finished, go back to the resettable counter application and click the increment counter, and you'll see a blue outline around the entire component flash briefly every time the counter increases. It should look like figure 5.26.

If you click the Reset button when the counter isn't at 0, you'll see the blue outline flash because the component renders. But if you click the Reset button when the counter is already at 0, no blue outline appears. React is smart enough to know that if the state is unchanged, the component output is (or at least should be) unchanged.

1. Open the Components tab in your browser developer tools.

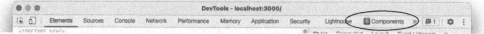

2. Click the circled gear icon to open settings (not the gear icon in the top-right corner).

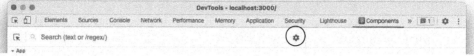

3. Check the Highlight Updates When Components Render check box.

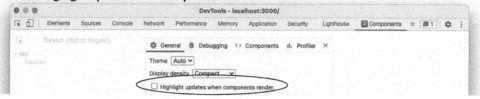

4. When checked, it should look like this.

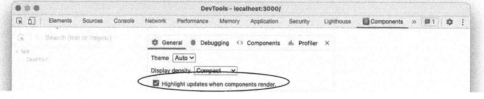

Figure 5.25   Open the Components panel for React Developer Tools, open the gear menu, and select the Highlight Updates When Components Render check box.

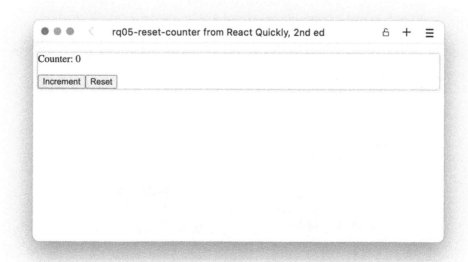

Figure 5.26   The blue outline around the entire component indicates that it has just rendered due to the state changing.

STATE MUST BE SET TO A NEW VALUE

This condition on the re-render also means that if you set the state value to the same object it already is, even if you changed the object "on the inside," nothing will happen because there isn't a re-render. This can occur, for example, if you have an array in your state. If you manipulate the array in place and set the same array as the state value again, the component won't render because nothing has changed (from a referential equality perspective, at least).

Let's see this in action and discuss how we can fix this. For that purpose, we're going to build a simple to-do application. We have a list of items we can tick off the list, and as we tick off an item, we remove it from the array and then render the list again.

The wrong way to do this is to set the state to the same array every time. It doesn't matter if we edit the array before setting it as state again because React doesn't look inside our state value, but only at the reference. This wrong approach in sketched out in figure 5.27.

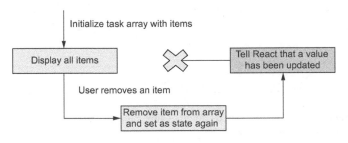

Figure 5.27   **The wrong way to use an array as a state value is to set the state to the same array every time. The problem here is that React actually won't see that anything changed, and it won't cause our component to re-render.**

While we now understand that this is wrong, let's try to implement it anyway, so we can also see that it actually doesn't work for real.

Listing 5.6   A broken to-do list application

```
import { useState } from "react";
function TodoApplication({ initialList }) {
  const [todos, setTodos] = useState(initialList);
  return (
    <main>
      {todos.map((todo, index) => (
        <p key={todo}>
          {todo}
          <button
            onClick={() => {
              todos.splice(index, 1);        ◄—  Modifies the
              setTodos(todos);        ◄—          array in place
            }}
          >                                 Updates the state to the
            x                               same value it already has
          </button>                         (which we changed
        </p>                                though, right?)
      ))}
```

```
    </main>
  );
}
function App() {
  const items = [
    "Feed the plants",
    "Water the dishes",
    "Clean the cat"
  ];
  return <TodoApplication initialList={items} />;
}
export default App;
```

> ### Repository: rq05-bad-todo
>
> This example can be seen in repository `rq05-bad-todo`. You can use that repository by creating a new app based on the associated template:
>
> `$ npx create-react-app rq05-bad-todo --template rq05-bad-todo`
>
> Alternatively, you can go to this website to browse the code, see the application in action directly in your browser, or download the source code as a zip file:
>
> https://rq2e.com/rq05-bad-todo

Let's try this out and click those Delete buttons shown in figure 5.28. Nothing happens when you click. If you try enabling update outlines in the React Developer Tools plugin, you'll see that the component doesn't actually re-render because the state value is identical by reference, even though it might have been "updated."

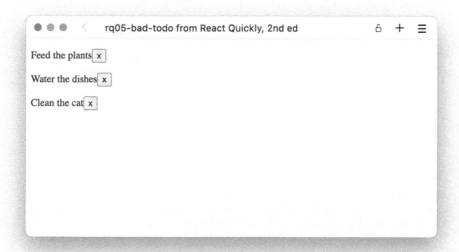

Figure 5.28 Our functional to-do list application looks right, but doesn't work—nothing happens when we click the buttons.

For this reason, it's not merely recommended that you don't mutate state directly, it's absolutely necessary that you don't. Doing this correctly requires setting the state value to a new array, which is a duplicate of the old one but without the spliced item. One way is to use the spread operator on a slice of the array before and after the item to be deleted. We can fix the model so it becomes like figure 5.29 by creating a new array and setting *that* as the new state. This is implemented in listing 5.7, which follows the figure.

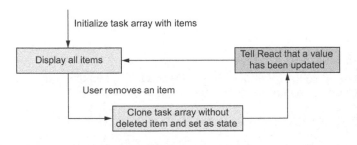

Figure 5.29 We now pass a new array to the setter function every time an item is removed. React correctly identifies that state as updated and will re-render the component.

Listing 5.7   A proper to-do list application

```
import { useState } from "react";
function TodoApplication({ initialList }) {
  const [todos, setTodos] = useState(initialList);
  return (
    <main>
      {todos.map((todo, index) => (
        <p key={todo}>
          {todo}
          <button
            onClick={() => {
              setTodos((value) => [
                ...value.slice(0, index),
                ...value.slice(index + 1),
              ]);
            }}
          >
            x
          </button>
        </p>
      ))}
    </main>
  );
}
function App() {
  const items = ["Feed the plants", "Water the dishes", "Clean the cat"];
  return <TodoApplication initialList={items} />;
}
export default App;
```

> Sets the state to a new array, which is the concatenation of two things: the old array sliced from the start to just before the deleted element, plus the old array sliced just after the deleted element to the end

This looks the same as before, but now we can actually delete items from the list, as you can see in figure 5.30.

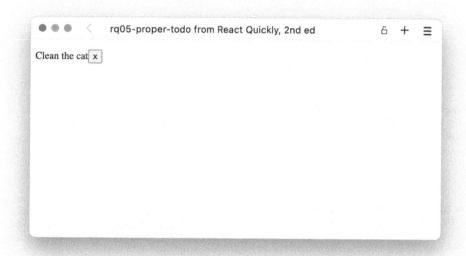

Figure 5.30   Our functional to-do list application now actually works as here we've completed two of the items on the task list for the day. Now, go run a bath; this is gonna be messy!

5.2.6   *Using multiple states*

We've hinted at this a few times, but just to confirm it—yes, you can have multiple use-State hooks in the same component, and you often will. As an example, let's expand our new to-do list application. Let's stop deleting items from the array when we complete them. Instead, we'll mark them as completed. Completed items will be rendered in the list with a strike-through. On top of that, we'll also add a new filter at the top, where you can decide if you want to see all items or only uncompleted items.

To filter the list, we need to remember whether we should filter out completed items or not. The perfect way to do this is to add another state value that holds this filter flag, as illustrated in figure 5.31. The implementation is shown in listing 5.8.

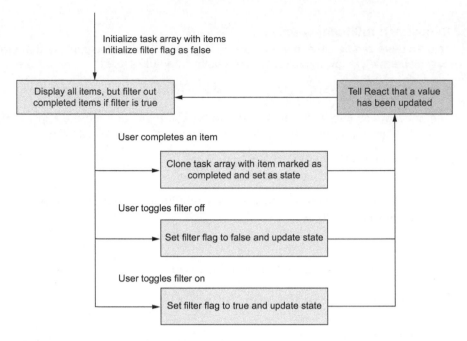

Figure 5.31 We can now update state in three different ways. If an item is marked as completed, we still have to remember to create a new array, but with the item in question marked as completed. If we toggle the filter flag, we simply set the relevant state flag.

Listing 5.8   To-do app with a filter

Uses the filter flag to optionally filter the list of to-do items to display

Creates a little utility function that takes an array of task objects and returns a new array of the same objects, except one of them will be marked as done, as indicated by the second argument

```
import { useState } from "react";
function markDone(list, index) {
  return list.map(
    (item, i) => (i === index ? { ...item, done: true } : item)
  );
}
function TodoApplication({ initialList }) {
  const [todos, setTodos] = useState(initialList);
  const [hideDone, setHideDone] = useState(false);
  const filteredTodos = hideDone
    ? todos.filter(({ done }) => !done)
    : todos;
  return (
    <main>
      <div style={{ display: "flex" }}>
        <button onClick={() => setHideDone(false)}>
          Show all
        </button>
        <button onClick={() => setHideDone(true)}>
          Hide done
```

Still initializes the task list using the useState hook

But now we have a second instance of the useState hook for the new filter flag, which we default to false.

The two filter buttons call the filter setter function with either true or false.

```
        </button>
      </div>
      {filteredTodos.map((todo, index) => (          ◄──    Now we must remember
        <p key={todo.task}>                                  to use the new (optionally
          {todo.done ? (                                      filtered) list.
            <strike>{todo.task}</strike>        ◄──┐   Renders the task with a
          ) : (                                      strike-through if it has
            <>                                       been completed
              {todo.task}
              <button
                onClick={() => setTodos((value) =>
                  markDone(value, todo.index)
                )}
              >
                x
              </button>
            </>
          )}
        </p>
      ))}
    </main>
  );
}
function App() {
  const items = [
    { task: "Feed the plants", done: false, index: 0 },
    { task: "Water the dishes", done: false, index: 1},
    { task: "Clean the cat", done: false, index: 2 },
  ];
  return <TodoApplication initialList={items} />;
}
export default App;
```

If not completed, renders a button that will call our utility function and updates the task list state

Creates the list of initial items as a list of objects, each marked as not done yet. Note that we need to remember the original position of each item, as the index in the filtered array will be different from the original index position.

Let's see this in action in figure 5.32 and try to use the various buttons.

Of course, you're not limited to two state values in a single component. You can use as many as you want, though it might get a bit hard to follow if the number exceeds 10. We suggest using either context providers, reducers, or custom hooks—or all three—if states get more complex. We'll get back to how these more advanced techniques work in chapter 10.

Figure 5.32   After completing the two easy items, we can decide whether to see the full list and bask in our 67% completed progress or only see the remaining items and get a bit overwhelmed because of the single daunting task.

5.2.7   *State scope*

In all the components we created previously, we accessed and updated the state inside the component itself, as opposed to accessing or updating the state outside the component, where we defined the state. But what if we want to have state that spans multiple components? What if we want to access the value in one component, but update it in another? We hinted at this at the beginning of the chapter, when we talked about the number of stateful components in the entire application component tree, but we haven't actually done it yet.

To do this, we can use properties to pass state values and state setters to the relevant components. The state flowchart is the same as before; the difference is the component tree. Where we just had a single component handle everything, we're now going to introduce a number of components. The `TodoApplication` component is still our stateful component holding the two state values. To aid this one, we add a `FilterButton` and a `Task`, which take care of rendering the top filter buttons and individual tasks in the list, respectively. Figure 5.33 shows this new component tree as well as all the properties.

Let's now put this all together in a single application in listing 5.9, and, while we're at it, let's also make things look a bit nicer with some styles.

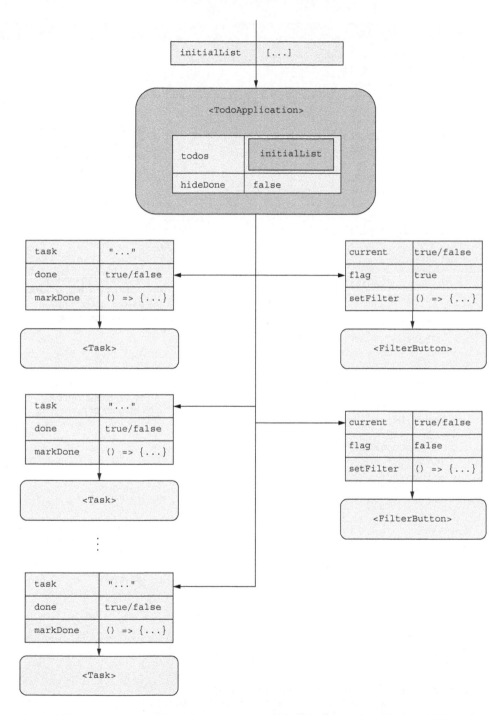

Figure 5.33 The component tree of our multicomponent to-do application. We render a variable number of Task instances, one for every item in the list, and always exactly two filter buttons.

Listing 5.9   **Advanced multicomponent to-do application**

```
import { useState } from "react";
function markDone(list, index) {
  return list.map(
    (item, i) => (i === index ? { ...item, done: true } : item)
  );
}
function FilterButton(
  { current, flag, setFilter, children }
) {
  const style = {
    border: "1px solid dimgray",
    background: current === flag ? "dimgray" : "transparent",
    color: current === flag ? "white" : "dimgray",
    padding: "4px 10px",
  };
  return (
    <button
      style={style}
      onClick={() => setFilter(flag)}
    >
      {children}
    </button>
  );
}
function Task({ task, done, markDone }) {
  const paragraphStyle = {
    color: done ? "gray" : "black",
    borderLeft: "2px solid",
  };
  const buttonStyle = {
    border: "none",
    background: "transparent",
    display: "inline",
    color: "inherit",
  };
  return (
    <p style={paragraphStyle}>
      <button
        style={buttonStyle}
        onClick={done ? null : markDone}
      >
        {done ? "✓ " : "◯ "}
      </button>
      {task}
    </p>
  );
}
function TodoApplication({ initialList }) {
  const [todos, setTodos] = useState(initialList);
  const [hideDone, setHideDone] = useState(false);
  const filteredTodos = hideDone
    ? todos.filter(({ done }) => !done)
    : todos;
```

The **FilterButton** takes four properties and renders a nice button based on these.

In particular, the onClick property on the button calls the passed setter function with the passed value.

Similarly, the Task component takes a number of properties, including a callback.

This time, we just invoke the passed callback when we click the button because it does the required work, but only if the item wasn't already done.

```
      return (
        <main>
          <div style={{ display: "flex" }}>
            <FilterButton
              current={hideDone}
              flag={false}
              setFilter={setHideDone}
            >
              Show all
            </FilterButton>
            <FilterButton
              current={hideDone}
              flag={true}
              setFilter={setHideDone}
            >
              Hide done
            </FilterButton>
          </div>
          {filteredTodos.map((todo, index) => (
            <Task
              key={todo.task}
              task={todo.task}
              done={todo.done}
              markDone={() => setTodos((value) =>
                markDone(value, todo.index)
              )}
            />
          ))}
        </main>
      );
}
function App() {
  const items = [
    { task: "Feed the plants", done: false, index: 0 },
    { task: "Water the dishes", done: false, index: 1 },
    { task: "Clean the cat", done: false, index: 2 },
  ];
  return <TodoApplication initialList={items} />;
}
export default App;
```

Two filter buttons in the final component with almost identical properties

For each task item, creates a Task component instance

Sets the markDone to the same updating function as before

Repository: rq05-nice-todo

This example can be seen in repository `rq05-nice-todo`. You can use that repository by creating a new app based on the associated template:

```
$ npx create-react-app rq05-nice-todo --template rq05-nice-todo
```

Alternatively, you can go to this website to browse the code, see the application in action directly in your browser, or download the source code as a zip file:

https://rq2e.com/rq05-nice-todo

And there we have it—our first complete, useful, and well-architected application in React! It looks just like before, except it looks a lot nicer, as you can see in figure 5.34.

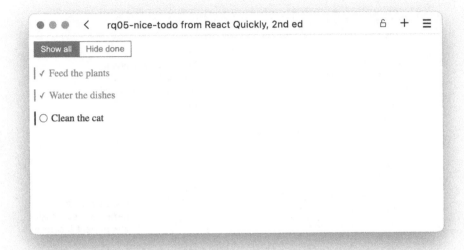

Figure 5.34 Our fully developed to-do application with a lovely UI, even! Currently, the filter is set to Show All, but if we toggle it to Hide Done, only the last item would be displayed—just like before.

The ideas used in this application are the same ideas that fuel any application. We store state in one level and pass it around to other components where applicable to render the result we need. In our latest to-do application, state is stored "globally" in the Todo-Application component and not just locally inside each of the child components.

If we were to add another component to this that existed next to the task list but would need access to the same state values as the task list does, we would need to lift the states from the TodoApplication component up to the App component and then pass the values and the setters down to the TodoApplication component. All of this work of passing state values and setters around can get a bit complex, but we'll see how to solve that in a better way in chapter 10 using React Context.

5.3 *Stateful class-based components*

So far, we've covered how to add component state to functional components. But stateful components existed before the emergence of hooks. In fact, state was a primary feature built into the functionality of class-based components.

In class-based components, state works the same way and has the same four steps shown in figure 5.5:

1 Initialize state.
2 Display current value.
3 Update state.
4 Inform React that state has been updated.

We've seen a ton of examples of how we do these four steps in a functional component. Now let's look at how to do the same in a class-based component. The API is similar, but the syntax is a bit different, and the behavior also varies slightly. The basic concept is the same, however.

The code for a (partial) counter component looks like this:

```
class Counter extends Component {
  state = { counter: 0 }
  render() {
    return (
      ...
      <p>Clicks: {this.state.counter}</p>
      <button onClick={() =>
        this.setState({ counter: this.state.counter + 1 })
      ...
    );
  }
}
```

Now, take a look at figure 5.35 for a quick overview of how the different parts relate to the different bits of the state cycle. Rather than store values as local variables as

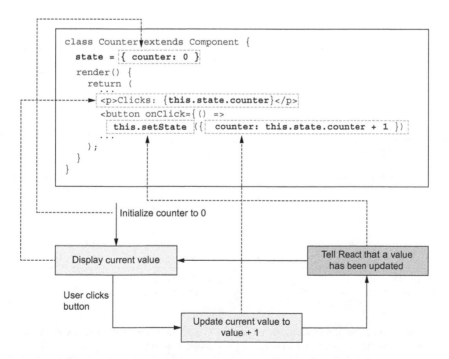

Figure 5.35   The flowchart of data in our click counter with code added. The dashed arrows connect the state in the flowchart to the corresponding bit of code responsible for that particular action.

we do in a functional component, we store the state values on the class member called `this.state`.

In this section, we'll first cover how adding state to class-based components is similar to adding state to functional components, but with a slightly different syntax; then, we'll discuss how this is also fundamentally different due to three larger changes in behavior; and, finally, we'll briefly go over how to convert a stateful class-based component to a functional component. Note that we're not going to provide full examples in this section, merely explain the differences.

5.3.1   Similarities with the useState hook

Everything we've done so far in functional components could just as well have been done in class-based components. Initializing, updating, and displaying state is the name of the game, and we can do that with a slightly different syntax. See table 5.1 for an overview of how the syntax deviates.

Table 5.1   State in functional components and class-based components

Functional component	Class-based component

`const [counter, setCounter] =`
`  useState(0);`
 	
This is the case if state is initialized to a static value.
	`state = {`
	`  counter: 0,`
	`}`
	
	When we initialize state to a static value here, we can use a class member.

`const [counter, setCounter] =`
`  useState(initialValue);`
 	
This is the case if state is initialized to a dynamic value from a property.
	`constructor(props) {`
	`  this.state = {`
	`    counter:`
	`      props.initialValue,`
	`  };`
	`}`
	
	Here, we have to access the property in the constructor and initialize the state using `this.state`.

`<p>`
`  Counter: {counter}`
`</p>`
	`<p>`
	`  Counter: {this.state.counter}`
	`</p>`

`onClick={() =>`
`  setCounter(0)`
`}`
 	
If we're setting the state to a fixed value, we can use the nonfunctional variant of the setter.
	`onClick={() =>`
	`  this.setState({ counter: 0 })`
	`}`
	
	We do the same thing here, except we need to make it an object.

Table 5.1   State in functional components and class-based components *(continued)*

Functional component	Class-based component
| ```
onClick={() =>
  setCounter(
    value => value + 1
  )
}
``` | ```
onClick={() =>
  this.setState(
    ({ counter }) =>
      ({ counter: counter + 1 })
  )
}
``` |
| If we use an update function, we simply use the old value and return a new one using whatever type we have in the state. | If we're setting the state to a dynamic value based on the current state, we can use the functional update variant of the setter, but we have to return an object based on the old state object. |

5.3.2   Differences from the useState hook

There are also differences in how state is used in class-based components. Those differences are significant and will affect how you use state in class-based components as opposed to functional components. The main differences are listed here:

- You can only have one state object, which is always an object.
- Components *always re-render if updated,* even if nothing changed.
- Objects are merged when you update the state, so *partial updates are possible.*

We'll go over each of these differences with a short example in the following subsections.

ONLY ONE STATE OBJECT

As you saw in table 5.1, class-based component state lives inside a state object. Even if you only have a single value—for example, a counter—you have to create it on the state object, update it on the state object, and display it from the state object.

The upside is that moving from a single state value to multiple state values is very smooth. You simply add a second property to the state object, and you're good to go. As soon as you have introduced state into a class-based component, you can support one or multiple state values without any problem.

COMPONENTS ALWAYS RENDER WHEN STATE IS UPDATED

We mentioned in section 5.2.5 that the useState hook will only cause the component to re-render if the state actually updates. If you set a state value to 0 when it's already 0, it won't update the component. React assumes that our components are pure and that the component will render the same if the state hasn't updated.

It was different in the old days, and some applications actually depended on this back then. In a class-based component, you can call setState with the same values or even no values, and React will re-render your component.

STATE OBJECTS ARE MERGED

Because the state in a class-based component is a single big object with potentially dozens of state values, it would be annoying to have to remember to set all of them.

Imagine that you reset a counter with the following snippet:

```
this.setState({ counter: 0 });
```

If you had a number of other state values in this same component, imagine that this would reset or even delete all these other state values because you didn't include them in the object that you passed to setState. That would be quite annoying. If that happened, you would have to do something like this every time to copy all the existing values into the new object:

```
this.setState(
  oldState => ({ ...oldState, counter: 0 })
);
```

Fortunately, you don't have to do that. React automatically does this for class-based components. When you pass a new object (or an update function that returns an object) to the setState method, React automatically merges this new object onto the existing state object. It will do exactly what is shown in the previous snippet, so you don't have to remember to do that every time.

5.4   Quiz

1 Which of the following would you store in component state?

   a Dynamic application data
   b Component properties
   c Constant values

2 Which of the following is the correct way to initialize a simple numeric state in a functional component?

   a `const { value, setter } = useState(0);`
   b `const [ value, setter ] = useState(0);`
   c `const { value, setter } = useState({ value: 0 });`
   d `const [ value, setter ] = useState({ value: 0 });`

3 You can only have a single useState hook in each functional component. *True or false?*

4 When updating a component state value through a useState setter function, the component will always re-render. *True or False?*

5 Which of the following would you use to read a single numerical value from state in a class-based component?

   a `<p>Value: {this.state}.</p>`
   b `<p>Value: {this.counter}.</p>`
   c `<p>Value: {this.state.counter}.</p>`

Quiz answers

1 You should definitely store dynamic application data in state but never properties (you already have them in the properties object), and neither should you store unchanging values in state.

2 `const [ value, setter ] = useState(0);`. You provide the initial value to use-State as a simple value and destruct the returned value as an array, not an object.

3 *False.* You can have as many `useState` hooks in each component as you desire.

4 *False.* The component will only render if the new value passed to the setter function is different from the existing value. The comparison is done using referential equality, so even if an object has updated internally, if it's still the same object, it won't cause a re-render.

5 `<p>Value: {this.state.counter}.</p>`. Remember that state in a class-based component is always an object, and your state values are properties of that object.

Summary

- Component state is used to make your application interactive. You'll get just about nowhere in your application development if you don't have stateful components.
- You can have state in both class-based components and functional components.
- State in functional components is initialized as separate distinct calls to use-State that have a separate setter per state value.
- You can initialize the value of a `useState` hook by providing a static value, a dynamic value, or even a function that returns the initial value.
- You can update the value of a `useState` hook at any time, but only in a callback or other hook, and never directly in the component definition.
- When updating the value of a `useState` hook, you can either provide a new value directly or provide a function that returns a new value based on the old value.
- State in class-based components is initialized as a single object and updated using the `setState` method.
- Conversion from a stateful class-based component to a stateful functional component might require a bigger refactor as the two approaches are significantly different.

Effects and the React component life cycle

6

This chapter covers

- Running effects inside components
- A complete guide to the React component life cycle
- Mounting, unmounting, and rendering components
- Introducing life cycle methods for class-based components

React components use JavaScript XML (JSX) to send information to the user in the form of HTML. But components need to do a lot more than that to be useful in an application. In React, everything that happens, happens in some component, so if your application wants to set a cookie, load some data, handle form input, display the user's camera, start or stop a timer, or a myriad of other dynamic capabilities, you need more than just JSX.

If you want your component to load some data from a server, you want the effect to run as soon as the component loads, but then you don't need the effect to run again even if your component re-renders. On the other hand, if you want to set a cookie with the last username entered into the login field, you want that effect to run every time the user types in the input field. If you want to display a timer inside your component, you want the timer to start ticking as your component loads, but you also want the timer to stop ticking as your component later unloads, to avoid unnecessarily clogging up resources.

What you need are effects. *Effects* are functions that run inside a component under certain circumstances. To run an effect, you have to specify under which circumstances the effect should run. To fully understand this, we have to dive into the topic of the React component life cycle.

We'll properly define some terminology that we've already used previously, but not properly explained, such as mounting, unmounting, and re-rendering. The latter is especially important. When and why do components re-render, and how can you hook into this process to either control it or react to it?

We'll finally give a brief introduction to how life cycle methods work in class-based components and what they compare to in functional components. The difference between the two component types becomes even more pronounced than what we've seen previously. The life cycle methods of a class-based component are extraordinarily complex and hard to understand compared with the simplicity of an effect in a functional component. With all that to cover, let's get started!

> **NOTE** The source code for the examples in this chapter is available at https://rq2e.com/ch06. But as you learned in chapter 2, you can instantiate all the examples directly from the command line using a single command.

6.1 Running effects in components

Let's say you have a timer component, and you want it to display the number of seconds it has been mounted. The first thing that comes to mind is to create an interval with `setInterval` inside the function body, which increments a counter state value every second. But when you change the state value, the whole component re-renders, which would start another interval rendering your component twice every second, which would start another two intervals rendering it four times every second, and so on. That's clearly not the way to do it.

Another idea is to use a timeout with `setTimeout`. In this situation, 1 second after the component renders, we increment the counter state value, which in turn causes a re-render, starting a new timeout. This seems like a reasonable approach. But what if your component re-renders for other reasons? A component can re-render because a property changes or because it has multiple state values that can change independently of the counter. If your component unmounts because it isn't needed anymore, the timeout continues to run and, after a second, will try to update a component that no longer exists. That's unfortunately also not a good way to do it.

To solve this problem, React introduced an *effect hook*, called `useEffect` (notice the important `use*` prefix used on all hooks). An effect in a `useEffect` hook is triggered when any value in a set of dependencies changes. Furthermore, when an effect in use-Effect runs, it can define a cleanup function that should run in one of two cases: before the effect is triggered again or if the component unmounts. Figure 6.1 shows this flow.

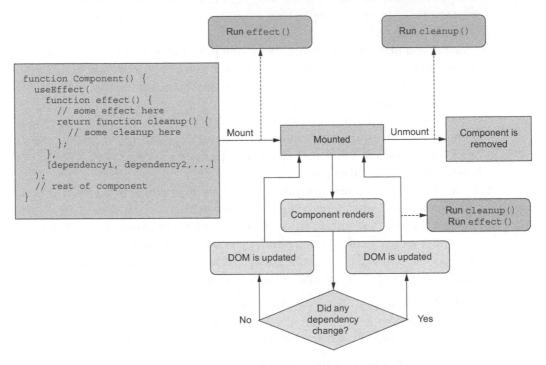

Figure 6.1   The useEffect hook here is displayed both as a code snippet and a flowchart. The hook contains an optional effect as well as an optional cleanup function. The effect runs on mount, and the cleanup runs on unmount—if they're defined, of course. Furthermore, if the effect has a dependency array, the cleanup and effect will also run every time any value reference in the dependency array changes.

This diagram is pretty complex, so we'll take you through it one step at a time by introducing functions that do just a few things at a time. The trick to this diagram is that you can set up your useEffect call so that you can define just the effect, just the cleanup function, or both, when it suits your needs. Furthermore, by carefully crafting the dependency array with the right values, you can trigger your effect and cleanup to run at exactly the desired instances.

There are five likely scenarios that you want your effect and cleanup function to run under. We'll go through all five scenarios with examples of each:

- You're loading some external data in a component. To correctly do that in an effect, you need it to run as your component mounts.
- You're creating a timer using an interval. To achieve this, you need to run such an effect as your component mounts, but also clean it up again as your component later unmounts.

- You want to track when a dialog is closed regardless of how it's closed. To do this properly, you need to run such an effect only as your component unmounts.
- You want to update the browser window (or tab) title with the title of the page currently displayed. To achieve this in an effect, you need it to run every time the title property changes, but not when any other property changes, as long as the title remains the same.
- You want to run a timer but only if the timer is active as denoted by an `isActive` flag. To achieve this, you need to run such an effect and its cleanup every time the `isActive` flag changes, but not if other properties or values change, as long as the `isActive` flag remains the same.

6.1.1   Running an effect on mount

Let's say we want to create a drop-down component that loads data from an external server to be displayed in the drop-down. We need to load this data as an effect that runs on mount, and then it shouldn't ever run again (because we already have the data). In this scenario, only the part of the diagram highlighted in figure 6.2 is relevant.

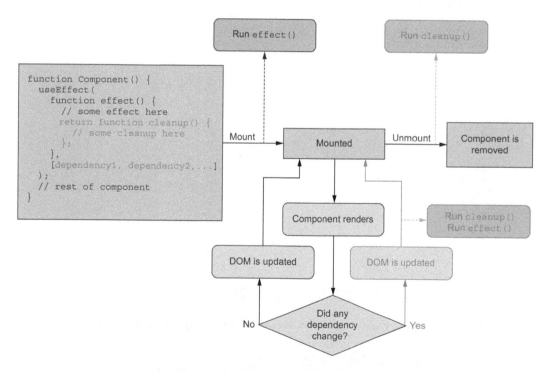

Figure 6.2   The execution of an effect hook when the effect is only desired as the component mounts. Note how the dependency array is kept empty, and there's no cleanup function. This means that the effect is only ever executed on mount and never as the component re-renders.

You can see the code in listing 6.1 and the result in figure 6.3.

Listing 6.1   Drop-down loading options from remote

```
import { useState, useEffect } from "react";
function RemoteDropdown() {
  const [options, setOptions] = useState([]);
  useEffect(() => {
    fetch("//www.swapi.tech/api/people")
      .then((res) => res.json())
      .then((data) => data.results)
      .then((characters) => characters.map(({ name }) => name))
      .then((names) => setOptions(names));
  }, []);
  return (
    <select>
      {options.map((option) => (
        <option key={option}>{option}</option>
      ))}
    </select>
  );
}
function App() {
  return <RemoteDropdown />;
}
export default App;
```

We need a state to have a place to hold the values once the options have been fetched.

In our effect hook, we load this URL (which is a list of characters in Star Wars).

As the result is parsed, we set our state value with an array of character names.

Finally, we make sure to pass an empty dependency array, so this effect only runs on mount and never again.

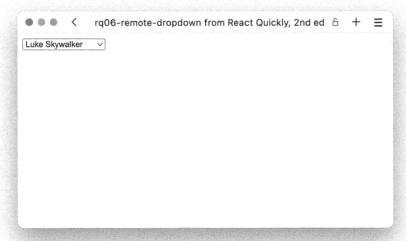

Figure 6.3   Our Star Wars character drop-down in action. May the source be with you!

Repository: rq06-remote-dropdown

This example can be seen in repository `rq06-remote-dropdown`. You can use that repository by creating a new app based on the associated template:

```
$ npx create-react-app rq06-remote-dropdown --template rq06-remote-dropdown
```

Alternatively, you can go to this website to browse the code, see the application in action directly in your browser, or download the source code as a zip file:

https://rq2e.com/rq06-remote-dropdown

This is a pretty classic setup that you'll often see in web apps loading data that is relevant only inside a small part of the overall application. It does have a small problem though. What happens if, for some reason, the component unmounts before the response comes back from the server—maybe because the internet connection is flaky or the server is experiencing a lot of load? We'll have to deal with that in a cleanup function. Cue next section.

6.1.2 Running an effect on mount and cleanup on unmount

We've been tasked with creating a stopwatch component. It should start an interval as soon as the component mounts that just keeps incrementing as time passes; however, if the component is ever unmounted in the future (e.g., because the user closes it), we must make sure to stop the interval. This requires an effect that runs on mount but also runs a cleanup function on unmount. In this scenario, only the part of the diagram highlighted in figure 6.4 is relevant.

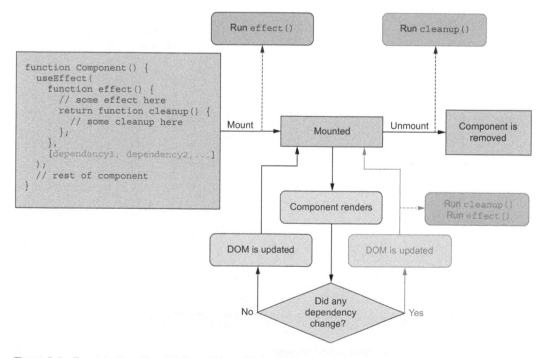

Figure 6.4 To make the effect hook activate with an effect and cleanup only on mount and unmount, respectively, you must add an empty dependency array to make sure that the effect and cleanup never runs just because the component is re-rendering.

You can see the code for such a component in the following listing. Figure 6.5 shows the component in action.

Listing 6.2   Stopwatch

In our effect function, we start an interval, to be run every second, that increments the counter.

```
import { useState, useEffect } from "react";
function Stopwatch() {
  const [seconds, setSeconds] = useState(0);
  useEffect(() => {
    const interval = setInterval(
      () => setSeconds((seconds) => seconds + 1),
      1000
    );
    return () => clearInterval(interval);
  }, []);
  return <h1>Seconds: {seconds}</h1>;
}
function App() {
  const [showWatch, setShowWatch] = useState(false);
  return (
    <>
      <button onClick={() => setShowWatch((b) => !b)}>Toggle watch</button>
      {showWatch && <Stopwatch />}
    </>
  );
}
export default App;
```

Using the browser built-in function setInterval, we can have our increment function invoked at a steady rate.

Cancels the ongoing interval in the cleanup function using the built-in function clearInterval

Conditionally renders the stopwatch to see the cleanup function do its job

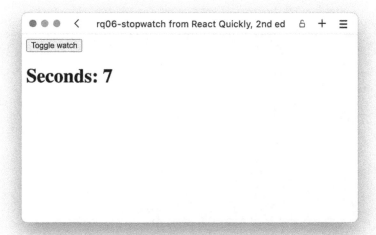

Figure 6.5   Our stopwatch is ticking away.

Even though we're using the variable `setSeconds` inside the effect, we don't list it as a dependency because it's a stable variable that doesn't change. The state update function as returned by the `useState` hook is always the same function by reference. You can include it in the array, and the hook works the same, so if you find this part a bit too complex to remember, just include the function in the array.

EVENTS

Another common example of using an effect only for mount and unmount is listening for events. For example, you might want your component to update itself when the whole web page resizes (listening to the resize event) or when a certain element scrolls (listening to the scroll event). We'll see a number of examples of this happening in chapter 8, which is dedicated to events.

CANCELING ACTION IF UNMOUNTED

The third type of use case for mount and unmount is an extension of the example in the previous section. Our `RemoteDropdown` loads data when mounted, but what would happen if the data transfer was slow, and the user somehow navigated away from the part of the application with the drop-down before the response came in? We would be trying to update state on a component that no longer existed!

This can be mitigated in one of two ways: you can either cancel the request in a cleanup function (in JavaScript, via `AbortController`), or you can have a local flag that remembers whether the component is still mounted and only updates the component state if the flag is true. If not, the component just ignores the returned response.

Canceling the request using an `AbortController` on unmount looks something like this:

```
useEffect(() => {
  const controller = new AbortController();     ◁──── Creates an abort controller
  fetch(url, { controller })                          inside the effect
    .then(data => {              ◁──── Makes sure to pass the
      // handle the data               abort controller to the
    });                                fetch function
```

```
  return () => {
    controller.abort();
  };
}, []);
```

In the cleanup function, we ask the abort controller to do its job. If the request already went through, nothing happens if we try to abort anyway.

The former option of aborting is the better option, as we can just cancel the request; however, that might not always be possible. If we can't cancel the request for some reason, we can keep track of whether the component is still mounted as follows:

```
useEffect(() => {
  let mounted = true;
  fetch(url)
    .then(data => {
      if (!mounted) {
        return;
      }
      // handle the data
    });
  return () => {
    mounted = false;
  };
}, []);
```

Keeps a local variable in our effect function that is initially set to true and reflects the fact that, as far as we know, the component is currently mounted

Once the data comes in, we'll first check whether the component is still mounted. If not, just abort now.

Flips the Boolean flag in a cleanup function, which will only be invoked if our component unmounts

This setup works for any type of delayed callback running in an effect hook. It could be a promise that resolves, a timeout that executes, or anything like that. You set a local variable inside the effect to false when the component unmounts and then make sure to just abort the callback when triggered.

6.1.3 Running cleanup on unmount

Imagine we're working on a large application with a dialog component that is displayed when some kind of alert has to be presented to the user. This dialog can be closed in a number of ways, including clicking the little x in the corner, pressing escape on the keyboard, clicking the OK button at the bottom, and so on. We're tasked with adding an analytics call as the dialog closes. We could manually add this little piece of code to all the different ways the dialog can be closed, but we know we can run an effect as a component unmounts instead. In this scenario, only the part of the diagram highlighted in figure 6.6 is relevant.

We can do this in our dialog as follows:

```
function Dialog() {
  useEffect(
    () => () => trackEvent('dialog_dismissed'),
    [],
  );
  // rest of component goes here
};
```

Double arrow notation is required, as we want our effect function to return a function when executed.

Note that this is only a partial example, as it assumes our dialog is part of a larger application with a lot more functionality.

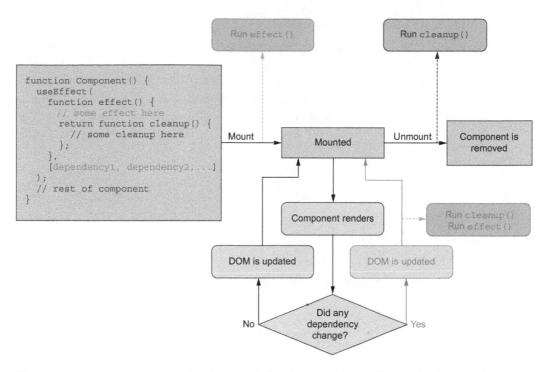

Figure 6.6 If only the cleanup function is relevant, there's no need to specify any effect code, only return a function from the effect function. With an empty dependency array once again, this code will never run just because the component re-renders.

Another example, which coincidentally also involves a dialog, is focus management. When you use a keyboard to tab your way to a button and press Enter to open a dialog, if you then later dismiss the dialog, you want the keyboard focus returned to that *same button*, so you can keep tabbing from there to other buttons in the user interface. When the dialog opens, we want the keyboard focus to move inside the dialog, but once unmounted, we must make sure to reset the keyboard focus to whatever element had focus before the dialog was opened. This could be done in a useEffect hook with only a cleanup function.

You might note that both of the preceding examples are a bit far-fetched or at least very specific to some narrow use cases. That's because this flow of only using a use-Effect hook for its cleanup function on unmount is a bit unusual and doesn't happen that often in components in the real world.

A much more common use case for the cleanup function is to do exactly what it's named for: clean up after a useEffect that leaves some sort of functionality in place after it unmounts, in order to not misuse resources or have memory leaks in our application. You saw an example of that in the previous subsection, and you'll see a lot more examples in the future.

6.1.4   *Running an effect on some renders*

Wouldn't it be wonderful if the title of the tab in the browser updates as the user navigates around on our blog? We created the whole blog website in React, and it has a component that can dynamically display any blog post. We now want to change the document title in an effect that runs every time the blog title changes, but it doesn't need to run if any other property changes. In this scenario, only the part of the diagram highlighted in figure 6.7 is relevant. You can see this component in listing 6.3.

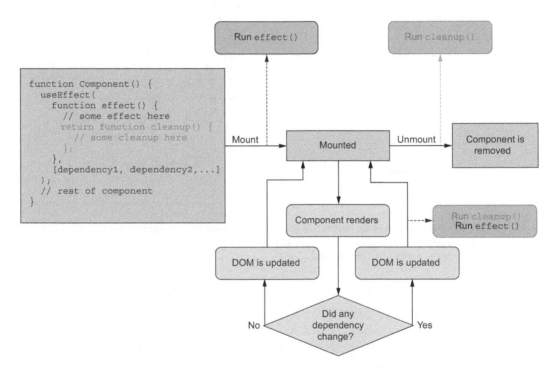

Figure 6.7   This time, we'll utilize the dependency array. We want our effect to run on mount, but also every time a certain property changes. However, we don't want it to run just because other properties change, so we're careful about including only the relevant variables in the dependency array.

Listing 6.3   Side effect executed in hook

```
import { useEffect } from "react";
function BlogPost({ title, body }) {
  useEffect(() => {
    document.title = title;
  }, [title]);
  return (
    <article>
      <h1>{title}</h1>
      {body}
```

Our effect inside useEffect sets the document title to the value of the title property.

Putting only the title in the dependency array ensures that the document title is updated only when the post title is.

```
    </article>
  );
}
function App() {
  return (
    <main>
      <BlogPost title="First post" body={
        <p>Welcome to my cool website.</p>
      } />
    </main>
  );
}

export default App;
```

> ### Repository: rq06-blog-title
> This example can be seen in repository `rq06-blog-title`. You can use that reposi-tory by creating a new app based on the associated template:
>
> ```
> $ npx create-react-app rq06-blog-title --template rq06-blog-title
> ```
>
> Alternatively, you can go to this website to browse the code, see the application in action directly in your browser, or download the source code as a zip file:
>
> https://rq2e.com/rq06-blog-title

This is probably the perfect textbook example of what `useEffect` is meant for, that is, to execute side effects of a component. You can't update the document title through the DOM, so it has to be a side effect; for that, `useEffect` is the perfect solution.

UPDATING FROM A PROPERTY

Another common use case is to update a state value based on a property. You might remember from the previous chapter that if we initialize a state in `useState` to the value of a property, it is only set to that property when the component renders the first time around on mount. If the component later re-renders with a new property value, the state won't automatically update to that value.

We can fix that using an effect that depends on the value of the property and updates the state value based on it. Let's build a very simple email input component where the user can input their email address. However, we'll allow the email address to be prefilled from the "outside" from a parent component using a property.

Listing 6.4 State updated from property

```
import { useEffect, useState } from "react";     We create a new state value,
function EmailInput({ value }) {                  but we don't initialize it to
  const [email, setEmail] = useState("");    ◁── anything.
```

```
    useEffect(() => setEmail(value), [value]);
    return (
      <label>
        Email address:
        <input
          type="email"
          value={email}
          onChange={(evt) => setEmail(evt.target.value)}
        />
      </label>
    );
  }
  const EMAIL1 = "daffyduck@looneytunes.invalid";
  const EMAIL2 = "bugsbunny@looneytunes.invalid";
  const EMAIL3 = "elmerfudd@looneytunes.invalid";
  function App() {
    const [defaultEmail, setDefaultEmail] = useState(EMAIL1);
    return (
      <main>
        <button onClick={() => setDefaultEmail(EMAIL1)}>Use {EMAIL1}</button>
        <br />
        <button onClick={() => setDefaultEmail(EMAIL2)}>Use {EMAIL2}</button>
        <br />
        <button onClick={() => setDefaultEmail(EMAIL3)}>Use {EMAIL3}</button>
        <br />
        <EmailInput value={defaultEmail} />
      </main>
    );
  }
  export default App;
```

That's because on every render where the property value changes, we'll (re)set the email state value to the property. We remember to add a dependency array, which is only the value property.

Finally, we update the state value every time the input changes.

We update the email input field in a new way in this component (discussed further in chapter 8).

The use case here can be a little hard to understand, but it's a pretty common pattern in controlled input components.

6.1.5   *Running an effect and cleanup on some renders*

This time, rather than a stopwatch that counts up, we're going to create a countdown component that—you guessed it—counts down. This countdown can now be paused and resumed. To do that, we still need to run an interval in an effect, but we need to stop and start this interval every time the countdown is paused and resumed, respectively. To do this, we need to create an effect (with a cleanup function) that has a dependency. In this scenario, everything in the diagram shown in figure 6.8 is relevant.

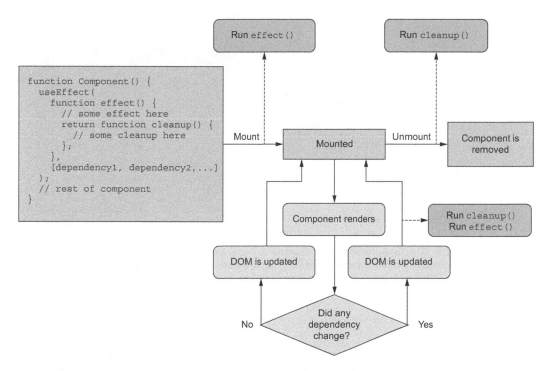

Figure 6.8   Everything in the effect hook is relevant when effect and cleanup on some renders are the goals.

A countdown component is an example of a component in which we want to run cleanup on unmount. This component is different from the stopwatch component from earlier in that you can pause, start, and stop the clock whenever you like without unmounting and remounting the component (the only way to stop the stopwatch component from earlier).

The countdown component will be initialized with the starting time of the counter, which is 10 in this example. It also has a Reset button that will reset the counter to the initial value at any point. Furthermore, there's a Pause/Resume button that will toggle whether the counter is running or not. Finally, there's the actual countdown decreasing every second, pausing the counter once it reaches 0. To make sure we can't start the counter again at 0, the Pause/Resume button is disabled if the countdown is over.

This sounds complicated, but take a look at the state flowchart for this component in figure 6.9.

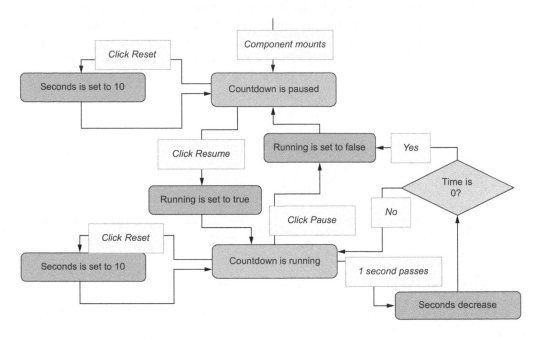

Figure 6.9 **The flow of state in the countdown component as time passes and the user interacts with the component. Notice in particular how clicking Reset doesn't stop or start the countdown, but just leaves it either running or not. In addition, note how the time stops when time runs out.**

You can see this implemented in the next listing. The result is shown in figure 6.10.

Listing 6.5 An interactive countdown

```
import { useEffect, useState } from "react";
function Countdown({ from }) {
  const [seconds, setSeconds] = useState(from);
  const [isRunning, setRunning] = useState(false);
  useEffect(() => {
    if (!isRunning) {
      return;
    }
    const interval = setInterval(
      () =>
        setSeconds((value) => {
          if (value <= 1) {
            setRunning(false);
          }
```

Initializes the seconds to the value of the initial property

Initializes the isRunning flag to false

The first thing we check in the effect is whether the countdown is running at all. If not, we just abort silently (and return nothing—nothing to clean up).

If the countdown is running, we define an interval that updates the state value every second.

When we update the state value, we check if the value was 1 (or less); if so, we make sure to stop the countdown.

```
        return value - 1;
      }),
    1000
  );
  return () => clearInterval(interval);
}, [isRunning]);
return (
  <section>
    <h2>Time left: {seconds} seconds</h2>
    <button onClick={() => setSeconds(from)}>
      Reset
    </button>
    <button
      onClick={() => setRunning((v) => !v)}
      disabled={seconds === 0}
    >
      {isRunning ? "Pause" : "Resume"}
    </button>
  </section>
);
}
function App() {
  return <Countdown from={10} />;
}
export default App;
```

Returns one less than the current value of the counter

Ensures our effect returns a cleanup function that cancels the interval completely

In our component JSX, we have a button that resets the counter and only that (it doesn't change the value of the run flag).

Another button flips the value of the run flag but doesn't change the counter. This button is disabled, however, if the counter is at zero.

We vary the text on the toggle button depending on the current state of the run flag.

We make our effect depend on the value of the isRunning state value. Whenever this value changes, our effect runs (and the cleanup of the last effect runs just before it).

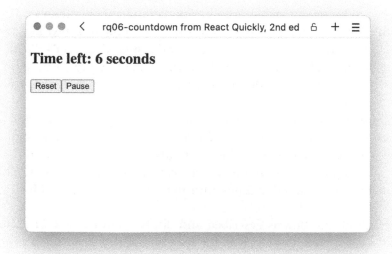

Figure 6.10   The countdown component while running

There's quite a lot happening in this component, and we use the three hooks in a clever combination to achieve the desired goals. One thing you might notice is that when our counter reaches zero, we don't directly stop the interval. In listing 6.5, we toggle the running flag to `false` with `setRunning(false);`. Doing so will force our component to re-render, causing the effect to rerun because `isRunning` is listed as a dependency for the effect. As the effect reruns, the cleanup function will stop the interval. So, setting the `isRunning` flag to `false` will indirectly stop the interval, but only through the magic of the hook.

This is a pretty advanced component, so it's okay if you don't understand it at first. We strongly recommend that you download the code for the preceding app and play around with it. Try changing parts of the code to see what makes it tick and how it works the way it does.

6.1.6 *Running an effect synchronously*

Now we're going to talk about an even more hypothetical situation than we normally do. Imagine that we're creating a component that has a bunch of text in it, and we want to count how many letters there are in total and display that number. The text is all static, so we could go ahead and count them all by hand before creating the component, but we want to make sure the component automatically updates the count if we change the text later.

One way to create this is to add a state value to the component that will contain the letter count and initialize this to zero. Then, we add an effect to the component that runs after the component has rendered, counts all the letters, and updates the state. When the component re-renders, it will display the correct count. This will combine the data flows of an effect hook with that of a state hook, as illustrated in figure 6.11.

The problem with the flow as described and displayed in figure 6.11 is that the browser updates the UI and displays it to the user before the effect hook runs. This means that the user will see the component render a 0 briefly before the component re-renders and displays the correct number of letters.

What if we instead could run an effect *after* React generates the required HTML but *before* the browser updates the UI and displays it to the user? Well, surprise, surprise,

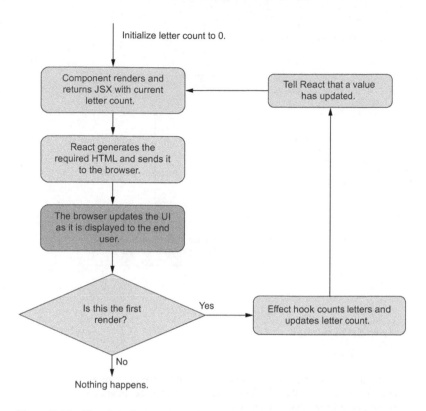

Figure 6.11   The state flow as we update state and run an effect. The problem here is the darker box. As we update the UI, the user will see the initial 0 displayed before the component quickly re-renders and displays the correct number of letters.

we can do exactly that. We can run a *layout effect hook* instead, which does two things differently than the regular effect hook. First, it runs before the browser updates the UI, but—just as important—it also runs instantly as the DOM is generated. If React detects a state update from a layout effect, it will immediately re-render the component with the updated state. We can see that in figure 6.12. By replacing useEffect with useLayoutEffect in this special instance, we can avoid a brief flash of the wrong content.

Do note that useEffect is the correct hook to use in almost all use cases, and use-LayoutEffect is only relevant in a few specialized instances. Always try useEffect first, and only if that doesn't work for your purpose, see if useLayoutEffect might be the right choice instead.

TECHNICAL DETAILS OF A LAYOUT EFFECT

The useLayoutEffect hook is a variant of useEffect. It's identical to useEffect in every way except *when* it's called. Similar to useEffect, the useLayoutEffect hook also takes a function and a dependency array as arguments. When any dependency changes, the cleanup function (if any) of the previous effect is run, and then the

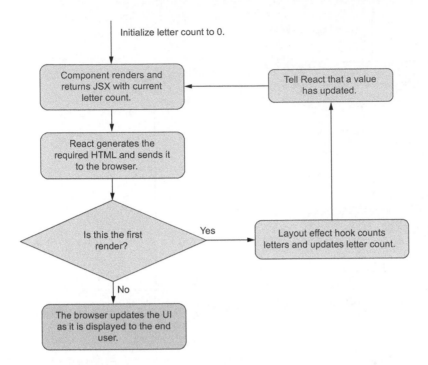

Figure 6.12   Now that we're using a layout effect, it will run before the browser UI is updated, and the new state will render immediately as the effect updates it, which makes the UI correct the first time around.

effect is run for this instance while capturing any potential returned cleanup function resulting from the effect.

The difference between useEffect and useLayoutEffect is a bit technical but boils down to timing. useLayoutEffect is called *synchronously* in the same execution cycle as when the components are rendered into the DOM (but before the browser has had a chance to *paint* the DOM to the browser window). On the other hand, useEffect is invoked *asynchronously* on the next execution cycle where the DOM has been painted to the window and all CSS has taken effect and been calculated. The timing of the two events is shown in figure 6.13.

As you can see in figure 6.13, we hid some details from the previous diagrams of useEffect execution. Note that here we have a useEffect and a useLayoutEffect with the same dependencies. These dependencies can vary, which would make the flow run differently for different renders, as some would only run layout effects and cleanups, others would run regular effects and cleanups, and still others might run both.

One consequence of a layout effect running synchronously after the render is that if the effect is complex, the screen doesn't update until the effect is complete. The UI is basically blocked while the layout effect runs. For this reason, extra caution should be used when writing layout effects to make sure they take up as few CPU cycles as possible.

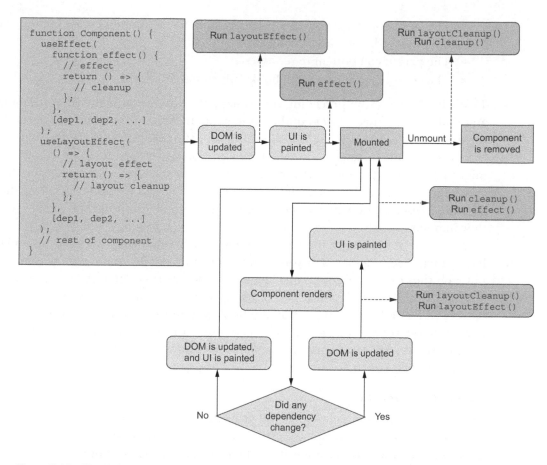

Figure 6.13   The timing of `useLayoutEffect` versus `useEffect`. Note how the layout effect is run just after the DOM is updated, but before the browser has had a chance to lay out the elements using CSS. (Sorry for the crowded diagram!)

If you don't fully understand the difference between regular effects and layout effects, you shouldn't worry too much about it. In 99% of cases, you ought to use the use-Effect hook. Only in very rare instances, where you need to update the DOM in an effect before it's painted to the window but after the component has rendered, do you need to use the `useLayoutEffect` hook.

6.2   *Understanding rendering*

In the previous section, we talked about components re-rendering many times. In this section, we'll go into some more technical details about what it means for a component to (re-)render. Note that this isn't directly useful in practice, but it's very important background information to understand what is going on in your application.

A functional component will render for one of three reasons:

- The component has just been *mounted* (as in, the component wasn't in the component tree before, and it is now).
- The parent component re-rendered.
- The component uses stateful hooks, which have updated.

That's it. If *none* of the preceding things happen, your component *won't* re-render, and that's a guarantee. If *either* of the three happens, your component *will* re-render, for sure. However, React might batch rendering after several of these happen, so if both a state value changes and the parent component re-renders, the component might only re-render once, or it might re-render twice. That is controlled by React and depends on subtle timing details. We'll give detailed examples of all of these scenarios, discuss how you can see these things happen, and what you can do when they happen.

Note that we're talking about your component re-rendering *as a whole.* You might have functions or callbacks in your component that render some part of your output, and they can re-render for any of a myriad of reasons depending on your usage. This is particularly the case if you're using so-called *render props*, which are often used in older codebases and in the non-hook variant of the React Context API. You might still see render props in modern and more complex codebases, as they can be used to render partial content in a generic component. We'll discuss this topic at the end of this section.

6.2.1   *Rendering on mount*

Imagine that we have a component that loads some external data. We can use the example of our remote drop-down from earlier. When it mounts, it loads data from a remote server and stores it locally in the component. When it unmounts, the data is forgotten.

The render of a component that happens on mount is the most trivial and obvious. Note that if a component is included *conditionally* in a parent component, it will mount and unmount depending on *that condition*. This isn't always what you want.

If we conditionally render the previously mentioned `RemoteDropdown` component in a parent component, thus toggling it on and off many times, we'll many times load the external data and throw it away, wasting time and bandwidth on the same request. While network caching will help somewhat, we can mitigate this in two ways. We can either move the data storage and data fetching up to a higher-level component, which is always included in the application, or we can conditionally render the component differently. You'll see this sometimes in everyday components. Normally we conditionally render a component like this:

```
return (
  <main>
    {hasDropdown && (<RemoteDropdown />)}
  </main>
);
```

> If the Boolean is true, we mount the component. If it is later set to false, the component is unmounted.

We can instead do it like this:

```
return (
  <main>
    <RemoteDropdown isVisible={hasDropdown} />
  </main>
);
```

> We always mount the component and simply toggle a flag as a property.

We would need to modify the component to use this flag as an indicator about whether to render anything at all:

```
function RemoteDropdown({ isVisible }) {
  const [options, setOptions] = useState([]);
  useEffect(() => {
    // Loading happens here
  }, []);
  if (!isVisible) {
    return null;
  }
  // Rest of component goes here
);
```

> We first include all the hooks that we need in the component.

> Only after all hooks have been evaluated can we check if we need to render anything at all.

While this approach to conditional rendering is generally not recommended (and the former approach is), this can be a handy tool when you don't want your component to mount and unmount again and again, but you want to keep it in the document all the time while only sometimes actually rendering anything.

6.2.2 *Rendering on parent render*

This might come partially as a surprise, but every child component also renders when their parent component renders. Let's create this simple example of an icon inside a push button:

> The icon component is extremely simple: it never changes nor updates based on anything.

> The button component has internal state and renders every time the state changes.

```
function Icon() {
  return <img src="/arrow.png" alt="" />
);
function Button() {
  const [enabled, setEnabled] = useState(false);
  const style = { border: `1px solid ${enabled ? "red" : "black"}`;
  return (
    <button style={style} onClick={() => setEnabled(b => !b)}>
      <Icon /> Toggle
    </button>
  );
}
```

If we test this out in the browser, what do you think will happen? Every time we click the button, the enabled flag flips, and the button renders again. But what about the icon? Will it render again (as in, will the function named Icon be executed again)? Yes, it will. React doesn't assume that components are "pure," and they might not be. For that reason, React will render the component every time that the parent renders. If the component takes properties, React will render the component every time, regardless of whether these properties change or not.

Let's imagine a different scenario, where we're actively utilizing this behavior. We can create a dice roller, where we can roll three dice. You can see the code in listing 6.6 and the output in figure 6.14.

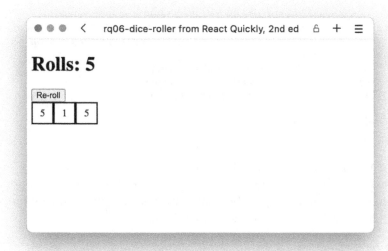

Figure 6.14   Our dice roller after five rolls

Listing 6.6   A dice roller

```
import { useState } from "react";
function Die() {
  const style = {
    border: "2px solid black",
    display: "inline-block",
    width: "2em",
    height: "2em",
    textAlign: "center",
    lineHeight: 2,
  };
  const value = Math.floor(6 * Math.random());
  return <span style={style}>{value}</span>;
}
function DiceRoller() {
  const [rolls, setRolls] = useState(1);
  return (
    <main>
      <h1>Rolls: {rolls}</h1>
      <button onClick={() => setRolls((r) => r + 1)}>
        Re-roll
      </button>
```

Even though our Die component appears to be pure, it actually has an external source of information (Math.random) and (potentially) returns something new on every render.

When we click the button, we increase the roll count, which forces a complete render of the component, causing all the child components to render and giving us new dice values in turn.

Our DiceRoller component is stateful.

```
      <div>
        <Die />        Three separate instances of the same
        <Die />        Die component—each with its own
        <Die />        internal random source of information
      </div>
    </main>
  );
}
function App() {
  return <DiceRoller />;
}
export default App;
```

> ### Repository: rq06-dice-roller
> This example can be seen in repository `rq06-dice-roller`. You can use that repository by creating a new app based on the associated template:
>
> ```
> $ npx create-react-app rq06-dice-roller --template rq06-dice-roller
> ```
>
> Alternatively, you can go to this website to browse the code, see the application in action directly in your browser, or download the source code as a zip file:
>
> https://rq2e.com/rq06-dice-roller

On a general level, you should always put such variable content (e.g., the value of a die roll) inside component state, and not depend on it just magically updating on every render as in the preceding example. Please don't do this at home. This makes the previous example a terrible React design pattern. For example, we can't display the sum of the dice in the parent component because it doesn't know the values of the child components.

A much better structure is for the parent component to generate three random numbers and pass them to the dice as properties. But for demonstration purposes, this does highlight how even seemingly pure components render when their parent component does.

6.2.3 Rendering on state update

When you update the state inside a stateful hook (see chapter 7 for more details about stateful hooks), your component using that hook will render. That's the whole purpose of updating the state, so this flow is pretty obvious and even desired.

But you can also render too often if your state contains data that updates often. You want to avoid components rendering all the time, as it can be very CPU and/or memory intensive for the browser, as well as annoying for the user.

A potential source of frequently updated information is something like the mouse position. A user can move the mouse around a lot—many times per second. If you have multiple components that store the mouse position in state, you'll have multiple components rendering many times per second, which will slow down your computer. Next, we'll look at two different instances with this setup and how you can minimize renders on state updates.

STORING HIGHER-LEVEL INFORMATION

Imagine a component that has a yellow background when the cursor is on the left side and a blue background when the cursor is on the right side. Let's say the component is 200 pixels wide, so if the cursor is more than 100 pixels from the left edge, the cursor is on the right; otherwise, it's on the left.

The first way to implement this is to save the cursor offset from the left side in a state value and, on each render, check which background color to display:

```
function BlinkingBackground() {
  const [left, setLeft] = useState(0);          ◁──  The state holds the
  const onMouseMove = (evt) =>                        mouse position.
    setLeft(evt.nativeEvent.offsetX);           │ Records the mouse position in the
  const style = {                               │ state when the mouse moves
    backgroundColor: left < 100 ? "blue" : "red",   ◁──  Determines which color
  };                                                       to use every time the
  return <div style={style} onMouseMove={onMouseMove} />;   component renders
}
```

This method wastes a ton of render cycles, though, because all the time you're moving the mouse around on only one side of the component, it will render again and again for every position. A much smarter approach is to just store in state whether the cursor is on the left or right side, and nothing else. That way, our component only renders when the cursor changes sides:

```
function BlinkingBackground() {
  const [isLeft, setLeft] = useState(true);     ◁──  The state holds only
  const onMouseMove = (evt) =>                        a Boolean flag.
    setLeft(evt.nativeEvent.offsetX < 100);     │ Records the mouse position in the
  const style = {                               │ state when the mouse moves
    backgroundColor: isLeft ? "blue" : "red"        ◁──  Determines which color
  };                                                       to use every time the
  return <div style={style} onMouseMove={onMouseMove} />;   component renders
}
```

In this example, we utilize the fact that React only renders a component on a state update if the state actually changed value. We call the setter function just as often as in the previous example, but because we only store a Boolean value, which only changes from true to false as the cursor moves over the center of the component, most calls to the setter are simply ignored, as they don't alter the component state. This new example results in a much cleaner data flow, and now our component only renders when something happens that affects the output.

MANIPULATING DOM ELEMENTS DIRECTLY

In this example, we want to have a component that moves an element in sync with the cursor at all times. It seems like we're doomed with this one. How can we update the style of an element in a component without storing it in component state?

For such a case, we might want to look at circumventing React and directly updating the DOM instead. To do this, we need a reference to the element in question (this requires another hook, `useRef`, discussed in chapter 7), and on mouse move, we'll update the style of the element directly:

```
function PhantomCursor() {
  const element = useRef();          ⟵  Creates a reference
  const onMouseMove = (evt) => {          that will point to our
    element.current.style.left =          DOM element
      `${evt.nativeEvent.offsetX}px`;
    element.current.style.top =        Directly updates the
      `${evt.nativeEvent.offsetY}px`;  DOM element through
  }                                     the reference whenever
  return (                              the mouse moves
    <div style={{ position: "relative" }} onMouseMove={onMouseMove}>
      <img
        style={{ position: "absolute" }}
        ref={element}              ⟵  Remember to put the ref
        src="/images/fake_cursor.png"     on the element that we
        alt=""                            want to manipulate.
      />
    </div>
  );
}
```

This component never re-renders. It renders as it's mounted, and then it just stays around. The mouse event will change the appearance of the component, but that is outside React's control. As seen from React's perspective, this is a static component that doesn't ever change.

The problem here is that if we need to use the mouse position for other things in our application—do some math, check collisions, and so on—we'll have to store it in state anyway. However, if at all possible, we want to avoid updating the state often.

6.2.4 Rendering inside functions

A component doesn't have to render directly inside another component; it can also render inside a function, for example. If that's the case, the component will render every time the function runs. Sometimes, such a function only runs when the parent component renders, so the result is the same; however, you might also have a function that can run at other times, causing the render to happen at different times.

Imagine a button component that allows the parent to specify an icon for the component. The button is a push button, so it has a state of either pressed or not pressed. Sometimes you want the icon to be different for those two states. You can make the component accept two different properties to use for the two states, or you can instead accept a function that will receive the state of the button as an argument and then return the proper icon.

> **Listing 6.7   A push button with an icon function**

```
import { useState } from "react";
function Icon({ type }) {
  return <img src={`/images/${type}.png`} width="16" alt="" />;
}
function Button({ label, getIcon }) {
  const [pressed, setPressed] = useState(false);
  return (
    <button onClick={() => setPressed((p) => !p)}>
      {getIcon(pressed)}
      {label}
    </button>
  );
}
function LockButton() {
  const getIcon = (pressed) =>
    pressed ? <Icon type="lock" /> : <Icon type="unlock" />;
  return <Button label="Lock" getIcon={getIcon} />;
}
function App() {
  return <LockButton />;
}
export default App;
```

A general icon component embeds an image loaded from the right folder.

Our button calls the getIcon function with its current state on every render.

Defines getIcon to return one of two icons

Repository: rq06-push-button

This example can be seen in repository rq06-push-button. You can use that repository by creating a new app based on the associated template:

```
$ npx create-react-app rq06-push-button --template rq06-push-button
```

Alternatively, you can go to this website to browse the code, see the application in action directly in your browser, or download the source code as a zip file:

https://rq2e.com/rq06-push-button

In this setup, we render the icon component inside a function and not directly inside our component. However, the function is only called inside the button component directly when it renders, so it's as if we include an icon conditionally directly in the render—we just do it through a function. This does change some of the things we know about components, however, and it can be a bit hard to optimize this bit of source code or even figure out exactly what's going on.

However, we can also achieve the same result in a much more familiar way. Take another look at that getIcon function. It's a function that returns JSX based on some arguments. Does that sound familiar? That's exactly what a functional component does. So, we can alter this slightly to instead make the `getIcon` function into a custom component.

Listing 6.8   A push button with an icon component

```
import { useState } from "react";
function Icon({ type }) {
  return <img src={`/images/${type}.png`} width="16" alt="" />;
}
function Button({ label, ButtonIcon }) {
  const [pressed, setPressed] = useState(false);
  return (
    <button onClick={() => setPressed((p) => !p)}>
      <ButtonIcon pressed={pressed} />
      {label}
    </button>
  );
}
function LockIcon({ pressed }) {
  return pressed ? <Icon type="lock" /> : <Icon type="unlock" />;
}
function LockButton() {
  return <Button label="Lock" ButtonIcon={LockIcon} />;
}
function App() {
  return <LockButton />;
}
export default App;
```

The button component now expects a (capitalized) ButtonIcon property rather than a getIcon function as before.

Because it's a component we expect, we can render it as such directly in the body.

Finally, we just supply LockIcon as a property, which is legal to do even though we haven't done it before.

getIcon is now not just a function, but a fully fledged functional component (by accepting properties rather than a simple argument).

> **Repository: rq06-push-button2**
>
> This example can be seen in repository rq06-push-button2. You can use that repository by creating a new app based on the associated template:
>
> ```
> $ npx create-react-app rq06-push-button2 --template rq06-push-button2
> ```
>
> Alternatively, you can go to this website to browse the code, see the application in action directly in your browser, or download the source code as a zip file:
>
> https://rq2e.com/rq06-push-button2

This works great—and looks so much cleaner! We can, of course, further optimize this (e.g., by moving the ternary conditional to the property that changes inside the Lock-Icon component), but that is beyond this example.

The concept of providing functions that render JSX is called *render props* and was a pretty common approach in older React codebases. However, with functional components, almost all such cases are better solved by converting the argument to a full component as we did here. It makes the whole flow of data much easier to understand and solves ~95% of the cases of a function (i.e., *not* a functional component) rendering JSX.

REACT CONTEXT

One of the remaining reasons for rendering JSX in functions is if you use the non-hook version of the React Context API with a `MyContext.Consumer` component. This component takes a function as a child component (a mind-blowing concept in itself). But that's quite a special case and not one that you're likely to encounter in a modern React codebase with functional components. If that does happen, you should check the online React documentation for how to use the React Context API. Even better, convert the component to a functional component and use the `useContext` hook if possible (see chapters 7 and 10 for more details on how to use this hook).

6.3 *The life cycle of a class-based component*

When a class-based component mounts, renders, and unmounts, rather than using hooks, you can use life cycle methods to react to the different stages in the component life cycle. The methods are named after what they do and where they fit into the life cycle, so they're fairly self-evident most of the time.

Some life cycle methods are executed in multiple events. Other life cycle methods allow you to interfere with React's regular scheduling of component updates if you have inside knowledge that React doesn't have. React used to have more life cycle methods, but they've been deprecated in newer versions of React because of their troublesome behavior.

You ought to be using functional components, but if you do come across a class-based component, and you want to refactor it to a functional one, there are some general tips for how to make this conversion. Note that this isn't an exact science, and rewriting or completely rethinking the feature might be required.

6.3.1 *Life cycle methods*

When a component mounts, these class methods are called (in this order):

1 `constructor()`
2 `static getDerivedStateFromProps()`
3 `render()`
4 `componentDidMount()`

When a class-based component updates (for any of the previously mentioned reasons), the following methods are invoked (in this order):

1 `static getDerivedStateFromProps()`
2 `shouldComponentUpdate()`
3 `render()`
4 `getSnapshotBeforeUpdate()`
5 `componentDidUpdate()`

Actually, that's not completely true. `shouldComponentUpdate()` is special here, in that if defined, you can halt the render loop if you return `false`. It seems like a great way to minimize renders, but it can be very tricky to do and, if used incorrectly, can lead to components that are out of sync with their actual DOM representation. When a component unmounts, the following method is invoked: `componentDidUnmount()`.

6.3.2 Legacy life cycle methods

A number of life cycle methods existed previously that you might still see in some legacy codebases, as these were quite popular to use, but came with a lot of problems, hence their deprecation. The methods have been renamed for now, but still exist in the React codebase—even in React 18. At some point, they will be removed and not work anymore, but they still work for now. Albeit, if you use them, you'll be aware of how fragile they are based on their current naming. The methods *were* called:

- `componentWillMount()`
- `componentWillUpdate()`
- `componentWillReceiveProps()`

All three have been renamed, and you now have to create the following class methods to be able to use the functionality:

- `UNSAFE_componentWillMount()`
- `UNSAFE_componentWillUpdate()`
- `UNSAFE_componentWillReceiveProps()`

Typing `UNSAFE` will get most developers to realize that they probably shouldn't be using this method or at least should have a plan for how to get rid of it fairly soon.

We won't cover their functionality, as they are strongly discouraged. If you find them in a codebase, check the online documentation for their functionality, so you're able to recreate the features without these methods.

6.3.3 Converting life cycle methods to hooks

Converting a class-based component can be tricky. We've already seen how to deal with some of the tasks involved, which got a bit complicated as we introduced stateful components. Now that we add life cycle methods, it gets even more daunting. The following lists these methods and describes how you can implement similar functionality using hooks:

- `constructor()`—This method can be implemented either using a `useEffect()` with no dependencies or, if used for precalculating expensive values, in `useMemo()` with no dependencies.
- `getDerivedStateFromProps()`—This can be implemented with a `useEffect()` hook with the relevant properties as dependencies.
- `render()`—The entire functional component is the render function.

- `componentDidMount()`—This method is mostly used for exactly what a `use-Effect()` hook with no dependencies achieves. It's often used together with `componentDidUnmount()`, which is then the equivalent cleanup function for the hook. Note that to be technically correct, `componentDidMount` runs *synchronously*, whereas `useEffect` runs *asynchronously*, so to achieve the same effect, you might have to use `useLayoutEffect`. Most of the time, however, `useEffect` will do just fine because the synchronous aspect is rarely a factor relevant for this life cycle method.

- `shouldComponentUpdate()`—This method has no hook equivalent, but it's also not necessary when using hooks. If you want to minimize the renders of a functional component, use the memoization hooks briefly introduced in the next chapter.

- `getSnapshotBeforeUpdate()`—This is a weird method that's seldom used. It's almost exclusively used for a single specific purpose, which is to record the scroll position of some part of a component *before* the component updates, so you can restore that position *after* the component updates with new data. This specific behavior can be emulated in a functional component by wrapping the state setter in a custom function that records the old scroll position in a reference before updating the component and causing a new render.

- `componentDidUpdate()`—This can be emulated with a `useEffect` hook with dependencies set to the relevant values that have changed and caused whatever changed behavior that you want to react to.

- `componentDidUnmount()`—Functionality in this method can be moved to a cleanup function in a `useEffect` (or `useLayoutEffect`) hook with no dependencies. This is often used to cancel subscriptions or intervals set on mount, so it goes together with the effect in the same hook.

6.4   Quiz

1   It's not possible to run side effects inside functional components, as only class-based components can do that. *True* or *false*?

2   When can you run an effect using an effect hook?

   a   As the component *mounts*
   b   As the component *unmounts*
   c   As the component *updates*
   d   All of the above

3   If you want to load data in a component as soon as it's displayed, but then not reload the data even if the component updates, your dependency array should

   a   Be skipped
   b   Be empty
   c   Contain only the URL of the data

4 When a parent component renders, the child components only re-render if their properties update. *True* or *false?*

5 What is the correct syntax for an effect hook that only runs as the component unmounts?

a `useEffect(() => runOnUnmount(), []);`

b `useEffect(() => () => runOnUnmount(), []);`

c `useEffect(() => runOnUnmount());`

d `useEffect(() => () => runOnUnmount());`

Quiz answers

1 *False.* Via the `useEffect` (and alternatively `useLayoutEffect`) hook, you can run side effects inside functional components too.

2 You can run an effect on any particular render of the component and even as it unmounts, so all of the scenarios are true.

3 If you want to run an effect only as a component mounts, you should supply an empty dependency array.

4 *False.* Any time a component renders, all the child components of that component will render too, regardless of whether their properties change or not.

5 `useEffect(() => () => runOnUnmount(), []);`. An unmount (also known as a cleanup) effect has to be returned by the effect function, so double function notation is required. In addition, the dependency array has to be empty, not skipped.

Summary

- A React component has an individual life cycle for each instance of the component.
- The `useEffect` hook is the primary way to trigger side effects that are relevant for the particular component as a component mounts, renders, and unmounts.
- By carefully crafting the dependency array, you can trigger an effect hook to run at exactly the times you need it to run, which is how you can make smart components that interact with the browser, network, and user in many different ways.
- Components render whenever React determines that they need to under three main circumstances: when the component mounts, when the state of the component updates, and when the parent component renders.
- Class-based components can't use hooks but rely on life cycle methods for similar behavior. These can be converted to hooks, but the conversion isn't always straightforward.

Hooks to fuel your web applications

7

This chapter covers
- A larger perspective on creating stateful components
- Introducing advanced topics solvable by hooks
- Rules to observe when using hooks in general

Hooks are what make modern React applications tick. They're a pretty small part of the overall React API, but very significant nonetheless. Hooks are also quite tricky to use. In this chapter, we'll discuss all the hooks, what they do, and some important things to know about using hooks in general.

Hooks are a special kind of creature in the React biosphere. From the outside, they seem completely unrelated in functionality, but when examined closer, they have some common traits and behaviors that we need to account for when using them. You could say that they stem from a common ancestor somewhere in the evolutionary tree, even though they have advanced to become very different beings.

We've dedicated this chapter to all the hooks for this very reason. So, while we're going to be covering some wildly different topics, all of them are concerned with using hooks. We'll tie a bow on it at the end by explaining how all of these hooks are, in fact, related, despite their seemingly divergent purposes.

You've seen three different hooks so far: useState (in chapter 5) and useEffect and useLayoutEffect (in chapter 6). At the time of writing, there are 15 built-in hooks in React (as of React 18), which we'll cover briefly, grouped by their functionality:

- *Stateful hooks*—These functions are concerned with making components and applications stateful on several different layers and levels of complexity: useState, useReducer, useRef, useContext, useDeferredValue, and useTransition.
- *Effect hooks*—These functions are concerned with running effects inside a component at different stages of the overall component life cycle as well as during each individual render cycle: useEffect and useLayoutEffect.
- *Memoization hooks*—These functions are used for performance optimization by avoiding recalculating values if their constituent parts haven't changed: useMemo, useCallback, useId.
- *Library hooks*—These advanced functions are almost exclusively used in larger component libraries that are created to be shared either with the community or internally in a larger organization. These functions are rarely used in smaller or medium-size applications: useDebugValue, useImperativeHandle, useInsertionEffect, and useSyncExternalStore.

These 15 hooks are the built-in "base" hooks that React comes with. You can build more hooks on top of them, but you can't build your own base hooks. You can only build hooks that utilize one or more of the existing hooks. We'll discuss custom hooks in chapter 10.

Note that React might be extended with more built-in hooks in future releases. React 18.0 came with five new hooks, and incremental releases after React 18 might come with even more.

> **NOTE** The source code for the examples in this chapter is available at https://rq2e.com/ch07. But as you learned in chapter 2, you can instantiate all the examples directly from the command line using a single command.

7.1 *Stateful components*

We've covered stateful components in general in chapter 5, but we'll gladly reiterate that information here for completeness. Stateful components and, in turn, stateful applications are essential for web applications to actually be interesting to use.

An application without state is completely static. The application will be identical for the entire time you have it open in the browser, and it will be identical for every user using the application. If you need login, sessions, interaction, and variability and changes over time, you need your application to be stateful.

However, stateful components aren't all the same, just like not all states are the same. One state is only kept briefly, another state is hyperlocal to an individual component, and yet another state is application-wide. In addition, state can be a single variable or a huge complex web of interdependent variables that have to update in unison. In this section, we'll cover some different use cases for stateful components and applications, and discuss how to solve the given challenge via the proper hooks.

7.1.1   Simple state values with useState

`useState` is the bread and butter of stateful applications. You'll probably find yourself using this hook the majority of times that you need state, so it's definitely an important one.

If you have a menu that can open and close, you keep its state in a local `useState` inside your menu component. This single simple value is only used inside this component, and it's unrelated to any other state values in the application.

We discussed all the ins and outs of `useState` in chapter 5, so we won't go into further detail on this hook here. However, in the rest of this section, we'll introduce some more complex scenarios where `useState` isn't enough or is suboptimal.

7.1.2   Creating complex state with useReducer

Imagine that we have a loader component, where we want to know whether loading succeeded or failed, what the error message is in case of failure, and what the data is in case of success. The value of the error message is only relevant if the loading fails. If loading succeeds, the error message is completely irrelevant and shouldn't even be set—and vice versa for the result data. This is an example of *interdependent* state. The individual values in the state depend on each other, and you'll often be updating multiple values at the same time.

`useReducer` is a stateful hook for exactly this purpose. It's an advanced version of `useState` where we can alter our state in a more complex and controlled way (almost like a state machine, but not really) if we have a setup that's more complex than a single state value can reasonably represent.

Using a reducer is a way to generate a new state ("reduce") solely based on the current state and some action that takes some payload. The concept of *reducing state* is known from other frameworks such as Redux (hence, the name), so it's already familiar to many React developers.

Note that `useReducer` is never strictly necessary—anything we can do with a reducer can also be done with a combination of simpler `useState`s. There are many cases where you would likely want to use a reducer rather than settle for multiple disparate states to ensure stricter data flow and better control.

We'll present some examples of a reducer in chapter 10 when we move to more complex application architecture. A reducer is only relevant for rather complex data flows, so it's not something we'll use a lot in the simple applications that we're building throughout this book.

7.1.3   Remembering a value without re-rendering with useRef

Imagine that we want to create a button that only works on double-clicking within a certain number of milliseconds. To create this, we need to remember how much time has passed between successive clicks. Remembering data inside a component is exactly what we have state for. We have a value that we want to persist between renders, but we don't use it for rendering. The button doesn't change when we click the first time. We just need to remember a value inside a component instance for some amount of time, but we won't use the value to determine the output of the component.

`useRef` is both one of the simplest hooks in React and also one of the least understood hooks. It's a hook with a *passive state*, which means the hook can contain state, but setting or updating the state doesn't cause a re-render.

`useRef` is used for a number of purposes, including remembering values between renders and serving as a reference to DOM elements used in the render. The latter is a very important use case (and the reason for the name, `useRef`), as it's the best and simplest way to address DOM elements through script in your components.

PASSIVE STATE VALUES

You can use the `useRef` hook to remember some value that is relevant between renders of the component but that doesn't directly affect the outcome of the component. That sounds a bit complex and even rare. When would you have such a value in a component? As an example, let's recreate our counter component once again, but this time with the added functionality that the increment button only works if double-clicked.

We need to store the time of the last click event somewhere in our component, and it needs to be in a place that persists between renders. We already know that we can store such a value in a state provided by the `useState` hook. A sketch of this scenario is shown in figure 7.1, and the implementation is shown in listing 7.1.

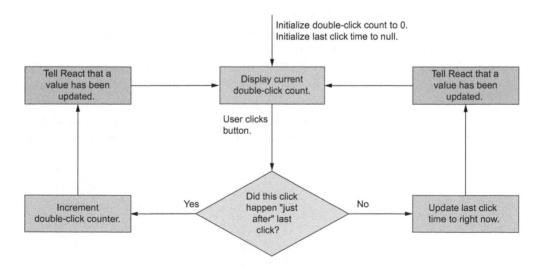

Figure 7.1 As the user clicks the button, the execution bifurcates based on whether this click happens within a very short time of the last recorded click.

Listing 7.1   A double-click counter with `useState`

```
import { useState } from "react";
const THRESHOLD = 300;
function DoubleClickCounter() {
  const [counter, setCounter] = useState(0);
  const [lastClickTime, setLastClickTime] =
    useState(null);
  const onClick = () => {
    const isDoubleClick =
      Date.now() - lastClickTime < THRESHOLD;
    if (isDoubleClick) {
      setCounter((value) => value + 1);
    } else {
      setLastClickTime(Date.now());
    }
  };
  return (
    <main>
      <p>Counter: {counter}</p>
      <button onClick={onClick}>Increment</button>
    </main>
  );
}
function App() {
  return <DoubleClickCounter />;
}
export default App;
```

Remembers the time of the last click in a state value

If the time since the last click is less than 300 ms, it's a double-click.

Increments the counter only if it's a double-click

Remembers the time of the current click if it's not a double-click

This isn't necessary, however, and will cause needless extra re-renders. When we call `setLastClickTime`, React will re-render the component because a state value changes. However, the JSX won't change in the component, and the same DOM output will be rendered to the screen. The code in listing 7.1 works, but it's less than optimal.

Because we only need the state value internally in the component and don't need the component to re-render just because the value is updated, we can instead use a reference via the `useRef` hook. To instantiate a `useRef` hook, you simply call the hook and store it in a variable. You can optionally pass an initial value to the hook as well. To read or update the current value of a `useRef` hook, you access the `.current` property on the hook return value. Compare the sketch of this scenario in figure 7.2 with the scenario in figure 7.1—we skip an entire cycle of rendering! This is implemented in listing 7.2.

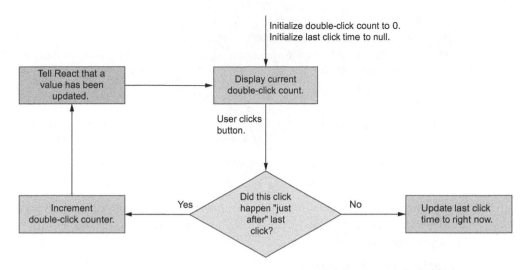

Figure 7.2 This time, if the user clicks the button the first time, the last click time is recorded, but it doesn't cause a re-render because it's not an active state value, but a passive one. This means that we can still access the value later (on this or future renders), but it doesn't cause a new render by itself.

Listing 7.2 A double-click counter with `useRef`

```
import { useState, useRef } from "react";
const THRESHOLD = 300;
function DoubleClickCounter() {
  const [counter, setCounter] = useState(0);
  const lastClickTime = useRef(null);                    Remembers the
  const onClick = () => {                                time of the last click
    const isDoubleClick =                                in a useRef value
      Date.now() - lastClickTime.current < THRESHOLD;    Performs the same
    if (isDoubleClick) {                                 check as before,
      setCounter((value) => value + 1);                  except now the value
    } else {                                             is accessed through
      lastClickTime.current = Date.now();                the .current property
    }
  };                                                     Updates the current
  return (                                               value of the state
    <main>                                               through the .current
      <p>Counter: {counter}</p>                          property
      <button onClick={onClick}>Increment</button>
    </main>
  );
}
function App() {
  return <DoubleClickCounter />;
}
export default App;
```

This is a much better version of our component, because we don't have needless re-renders. We persist the state properly in a way that works, even if the component does re-render for some other reason.

REFERENCES TO DOM ELEMENTS

The other use case for `useRef` is, as mentioned, to get references to DOM elements. You'll see this used many times throughout the remainder of this book. We use it to have a reference to the actual DOM element that is rendered in the document as a consequence of the JSX element that we've created. The syntax is very simple:

```
function Component() {
  const ref = useRef();          ← Creates a reference
  return <div ref={ref} />;            using the hook
}
                        ← "Assigns" the reference to the DOM node, which, when
                          the component is rendered, assigns a reference to
                          the DOM node inside the ref object
```

This doesn't use the reference for anything, but merely creates it. You can use the reference in an effect hook to, for example, invoke methods on the element, which isn't directly possible through properties of the DOM element.

For instance, let's autofocus an input field when a component is mounted:

```
function AutoFocusInput() {
  const ref = useRef();
  useEffect(() => ref.current.focus(), []);   ← Creates an effect that runs on mount
  return <input ref={ref} />;                     only (empty dependency array) and
}                                                  focuses the element through the ref
                                                   object. Note that it uses the ref.current
                                                   syntax as mentioned previously.
```

This latter use of `useRef` is the more common use (and the originally intended purpose). There's quite a bit more to say about how both `useRef` and the JSX `ref` property work, but we'll leave it here for now. We'll expand a bit on this in future chapters where relevant.

7.1.4 *Easier multicomponent state with useContext*

`useContext` is a stateful hook, meaning that it works similarly to `useState`. But rather than load and update values in a local store, `useContext` works in a store in a parent component somewhere up the component tree. This is the hook version of the React Context API, and we'll see a lot more about how this works in practice in chapter 10. We can reveal that it's one of the more powerful hooks when it comes to building good architecture.

7.1.5 Low-priority state updates with useDeferredValue and useTransition

> **NOTE** This topic is both fairly advanced and also brand new. These are features only just added with React 18, so there's still a lot of discoveries around best practices yet to be made. It's also an advanced topic that probably isn't relevant for everyday applications. We won't cover the functionality of these hooks in full in this section, but we'll only briefly outline why they exist. If you don't care about them at this point, feel free to skip this section.

Imagine that we've created an online document editor application similar to Google Docs, and we've added many features to it. We're now adding a spell-checker to the application and want to do this by adding a button that can be clicked to enable spell-checking and clicked again to disable it. The button has a different background color if enabled.

When a user clicks this button, it should react instantly. The button should change display within a few milliseconds for the user to feel like the button works. We can implement this using state by just toggling an enabled property inside the button using a `useState` setter.

But our button is going to do more than that. When spell-check is enabled, all the typos in the document should be highlighted with a red line underneath them. If the user is working on a large document, finding and highlighting all the errors might be an expensive operation. You have to run a lot of operations on all the words in the document to find errors and maybe even find suggestions for correct spellings for each. These tasks can easily take tenths of a second or even whole seconds to execute.

If we update both the internal enabled state flag inside the button as well as the global flag that triggers the spell-check calculation with the same priority at the same time in React, React's internals will treat both updates as happening at the same time and won't render anything until both updates have been fully calculated. This isn't ideal because the spell-check button will seem nonfunctional. When the user clicks the button and nothing happens, they will click it again. Then, all of a sudden, the button will actually work after the calculation is completed, but because the user had already clicked it again, the user disables the functionality. That's a horrible user experience.

What if we could inform React that updating the button state is high priority and should happen right away, whereas highlighting all the spelling errors in the document is lower priority, and we don't mind if that trails the button click by several render cycles? React 18 introduced a brand-new concept, Concurrent Mode, which allows exactly that. The `useDeferredValue` and `useTransition` hooks are two different ways of specifying low-priority state updates from two different angles. Given the complexity of these hooks, we won't cover them further in this book, but please refer to the following online materials for more information:

- Article: http://mng.bz/jPAP
- Video: http://mng.bz/WzM1

7.2   Component effects

This section is going to be short, so try not to blink or you might miss it completely! *Component effects* are a group of hooks dedicated to running side effects from within hooks with three different purposes:

- To influence the outside based on the component state
- To update the component state based on something from the outside
- To both influence the outside and update the component state at the same time

We've seen two such hooks already presented in the previous chapter, `useEffect` and `useLayoutEffect`. There is only one more such hook, `useInsertionEffect`, but it's reserved for advanced use by specific libraries, so it's not recommended to be used by "regular" developers.

We won't add any information on `useEffect` and `useLayoutEffect` in this chapter, as we covered everything there is to know in chapter 6. The last effect hook, `useInsertionEffect`, will be briefly covered in section 7.4.

7.3   Optimizing performance by minimizing re-rendering

> **NOTE**   This is an advanced topic not required by most simple applications. We'll only quickly introduce the topic here and not cover it in detail, as it's not necessary for your first, your second, or even your tenth application. Only once you start moving into larger applications with dozens or even hundreds of components do these hooks start to shine.

If you're working on a larger application with many moving parts, data updating from many sources, and events listening to many types of input, performance might start to degrade if components render unnecessarily. Once your application gets to that point, memoization might be the trick that can help your application regain its responsiveness.

At its core, *memoization* is the principle of caching the result of a given calculation so that if the same calculation is performed later, the cached result is returned. This can be used in React in a number of ways, including the three hooks we'll introduce in this section.

As mentioned, we won't go into detail about these hooks in this chapter, as they aren't necessary when starting out as a React developer. In fact, wrongly applying memoization might lead to worse performance, not better. So given the advanced nature of this topic, we don't use memoization at all in this book, and we'll only briefly introduce the three hooks in the following subsections.

You can read more about optimizing React performance in *Job-Ready React* (Morten Barklund, Manning, 2024), which covers not only these hooks and memoization in general, but also other ways to make your application more performant.

7.3.1 Memoizing any value with useMemo

Let's say you need to display the cryptographic hash of a given password as entered in an input field. The calculation of such a hash is pretty expensive, so you don't want to perform the calculation if the password doesn't change. But your component re-renders several times, even without the password changing. For this and similar occasions, you can use the `useMemo` hook to recalculate a given value in a component only if its dependencies change.

7.3.2 Memoizing functions with useCallback

`useCallback` is just a specialized version of `useMemo`, which is useful when `useMemo` is used to memoize a function. But because this happens so often, the `useCallback` hook exists for this purpose and is often used more than `useMemo`.

7.3.3 Creating stable DOM identifiers with useId

This is an even more advanced topic that is only relevant for server-generated React. It requires quite a buildup of knowledge to understand the circumstances for this hook that has such an extremely narrow usage.

`useId` makes sure that for two completely identical component trees, if a particular component inside either tree calls `useId`, it will get the same ID returned regardless of which platform the hook is run on. This is used to ensure that generated HTML is identical on the client and on the server.

7.4 Creating complex component libraries

This section is only included for completion, so we cover all the hooks in React. The four hooks described in the next subsections are all very advanced and rarely used. They are meant for reusable packages such as component libraries or open source modules.

The last two hooks mentioned in this section are introduced in React 18 as a consequence of the new Concurrent Mode. Some libraries have to be updated to correctly render in Concurrent Mode to avoid calculating logic that isn't required or is premature because of concurrency. Feel free to skip this section and go on to section 7.5 if you want to get on with the more practical stuff.

7.4.1 Creating component APIs with useImperativeHandle

This hook is used for advanced component libraries where you want to expose an API to parent components that is either custom for your particular component or that mimics a built-in DOM element for ease of use. It's almost exclusively used with `forwardRef`, which allows you to create your own components that accept refs, but pass them on to other elements or make a custom reference.

A quick example of this is a generalized custom input component where you want the parent component to be able to focus the input. Maybe you have an error message saying "missing field," and if the user clicks the error message, the correct field is focused. However, inside your component, the input can be many different types of elements (input, text area, or select) and can even have multiple input fields (imagine a phone form field, consisting of both a country prefix field and another phone number field).

To generalize this and make a unified API for all of these cases, you can use the hook useImperativeHandle to expose a focus() method for your component. This method can be used in imperative code (rather than declarative code through properties only), which will make sure to focus the proper element when invoked.

We won't go into details about how this hook nor forwardRef work in this book, as that is an advanced subject beyond the scope of this chapter, but it's good to know this hook exists if you want to create an advanced custom component that exposes a custom API through a reference. For more information, see this "ultimate guide" to useImperativeHandle: http://mng.bz/EQ0O.

7.4.2 *Better debugging of hooks with useDebugValue*

This is a hook only meant for developer experience. It doesn't change nor improve the user experience of your application regardless of how it's used.

The useDebugValue hook allows you as a React library developer to display a custom message when other developers are inspecting your custom hooks in their React application using the React Developer Tools plugin in their browser.

Normally a custom hook would display all of its internal states in the React Developer Tools explorer, but that might be confusing to someone who doesn't care about the internals of your custom hook. With the useDebugValue hook, you can expose only what the developer using your hook cares about. For more information, see "How to Use useDebugValue in React" at http://mng.bz/N251.

7.4.3 *Synchronizing non-React data with useSyncExternalStore*

In Concurrent Mode, React can be updating a state value with low priority, and while calculating the consequences of said update, an urgent update comes in that has to be calculated irrespective of the incomplete update. Because React is running concurrently, React will have several completely separate instances of the application running and can thus spin off a new calculation based on a former state when an urgent update comes in.

If an application uses an external library to keep state updated, this external library has to be able to support this kind of concurrent state logic so it, too, can keep multiple instances of the state running at the same time. React 18 introduces the useSyncExternalStore for that exact purpose. For more information, see this article on useSyncExternalStore: http://mng.bz/8r1K.

7.4.4   *Running effect before rendering with useInsertionEffect*

If you have a library that creates stylesheets or similar HTML nodes in the document as a side effect of component rendering, your library now needs to be aware of Concurrent Mode to render the correct nodes at the correct time. For that specific purpose, React 18 introduces the `useInsertionEffect` hook.

While this is and looks like an effect hook in the same vein as `useEffect` and `useLayoutEffect`, the `useInsertionEffect` hook is never applicable to regular components. It was only created as a consequence of how some general-purpose libraries have to be updated to account for the consequences of concurrency. For a bit more detail, see this short article on `useInsertionEffect`: http://mng.bz/EQlq.

7.5   *The two key principles of hooks*

You only need to obey two rules regarding React hooks:

- Only call hooks *unconditionally* at the *top level* of functional components.
- Only call hooks *inside* functional components.

The first rule, we already discussed: you can only use hooks directly in your components, and you must always include the same number of hooks. That means you can never call hooks inside a function (including inside a function used in a hook) or a nested block (either a conditional or loop), and you can't have early returns in your component before you've rendered all your hooks.

The second rule is kind of obvious, but maybe kind of *not* obvious: you can only use hooks inside functional components. You can't create some helper function or callback that calls a hook. You also can't use them inside class-based components.

The only exception to this rule is that you can use hooks inside other hooks, which are called *custom hooks*, and you can again use custom hooks inside other custom hooks, and so on. But you can only use those custom hooks either in other custom hooks or in your components, so you can't circumvent this rule—you can just hide it one layer (or multiple layers) down. We'll cover custom hooks in chapter 10.

7.6   *Quiz*

1   React has always had and will always have 15 hooks. *True* or *false?*
2   Which of these are considered *stateful* hooks?

    a   `useState`

    b   `useValue`

    c   `useId`

    d   `useReducer`

3   `useMemo` is a specialized version of `useCallback`. *True* or *false?*
4   You can't call a hook inside a function unless it's a functional component or a custom hook. *True* or *false?*

5 Which of the following constructions aren't allowed?

a   ```
    function Component({ isVisible }) {
        if (!isVisible) return false;
        useEffect(() => { ... }, []);
        ...
    }
    ```

b   ```
    function Component({ hasEffect }) {
        if (hasEffect) {
          useEffect(() => { ... }, []);
        }
        ...
    }
    ```

c   ```
    function Component({ shouldRender }) {
        useEffect(() => { ... }, []);
        if (!shouldRender) return false;
        ...
    }
    ```

## Quiz answers

1  *False.* React 16.8 introduced the first 10 hooks, and React 18.0 added another 5. More will definitely come in future releases.

2  `useState` and `useReducer` are stateful hooks. `useValue` isn't a built-in hook (but you could make a custom hook named this if you wanted), and `useId` is instead used for a rather specific memoization purpose.

3  *False.* It's the other way around. `useMemo` is a general hook for memoizing *any value*, whereas `useCallback` is a hook for memoizing *functions* only.

4  *True.* You shouldn't attempt to call hooks inside functions that aren't themselves custom hooks. Even though it might seem to work at first, it will only lead to problems down the line if you suddenly start calling one of these functions outside of a functional component. Obey the principles of hooks!

5  The illegal constructions are a and b. Only version c is a valid component. Versions a and b both use conditional rendering of hooks, which isn't allowed.

## Summary

- React has 15 different built-in hooks, but several of them are rarely used, leaving about 10 as the core API on which all React applications are built.
- Hooks are used for a variety of purposes that make components smart and able to interact with the web page as a whole. Even though all the hooks vary wildly in their purposes, they all have some common features.
- Stateful hooks are required to make applications stateful. You can use several different hooks depending on the complexity of your application and the values in your state. With React 18, you can even make lower priority and higher priority state updates to help React make your UI as responsive as possible.
    ```

- Effect hooks are used to run side effects inside components, as you learned in chapter 6. By using the dependency array, you can trigger your effect to run at the desired time(s).
- Memoization hooks are used for optimization of rendering in React, once your application grows large and complex.
- Library hooks are meant for more complex codebases only and probably aren't relevant for your everyday applications.
- If you use a hook, you must obey the two laws of hooks: only call hooks at the top level of a component (so no conditional hooks or loops of hooks), and only use hooks inside functional components (so no hooks outside a component, in a helper function, or even in a class-based component).

Handling events in React

8

This chapter covers

- Reacting to user input using events
- Handling event capturing and bubbling
- Managing default event actions
- Attaching event listeners directly to the DOM

Events are the way that users interact with a JavaScript web application. Events can be caused by mouse movement or clicking, touch interface clicks and drags, keyboard button presses, scrolling, copying and pasting, as well as indirect interactions such as focusing and unfocusing elements or the entire application.

So far, we've created React applications with very little user interaction. We've handled clicking a button here and there, but not really talked in depth about how the click event works, and how we as developers handle it. We're going to change that in this chapter, which is dedicated to event handling.

You can think of events as the way to handle inputs from a user. Our web application creates JavaScript XML (JSX), which is converted to HTML. The user then interacts with that HTML, and the result of those interactions are events dispatched from the HTML elements to our React application. This simple flow of information is illustrated in figure 8.1.

Figure 8.1 Information flow between React and the user goes through the HTML. Imagine the user visiting a login page. The user inputs the email and password, the browser forwards those interactions as events to React, the application then generates the JSX required to display a green checkmark next to each input as it's filled, and the browser renders the corresponding HTML to display to the user.

Events are also used internally in the browser to signify when things change between elements. It can be when a video is playing/pausing/buffering, an animation is completed, a DOM node is mutated, data is loaded (or failed to load), and so on. There are hundreds of possible events, and any interactive web application will be using a sizable chunk of them. (You can read more about all the possible DOM events in the event reference document at http://mng.bz/9D1j.)

There are two ways to handle events in React:

- You can use React to manage your event listener.
- You can manually add and remove your event listener directly on a DOM node.

Relying on React to handle listeners saves a bunch of tedious work and headaches (and potential memory leaks), but it comes with a minor loss of flexibility. Directly adding event listeners allows you to listen for all kinds of events and assign listeners to whichever nodes you feel like when you need to, but comes with the cost of having to manage listeners (and remember to remove them again) as well as dealing with native events that might differ between browsers.

In this chapter, we'll show you both approaches and discuss when best to apply one or the other. Note that handling events *in React* is both a whole lot easier as well as recommended. Therefore, this scenario will be covered in a lot more detail in this chapter.

As we cover how you can listen to events using React's interface, we'll discuss a number of topics about how React handles events and how you can work with the React API to listen to the specific events that you need. We'll answer the following questions:

- Which events are supported?
- How do you create the event handler function?
- What event objects will you receive?
- How do event phases and propagation work?
- How do you handle events in the capture phase of the event dispatch?
- What are default actions and how do you prevent them?

- When should you persist an event?
- Can you use properties as event handlers?
- What are event handler generators?

We'll then proceed to situations where React's built-in event handling isn't capable enough, and we need to handle events manually in the DOM. We'll give you all the insights into how to do this best, as well.

All of this will lead to the next chapter, where we'll use our newfound understanding of event handling to create interactive form inputs and forms in general, which is a cornerstone of many web applications.

> **NOTE** The source code for the examples in this chapter is available at https://rq2e.com/ch08. But as you learned in chapter 2, you can instantiate all the examples directly from the command line using a single command.

8.1   Handling DOM events in React

Events are an essential way of communicating in the browser between the user and the script as well as between different elements in the application. Because of this, proper event handling is a first-class citizen in React, meaning that React has dedicated a big part of its core API to this exact purpose.

The API is very simple. If you define a property on a JSX element that references an HTML node, and that property matches a known event from React's list of supported events, React will treat the property as an event listener rather than as a DOM attribute. React will then make sure to correctly add and remove the event listener, as the component mounts and unmounts.

8.1.1   Basic event handling in React

The most important event of all in almost any web application is the click event. Contrary to its name, it's not only used to accept clicks from a mouse. The click event in HTML is also invoked when a touchscreen user taps on a button (or a link) or when a keyboard user activates a button (or a link) using the Enter key.

Let's go back to our trusted counter component and take a closer look at how we handle the click event. If you remember, this application had a button, and we incremented the state value as a response to the user clicking. First, let's repeat the code for this simple application.

Listing 8.1   Counter component

```
import { useState } from "react";
function Counter() {
  const [counter, setCounter] = useState(0);
  const onClick = () =>
    setCounter((value) => value + 1);
```

Creates a local variable, which is a function, that will increment the state value when invoked

```
    return (
      <>
        <h1>Value: {counter}</h1>
        <button onClick={onClick}>Increment</button>      <──┐
      </>
    );                                                        Assigns that local
}                                                             variable to the onClick
function App() {                                              property on our button
  return <Counter />;
}
export default App;
```

In this example, we handle a click event on an HTML object, which is a `<button>`. Any HTML element will dispatch a click event if clicked, so we could have changed this element to a `<div>` or any other type of element.

Another event that we can listen for on all objects is the mouse (or pointer) event. Any element can dispatch, for example, a `mousemove` event, when a mouse moves inside that element's boundary. We can listen for such an event in the same way.

Let's create a component that shows a checkmark if the mouse is moving around inside the element, but changes to a cross if the mouse has stopped moving for half a second or if the mouse moved outside the element.

To do that, we need to listen for the `mousemove` event. In React, that means we assign a function as the `onMouseMove` property on our target element. In this case, we'll use a `<section>` element and display our result in a heading inside of that. See this implemented in the following listing and the result in figure 8.2.

Listing 8.2 Is the mouse moving?

```
import { useState, useEffect } from "react";        Creates a local variable,
function MouseStatus() {                             which is a function that
  const [isMoving, setMoving] = useState(false);     will set the moving flag
  const onMouseMove = () => setMoving(true);   <──┘  to true when invoked
  useEffect(() => {
    if (!isMoving) return;
    const timeout = setTimeout(() => setMoving(false), 500);
    return () => clearTimeout(timeout);
  }, [isMoving]);
  return (
    <section onMouseMove={onMouseMove}>                    <──┐
      <h2>                                                     │
        The mouse is {!isMoving && "not"} moving: {isMoving ? "√" : "X"}
      </h2>
    </section>                              Assigns that local variable to the
  );                                        relevant property on our element—
}                                           this time, the onMouseMove property
function App() {                            on our section element
  return <MouseStatus />;
}
export default App;
```

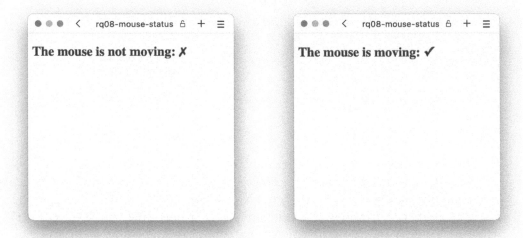

Figure 8.2 Our mouse status component when the mouse isn't moving or is moving, respectively

---

Repository: rq08-mouse-status

This example can be seen in repository `rq08-mouse-status`. You can use that repository by creating a new app based on the associated template:

```
$ npx create-react-app rq08-mouse-status --template rq08-mouse-status
```

Alternatively, you can go to this website to browse the code, see the application in action directly in your browser, or download the source code as a zip file:

https://rq2e.com/rq08-mouse-status

Not all events are dispatched by all types of elements, though. Video (and audio) elements dispatch a play event once the video (or audio) starts playing. Buttons don't dispatch that event because they aren't videos (or audios) that play.

Let's create an application that displays a Play/Pause button next to a video. When the video is playing, the button is a Pause button; when the video is paused, the button is a Play button.

For this, we need a total of four listeners. We need to listen to the play and pause events on the video object, and we need to listen for the click event on our button, but with two different event listeners depending on whether the video is playing or not. We'll implement this in the next listing. If you run this application, you should see something similar to figure 8.3 in your browser.

Listing 8.3   A very simple video player

```
import { useState, useRef } from "react";
const VIDEO_SRC =
```

```
"//images-assets.nasa.gov/video/One Small Step/One Small Step~orig.mp4";
function VideoPlayer() {
  const [isPlaying, setPlaying] = useState(false);
  const onPlay = () => setPlaying(true);
  const onPause = () => setPlaying(false);
  const onClickPlay = () => video.current.play();
  const onClickPause = () => video.current.pause();
  const video = useRef();
  return (
    <section>
      <video
        ref={video}
        src={VIDEO_SRC}
        controls
        width="480"
        onPlay={onPlay}
        onPause={onPause}
      />
      <button onClick={
        isPlaying ? onClickPause : onClickPlay
      }>
        {isPlaying ? "Pause" : "Play"}
      </button>
    </section>
  );
}
function App() {
  return <VideoPlayer />;
}
export default App;
```

Toggles the state flag to true when the video starts playing

Invokes play on the reference to the video DOM element when the button is clicked to play the video

Pauses the video when the button is clicked while the video is already playing

Toggles the flag to false when the video pauses

Assigns the two video event listeners to the video element using the appropriate properties

Assigns one of the button click event listeners to the onClick property depending on the flag

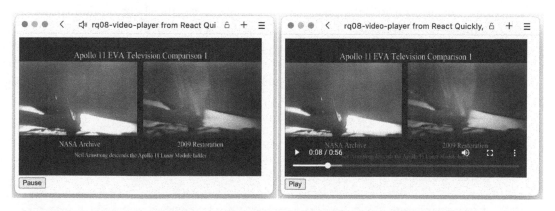

Figure 8.3 The video player interface when the video is playing and paused, respectively

Listening to events in React is really only about three things:

- Knowing what event to listen for
- Knowing which element to listen on
- Assigning a listening function to the correct property on the correct element

That's really all there is to it. The rest of this chapter walks through a number of event examples, so your toolbox will be ready to handle any event scenario that you come across.

EVENTS SUPPORTED BY REACT

You can only use React to listen for events that are supported by React. Normally, this isn't something you have to worry about because almost all DOM events are supported by React. You can see a full list of all the supported events in table 8.1.

However, there are some JavaScript events that aren't supported in React—mostly because these events are dispatched from objects that aren't in the DOM, but are objects that you create in JavaScript only. These include events from objects such as socket connections and request objects.

Some other unsupported DOM events are events that are only sent to the window or document nodes. They aren't supported by React because these two nodes are never inside your React application. React only lives somewhere inside the document element, never above it.

Note that if you set a property on a JSX element that matches a known event type listed in table 8.1, React will convert that property to a listener on that element, regardless of whether that element can dispatch that event at all. You can, for instance, assign an `onPlay` event listener to an `<h1 />` element, even though that event will only ever be dispatched from `<video />` and `<audio />` elements.

Table 8.1   List of events directly supported in React

Clipboard events	`onCopy onCut onPaste`
Composition events	`onCompositionEnd onCompositionStart onCompositionUpdate`
Keyboard events	`onKeyDown onKeyPress onKeyUp`
Focus events	`onFocus onBlur`
Form events	`onChange onInput onInvalid onReset onSubmit`

Table 8.1 List of events directly supported in React *(continued)*

Generic events	`onError onLoad`

Mouse events	`onClick onContextMenu onDoubleClick onDrag onDragEnd`
	`onDragEnter onDragExit`
	`onDragLeave onDragOver onDragStart onDrop onMouseDown`
	`onMouseEnter onMouseLeave`
	`onMouseMove onMouseOut onMouseOver onMouseUp`

Pointer events	`onPointerDown onPointerMove onPointerUp onPointerCancel`
	`onGotPointerCapture`
	`onLostPointerCapture onPointerEnter onPointerLeave`
	`onPointerOver onPointerOut`

Selection events	`onSelect`
Touch events	`onTouchCancel onTouchEnd onTouchMove onTouchStart`
UI events	`onScroll`
Wheel events	`onWheel`

Media events	`onAbort onCanPlay onCanPlayThrough onDurationChange`
	`onEmptied onEncrypted`
	`onEnded onError onLoadedData onLoadedMetadata onLoadStart`
	`onPause onPlay`
	`onPlaying onProgress onRateChange onSeeked onSeeking`
	`onStalled onSuspend`
	`onTimeUpdate onVolumeChange onWaiting`

Image events	`onLoad onError`
Animation events	`onAnimationStart onAnimationEnd onAnimationIteration`
Transition events	`onTransitionEnd`
Other events	`onToggle`

8.2 *Event handlers*

To handle an event, simply assign any function to the relevant property of a JSX element that might dispatch such an event. Your function doesn't have to behave in any particular way or accept any particular argument. The event handler function will be called with a single argument—the event object—but you don't have to accept it.

Because there are no restrictions nor any defined best practices from an "official" source on how to define an event handler function, you'll see people do it in many different ways. In this section, we'll cover some of the different options and some conventions that we've seen used in larger codebases.

8.2.1 *Definition of event handlers*

NOTE This subsection doesn't teach you anything new React-wise. It mainly reiterates how you can define functions in different ways in JavaScript inside other functions. If you're a JavaScript expert, feel free to skip this section and go straight to section 8.2.2.

You can define the event function any way you like. If it's a valid function, it's valid as an event handler. Common options include the following:

- Define the function as a local variable using an arrow function.
- Define the function as a local variable using a function expression.
- Define the function as an inline function using an arrow function directly assigned to the property.

Here's an example of our counter component once again with a local variable using an arrow function:

```
function Counter() {
  const [counter, setCounter] = useState(0);
  const onClick = () => setCounter(c => c + 1);
  return (
    <>
      <h1>Value: {counter}</h1>
      <button onClick={onClick}>Increment</button>
    </>
  );
}
```

Creates a variable using const and assigns a function using the arrow function notation

Assigns that variable to the onClick property

Here's the very same component, but with the handler function defined using a function expression:

```
function Counter() {
  const [counter, setCounter] = useState(0);
  function onClick() {
    setCounter(c => c + 1);
  }
  return (
    <>
      <h1>Value: {counter}</h1>
      <button onClick={onClick}>Increment</button>
    </>
  );
}
```

Creates the function using a function expression, which will scope the variable as a local variable

Assigns that variable to the onClick property

And, finally, here's the same component with the handler defined inline using an arrow function:

```
function Counter() {
  const [counter, setCounter] = useState(0);  return (
    <>
```

```
      <h1>Value: {counter}</h1>
      <button onClick={() => setCounter(c => c + 1)}>      ◄──────┐
        Increment                                                 │
      </button>                           Creates the event handler inline and
    </>                                   directly assigns it to the relevant
  );                                      property on the HTML element
}
```

The second approach, with a function expression inside your component, is a bit unusual, albeit fully valid. We won't use that syntax, and we haven't seen it much in the wild.

Whether you define your event handler in a variable or inline in the JSX is up to you. Many will mix and match the two options, and so will we throughout this book. Your team will most likely find a convention that works for them, and if you're working alone, find what works for you.

A common convention is to define single-line event handlers inline, but multiline event handlers in a separate variable. So, there's nothing stopping you from doing this:

```
return (
  <button onClick={() => {
    setCounter(count => count + 1);
    toggleState();
  }}>Button</button>
);
```

But some developers will find it a bit messy and will prefer to have such multiline event handlers defined separately in a variable before the JSX is returned:

```
const onClick = () => {
  setCounter(count => count + 1);
  toggleState();
};
return <button onClick={onClick}>Button</button>;
```

8.2.2   Event objects

When an event handler is invoked because an event has occurred, the event handler is invoked with a single argument—the event object. This happens both in regular HTML and JavaScript, as well as in React.

React event objects are a bit special, but we'll get to that in the next subsection. For now, we'll showcase a few things that regular JavaScript event objects and React event objects have in common.

Let's try to build our counter component with both increment and decrement buttons again, but this time we'll use the same event handler function to handle the click event on both buttons. We do this to display an alternative way of structuring the code. It's not faster or better in terms of code performance, but some will prefer this style over the previous one.

To do this, we need to know which button caused the event that was sent to the event handler. We can do that by looking at the event object passed. It will have a property, `.target`, that points to the HTML node that was clicked. To compare this target property with the actual node, we need a reference to one of the nodes in our component. Let's implement this in the following listing.

Listing 8.4   Increment and decrement with a single event handler

```
import { useState, useRef } from "react";
function Counter() {
  const [counter, setCounter] = useState(0);
  const increment = useRef();
  const onClick = (evt) => {
    const delta =
      evt.target === increment.current ? 1 : -1;
    setCounter((value) => value + delta);
  };
  return (
    <section>
      <h1>Value: {counter}</h1>
      <button ref={increment} onClick={onClick}>
        Increment
      </button>
      <button onClick={onClick}>Decrement</button>
    </section>
  );
}
function App() {
  return <Counter />;
}
export default App;
```

First, we need a ref, so we can access the HTML node.

Then, in our single event handler, we compare the event target with the increment node. If it's not that button, it must be the other one.

Adds the delta to the currently stored value

Assigns the same event handler to both buttons but only a ref to the increment button

---

Is this better than having two separate event handlers? That's a subjective question. Both solutions are fine. Sometimes one seems more appropriate, and other times, the other one does. The choice mostly comes down to personal preference. Do you feel that having a single event handler makes the code more readable, or do you prefer having separate handlers? There's no difference in performance, so it's completely up to your preferred style.

Event objects always have a target property that refers to the target of the event. Another property that all events have is the type property. The value of this property is the type of event invoked. Imagine that we assigned the same event handler to both the `onMouseEnter` and the `onFocus` property of an input field. Then, our event handler would fire if the user either moved their mouse over the field or used the keyboard to tab into the field. We could tell which event occurred by looking at the `evt.type` property.

Some event objects have extra properties that are specific for the event types that dispatched them. For instance, mouse event objects always have the properties `.clientX` and `.clientY`, which indicate where in the document the mouse event occurred, as well as .ctrlKey and .shiftKey, which indicate whether either of those keys were pressed while the mouse event occurred. Mouse event objects have many other properties than these, though. To see the full list of available properties for all the different event objects in React, check the online documentation here: http://mng.bz/D4Zy.

8.2.3 React event objects

React event handlers aren't the same as "true" DOM event handlers. A DOM event handler is added to a DOM node and passed a DOM event object when invoked. A React event handler isn't directly added to any DOM node and will be invoked by React with a React event object when React detects that an event of the given type happened on that node. Compare and contrast the two approaches in figure 8.4.

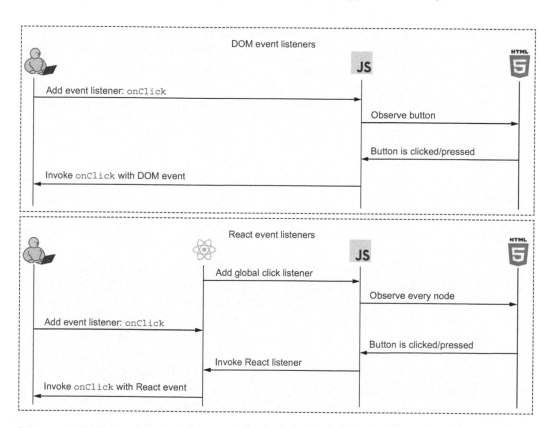

Figure 8.4 React doesn't add a listener on the individual node, but listens to any event on any node, unlike native DOM listeners.

In figure 8.4, notice that when you add a listener to a JSX element, React *doesn't* add a new listener anywhere. Instead, it just remembers that you want to be informed about this specific type of event for this specific node. React already listens to all events on all nodes, so when an event of the specified type occurs, React will check if the target matches the one you asked about; if so, React will invoke your event listener with a custom React event object. The reasoning for React implementing this new event system on top of the already existing native browser event system is two-fold: performance and consistency.

PERFORMANCE

As we just mentioned, React doesn't add listeners to individual nodes. React adds a single listener of every event type to the document, and this is done for performance reasons.

The performance gain is real. If you add a thousand buttons and assign a click event listener to each node in pure JavaScript, it requires a lot of memory. But if you use React to do the same, React will only ever create a single click event listener on the document as a whole and, when invoked, check if the target matches any that you asked for. This significantly reduces memory usage.

For this reason, you don't have to worry about adding too many event listeners in React. If you were implementing a web app in plain JavaScript, you might have to create some workarounds to reduce how many listeners you have. When using React, this is all taken care of for you, so you can just add listeners as you like and know that you still have great performance.

CONSISTENCY

Despite browsers being more and more standards compliant, there are still older browsers out there, and they might do things a bit differently. This is particularly relevant when it comes to the event API. A lot of this concern is about browsers that are 5+ years old (older versions of Firefox and especially Internet Explorer 9 and earlier), so it doesn't seem extremely important today, but these browsers might still exist in the wild.

Another big reason for consistency might be slightly surprising. Some events aren't standardized but are still implemented by every browser. This includes events such as the mouse wheel event. There is no standard for this event, nor is any such on the way, but all browsers still support it, so React does as well. Because there is no standard, browsers handle the mouse wheel event slightly differently when it comes to naming. The scroll wheel change in the x direction is stored in a property called either `.deltaX` or `.wheelDeltaX` in different browsers. React's synthetic mouse wheel event takes care of this and unifies this naming as `.deltaX` always. Similar unification happens for some other nonstandard properties on this and other event types.

For this reason, you don't have to worry about browser differences at all when using React events. You can rely on the React documentation only and trust that React will take care of all the underlying details for you. Due to browser differences disappearing as the use of older browsers decreases, it's likely that this feature of the React synthetic event system will disappear at some point in the future and be replaced exclusively with browser-native events.

THE SYNTHETIC EVENT API

React's synthetic events have an API that's based on the standard API model as defined in the HTML specification. This means that you can use all the properties and methods that you expect from an event.

All synthetic events share a set of common properties and methods, and more specialized events have extra properties specific to certain events. For instance, all events have a `.type` property and a `.target` property. They also all have `.preventDefault()` and `.stopPropagation()` methods. We'll get back to how these work later.

Individual event types have extra properties as needed for specific events, including, for example, the `.pageX` and `.pageY` properties on mouse and pointer events, which include the coordinates of the clicks on the page.

> **NOTE** For details on the specific properties and methods, please see the React synthetic event API documentation: http://mng.bz/D4Zy.

ACCESS TO NATIVE EVENTS

If for some reason you need access to the underlying native event, maybe because you're doing something for a specific browser that can include some extra information that is useful for your particular application, you can access it via the `.nativeEvent` property. This is a nonstandard property and a React-only extension of the event API.

8.2.4 Synthetic event object persistence

Events need no longer be persisted. That's it, next section. Wait, what? This might seem odd, but event persistence was a thing you had to do in earlier versions of React up until the release of React 17, after which it was no longer needed.

However, because persistence was a commonly used "feature" that only fairly recently became obsolete, we'll still cover it here in case you stumble upon it in the wild. You'll find event persistence in a codebase that hasn't been fully updated when moving to newer versions of React or even in tutorials and guides about React that aren't completely up to date.

Back in the day, for performance reasons, React's synthetic events were pooled in order to not create too many objects all the time. Before version 17, React didn't create new event objects every time an event was dispatched. React instead held an internal pool (an array, basically) of events, and when it needed to send an event, React would get one from the pool, and then immediately after dispatching the event, return the event object to the pool. As the event object returned to the pool, the event was "cleared out," meaning that all properties were reset to have no value.

As a developer, this meant that if you received an event in an event handler, you had to *consume* the event right away. You couldn't save it or otherwise access it in a delayed manner.

Let's say that we want to create a counter that we can increase by a value selected from a drop-down. We've created a ton of counters, but this is a new variant. The goal is to display the current counter value (starting at 0) and also a drop-down with values from 1 to 5. When you select one of the values, the counter will increase by that amount. When you then select a new value, the drop-down will again increase by that new amount, and so on. Let's implement this in the next listing.

Listing 8.5   Drop-down counter

```
import { useState } from "react";
function DropdownCounter() {
  const [counter, setCounter] = useState(0);
  const onChange = (evt) => setCounter(
    (value) => value + parseInt(evt.target.value)
  );
  const values = [1, 2, 3, 4, 5];
  return (
    <section>
      <h1>Counter: {counter}</h1>
      <select onChange={onChange}>
        {values.map((value) => (
          <option key={value} value={value}>
            {value}
          </option>
        ))}
      </select>
    </section>
  );
}
function App() {
  return <DropdownCounter />;
}
export default App;
```

> Adds the selected option to the current counter value in our change event handler by using an update function

> Assigns the event handler to the select element

Repository: rq08-persistence

This example can be seen in repository `rq08-persistence`. You can use that repository by creating a new app based on the associated template:

```
$ npx create-react-app rq08-persistence --template rq08-persistence
```

Alternatively, you can go to this website to browse the code, see the application in action directly in your browser, or download the source code as a zip file:

https://rq2e.com/rq08-persistence

This works and all is well. However, if you were to create this in React 16.8 (when React hooks were introduced) through React 16.14 (the latest React 16 version before React 17 was introduced), this wouldn't work. Instead, `evt.target.value` would throw an error in the console because `evt.target` is undefined. This happens because we pass an update function to the state setter, and that update function is invoked asynchronously. By the time the function is invoked, React already has returned the event object to the pool and reset it, including clearing `evt.target`. We could have solved this in React 16 in one of two ways:

- Make a local copy of the value from the event object we needed right away and use that value asynchronously in our update function.
- Persist the event, meaning that React would know not to return this particular event object to the pool, and instead discard it as a "one-time event object" and create another new event object to return to the pool instead.

The first approach for copying the values we need would look like this:

```
const onChange = (evt) => {
  const delta = parseInt(evt.target.value);      ⟵—— First, we copy the value
  setCounter((value) => value + delta);          ⟵⌐   from the event object we
};                                                   |   need to access later.
                                                     Then, we use
                                                     that value.
```

The second approach, where we persist the event object, would look like this:

```
                                           We instruct React to not reuse this
                                           event object, but persist it for our
const onChange = (evt) => {                 use indefinitely.
  evt.persist();                   ⟵—————⌐
  setCounter((value) =>
    value + parseInt(evt.target.value));   ⟵——— Then, we can freely use the event
};                                                object even in asynchronous code.
```

This whole mess of having to remember to persist events if used asynchronously was pretty annoying. It didn't happen very frequently and was a very common source of confusion and errors, even for experienced developers, which is partially why it was abandoned. The other reason was that the performance gained by pooling events decreased as devices grew faster, so it became an unnecessary optimization.

8.3   Event phases and propagation

Events are not *just* sent to the target object. When you click a link, the link dispatches a click event. But if the link had a bold text element inside it (e.g., `<a href>A <strong>bold</strong> link</a>`), you actually click the bold text element. The link then dispatches a click event because you also click the link element. You "click" all the parent elements of the bold text element. This is called *event propagation.*

To introduce the concept of event propagation, let's consider a new example. We want to build a contact form that contains two different sections (field sets). The first section is information about the user (name and email), and the second is about why they are sending this contact request (subject and body).

Because we want the form to look nice and user friendly, we'll highlight the section in which the user is currently inputing data. We want the result to look like what you see in figure 8.5.

To achieve this goal, we need to listen to the focus and blur events on the input fields. When an input receives focus, store its section as the focused one. When an

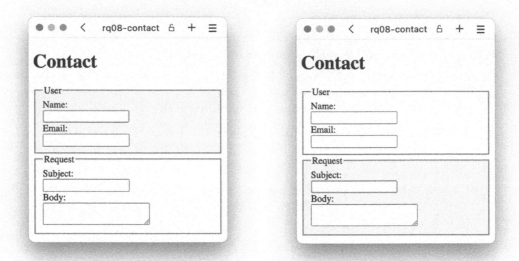

Figure 8.5   Our finished form when the user is inputting data into either section

input field loses focus, remember that no section has focus. With this approach, we need to put two event listeners on every input in both sections. In this example, we only have two inputs in each section, so that's a total of eight listeners, but what if we had a lot more inputs? We would have to duplicate the same two listeners to every input field. If that seems like a terrible way to do this, it is. You should avoid repeating yourself if possible. In this instance, it's very much avoidable because events bubble!

Every event in React *bubbles* up through all the nodes in the document tree above it. To know which section has focus, we just need to listen for when anything inside a section receives focus. Likewise, to know that an element loses focus, we just need to know whenever any element inside the form loses focus. We can use this trick to place our focus listeners on the two sections and the blur listener on the form itself. Then, we only need a total of three event listeners to achieve this result rather than eight different listeners, of which most are identical. Let's look at the resulting JSX structure and where we want to put our listeners in figure 8.6.

When you focus any input field, the event will first dispatch on the input field itself, but after that, the same event will dispatch on every ancestor to the target element in order from the parent all the way up to the root node of the React application. When the bubbling reaches the field set, React will invoke our onFocus listener placed there. Similarly, when an input blurs, React will invoke the onBlur listener placed on the form element.

Now that we know what we want to achieve and what the resulting JSX is going to look like, all that remains is to put it all together into a single component. Let's do that in listing 8.6.

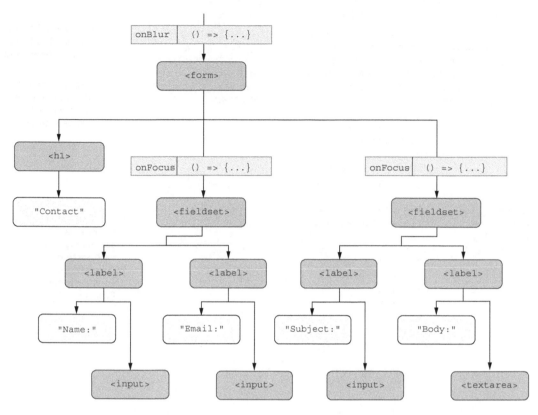

Figure 8.6 We add a blur listener to the entire form and focus listeners on both field sets. When an event occurs on any input (in the bottom row), the event will travel up the tree and be handled by the proper event handler.

Listing 8.6 Highlighting contact form sections

```
import { useState } from "react";
const FOCUS_NONE = 0;
const FOCUS_USER = 1;
const FOCUS_REQUEST = 2;
function getStyle(isActive) {
  return {
    display: "flex",
    flexDirection: "column",
    backgroundColor: isActive ? "oldlace" : "transparent",
  };
}
function Field({ label, children }) {
  return (
    <label>
      {label}:
      <br />
      {children}
    </label>
```

First, we add a helper function to generate the style for a section depending on whether it's the active section or not.

```
    );
  }
  function Contact() {
    const [focus, setFocus] = useState(FOCUS_NONE);
    const onUserFocus = () => setFocus(FOCUS_USER);
    const onRequestFocus = () => setFocus(FOCUS_REQUEST);
    const onBlur = () => setFocus(FOCUS_NONE);
    return (
      <form onBlur={onBlur}>
        <h1>Contact</h1>
        <fieldset
          onFocus={onUserFocus}
          style={getStyle(focus === FOCUS_USER)}
        >
          <legend>User</legend>
          <Field label="Name">
            <input />
          </Field>
          <Field label="Email">
            <input type="email" />
          </Field>
        </fieldset>
        <fieldset
          onFocus={onRequestFocus}
          style={getStyle(focus === FOCUS_REQUEST)}
        >
          <legend>Request</legend>
          <Field label="Subject">
            <input />
          </Field>
          <Field label="Body">
            <textarea />
          </Field>
        </fieldset>
      </form>
    );
  }
  function App() {
    return <Contact />;
  }
  export default App;
```

Second, we need to remember what section has focus right now (at the start, none of them do).

Creates three different and very simple listeners that we need to use

Assigns the listeners where we need them

Assigns the correct style to each section depending on whether it has focus or not

Repository: rq08-contact

This example can be seen in repository `rq08-contact`. You can use that repository by creating a new app based on the associated template:

```
$ npx create-react-app rq08-contact --template rq08-contact
```

Alternatively, you can go to this website to browse the code, see the application in action directly in your browser, or download the source code as a zip file:

https://rq2e.com/rq08-contact

That's it! We now have a fancy styled contact form with some pretty clever focus listeners. If you run this in a browser, you'll get exactly the desired result that we saw in figure 8.5.

In the rest of this section, we'll discuss in a lot more detail how event propagation works from a technical perspective. First, we'll cover events in HTML and JavaScript in general, and later, events in React specifically.

8.3.1 How phases and propagation work in the browser

React events bubble, as just mentioned. HTML events also bubble. When you click a button, every ancestor of that button will dispatch an event. They will dispatch two events—one *before* the target element itself and one *after* the target element itself.

> **NOTE** This subsection is about events in HTML in general, and not React specifically. We need to cover this topic first in order for you to better understand how events in React work. In the next subsections, we'll discuss event phases in React specifically, which are slightly different.

Previously, we discussed events bubbling, which is what happens when the ancestors dispatch an event *after* the event has already dispatched to the target element. However, all events also *capture*, which is what happens *before* the event is dispatched to the target element. The three stages of event dispatches are as follows:

- *Capture phase*—Events are dispatched to all parent DOM nodes in descending order, starting with the window element, going through every ancestor, and ending at the parent of the target element.
- *Target phase*—An event is dispatched to the target element itself.
- *Bubble phase*—Events are dispatched to all parent DOM nodes in ascending order, starting with the parent of the target element and moving up through the ancestors until the window element

See figure 8.7 for an illustration of this. This entire concept is called *event propagation*. An event propagates first in the capture phase from the window object "down" to the target element and then proceeds to propagate back "up" to the window object in the bubble phase.

When you want to listen for an event on a particular element, you can specify in which phase you're listening to the event. The default is to listen for an event in the bubbling and target phases, but you can add an argument to listen for events in the capture phase specifically.

In JavaScript, you add a listener (bubble and target) by simply calling `addEvent-Listener` with the event and callback function:

```
element.addEventListener("click", onClick);
```

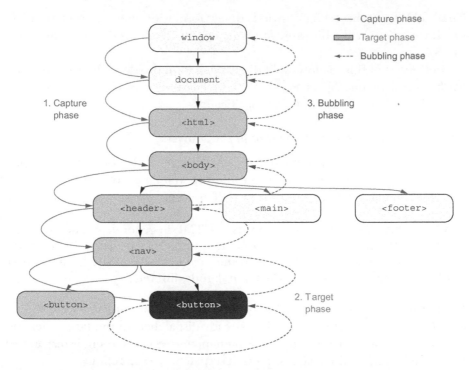

Figure 8.7   When you click the black button, the browser will start propagating events throughout the nodes in the document starting at the window, moving down through the document tree in the capture phase until the target, and then moving back up the tree in the bubbling phase until it reaches the window.

If you wanted to use a capture listener instead, you would have to add a third argument with an object:

```
element.addEventListener("click", onClick, { capture: true });
```

When you receive an event, you can check the `.eventPhase` property of the event object to see which event phase it belongs to. The possible values are listed here:

- `Event.CAPTURING_PHASE` (1) for capture
- `Event.AT_TARGET` (2) for target
- `Event.BUBBLING_PHASE` (3) for bubble

In the example in figure 8.7, a total of 14 potential events will be sent in this exact order:

1 Capture phase:
  a Capture event dispatched on `window`
  b Capture event dispatched on `document`
  c Capture event dispatched on the `<html>` element

   d Capture event dispatched on the `<body>` element

   e Capture event dispatched on the `<header>` element

   f Capture event dispatched on the `<nav>` element

2 Target phase:

   a Target event (registered as capture listener) dispatched on the `<button>` element

   b Target event (registered as bubble listener) dispatched on the `<button>` element

3 Bubbling phase:

   a Bubble event dispatched on the `<nav>` element

   b Bubble event dispatched on the `<header>` element

   c Bubble event dispatched on the `<body>` element

   d Bubble event dispatched on the `<html>` element

   e Bubble event dispatched on `document`

   f Bubble event dispatched on `window`

Events 2.a and 2.b might seem similar, but they will be grouped first into all dispatches to listeners defined as capture listeners, and then into dispatches to listeners defined as bubble listeners. You can, of course, have multiple listeners listening to the same event on the same target. If that happens, events will be dispatched in order of assignment of the listeners.

Let's make a simplified view of the previous figure with only three elements in descending order in figure 8.8.

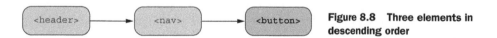

Figure 8.8 Three elements in descending order

Let's say that we add a number of listeners to the different elements in this order:

   A Add a capture listener to `<nav>` element

   B Add a bubble listener to `<button>` element

   C Add a capture listener to `<button>` element

   D Add a capture listener to `<header>` element

   E Add a capture listener to `<nav>` element (again)

   F Add a capture listener to `<button>` element (again)

   G Add a bubble listener to `<nav>` element

These eight listeners (A through G) will be invoked in this order:

1 Capture listeners on `<header>`: D (`eventPhase=CAPTURING_PHASE`)

2 Capture listeners on `<nav>`: A, E (`eventPhase=CAPTURING_PHASE`)

3 Capture listeners on `<button>`: C, F (`eventPhase=AT_TARGET`)

   4 Bubble listeners on `<button>`: B (`eventPhase=AT_TARGET`)

   5 Bubble listeners on `<nav>` element: G (`eventPhase: BUBBLING_PHASE`)

   6 Bubble listeners on `<header>` element: *None*

Note that even though the listeners on the target element itself will be dispatched in the order of capturing listeners first, then bubbling listeners second, they will all be invoked with an event phase of `AT_TARGET`, rather than capturing and bubbling phases, respectively.

8.3.2 Handling event phases in React

Events in React aren't added by adding a listener to a node using a method. Events in React are added by assigning a property to the JSX element that represents that node. Because of that, you can't add an argument to say which phase you're listening to an event in. In React, as in JavaScript, the default is to add events as bubble listeners. When you write

```
<main onClick={onClickHandler}>
  ...
</main>
```

this `onClickHandler` would be added as a bubble phase listener. If you want to add a capture event listener, you have to postfix the event with `*Capture`. For a click handler, that would be `onClickCapture`. So, if you have

```
<main onClickCapture={handler1} onClick={handler4}>
  <button onClickCapture={handler2} onClick={handler3} />
</main>
```

these click handlers would be invoked as `handler1`, `handler2`, `handler3`, and then `handler4`.

Capture handlers are pretty rare. You'll likely never use them or maybe use them only once or twice in a huge application, but they're a great tool to have available when you really need them. They're the julienne peelers of React—rarely used, but when they are, they are perfect for the job!

8.3.3 Unusual event propagation

Four event types have a very unusual event propagation flow in React. This concerns the pairs `mouseEnter`/`mouseLeave` and `pointerEnter`/`pointerLeave`. These pairs of events are related, as the mouse or pointer will enter one element as it leaves the other. The propagation of these events bubble from the element being left to the element being entered, and they don't capture.

Please see the following article for details on this flow if you ever need it: https://barklund.dev/mouseevents. It would only come up in some very specialized cases though, so this is probably not something you need to worry about.

8.3.4 Nonbubbling DOM events

In the DOM, some events don't bubble at all, but they still capture. This only happens for blur and focus events. However, in React, for ease of use, both of these events still bubble as normal, like other events. So, let's say you have this structure in React:

```
<label onFocusCapture={handler1} onFocus={handler3}>
  <input onFocus={handler2} />
</label>
```

If you put the cursor inside the input field, the three event handlers would fire in this order: `handler1`, `handler2`, `handler3`. If you implemented the same thing without React and added the event listeners using JavaScript, `handler3` would never fire because it's an event in the bubbling phase of an event type that doesn't bubble.

There is a technical reason for these events not bubbling in HTML, but because it's pretty confusing for developers (and very easy to forget), React simply bubbles these events as well. As a React developer, you don't need to worry about this and can just use the focus and blur events as normal events, which we actually already did in the beginning of this section.

> **Why focus and blur events don't bubble in HTML**
>
> When the window loses focus by the user (because the user switches tabs in the browser or even switches to a different program), a blur event will be dispatched on the window object. Similarly, when the window regains focus by a user returning to the same window/tab in the browser, a focus event will be dispatched on the window object.
>
> If a focus or blur event on an input field or button bubbled, it would have to bubble all the way up to the window object. Then, you as a developer could be confusing the event for the window losing/gaining focus by the user. You would be able to tell the two occurrences apart by examining the `.target` property of the event, but for historical reasons, these events don't bubble simply to make sure this confusion doesn't happen.
>
> In React, that's not a problem because you can't assign a React event listener to the window object. You can only assign React event listeners to actual HTML elements (and the window object isn't an HTML element) and only those inside your application (which goes somewhere inside the `<body>` element). For this reason, focus and blur events *do* bubble in React.

8.4 Default actions and how to prevent them

Browsers have default actions as the consequence of some events. Most of the time, you as a developer want these default actions to occur, but sometimes you don't. In this next example, we'll see a default action that you don't want the browser to do, and we'll see how to prevent it from happening.

Let's say we want to create an administrator login form in React with a password field and a login button. When the user clicks the button, we want our code to check if the password matches the secret string "platypus". If it does, whatever secret information we have inside our application should be revealed to the clearly legit administrator. Let's start by creating this in the following listing.

Listing 8.7   Admin form (potentially broken?)

```
import { useState } from "react";
function Admin() {
  const [password, setPassword] = useState("");
  const [isAdmin, setAdmin] = useState(false);
  const onClick = () => {
    if (password === "platypus") {
      setAdmin(true);
    }
  };
  return (
    <>
      {isAdmin && <h1>Bacon is delicious!</h1>}
      <form>
        <input
          type="password"
          onChange={
            (evt) => setPassword(evt.target.value)
          }
        />
        <button onClick={onClick}>
          Login
        </button>
      </form>
    </>
  );
}
function App() {
  return <Admin />;
}
export default App;
```

- Stores the entered password in a state value
- Stores whether the user is approved as an admin user in another state value
- When the user clicks the button, checks if the entered password matches the expectation and, if so, updates the state
- Displays conditional JSX depending on whether the user is approved as an admin user or not
- Our input field will update the state password when changed.
- Our button will call the event handler when clicked.

If you spin this up in a browser, enter something into the input field, and click the button, something unexpected happens. The whole page reloads, and the input field is cleared. That's not at all what we wanted here and seems like a completely arbitrary result. Why did this happen?

8.4.1   *The default event action*

If we create an HTML form with a button on a webpage and click the button, the page will reload. This is the default behavior in HTML.

Let's say we put this HTML (note that we're talking about plain HTML at this point, not JSX) into a file and open it in a browser:

```
<form>
  <button>Click me</button>
</form>
```

Clicking this button reloads the page. That's because a button inside a form causes the form to submit, and when a form submits, the variables inside the form will be sent to the target URL of the form. This happens even if the form doesn't have any inputs and even if the form doesn't have an explicit target URL (the default target URL is the page itself).

Knowing this information, we now see what we did wrong before. Our button inside our application would submit the form, and submitting a form causes the page to reload by default.

8.4.2 Preventing default

With our newfound knowledge, we'll do two things in our form to make it work correctly. First, we'll move the event handler from clicking the button to submitting the form. It's the same handler, we just assign it to the onSubmit property of the form rather than the onClick property of the button.

Second, we need to tell the form not to perform the default action that it normally does when submitting. We do that by invoking evt.preventDefault() on the event object passed to the event handler. Let's implement this in the next listing.

> **Listing 8.8 Admin form (potentially fixed?)**

```
import { useState } from "react";
function Admin() {
  const [password, setPassword] = useState("");
  const [isAdmin, setAdmin] = useState(false);
  const onSubmit = (evt) => {                 ⟵──┐  Accepts the event object as
    evt.preventDefault();               ⟵─────┐  │  an argument to the event
    if (password === "platypus") {            │  │  handler in order to prevent
      setAdmin(true);                          │  │  the default action
    }
  };                                           │
  return isAdmin ? (                       Invokes the evt.preventDefault
    <h1>Bacon is delicious!</h1>           method in the submit handler
  ) : (                                    regardless of what else happens
                                           in the handler
    <form onSubmit={onSubmit}>
      <input
        type="password"
        onChange={(evt) => setPassword(evt.target.value)}
      />
      <button>Login</button>
    </form>
  );
}
function App() {
  return <Admin />;
}
export default App;
```

Connects the event handler to the form element

And there we go. Our admin form works as intended! We prevented the default event from happening in our form, so the browser native event handler didn't kick in. You can see the result in figure 8.9.

Figure 8.9   The admin login form works, and when we enter the correct password, the secrets of the universe are revealed to us (and apparently those secrets are delicious).

If you press Enter while focusing an input field inside a form that also has a Submit button, the form will be submitted. If we just put our event handler on the button as `onClick`, submitting the form by pressing Enter with focus in the input field would not work as intended, and it would still reload the page because of form submission. By moving our handler to the form's submit event, we handle both ways of submitting a form.

> **NOTE**   This example is, of course, not in any way proper web security. Anything that happens in React is readable by any visitor on your web page, and the preceding security would be compromised in seconds. Be sure to use proper web architecture for creating secure logins.

8.4.3   *Other default events*

Form submit events have a default action, where the form actually submits to the target URL with all the values entered into the form. This is one of the default events used in the browser, but definitely not the only one.

Clicking a link will create a click event on the link element. The default action for this event is to follow the link and go to the new URL as indicated by the `href` property. Again, you can prevent this default behavior by invoking the `.preventDefault()` method on the click event object received in an event handler. This would mean the browser wouldn't go to the target URL, and effectively nothing would happen.

You can check if an event is cancellable by checking the `.cancellable` property. If true, `.preventDefault()` can be invoked to stop whatever the browser's default action would have been. If false, invoking `.preventDefault()` is still possible, but it just doesn't do anything. Here's an inexhaustive list of cancellable events:

- Scroll events are cancellable, which causes the scroll not to occur and the scroll offset to remain unchanged.
- Key-down, key-press, and key-up events are cancellable and cause the character to not be inserted (if invoked on an input field or text area) or cause whatever the browser would do in case of the given key *not* to happen (e.g., make the browser not scroll the page when canceling the press of Page Up). On the other hand, input events aren't cancellable as they are dispatched after the fact (e.g., after the user typed something or pasted something).
- Drag-start and drag-enter events are cancellable (respectively, causing the drag not to happen at all or causing the drag effect to remain unchanged), but the drag-end and drag-leave events aren't cancellable.

React follows the same procedures for default actions and preventable actions as HTML, so refer to any online HTML guide on which events are cancellable and what the default action is.

8.5   *React event objects in summary*

We've seen a number of different ways to use the event object that React sends to an event handler. Table 8.2 lists a subset of properties that all event objects have in common. A lot of these properties have already been explained in detail in this chapter. These aren't all the properties available on all event objects, but in our opinion, they are the most important ones.

Table 8.2   Important properties common for all event objects in both React and HTML

Property	Purpose
`bubbles`	A Boolean value indicating whether or not the event bubbles
`cancelable`	A Boolean value indicating whether or not the event can be canceled

Table 8.2 Important properties common for all event objects in both React and HTML *(continued)*

Property	Purpose
eventPhase	A numerical value indicating which phase in the event propagation this event belongs to
preventDefault	A method to prevent the browser from handling the event with its default action
stopPropagation	A method to prevent the event from propagating any further
target	The target node that this event was assigned to
timestamp	The time at which the event was created in milliseconds
type	The type of event that caused this event object to be dispatched

8.6 *Event handler functions from properties*

When you're creating reusable UI elements, a vital part is to create generalized interface elements that you can then use in other locations without having to style them every time. For this purpose, let's now create a styled generalized button component that can be reused over and over. We'll use this generalized button component to create a counter with Increment and Decrement buttons—but styled. We want to create something that looks like figure 8.10—look at those stylish buttons.

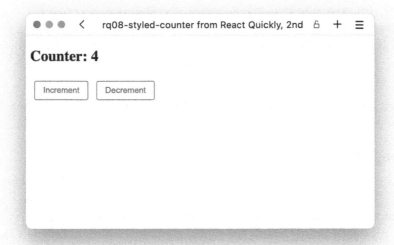

Figure 8.10 The final application with the counter already increased a few times. Don't these buttons look just a bit nicer than the default ones we're used to seeing?

We'll structure the application shown in the JSX diagram in figure 8.11.

As you can see, we'll pass a function, `handleClick`, to each of the button component instances, which should internally be assigned to the button as the click handler. Let's implement this in listing 8.9.

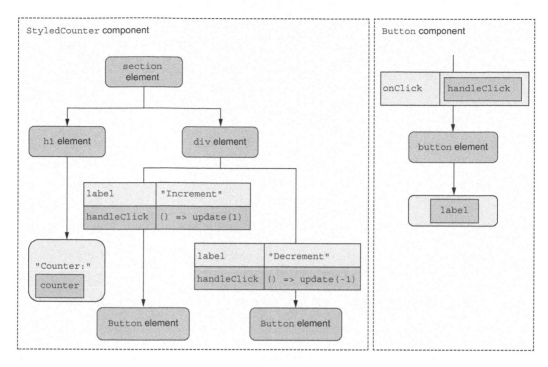

Figure 8.11   Our styled counter application will include two instances of our button component with slightly different properties.

Listing 8.9   Styled counter

```
import { useState } from "react";
function Button({ handleClick, label }) {
  const buttonStyle = {
    color: "blue",
    border: "1px solid",
    background: "transparent",
    borderRadius: ".25em",
    padding: ".5em 1em",
    margin: ".5em",
  };
  return (
    <button style={buttonStyle} onClick={handleClick}>
      {label}
    </button>
  );
}
function StyledCounter() {
  const [counter, setCounter] = useState(0);
  const update = (d) => setCounter((v) => v + d);
  return (
    <section>
      <h1>Counter: {counter}</h1>
      <div>
```

> Directly assigns the received
> handleClick property as the
> onClick event handler inside
> the button component

```
      <Button
        handleClick={() => update(1)}          ◁——   When buttons are clicked,
        label="Increment"                              sets the handleClick
      />                                               property to a function
      <Button                                          updating the state
        handleClick={() => update(-1)}        ◁——
        label="Decrement"
      />
    </div>
  </section>
  );
}
function App() {
  return <StyledCounter />;
}
export default App;
```

> ### Repository: rq08-styled-counter
> This example can be seen in repository `rq08-styled-counter`. You can use that
> repository by creating a new app based on the associated template:
>
> `$ npx create-react-app rq08-styled-counter --template rq08-styled-counter`
>
> Alternatively, you can go to this website to browse the code, see the application in
> action directly in your browser, or download the source code as a zip file:
>
> https://rq2e.com/rq08-styled-counter

This looks pretty good and is a nice, compact, well-defined application. However,
something is slightly weird. When we use our button components, we assign a function
that should be invoked when the button is clicked. However, in listing 8.9, because we
assign the function directly as the `onClick` property to the button, the function is
invoked with an event object as the first and only argument. Sometimes, this might be
a good solution, but other times this isn't ideal. The outside component should not
have access to this event object because it's an internal implementation detail of the
button component.

   To remove this event from the function invocation, we have to create another function as the event handler and, when invoked, call the `handleClick` property (without
any arguments). That would look something like this:

```
function Button({ handleClick, label }) {      ◁—┤  Still receives a handleClick
  const buttonStyle = {...};                          property as before
  const onClick = () => handleClick();        ◁————————      Now creates a local
  return (                                                    function that, when
    <button style={buttonStyle} onClick={onClick}>  ◁—┐      called, invokes the
      {label}                                            passed property
    </button>         Assigns this local function as
  );                   the event handler, not the
}                          passed property
```

Note that we've named the event listener as a property `handle*`. That is a fairly common practice when passing functions as properties to elements that aren't directly event listeners themselves, but rather just callbacks that will be invoked by event listeners or effects as needed. We could also have named this property `onClick`, but that would make it seem like an event listener, and users would expect it to act as an event listener (and we would definitely have to send the event object to it as an argument).

You'll see many examples of function properties invoked as callbacks (either directly as event listeners or inside event listeners) in real-life codebases because it's a very common way to design reusable UI component libraries. We'll also use this structure in future chapters. We'll use `on*` naming for direct event handlers (that receive an event object) and `handle*` naming for callbacks (that either don't take any arguments or take some custom arguments).

8.7 Event handler generators

If you have many event handler functions that only vary slightly, you might want to generalize them into an *event handler generator*. Let's take our earlier example of a counter with Increment and Decrement buttons. We generalized these two different functions into a single function that updates the value based on an argument, and then we called *that* function with different arguments in the click event handler on the two buttons:

```
function Counter() {
  const [counter, setCounter] = useState(0);
  const update = (delta) =>           A generic function for updating
    setCounter((c) => c + delta);     the counter value with a delta
  return (
    <>
      <h1>Value: {counter}</h1>
      <button onClick={() => update(1)}>      Invokes update with two
        Increment                             different values in the
      </button>                               event handlers
      <button onClick={() => update(-1)}>
        Decrement
      </button>
    </>
  );
}
```

We can take this concept one step further. Note that in both event handlers, we're still defining a function that then calls `update` (both have an arrow definition such as `() =>` `update`). We can move that function definition inside the `update` function with a *curried* function. This turns the `update` function into an event handler *generator*, which returns an event handler when invoked. So, it's a function that returns another function:

```
function Counter() {
  const [counter, setCounter] = useState(0);
  const update = (delta) => () =>          A generic event handler generator for
    setCounter((c) => c + delta);          updating the counter value with a delta
```

```
return (
  <>
    <h1>Value: {counter}</h1>
    <button onClick={update(1)}>Increment</button>
    <button onClick={update(-1)}>Decrement</button>
  </>
);
}
```

Invokes the event handler
generator in the event
handlers to generate an
event handler with a
specific delta

This might look a bit esoteric, and it's not essential that you fully understand the logic here. Just note that this is a fairly common approach used by many developers, so you might see it in your everyday work. We'll revisit this approach of using event handler generators in the next chapter on event handling in forms, so you'll get some more experience with the concept there.

8.8   Listening to DOM events manually

Sometimes, you want to be able to listen for events on nodes not directly controlled by React, whereas other times, you want to manually control whether to listen for events at all. For both of these purposes, you can listen for events directly on the DOM nodes in regular JavaScript, circumventing React's event listener setup. Here are some example situations where you might want to manually manage event listeners:

- You want to listen for events on the window or document object.
- You want to listen for events on HTML nodes not directly included inside the React application, such as body, which can never be inside your React application, but could also just be some node outside of the control of the React application.
- You want to listen for events on non-DOM objects, such as a request, socket, or any other JavaScript object.
- You want to listen for a single event on a particular node but don't care about more than one instance of the event occurring.
- You want to conditionally listen for an event on a node.

The first three examples in this list are only possible by listening directly on the nodes, but the two latter two are still possible using React. However, both would require extra work that might not be necessary. In the following subsection, you'll see how to achieve each of the items in the preceding list through manually listening to DOM events by going outside of the React architecture.

8.8.1   Listening for window and document events

Let's say that we want to display the size of the browser window in our application. We can display the size of the browser window when the component renders the first time by looking at window.innerWidth and window.innerHeight. But if the user resizes the window while our component is mounted, it won't automatically re-render, and we won't update our displayed value.

To make sure our component updates when the window resizes, we need to listen for the resize event on the window object. Because this is an event not managed by React, we need to attach our listener directly on the window object using `window .addEventListener`. But we also need to make sure to remove our event listener again if our component unmounts by calling `window.removeEventListener`.

If you remember back to chapter 6 on component life cycles, this might seem like a perfect candidate for a `useEffect` hook—and, it is! We'll combine this with a `use-State` hook to achieve a component that works something like the flowchart outlined in figure 8.12. The implementation in shown in listing 8.10.

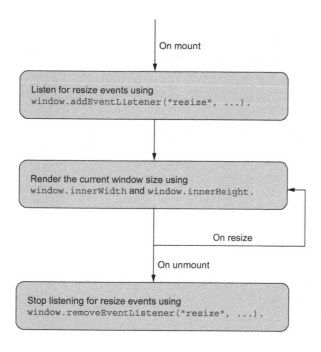

Figure 8.12 The `WindowSize` component must add a listener on mount and remove it again as the component unmounts. While mounted, the browser will invoke our callback if the browser window ever resizes.

Listing 8.10   Window size display

First, a little utility function to get a nice display value for the size of the browser window

```
import { useState, useEffect } from "react";
function getWindowSize() {
  return `${window.innerWidth}x${window.innerHeight}`;
}
function WindowSize() {
  const [size, setSize] = useState(getWindowSize());
  useEffect(() => {
    const onResize = () => setSize(getWindowSize());
    window.addEventListener("resize", onResize);
```

Uses that utility function to initialize our state value

Inside this hook, we define a function to be called when the window resizes.

Sets up an effect hook

Assigns this function as an event listener directly on the window object

```
    return () =>
      window.removeEventListener("resize", onResize);
  }, [setSize]);
  return <h1>Window size: {size}</h1>;
}
function App() {
  return <WindowSize />;
}
export default App;
```

Because it's an effect hook, we need to set up our dependencies. They only contain the setSize function, which we know to be stable, but is included anyway for transparency.

Renders the actual window size in the returned JSX

Makes sure that our effect hook returns a cleanup function, which removes the listener again

---

Repository: rq08-window-size

This example can be seen in repository rq08-window-size. You can use that repository by creating a new app based on the associated template:

```
$ npx create-react-app rq08-window-size --template rq08-window-size
```

Alternatively, you can go to this website to browse the code, see the application in action directly in your browser, or download the source code as a zip file:

https://rq2e.com/rq08-window-size

If you run this app in a browser, you'll see something like figure 8.13.

Figure 8.13   The window size app in action with a small window

This is a very basic example of how to listen for events on a permanent object such as a window or document. This is a common approach for a number of events that only occur on those two objects or to catch all events of some type that bubble all the way up to them.

Note the clever use of a cleanup function in our useEffect. Because we define our listener function inside the effect, add the listener in the effect, and—in case we need to clean up—remove the listener again, this structure works regardless of our dependencies and regardless of whether our function mounts and remounts several times.

However, also note that because we're not using React's clever trick of only listening to events once and manually remembering who listens for what, we're adding a listener to the window object for every instance of our component. If this was an element in a long list of similar elements, we would be adding a new listener for every element that we added. That definitely seems pointless if we could instead be adding a single listener. When adding events directly on DOM nodes, you might have to pay extra attention to how to optimize them.

8.8.2   Dealing with unsupported HTML events

Now let's look at how to listen for the few DOM events that are *not* supported by React, for example, transition events. These events are dispatched by CSS actually, when a CSS transition is assigned, started, ended, and canceled. Of these four events, only the ended event is supported directly in React, using the onTransitionEnd property.

Let's create a component with an element with a transition. We want to display a text in a transition from red to blue and back again. We'll trigger this transition with two different buttons that set the color directly on the HTML node using the node's style object. We then want to display in the headline whether the transition is running or not.

While we can listen for the transitionend event in React using the onTransition-End property, we can't listen to the transitionstart event in the same way. So, for ease of use, we'll listen for both events using a regular DOM listener. Let's combine all of this in the following listing. You can see the result in figure 8.14.

Listing 8.11   Transition events

We also need a local variable that points to the DOM element so we can access the element in the cleanup function.

```
import { useState, useRef, useEffect } from "react";
function Transition() {
  const [isRunning, setRunning] = useState(false);
  const div = useRef();
  useEffect(() => {
    const onStart = () => setRunning(true);
    const onEnd = () => setRunning(false);
    const node = div.current;
    node.addEventListener("transitionstart", onStart);
    node.addEventListener("transitionend", onEnd);
    return () => {
      node.removeEventListener(
        "transitionstart", onStart
      );
      node.removeEventListener("transitionend", onEnd);
    };
  }, [setRunning]);
```

Because we need to reference an HTML element, we need to use the useRef hook.

Creates two callbacks inside an effect hook to use as listeners

Adds the listeners in the effect hook directly on the DOM element

Removes the same listeners from the same object on cleanup

```
    return (
      <section>
        <h1>Transition is {!isRunning && "not"} running</h1>
        <div
          style={{ color: "red", transition: "color 1s linear" }}
          ref={div}                                              ◁──┐  Sets the ref
        >                                                            │  property on our
          COLORFUL TEXT                                              │  target element
        </div>
        <button onClick={() => (div.current.style.color = "blue")}>
          Go blue
        </button>
        <button onClick={() => (div.current.style.color = "red")}>
          Go red
        </button>
      </section>
    );
}
function App() {
  return <Transition />;
}
export default App;
```

Figure 8.14 If you click the two buttons, you'll see the text change color from red to blue to red, and the headline will reflect whether the animation is running or not. As a bonus, notice that if you click the Go Red button while the text is already red, the transition never starts, so the headline never changes.

Repository: rq08-transition

This example can be seen in repository rq08-transition. You can use that repository by creating a new app based on the associated template:

```
$ npx create-react-app rq08-transition --template rq08-transition
```

> Alternatively, you can go to this website to browse the code, see the application in action directly in your browser, or download the source code as a zip file:
>
> https://rq2e.com/rq08-transition

This is an example of one of those unique cases where you need to listen for one of the few events not directly supported in React. That's because this event is rarely used in an application, but that doesn't mean it doesn't have its use cases.

Applications with complex scenarios are more likely to use direct DOM listeners on HTML nodes. In these situations, listeners can change based on other criteria, and it makes more sense to manage the event listeners manually rather than relying on JSX and React to add and remove listeners for us. We have an example of that coming up next.

8.8.3   *Combining React and DOM event handling*

In this example, we'll use a combination of React's event listeners with manual DOM event listeners. Let's create a menu that pops up when we click a button, and then closes again when we click the mouse anywhere outside the menu. We'll create this application in two iterations. We'll first implement it in a slightly naive way, but as we find a bug, we'll fix that bug and then implement the component correctly.

For now, let's consider the flow of events. We need to listen for clicks on the button that open the menu. We know how to do that using `onClick` in React. But then we also need to listen for mouse-down events anywhere when the menu is opened. To do that, we need to listen for any mouse down (or pointer down, so we also catch touch events) on the window object, and we need to assign this handler in an effect hook. This flow of events is illustrated in figure 8.15, and the implementation is shown in the next listing.

Listing 8.12   An expandable menu (naive version)

```
import { useState, useEffect } from "react";        Stores whether the menu is
function Menu() {                                    expanded or not in a state
  const [isExpanded, setExpanded] = useState(false); ◁─ value (default false)
  useEffect(() => {
    if (!isExpanded) {          ◁──────────    Aborts early inside our effect hook
      return;                                  if the menu isn't expanded (nothing
    }                                          to do, in this case)
    const onWindowClick = () => setExpanded(false);  ◁──
    window.addEventListener(                              If the menu is expanded,
      "pointerdown", onWindowClick                        we create a listener that
    );                                                    will collapse the menu
    return () => window.removeEventListener(              again to be invoked
      "pointerdown", onWindowClick                        when the mouse is
    );                                                    clicked anywhere inside
                                                          the window.
```

Adds the listener to the window object

Removes the listener again on cleanup

```
        }, [isExpanded]);
        return (
          <main>
            <button onClick={() => setExpanded(true)}>
              Show menu
            </button>
            {isExpanded && (
              <div style={{ border: "1px solid black", padding: "1em" }}>
                This is the menu
              </div>
            )}
          </main>
        );
      }
      function App() {
        return <Menu />;
      }
      export default App;
```

Causes the menu button to simply toggle the expanded flag to true

Renders our menu if the expanded flag is true

Because we have isExpanded in the dependency array, this hook will rerun every time the menu changes state from expanded to collapsed and vice versa.

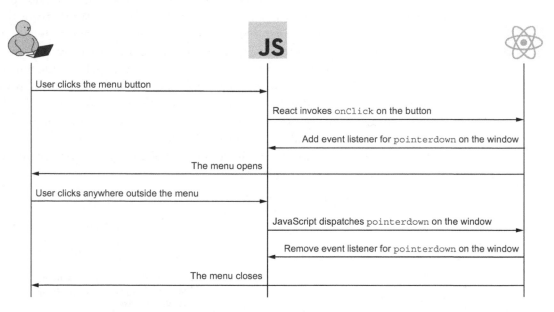

Figure 8.15   The flowchart that governs our menu component

Repository: rq08-naive-menu

This example can be seen in repository rq08-naive-menu. You can use that repository by creating a new app based on the associated template:

```
$ npx create-react-app rq08-naive-menu --template rq08-naive-menu
```

Alternatively, you can go to this website to browse the code, see the application in action directly in your browser, or download the source code as a zip file:

https://rq2e.com/rq08-naive-menu

Figure 8.16 shows this application running in the browser. However, there is a slight problem. If you try this out, and click *outside* the menu when it's expanded, the menu does correctly close. However, if you click *inside* the menu, it also closes. That's not good. We want the user to be able to interact with our menu because we'll probably have some buttons or links in there at a later point.

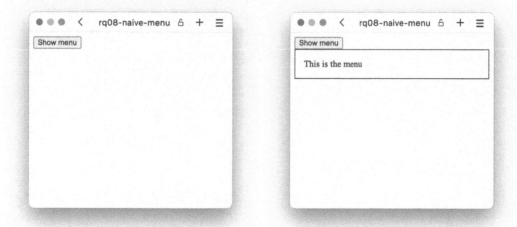

Figure 8.16   The menu app when collapsed and expanded, respectively

What we want is to close the menu only when the user clicks the mouse outside the menu, not when they do it inside the menu. The tricky part is to do something when clicking the mouse "anywhere" except in a specific location. To do this, we'll use three techniques that we've learned so far:

- When we expand the menu, we'll add a listener on the window object for any pointer-down events that happen on the window. When invoked, we'll collapse the menu just like before.
- This time, we'll also add an event listener on the menu itself that will block these pointer events inside it from bubbling to the window object. We do this by stopping the propagation of those events.
- Because we're going to need a reference to our menu DOM node, we need to use a `useRef` hook.

By combining these three things, we'll ensure that any mouse down *inside the window* (even on elements completely outside React's control) will cause our menu to collapse, but any mouse down *inside the menu* won't cause our menu to collapse because we've ensured that these events don't bubble to the window object. We've captured this flow of events in figure 8.17 and implemented it in listing 8.13.

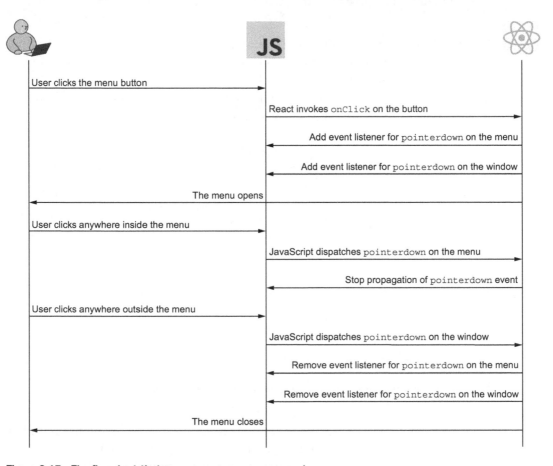

Figure 8.17   The flowchart that governs our menu component

Stops pointer events inside the menu itself to close the menu by suppressing propagation of pointer events from "escaping" beyond the menu node

```
import { useRef, useState, useEffect } from "react";
function Menu() {
  const [isExpanded, setExpanded] = useState(false);
  useEffect(() => {
    if (!isExpanded) {
      return;
    }
    const onWindowClick = () => setExpanded(false);
    const onMenuClick = (evt) => evt.stopPropagation();
```

```
      const menu = menuRef.current;
      window.addEventListener("pointerdown", onWindowClick);
      menu.addEventListener("pointerdown", onMenuClick);
      return () => {
        window.removeEventListener(
          "pointerdown", onWindowClick
        );
        menu.removeEventListener(
          "pointerdown", onMenuClick
        );
      };
    }, [isExpanded]);
    const menuRef = useRef();
    return (
      <main>
        <button onClick={() => setExpanded(true)}>Show menu</button>
        {isExpanded && (
          <div
            ref={menuRef}
            style={{ border: "1px solid black", padding: "1em" }}
          >
            This is the menu
          </div>
        )}
      </main>
    );
}
function App() {
  return <Menu />;
}
export default App;
```

Adds a listener to the menu element — Adds a listener to the menu element

Before we assign a listener to the menu element, we need to capture a reference to said element via the ref.

Removes both of these listeners on cleanup

We need a useRef to store our reference to the menu element.

Assigns our reference to the proper JSX element

Repository: rq08-menu

This example can be seen in repository `rq08-menu`. You can use that repository by creating a new app based on the associated template:

```
$ npx create-react-app rq08-menu --template rq08-menu
```

Alternatively, you can go to this website to browse the code, see the application in action directly in your browser, or download the source code as a zip file:

https://rq2e.com/rq08-menu

If you run this app in a browser, you'll see the same thing as before in figure 8.16. Observe that when you expand the menu, you can collapse the menu by clicking anywhere except on the menu itself (i.e., except when inside the big box with a black border).

Notice how we use a variety of hooks and even combine React event listeners with DOM event listeners to achieve this result. All of these low-level elements go together nicely in a simple component that does exactly what we want it to do.

8.9   Quiz

1 What is the correct way to add a click listener to a JSX button?

  a `<button click={onClick}>Click me</button>`

  b `<button click="onClick">Click me</button>`

  c `<button onClick={onClick}>Click me</button>`

  d `<button onClick="onClick">Click me</button>`

2 React event handlers can also be assigned by calling `addEventListener` on the JSX element. *True* or *false?*

3 Event bubbling is rare and only happens for a few event types. *True* or *false?*

4 If you don't want a form to reload the page when submitted, what do you do?

  a Assign the listener as a capture listener.

  b Invoke `evt.preventDefault()` on the event object.

  c Assign the listener manually on the HTML node.

  d Invoke `evt.stopPropagation()` on the event object.

5 You can't listen to events on HTML nodes that aren't inside the React application. *True* or *false?*

Quiz answers

1 `<button onClick={onClick}>Click me</click>`.

2 *False.* React event handlers can only be assigned using a property, for example, `onClick`. They can't be assigned using `addEventListener`.

3 *False.* All events bubble in React—even some events that don't bubble in HTML.

4 If you want to cancel the default action, you must invoke `evt.preventDefault()` on the event object. An HTML form would cause the page to reload on submission as the default action.

5 *False.* You can use manual DOM event listeners to listen for events on any HTML node as long as you have a reference to it.

Summary

- Events are essential to creating interactive web applications. Events are the way an application reacts to user input.

- Events are also used to communicate between HTML nodes and the React application, for example, when a resource has loaded or a video has finished playing.

- React event listeners are assigned to JSX elements using a property. A click listener is assigned using `onClick`, a paste listener is assigned using `onPaste`, and so on.

- Event listeners are invoked with an event object, which can be used to tell which event occurred, which node caused the event to happen, which phase in the event propagation is currently in process, and several other properties relevant for the specific event.

- Event objects are also used to interrupt the normal progression of event handling by either preventing the browser's default action, stopping further propagation of the event to other event listeners, or both.
- Events propagate from the window object down to the target node and back up to the window again. You can assign listeners to listen for events as they go up or down the tree in order to, for example, interrupt the regular flow or listen for events on multiple targets.
- You can still assign regular event listeners to JavaScript objects and HTML nodes using regular JavaScript. You have to do this sometimes, as not all event types are supported in React, nor are all HTML nodes accessible through React.

Working with *9* forms in React

Imagine the web without forms: You can't log in anywhere. You can't order anything in a web shop. You can't chat with anyone. And, you can't even complain about it because there's no contact form!

Forms are the backbone of many interactive web applications. Forms, and form elements in particular, are the primary way to capture user input in input fields, check boxes, drop-downs, file uploads, and a bunch more related elements.

Because forms are so important, any decent web framework has to support handling form data. React is very capable of dealing with forms. In fact, proper handling of form data was one of the earliest priorities in the React codebase because it was essential for the work React was developed for.

You can work with forms in React in one of two ways. You can let React control the state of the form and store the current values in the component state, which is the recommended and primary way. It's the recommended way because you keep the logic and data flow inside React. Having your React application be in control of your entire application is often preferred over handing out control to other parties or applications. In this instance, you take control from the browser's automatic form handling and let React deal with it.

Alternatively, you can let HTML have the responsibility of the form state and only read it in React when required. This has the benefit of using the browser's built-in form handling, but it comes with a loss of control in your application. An uncontrolled input value is at the mercy of the user and the browser. Your application can't (easily) force it to conform to any rules you might want to apply.

We call these two options *controlled* and *uncontrolled*, respectively. We'll dig into what those two different modes entail and how they affect your options and your architecture in this chapter.

By the end of this chapter, you'll be able to create complex forms with all sorts of inputs, including text fields, date fields, number inputs, ranges, buttons, and dropdowns. Figure 9.1 shows a full list of all the input variants that you can use in React, and, by the end of this chapter, you'll be able to wield all of them in your React applications. You'll also be able to spot the instances where an uncontrolled form might be better than the default of using a controlled form, although those instances are likely rare.

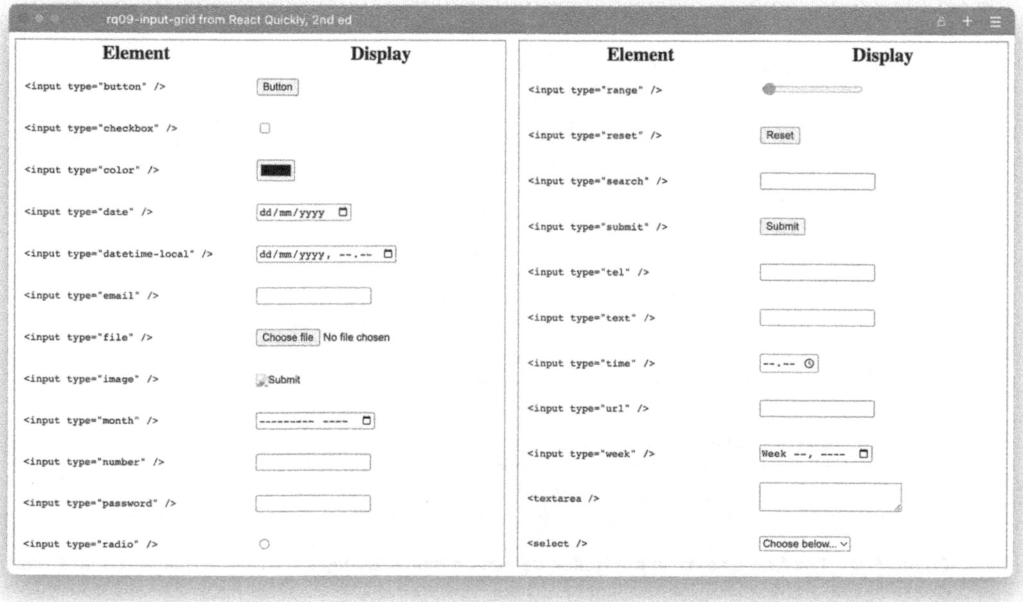

Figure 9.1 All the different HTML input controls that you can also use in React

NOTE   The source code for the examples in this chapter is available at https://rq2e.com/ch09. But as you learned in chapter 2, you can instantiate all the examples directly from the command line using a single command.

9.1 Controlled vs. uncontrolled inputs

When an input is controlled, React is in charge of what gets displayed. React has to "confirm" that a given change to the input value is going to cause the input to change. When an input is uncontrolled, the input changes based on the user's interactions, and React can only passively read the state, but not affect or change it.

The difference between these two approaches is highlighted in figure 9.2. Note actions 4 and 5 on the controlled version of the diagram, in particular. These two interactions are mandatory. On the other hand, in the uncontrolled version, action 4.b is optional, and action 5.b is completely missing because this action isn't possible.

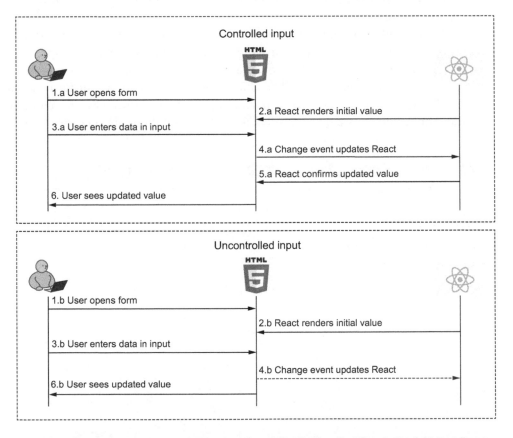

Figure 9.2   **The flow of data in controlled versus uncontrolled inputs differs in the fact that React doesn't control the value after the input has been rendered. Action 5.a highlights React's control over the input even after the user interacts with it—React can intercept updates and change them on the fly or even ignore them. In the uncontrolled input on the bottom, React has no such control, and whatever the user enters will be displayed in the input.**

On both versions of the diagram, React can decide what the initial value is. But only on the controlled version of the diagram can React control what the value is after the user starts inputting data.

In situations where you don't need to control the input after the initial value, you can use either mode. In situations where you want to control the input as the user is entering data—for example, when you want to filter the input or apply some formatting mask on it—then you have to use a controlled input. There are never situations where you *must* use an uncontrolled input, so there is no reason to use it. The option exists mostly for performance reasons. In the next two sections, we'll look at some examples of how to indicate that your input is of the given type and then use it.

9.2 Managing controlled inputs

For this example, we want to create a very basic input form. We'll build a simple calculator with two different inputs and an output, which will display the sum of the two values. To achieve this result, we need to create JSX, as shown in figure 9.3.

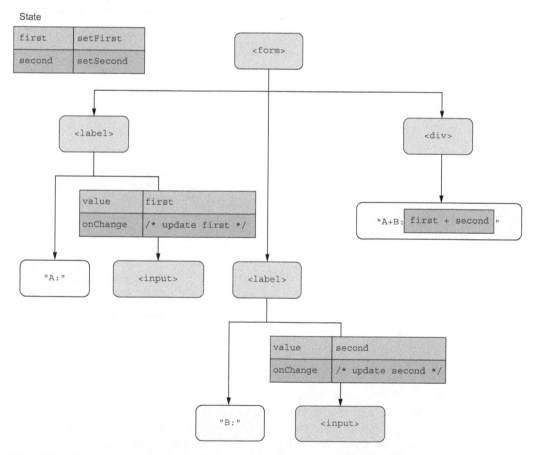

Figure 9.3 The desired output JSX for our calculator contains two inputs. Note how we pass two specific properties to both inputs: `value` **and** `onChange`.

As you can see, we specify both the `value` and `onChange` properties for our inputs, which is required to make a controlled input. In fact, this is the definition of a controlled input. If you set the value directly in React, you must also listen for the change event and update the value, which makes your input controlled. If you don't set a value in React, you don't need to listen for updates because you can't control the input anyway.

As a bonus, to make sure the inputs are numbers, we'll also set their types to `"number"`. Let's go ahead and implement this in the following listing. If you try this out in the browser, you should see something like figure 9.4.

Listing 9.1   Summation

```
import { useState } from "react";
function Sum() {
  const [first, setFirst] = useState(0);
  const [second, setSecond] = useState(0);
  const onChangeFirst = (evt) =>
    setFirst(evt.target.valueAsNumber);
  const onChangeSecond = (evt) =>
    setSecond(evt.target.valueAsNumber);
  return (
    <form style={{ display: "flex", flexDirection: "column" }}>
      <label>
        A:
        <input
          type="number"
          value={first}
          onChange={onChangeFirst}
        />
      </label>
      <label>
        B:
        <input
          type="number"
          value={second}
          onChange={onChangeSecond}
        />
      </label>
      <div>A+B: {first + second}</div>
    </form>
  );
}
function App() {
  return <Sum />;
}
export default App;
```

Initializes two state values. We don't have to initialize them to 0; any start numbers will work here.

Creates two almost identical change handlers that just update different state values from the input events

Assigns the correct values and change listeners to the two inputs

Displays the output in the end, which is the sum of the two state values

---

Repository: rq09-controlled-sum

This example can be seen in repository `rq09-controlled-sum`. You can use that repository by creating a new app based on the associated template:

```
$ npx create-react-app rq09-controlled-sum --template rq09-controlled-sum
```

Alternatively, you can go to this website to browse the code, see the application in action directly in your browser, or download the source code as a zip file:

https://rq2e.com/rq09-controlled-sum

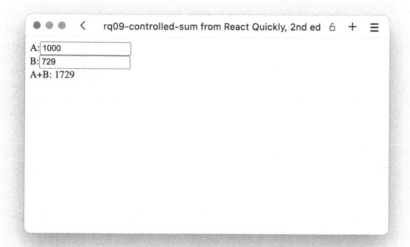

Figure 9.4   Our summation component in action. The sum of 1000 and 729 is indeed 1729 (as Ramanujan pointed out).

Note that we've set both `value` and `onChange` as properties on the inputs—that's not a coincidence. These two properties are the exact properties you need to specify to use a controlled input, and you need to make sure that the value changes when the change handler is invoked. You can also change the value at other times, but you *must* update the value when the change handler updates. If not, the information entered by the user will be ignored.

9.2.1   *Filtered input*

If you don't update the state value when data has been entered, the input field doesn't update. You can, of course, use this behavior selectively. Let's say we want to add an input for a hex color and next to that a small square that displays that same color.

A hex color is six hexadecimal digits, so 0–9 and A–F. Because nondigits are allowed, we can't rely on `type="number"` as we did before. We'll use a regular `type="text"` input for this, but we need to filter the input so only the valid characters make it into the actual text field after the user has entered some data. See the diagram in figure 9.5.

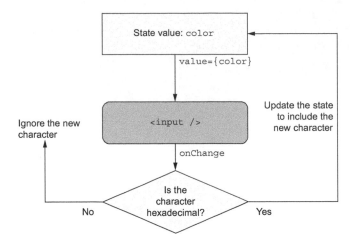

Figure 9.5   The data flow in our color display component includes a filter in the `onChange` event handler. We'll strip out nonhexadecimal characters from the input string before we "confirm" the value back to JSX.

NOTE   We're aware of the special input for selecting colors, namely, `<input type="color" />`, which is supported by all modern browsers. We won't use it here, however, as that would make it too easy.

To do this, we simply apply a filter in the `onChange` function before setting the state value. The input field will then correctly update when we enter valid characters, but ignore any invalid characters. On top of this, we're also going to force all the characters to be uppercase because it just looks nicer. When we display the color, we only display six-character color strings. If the string isn't six characters long, we display a placeholder background to indicate no valid input. Let's implement this in the next listing. If you run this in the browser, you get the result in figure 9.6.

Listing 9.2   Hex color display

```
import { useState } from "react";
const PLACEHOLDER = `conic-gradient(
  gray 0.25turn, white 0 0.5turn,
  gray 0 0.75turn, white 0 1turn
)`;
function HexColor() {
  const [color, setColor] = useState("BADA55");
  const onChange = (evt) =>
    setColor(
      evt.target.value
        .replace(/[^0-9a-f]/gi, "")
        .toUpperCase()
    );
  const outputStyle = {
    width: "20px",
    border: "1px solid",
```

> Defines a static placeholder, which uses a conic gradient to display a checkered background

> Initializes our state to a valid color input

> In the change handler, examines the current value of the input field after the event, filters the input against a regular expression, and uppercases the entire result

```
      background: color.length === 6
        ? `#${color}`
        : PLACEHOLDER,
    };
    return (
      <form style={{ display: "flex" }}>
        <label>
          Hex color:
          <input value={color} onChange={onChange} />
        </label>
        <span style={outputStyle} />
      </form>
    );
  }
  function App() {
    return <HexColor />;
  }
  export default App;
```

> **When we want to output the color value, we first check if the color string is exactly six characters. If good, we precede it with a hash mark in front; otherwise, we display the placeholder instead.**

⟵ **Adds the value and change handler to the input field as before**

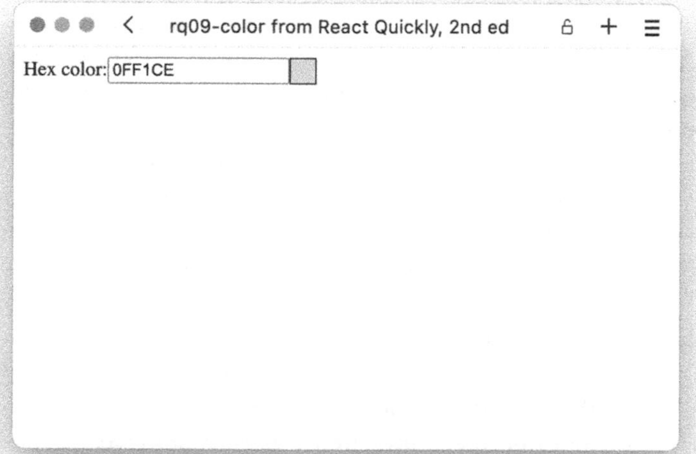

Hex color: `0FF1CE`

Figure 9.6 `0FF1CE` is a valid color—a nice cyan shade.

Repository: rq09-color

This example can be seen in repository `rq09-color`. You can use that repository by creating a new app based on the associated template:

```
$ npx create-react-app rq09-color --template rq09-color
```

Alternatively, you can go to this website to browse the code, see the application in action directly in your browser, or download the source code as a zip file:

https://rq2e.com/rq09-color

Note that in the diagram in figure 9.5, we discussed evaluating the newly input character to either include or discard it, but in the actual source code in the onChange callback in listing 9.2, we don't look at an individual character, but the entire input value every time. This is because inputs aren't necessarily entered one character at a time. The user could paste in a string of characters from their clipboard. If they did so, we would have to check the entire new input rather than a single character. The user can also decide to enter a new character anywhere in the new string, which would complicate things even further. To circumvent all such extra work, we always evaluate the whole input and validate it against our filter.

In addition, note that we decided to initialize the state value to something other than just the empty string this time. This is literally all it takes to set a default value in the input field.

9.2.2   *Masked input*

A more advanced variant of a change handler is to apply a mask to a given input field as the user is typing. For this example, we want to add an input for entering a ticket number for a fictional website. These fictional ticket numbers are defined as three alphanumeric characters followed by a dash followed by another three alphanumeric characters, for example, R1S-T2U.

When we have an input like that, it makes sense to help the user as they are typing. For one thing, we want to display the characters in uppercase regardless of the user entering them as such (we already know how to do that!). Secondly, we want to add a dash after the first three characters. Finally, we want to limit the input to only seven characters total.

This does sound complicated, but it's fairly easy. We just have to modify our onChange to only update the state value with the valid and correctly formatted string and ignore any other input. The actual JavaScript code to accomplish this task is a set of string-formatting operations that together achieve the desired business logic.

This time, we also want to add a placeholder to our input, guiding the user as they are about to enter some data. Let's implement all of this in the next listing. If you run this in the browser, you get the result shown in figure 9.7.

Listing 9.3   Ticket number input

```
import { useState } from "react";
function TicketNumber() {
  const [ticketNumber, setTicketNumber] = useState("");
  const onChange = (evt) => {
```

```
    const [first = "", second = ""] = evt.target.value
      .replace(/[^0-9a-z]/gi, "")
      .slice(0, 6)
      .match(/.{0,3}/g);
    const value = first.length === 3
      ? `${first}-${second}`
      : first;
    setTicketNumber(value.toUpperCase());
  };
  const isValid = ticketNumber.length === 7;
  return (
    <form style={{ display: "flex" }}>
      <label>
        Ticket number:
        <input
          value={ticketNumber}
          onChange={onChange}
          placeholder="E.g. R1S-T2U"
        />
      </label>
      <span>{isValid ? "✓" : "✗"}</span>
    </form>
  );
}
function App() {
  return <TicketNumber />;
}
export default App;
```

If there are exactly three characters in the first part, we help the user by adding a dash to the input field.

If the input is exactly seven characters long, it must be a valid ticket number.

Adds all the properties to the input field, including a placeholder value

Displays an icon at the end indicating whether the input is valid or not

This time we have some more validation of the input value, which results in breaking it down into at most two parts of up to three characters.

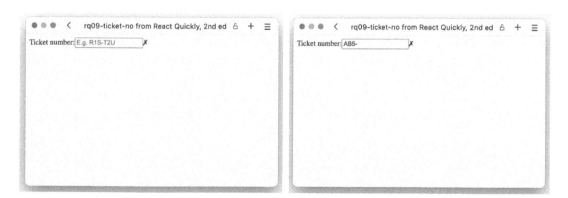

Figure 9.7 This is the output of the Ticket Number input field before and while entering a value. When you try this out, note how the dash is automatically added after entering three characters.

Note that this isn't a perfect solution. If you press Backspace to delete some of the characters, you're prohibited from deleting the dash character because after deleting it, the script will notice that the string is three characters long and automatically add the dash again. Creating such masked inputs can be very tricky. There are some libraries and tutorials out there that can help you if you need to create complex masked inputs like this.

9.2.3   *Many similar inputs*

If you have a form with many inputs, it can get tedious (and cause duplicated code) to create separate state values and change handlers for all of them. Instead, you can have a single state value that contains all your form values and a generic change handler generator that can update any input.

For example, this works for a simple address form that has inputs for address line 1, address line 2, city, zip code, state, and country. We're using plain input fields for all of these without validation because different countries have all sorts of different rules for validating them. Without more information, we'll just let the users enter any data they like in these fields.

We'll keep a single object in state with all the relevant form data, initialized to an empty string. Because we have all the values in the same object indexed by a key, we can use that single key to identify which field to update on each update handler. The resulting JSX will look something like the partial JSX tree displayed in figure 9.8.

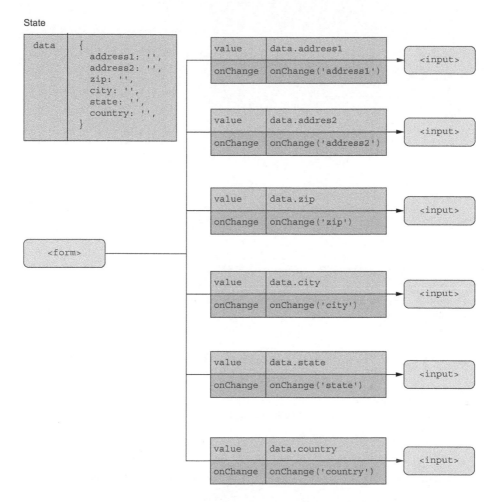

Figure 9.8 A partial DOM tree (it doesn't show labels and other trivial elements) that focuses on the inputs and their properties. Note that we've switched to a left-to-right tree rather than a top-to-bottom tree merely to fit all the elements in.

All we need to do now is create an event handler generator function that takes the property of the state object to set and updates it with the input value from the event object as the event handler is invoked. For this, we must create a function that returns a function, as we saw in chapter 8. Let's put this all together in listing 9.4. If you run this in the browser, you get the result shown in figure 9.9.

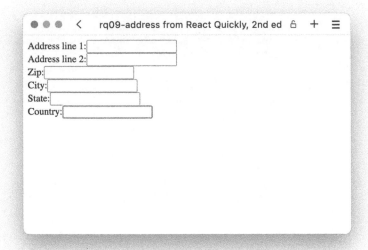

Figure 9.9   The complete address form in the browser—not the prettiest, but fully functional.

Listing 9.4   Address form

```
import { useState } from "react";
function Address() {
  const [data, setData] = useState({
    address1: "",
    address2: "",
    zip: "",
    city: "",
    state: "",
    country: "",
  });
  const onChange = (key) => (evt) => {
    setData((oldData) =>
      ({ ...oldData, [key]: evt.target.value })
    );
  };
  return (
    <form style={{ display: "flex", flexDirection: "column" }}>
      <label>
        Address line 1:
        <input
```

The state is an object this time, holding all the variables that we need.

The onChange function is now a generator that first takes a key and then returns an event handler.

When an input changes, we update the state with the entire old state (to not override any existing values), but we then add in the new value with the indicated key.

```
          value={data.address1}
          onChange={onChange("address1")}
        />
    </label>
    <label>
      Address line 2:
      <input
        value={data.address2}
        onChange={onChange("address2")}
      />
    </label>
    <label>
      Zip:
      <input
        value={data.zip}
        onChange={onChange("zip")}
      />
    </label>
    <label>
      City:
      <input
        value={data.city}
        onChange={onChange("city")}
      />
    </label>
    <label>
      State:
      <input
        value={data.state}
        onChange={onChange("state")}
      />
    </label>
    <label>
      Country:
      <input
        value={data.country}
        onChange={onChange("country")}
      />
    </label>
    </form>
  );
}
function App() {
  return <Address />;
}
export default App;
```

Applies the value
and change handler
to all the inputs

Repository: rq09-address

This example can be seen in repository `rq09-address`. You can use that repository
by creating a new app based on the associated template:

```
$ npx create-react-app rq09-address --template rq09-address
```

(continued)

Alternatively, you can go to this website to browse the code, see the application in action directly in your browser, or download the source code as a zip file:

https://rq2e.com/rq09-address

USING THE NAME PROPERTY

We can take this idea one step further. Form elements can have a name attribute, which is the ID of the field that will be submitted if you use a regular HTML form. We can use that property to contain the key to be updated in the change handler. Then, we don't need to pass the key to the change handler at all because it can examine the name property of the event target. Our JSX would look like figure 9.10 instead (compare with figure 9.8).

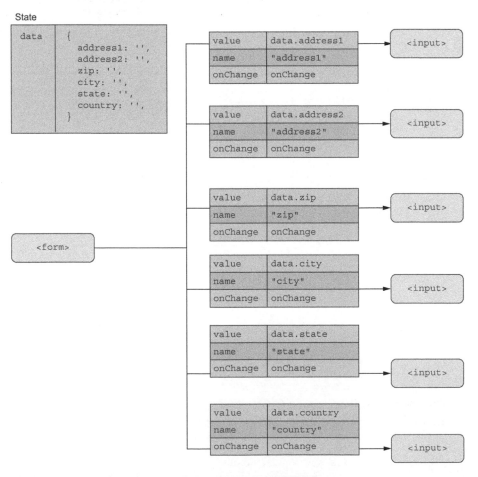

Figure 9.10   A partial DOM tree with our simpler event handlers

Now, we can use the same event handler for every element. The event handler will update the state object with the key taken from the event target name and the value taken from the event target value.

This time, we also want to see that our state actually contains what we think it does. So, at the end, we'll include a `<pre>` element, which dumps out the data variable as a JSON document. We put this all together in the following listing. Take a look at figure 9.11 to see this in action.

Listing 9.5   Simpler address form

```
import { useState } from "react";
function Address() {
  const [data, setData] = useState({
    address1: "",
    address2: "",
    zip: "",
    city: "",
    state: "",
    country: "",
  });
  const onChange = (evt) => {
    const key = evt.target.name;
    const value = evt.target.value;
    setData((oldData) =>
      ({ ...oldData, [key]: value }));
  };
  return (
    <form style={{ display: "flex", flexDirection: "column" }}>
      <label>
        Address line 1:
        <input
          value={data.address1}
          name="address1"
          onChange={onChange}
        />
      </label>
      <label>
        Address line 2:
        <input
          value={data.address2}
          name="address2"
          onChange={onChange}
        />
      </label>
      <label>
        Zip:
        <input
          value={data.zip}
          name="zip"
          onChange={onChange}
        />
      </label>
      <label>
```

The onChange function is now back to being a simple event handler, and we extract the name of the input from the target.

Also extracts the current value in the input field the same way

Updates the state object with the newly changed input

Assigns the name property and a simple event handler to each input node

```
      City:
      <input
        value={data.city}
        name="city"
        onChange={onChange}
      />
    </label>
    <label>
      State:
      <input
        value={data.state}
        name="state"
        onChange={onChange}
      />
    </label>
    <label>
      Country:
      <input
        value={data.country}
        name="country"
        onChange={onChange}
      />
    </label>
    <pre>{JSON.stringify(data, true, 2)}</pre>
  </form>
);
}
function App() {
  return <Address />;
}
export default App;
```

Assigns the name
property and a
simple event handler
to each input node

Prints out a nice JSON
representation of the
current data state so we
can see that we're doing
everything correctly

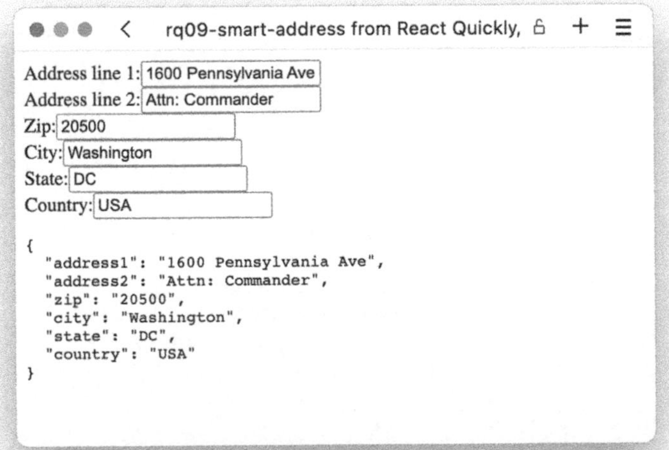

```
●  ●  ●     <     rq09-smart-address from React Quickly,  🔒  +  ☰

Address line 1: 1600 Pennsylvania Ave
Address line 2: Attn: Commander
Zip: 20500
City: Washington
State: DC
Country: USA

{
  "address1": "1600 Pennsylvania Ave",
  "address2": "Attn: Commander",
  "zip": "20500",
  "city": "Washington",
  "state": "DC",
  "country": "USA"
}
```

Figure 9.11   Our smart but simple address form seems to be working
exactly as designed!

Repository: rq09-smart-address

This example can be seen in repository `rq09-smart-address`. You can use that repository by creating a new app based on the associated template:

```
$ npx create-react-app rq09-smart-address --template rq09-smart-address
```

Alternatively, you can go to this website to browse the code, see the application in action directly in your browser, or download the source code as a zip file:

https://rq2e.com/rq09-smart-address

This idea of using the input name property to store the key for the information entered in the input is very common. It's not a requirement but is a very convenient way of organizing forms, especially if they grow large.

This form (and all the forms we created previously in this chapter) is missing something, however. How do we submit this form? What do we do with the data when we submit it? Let's get to that in the next section.

9.2.4   *Form submission*

Let's create a very simple to-do application that is complete, useful, and fully functional. It's a classic exercise to complete in a web framework, so we might as well get it over with.

We want to be able to create new to-do items with a title, category, duration, and due date. We then want to be able to see a list of to-do items created, and, of course, delete items as we complete them. We'll have two different screens: one for displaying the list of items and another for adding a new item.

The important part at this stage is the form handling. We want to create a form with some inputs. When the user submits the form, we want to create a new data object based on the entered data, add it to the list of items, clear the form, and allow the user to add a new one. This flow is shown in figure 9.12.

In this application, we'll store the list of to-do items in memory only, so if you reload the page, you lose all the data. Persisting the data isn't the interesting part; for now, we just want to handle the form data in a logical way. Let's create this application using three components (see their structure in figure 9.13):

- `<App />`—This main component contains the list of items as local state as well as methods for adding and deleting items. It also knows whether we're currently adding an item or looking at the list of all items and provides a small menu for switching between the two views.
- `<List />`—This component accepts a list of items to display as well as a function to call when deleting an item.
- `<Add />`—This component contains a form for entering information about a new item and submitting it. When an item is submitted, you go back to the list. You can also cancel the submission and go back to the list without adding anything.

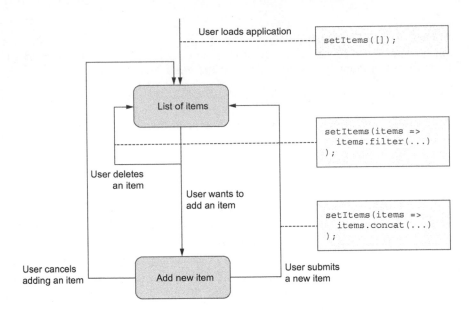

Figure 9.12   The flow of data in our to-do application

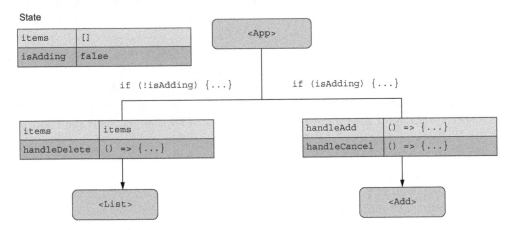

Figure 9.13   A very rough overview of the three components in our application and their relationships

In the end, we want to create an application that looks like figure 9.14.

Now, let's start implementing the main `<App />` component. For this example, we'll use multiple files, so the app component goes in the `App.js` file. The contents are shown in listing 9.6

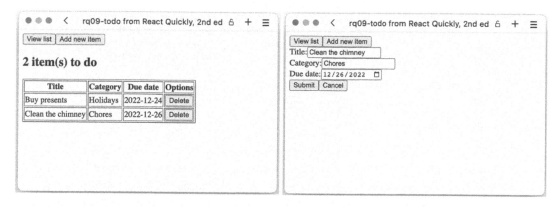

Figure 9.14   The final application when viewing a list of items and adding a new item

Listing 9.6   The main component in `App.js`

When we add an item, we update the state with
all the existing items plus the newly added item.
We then return to the list view.

```
import { useState } from "react";
import List from "./List";
import Add from "./Add";
function App() {
  const [items, setItems] = useState([]);
  const [isAdding, setAdding] = useState(false);
  const handleDelete = (item) =>
    setItems((oldItems) =>
      oldItems.filter((oldItem) => oldItem !== item));
  const handleAdd = (newItem) => {
    setItems((oldItems) => oldItems.concat([newItem]));
    setAdding(false);
  };
  const handleCancel = () => setAdding(false);
  return (
    <main>
      <nav>
        <button onClick={() => setAdding(false)}>
          View list
        </button>
        <button onClick={() => setAdding(true)}>
          Add new item
        </button>
      </nav>
      {isAdding ? (
        <Add
          handleAdd={handleAdd}
          handleCancel={handleCancel}
        />
      ) : (
```

Imports the two detail
views from separate files

The initial state of the
application reflects an
empty list of to-do items
and that we're not
currently adding an item.

When we delete an item,
we update the state with
all the items except the
one to be deleted.

When we cancel adding
an item, we just return
to the list view.

The main
part of the
application
depends on
the current
state—are
we adding an
item or not?

Our menu simply toggles the
flag about whether we're
adding an item or not.

If we're adding an item, we
include the relevant component
with the two necessary callbacks
as properties.

```
        <List
          items={items}
          handleDelete={handleDelete}
        />
      )}
    </main>
  );
}
export default App;
```

> If we're not adding an item, we display a list of all the items, so we need to pass the relevant properties here as well.

With the main `<App />` component out of the way, let's turn our focus to the `<List />` component in `List.js`. It's a lot simpler because it just displays a table of all the items and includes a button next to each one that allows you to delete that item. The component takes two properties: the list of items to display and the callback to call when deleting an item, as implemented in the next listing.

Listing 9.7   The list component in `List.js`

```
function List({ items, handleDelete }) {
  if (!items.length) {
    return <h2>To-do list empty, go out and play!</h2>;       ◄──
  }
  return (
    <>
      <h2>{items.length} item(s) to do</h2>
      <table border="1">
        <thead>
          <tr>
            <th>Title</th>
            <th>Category</th>
            <th>Due date</th>
            <th>Options</th>
          </tr>
        </thead>
        <tbody>
          {items.map((item) => (                               ◄──
            <tr key={JSON.stringify(item)}>
              <td>{item.title}</td>
              <td>{item.category}</td>
              <td>{item.date}</td>
              <td>
                <button
                  onClick={() => handleDelete(item)}           ◄──
                >
                  Delete
                </button>
              </td>
            </tr>
          ))}
        </tbody>
      </table>
    </>
  );
}
export default List;
```

> The important part of this component is the early return in case of no items. There's no need to display a table if there's nothing to fill it with.

> When there is something to display, we loop over all the items and display a table row for each.

> The Delete button invokes the cancel callback function with the entire item as an argument.

Finally, we need to implement the important component for this application: the form to add a new item in the <Add /> component in Add.js. We'll use all the tricks we've seen in this chapter, including a generic change handler for all the inputs that update the component state, based on the input name property. Let's implement this in listing 9.8.

Listing 9.8 The form component in `Add.js`

```
import { useState } from "react";
function Add({ handleAdd, handleCancel }) {
  const [data, setData] = useState({
    title: "",
    category: "",               Initializes our
    date: "",                   state as before
  });
  const onChange = (evt) => {
    const key = evt.target.name;        This is the same change
    const value = evt.target.value;     handler we used in listing
    setData((oldData) =>                9.5—it's a very versatile
      ({ ...oldData, [key]: value }));  construct!
  };
  const onSubmit = (evt) => {       When we submit the form, we need to send the form
    handleAdd(data);               data to the relevant callback and prevent the default
    evt.preventDefault();          form action. If we forget the latter, the page will
  };                               reload and all data will be lost.
  return (
    <form
      onSubmit={onSubmit}
      style={{ display: "flex", flexDirection: "column" }}
    >
      <label>
        Title:
        <input
        value={data.title}
        name="title"
        onChange={onChange}
        />
      </label>
      <label>
        Category:
        <input
        value={data.category}
        name="category"
        onChange={onChange}
        />
      </label>
      <label>
        Due date:
        <input
        type="date"
        value={data.date}
        name="date"
        onChange={onChange}
```

Assigns the submit handler to the form

Assigns the properties to the inputs as normal. Note how we also add type="date" to the due date input.

```
          />
        </label>
        <div>
          <button>Submit</button>
          <button type="button" onClick={handleCancel}>
            Cancel
          </button>
        </div>
      </form>
    );
  }
export default Add;
```

A button is by default a Submit button unless explicitly set to type="button", so this is the Submit button. We don't need a click handler because the form submit handler will take care of that.

The Cancel button must not submit the form, so we have to add an explicit type and then invoke the cancel callback on click.

> **Repository: rq09-todo**
>
> This example can be seen in repository `rq09-todo`. You can use that repository by creating a new app based on the associated template:
>
> ```
> $ npx create-react-app rq09-todo --template rq09-todo
> ```
>
> Alternatively, you can go to this website to browse the code, see the application in action directly in your browser, or download the source code as a zip file:
>
> https://rq2e.com/rq09-todo

This is our first larger application, so we strongly encourage you to play with the source code for this one, if you aren't already doing that for every example. You should begin to see how all the things we've discussed about properties, events, state, JSX, and component composition go together in this application and are rounded off by our new knowledge about form handling to create a small but very powerful application.

Nothing is stopping us from expanding this to include all sorts of new elements. We can have a separate form for creating categories for new items and then display a drop-down of categories to choose from in the form. We just need to know how to use drop-downs, but we'll get to that in the next section. We can also create a calendar display mode, where all the items will be displayed in a grid. We can add all the extra properties we want on the items, for example, expected duration. We can then summarize the expected duration for all items each day.

FORM SUBMISSION VERSUS BUTTON CLICK

When you want to submit your form, you basically want to collect the data in the form and send it to a remote service or some other storage location. Because we're using controlled inputs in this section, the React component state is the source of truth, so we can read the value directly from the state.

We want to create a submit handler on the form. As we've previously discussed, a form's submit handler will automatically be invoked by the browser in two different instances:

- If the user clicks a Submit button inside the form
- If the user has focus inside an input field in the form with a Submit button and presses Enter

Because the form's submit handler handles both of those use cases, it's the proper place to deal with it. If we placed the handler directly as a click handler on the Submit button, we would be mishandling form submission if the user has focus inside an input field with a Submit button and presses Enter.

9.2.5 Other inputs

We briefly saw a different type of input in that previous example. We had a date input and, as you could see in figure 9.14, it displayed differently in the browser. That's not the only special type we have, as there are many other useful input variants. Figure 9.15 (a copy of figure 9.1) shows a list of all the input types that you can use in HTML forms in general and in React forms in particular.

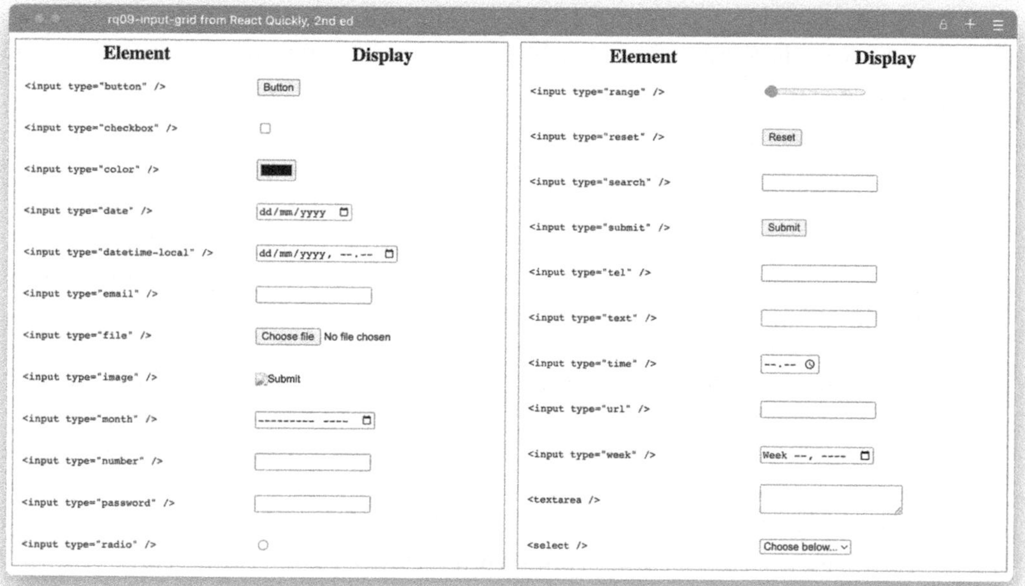

Figure 9.15   A table of various inputs available in HTML and React forms. Note how this includes mostly variations of input fields, but also a range of buttons and a drop-down.

Some of these inputs are merely variants that make it easier to input data on smaller devices. For instance, `type="tel"`, when focused on a mobile device, will display a keyboard with only the buttons that are relevant for entering phone numbers (digits, +, -, and a few others). Others are a lot more complex and have more intricate interfaces.

A few of these inputs aren't actually inputs, but just buttons. These include the reset, submit, button, and image types that you can see in figure 9.15.

Most of these inputs have the same API as text input fields though, so they are very easy to work with from a React perspective. Notice how, in the previous example, we didn't have to change anything in React just because we used a date field. We used the properties and events in the same way.

However, some of these input types are slightly different and require you to use the inputs and the events in a different way. We'll go over each input type in the next subsections with some small examples to display how you can use the different input types.

> **NOTE** All the examples in this section will be included in the `rq09-todo` repository mentioned previously, as they are all variants of the add form used in that example. These files will only be partially functioning though, as the list component in that application is only set up to work with the regular add form we used previously.

One input type will be skipped. The file input isn't possible to use in a controlled input, so we'll describe that one a bit later, when we get to the uncontrolled inputs.

NUMERIC INPUTS

Number inputs are almost identical to text inputs with a single exception. The normal value property on the target object is a string, but because we're working with numbers, we want to get the current value of the input field as a number. To do that, we can look at the `evt.target.valueAsNumber` property rather than the regular `evt.target.value` property. We don't have to manually parse the input and convert it to a string using a given base because JavaScript will do that for us automatically.

There are two categories of numeric inputs: number inputs and calendar inputs. Number inputs include the input types `"number"` and `"range"`, and the calendar inputs include the input types `"date"`, `"datetime-local"`, `"month"`, `"time"`, and `"week"`.

If you have a calendar input, the value property will return the selection as a string, depending on your local language and other settings. So, for a `type="week"` input, the value might return `"2022-W52"` as a string. The `valueAsNumber` property, on the other hand, returns a timestamp for most calendar input types, which is the number of milliseconds between midnight on January 1 in 1970 and the selected date and/or time. So, for the same week 52 in 2022, this would return the number `1672012800000`.

Month inputs are again a special variant of the calendar inputs as they return the number of months between January 1970 and the selected month. So, if you select December 2022 in the input, the `valueAsNumber` would return `635`, as that is the number of months passed since then. Numeric inputs also take `min`, `max`, and `step` properties that indicate the valid value range as well as the default amount the input can change by if you're using the keyboard to change the value.

React doesn't care if you set the value of a number input as a number or a string. It will be converted to a number before being displayed though, so if you pass something that can't be displayed in the given input, it will display incorrectly. For this reason, it makes sense to store the values as numbers in JavaScript to avoid conversion problems.

CHECK BOXES AND RADIO BUTTONS

Check boxes and radio buttons are special because they don't have a value—or at least they don't have a value that changes. The value is just an identifier that denotes what the check box or radio button signifies, but it doesn't hold information about whether the input is checked or not.

For instance, consider the form shown in figure 9.16. The four radio buttons are all independent `<input>` elements, but their values are static—they are just the four priorities. The dynamic part of this input element is the information about which radio button is currently selected in the list. For this reason, these two types of input, check boxes and radio buttons, have a `checked` property that you have to set to `true` or `false` to control the state of the component.

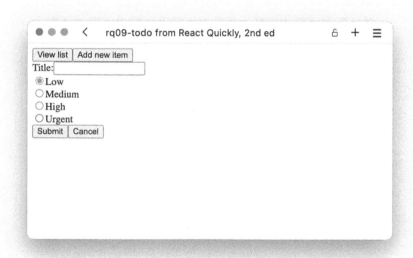

Figure 9.16   Radio buttons are used to set a priority.

First, we'll create the form with the four radio buttons. The following listing shows what that will look like.

Listing 9.9   The form component if we want radio buttons (excerpt)

```
import { useState } from "react";
function Radio({ value, label, onChange, current }) {        ⟵── Creates a helper
  return (                                                        component to
    <label>                                                       render a label
      <input                                                      with a radio
        type="radio"                                              button inside
        name="importance"        ⟵──
```

> Set the name of all the radio buttons to the same name in this component so they are part of the same radio button group.

Adds the same change handler to all of them

```
        checked={value === current}
        value={value}
        onChange={onChange}
      />
      {label}
    </label>
  );
}
function Add({ handleAdd, handleCancel }) {
  const [data, setData] = useState({ title: "", importance: "low" });
  const onChangeTitle = (evt) =>
    setData((oldData) => ({ ...oldData, title: evt.target.value }));
  const onChangeImportance = (evt) =>
    setData((oldData) =>
      ({ ...oldData, importance: evt.target.value }));
  ...
      <Radio
        value="low"
        label="Low"
        current={data.importance}
        onChange={onChangeImportance}
      />
      <Radio
        value="medium"
        label="Medium"
        current={data.importance}
        onChange={onChangeImportance}
      />
      <Radio
        value="high"
        label="High"
        current={data.importance}
        onChange={onChangeImportance}
      />
      <Radio
        value="urgent"
        label="Urgent"
        current={data.importance}
        onChange={onChangeImportance}
      />
  ...
```

Sets checked to true on only the radio button that is currently selected

Sets the value that is static for each instance of this component

The change handler works as usual.

Creates four instances of the Radio component

Let's create another variant of our to-do form from earlier. This time, we just want to record the title of the task and whether this is an urgent task or not. This will be a Boolean flag that we store in the item object. We'll use a check box for this purpose.

Listing 9.10   The form component with a check box (excerpt)

```
import { useState } from "react";
function Add({ handleAdd, handleCancel }) {
  const [data, setData] = useState({ title: "", isUrgent: false });
```

```
const onChangeTitle = (evt) =>
  setData((oldData) =>
    ({ ...oldData, title: evt.target.value }));
const onChangeUrgent = (evt) =>
  setData((oldData) =>
    ({ ...oldData, isUrgent: evt.target.checked }));
```

The change handler for the title input works, as we've seen many times, by looking at the value on the target property.

```
...
    <label>
      Title:
      <input
        value={data.title}
        onChange={onChangeTitle}
      />
    </label>
    <label>
      <input
        type="checkbox"
        checked={data.isUrgent}
        onChange={onChangeUrgent}
      />
      Urgent?
    </label>
...
```

Assigns the value and onChange properties as normal to the regular text input

Assigns checked and onChange properties to our check box input. Note that we don't need a value property because it doesn't serve any useful function in this instance.

The change handler for the check box is different, though. It examines the Boolean property .checked on the target property.

SELECT BOXES

Select boxes, also known as drop-downs, are seemingly very different from other input types in HTML. Select boxes use multiple elements and have their selection indicated in a completely different way. But React makes it easy to use this input type. You can use select boxes identically to regular input elements in terms of the properties to use. Of course, you still have to add the option elements.

Let's implement the priority example we saw in figure 9.16, but with a drop-down instead. This would look something like figure 9.17. This is surprisingly simple to do because React makes it easy for us.

Listing 9.11 The form component with a drop-down (excerpt)

```
import { useState } from "react";
function Add({ handleAdd, handleCancel }) {
  const [data, setData] = useState({
    title: "",
    priority: "low",
  });
  const onChange = (evt) => {
    const key = evt.target.name;
    const value = evt.target.value;
    setData((oldData) =>
      ({ ...oldData, [key]: value }));
  };
```

Initializes the priority to a simple string

We can use the same change handler for regular inputs as well as for select boxes.

```
...
    <label>
      Priority:
      <select
        value={data.priority}              Assigns the value and onChange
        name="priority"                    properties like on a regular input
        onChange={onChange}                directly on the select element
      >
        <option value="low">Low</option>
        <option value="medium">Medium</option>     Adds the options using
        <option value="high">High</option>         option elements with a
        <option value="urgent">Urgent</option>     value and a display text
      </select>
    </label>
...
```

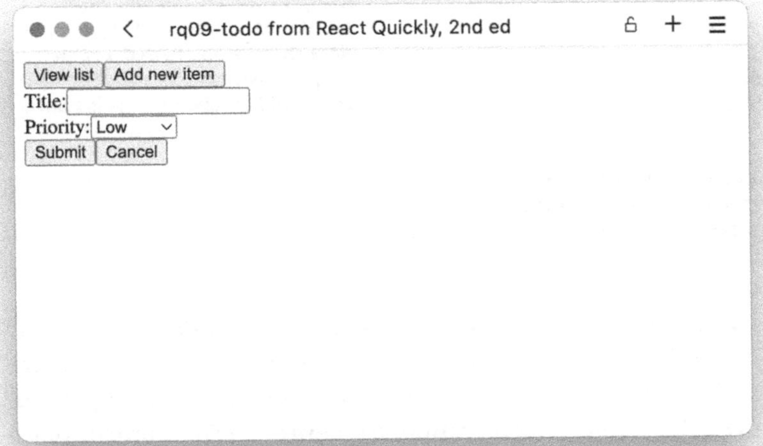

Figure 9.17   Priority can now be set using a drop-down.

If you've used select boxes in HTML before, you know that you normally have to set the `selected` property on the individual `<option>` elements to indicate which one is selected. There is no `value` property on the select element in HTML. But React has made sure to make this easy to use, so the API is the same for inputs as it is for select boxes, and that's pretty nifty!

You can even use multiselect boxes, where the user is able to select more than one option. Imagine if we had a select box with a list of people, where the user could select which persons were involved in a given task. If we store an array of people in the local state, we can use the array of selections as the value for the component, as shown in the next listing.

Listing 9.12   The form component with multiselect (excerpt)

```
import { useState } from "react";
function Add({ handleAdd, handleCancel }) {
  const [data, setData] = useState({
    title: "",
    people: [],                    ◁──────────    The state value is just an
  });                                             array, and we can initialize
                                                  it to an empty array.
  const onChange = (evt) => {
    const key = evt.target.name;
    const value = evt.target.value;                       We need to create a
    setData((oldData) => ({ ...oldData, [key]: value }));  custom change handler,
  };                                                        however, because we
  const onChangePeople = (evt) => {                         have to look at the list of
    const options =                                         selected options on the
      Array.from(evt.target.selectedOptions);              target object.
    const value = options.map((opt) => opt.value);   ◁──
    setData((oldData) => ({ ...oldData, people: value }));    For each of the
  };                                                           selected options, we
  ...                                                          have to extract the
      <label>                                                  value property. We
        People:                                                can then store the
        <select                                                resulting array of
          value={data.people}                                  option values in
          name="people"              We assign the             the state.
          onChange={onChangePeople}  properties as normal,
          multiple                   but now we also set
        >                            the "multiple"
          <option>Tinky Winky</option>   property.
          <option>Po</option>
          <option>Laa-Laa</option>
          <option>Dipsy</option>
        </select>
      </label>
  ...
```

Handling multiselect boxes is a bit more work, but it's rarely required. However, it's a great tool to have in the toolbox for those once-in-a-blue-moon occasions.

MULTILINE INPUTS

Multiline inputs are known as text areas in HTML. Text areas are seemingly identical to inputs in HTML with the main exception that the value of the text field isn't added as the value property on the element but as a child text node. If we want to set the value of an input field in HTML to "this text", we do it using the value property:

```
<input value="this text" />
```

If we want to do the same in a text area, we have to set it as the child of the element:

```
<textarea>this text</textarea>
```

However, in React, we don't do that. In React, we use text areas as if they are text fields. So, if we wanted to add a description field to our to-do form, we would simply extend the form.

Listing 9.13   The form component with `textarea` (excerpt)

```
import { useState } from "react";
function Add({ handleAdd, handleCancel }) {
  const [data, setData] = useState({
    title: "",
    description: "",          ◁──┐  The state value is
  });                            │  again initialized
  const onChange = (evt) =>      │  to a string.
    setData((oldData) =>
      ({ ...oldData, [evt.target.name]: evt.target.value }));
  ...
      <label>
        Description:                    ┐  Sets the value property
        <textarea                       │  directly on the textarea
          value={data.description}   ◁──┘  element—no need to set
          name="description"                 it as a child node
          onChange={onChange}      ◁──┐  Uses the same generalized change
        />                             │  handler as before as long as we make
      </label>                         │  sure to set the name property as well
    ...
```

With all these extra input types, you should now be well equipped to create even the most complex forms and handle the data both properly and cleverly with a great deal of code reuse, to avoid repeating yourself.

9.2.6   *Other properties*

All the other properties still work as expected on all the different types of inputs. That is because most of the extra functionality is managed in HTML, so we don't need to do anything in React to get the benefits from these extra capabilities. Following is a an inexhaustive list of extra properties you can add to your inputs to change how your form works:

- `required`—If set on an input field, the input will be required. If the field is left empty, the form cannot be submitted—the browser won't invoke the `onSubmit` callback. If the field is non-empty, submitting works as normal. This is a Boolean property, so you just need to include it as `<input required />`.
- `min`, `max`, *and* `step`—The properties are used for number inputs and ranges to control the allowed ranges for the values. You can use them in a range input like so: `<input type="range" min="100" max="200" step="10" />`.
- `readOnly`—This property does exactly what it says: makes your input read-only. You can't edit the value in the input field, nor will it ever invoke the `onChange` handler. This is also a Boolean property. Note the spelling with a capital `O`.

- disabled—If set, the input is disabled. This is different from a read-only input in that you can can't focus a disabled input like you can a read-only input. Read-only inputs are also still considered part of the submittable data in a form, but disabled inputs aren't. This is a Boolean property.
- list—If set to the ID of a <datalist> element elsewhere in the document, that data list will serve as a list of options that you can enter into the input. It's kind of like a drop-down, except that the list is only a list of suggestions, so the input isn't limited to those values.
- maxLength—This indicates the maximum number of characters allowed in the input and is managed by most browsers automatically. Note the capital L in the spelling.

There are many more properties not covered here. None of these are React-specific but work in HTML in general. We suggest checking the MDN documentation for input fields if you would like to know more: http://mng.bz/WzAg.

9.3 Managing uncontrolled inputs

Let's create another very simple calculator—this time with only a single input. We want to create a component that, given an input, will return the sum of all the integers leading up to that number. So, given an input of 4, it would return 1+2+3+4=10. There's a very simple formula for this, which is just n*(n+1)/2, with n being the number to calculate the sum for. This time we're not going to calculate the final value until the user clicks the Submit button. The component tree for creating this as a controlled component is shown in figure 9.18.

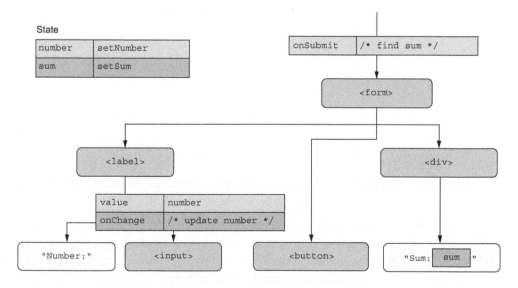

Figure 9.18 The output JSX for an integer sum calculator. When the form submits, we calculate the sum, which is displayed in the output element.

As we've done many times, we create a local state variable that holds the input value. This time, we also need another variable to hold the sum, as the sum only changes when the form is submitted.

So, what do we need the number variable for at all? The only reason for the number variable is to be able to pass it back into the controlled input component. Sure, it's very convenient to have, and we have full control over the input, but we don't really need that control because the user can enter whatever they want (as long as we set `min="0"`, as you can't calculate the sum for negative numbers).

There is another way we could do this. We could let go of all control of the input and just have the HTML control and keep it there until we need it. We only need the value when the form submits and don't really need to burden our component with controlling the state of the input while we work.

The downside to this is that we can only control the initial value in the component; after that, we can't really do anything. But we also don't need to keep control of the value in this component, so that's fine. If we implemented this, we would only have the `sum` variable in the state and calculate that in the form submit event handler. The resulting component tree is shown in figure 9.19.

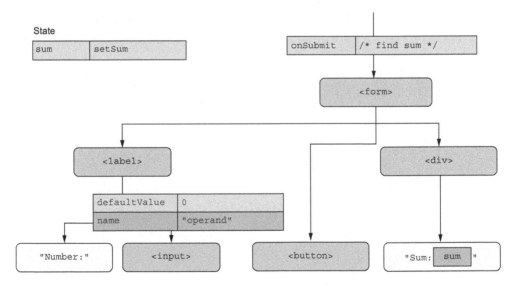

Figure 9.19 The output JSX for the integer sum calculator with an uncontrolled input component

The trick now becomes how to access the number in the input. We could make a reference to the input and go through `ref.current.valueAsNumber`, but that's not necessary. The submit event will have a target property, which is a reference to the form element, and the form element has a direct reference to all its inputs by name through the `.elements` collection. So, because we've named the input `"operand"`, we can access it through the form submit event object as `evt.target.elements.operand.valueAs-Number`. That's not too shabby. Let's implement this as shown in the next listing.

Listing 9.14   The sum of natural numbers

```
import { useState } from "react";                    We don't store
function NaturalSum() {                               the input data
  const [sum, setSum] = useState(0);     ◀─────       in state at all.
  const onSubmit = (evt) => {
    const value =                                     Instead of reading input
      evt.target.elements.operand.valueAsNumber;      values from the state, we
    const naturalSum = (value * (value + 1)) / 2;     must read them through
    setSum(naturalSum);                               the DOM. Fortunately, that's
    evt.preventDefault();                             very easy to do for form
  };                                                  elements.
  return (
    <form
      onSubmit={onSubmit}
      style={{ display: "flex", flexDirection: "column" }}
    >
      <label>
        Number:
        <input
          type="number"
          min="1"
          defaultValue="1"              Sets defaultValue but not
          name="operand"                value on the input element,
        />                              and sets the name so it's
      </label>                          easy to find via the form
      <div>
        <button>Submit</button>
      </div>
      <div>Sum: {sum}</div>
    </form>
  );
}
function App() {
  return <NaturalSum />;
}
export default App;
```

Repository: rq09-natural-sum

This example can be seen in repository `rq09-natural-sum`. You can use that repository by creating a new app based on the associated template:

```
$ npx create-react-app rq09-natural-sum --template rq09-natural-sum
```

Alternatively, you can go to this website to browse the code, see the application in action directly in your browser, or download the source code as a zip file:

https://rq2e.com/rq09-natural-sum

This should work. Let's try to run it in the browser, where you should see something like figure 9.20.

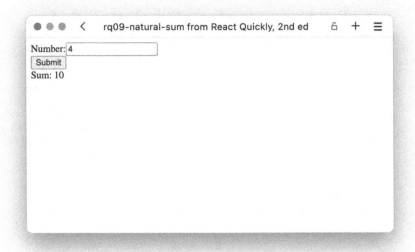

Figure 9.20   The natural sum calculator in action correctly calculating the sum for the input 4

Note that we could have had a change event handler on the input, reading the value as it changes, but we didn't need to.

So, what did we gain here and what did we lose? We've summarized the differences of the two approaches in table 9.1.

Table 9.1   Differences between controlled versus uncontrolled inputs

	Controlled input	**Uncontrolled input**
Set initial value	Yes.	Yes.
Read value as it changes	We have to.	We can if we want to, but we don't have to.
Read values on submit	Easy, we have them in state.	We have to go through the DOM, but definitely possible.
State values	We need them for every input.	We don't need any at all.
Change values on the fly	Easy.	Very difficult (but could be done through the DOM).
Source of truth	Component state value.	DOM value.

9.3.1 Opportunities

When would you want to use an uncontrolled input, then? Table 9.1 gives us some hints. If you think back to the previous address form we had in listing 9.5, we needed a bunch of state values and change handlers, but we didn't actually do anything with all of them. We simply copied the DOM values to state values and back again.

If we want to implement that same form with uncontrolled inputs, it would be surprisingly simple. Recall that in listing 9.5 we didn't actually use the form for anything. We didn't have a submit handler on the form. We edited the data, but didn't send it anywhere.

So, let's say we want to make an address form, and on submit, we want to send the data to a remote service using a POST request at this URL: //salespower.invalid/api/address. Note that this is just an example URL; it doesn't work (the .invalid top-level domain also indicates that). If we expand the example in listing 9.5 with a submit handler that sends the data as post data to this URL, it becomes listing 9.15.

Listing 9.15 Controlled address form with submit

```
import { useState } from "react";
const URL = "//salespower.invalid/api/address";
function Address() {
  const [data, setData] = useState({       Initializes
    address1: "",                          state first
    address2: "",
    zip: "",
    city: "",
    state: "",
    country: "",
  });
  const onChange = (evt) => {              Creates a change
    const key = evt.target.name;           handler that can
    const value = evt.target.value;        update the state
    setData((oldData) =>
      ({ ...oldData, [key]: value }));
  };
  const onSubmit = (evt) => {
    fetch(URL, {
      method: "POST",
      body: JSON.stringify(data),     ◁──  Uses the state as
    });                                    the data to send
    evt.preventDefault();                  in the submit
  };                                       handler
  return (
    <form
      onSubmit={onSubmit}
      style={{ display: "flex", flexDirection: "column" }}
    >
      <label>
        Address line 1:
        <input
          value={data.address1}
```

```
        name="address1"
        onChange={onChange}          ←
     />
   </label>
   <label>
     Address line 2:
     <input
       value={data.address2}
       name="address2"
       onChange={onChange}          ←
     />
   </label>
   <label>
     Zip:
     <input
       value={data.zip}
       name="zip"
       onChange={onChange}          ←
     />
   </label>
   <label>
     City:
     <input
       value={data.city}
       name="city"
       onChange={onChange}          ←
     />
   </label>
   <label>
     State:
     <input
       value={data.state}
       name="state"
       onChange={onChange}          ←
     />
   </label>
   <label>
     Country:
     <input
       value={data.country}
       name="country"
       onChange={onChange}          ←
     />
   </label>
   <button>Submit</button>          ←
 </form>
);
}
export default Address;
```

Assigns an onChange handler to every input

The Submit button

Let's look at this with uncontrolled inputs. First of all, we don't need any state value at all, and we don't need any change handlers anywhere. Just those two things will greatly reduce the complexity of our form.

The submit handler will get a bit more complex, though, because even though we have an object of the state values in `evt.target.elements`, it's not directly a list of state values, but an object of the input elements themselves. However, this object also contains all the form inputs as numbered indices, so `form.elements[0]` is the first element in the form, and so on. The Submit button is also an element of the form, but we can look at only the first six form inputs because we know they are the only relevant ones. We need to go over this list of elements, extract the name and value of each, and put that into an object.

Listing 9.16 Uncontrolled address form with submit

```
const URL = "//salespower.invalid/api/address";
function Address() {
  const onSubmit = (evt) => {
    const data = Object.fromEntries(
      Array.from(evt.target.elements)
        .slice(0, 6)
        .map((input) => [input.name, input.value])
    );
    fetch(URL, {
      method: "POST",
      body: JSON.stringify(data),
    });
    evt.preventDefault();
  };
  return (
    <form
      onSubmit={onSubmit}
      style={{ display: "flex", flexDirection: "column" }}
    >
      <label>
        Address line 1:
        <input name="address1" />
      </label>
      <label>
        Address line 2:
        <input name="address2" />
      </label>
      <label>
        Zip:
        <input name="zip" />
      </label>
      <label>
        City:
        <input name="city" />
      </label>
      <label>
        State:
        <input name="state" />
      </label>
      <label>
        Country:
        <input name="country" />
```

The primary change here is in the submit handler, where we extract the current data directly from the form rather than reading it from the local component state as before.

Adds the submit handler to the form object

```
      </label>
      <button>Submit</button>                ◁─┐   The Submit
    </form>                                     │   button
  );
}
export default Address;
```

If we count characters in the two different listings, the controlled variant in listing 9.15 comes in at 1,441 characters, whereas the uncontrolled example in listing 9.16 is only 1,022 characters. That's an ~30% reduction in code! Plus, the controlled component renders every time the user types something, whereas the uncontrolled component never re-renders at all!

This almost sounds like an uncontrolled form is better, and it is in this extremely simple case with a form, where you don't need to control anything. But if you want to control the form smartly with things such as validations, limitations, formatting, and so on, then you do need to make at least those fields controlled. To be honest, if you have such a simple address form that has no validation or rules and just sends the input values to a target URL using POST, you don't need React (or JavaScript) at all. A regular old HTML form can do that for you.

React only really shines once web applications become complex, and ditto for your forms. If you want to add something such as validation to any of the two preceding forms, it's so much easier to do in the controlled example in listing 9.15 than in the uncontrolled one in listing 9.16. If you don't need any of that, you might not need to control your inputs inside your React component. In fact, you might not even need React at all.

9.3.2 *File inputs*

File inputs can *only* be uncontrolled because the value property is protected in the DOM as a browser security feature. You can't directly set the value of a file input; you can only read it once the user selects a file to upload. The only thing you can do is clear the value, but you can't in any way alter or set it to an initial value.

Thus, in React, file inputs can never be controlled. If you create a component with `<input type="file" value={file} />`, the browser will tell you to stop fooling around with a message like this:

```
Uncaught DOMException: Failed to set the 'value' property on
'HTMLInputElement': This input element accepts a filename, which
may only be programmatically set to the empty string.
```

It's not something React prevents you from doing. It's just that the browser simply won't allow you to try to set the value of a file input.

So, if you need a file input in your React form, you must make (at least) that input uncontrolled. But because you never need to validate, limit, or format the current value of a file input anyway, this should be just fine.

9.4 Quiz

1. You can only specify an initial value in a controlled input, not in an uncontrolled input. *True* or *false?*

2. Which event handler do you use to handle input in a select box?
   a. `onValue`
   b. `onChange`
   c. `onSelect`
   d. `onClick`

3. Which of the following properties would you use to read the new state of a check box input in the event handler?
   a. `evt.target.value`
   b. `evt.target.selected`
   c. `evt.target.checked`
   d. `evt.target.valueAsBoolean`

4. When you need to target an uncontrolled input node with the name `"email"` in a form submit handler, which of the follow is the correct way to do it?
   a. `evt.target.inputs.email`
   b. `evt.target.email`
   c. `evt.target.nodes.email`
   d. `evt.target.elements.email`

5. Which two properties are required on a controlled input element?
   a. `name`
   b. `value`
   c. `defaultValue`
   d. `onChange`

Quiz answers

1. *False.* Setting the initial value is possible in both modes. You can't update the value after the initial value in the uncontrolled input, but you *can* set the initial value.

2. You always use the `onChange` event handler, regardless of which form input element you're using.

3. The state of a check box input element is stored in the `checked` property, so you would access it as `evt.target.checked` in the change handler.

4. Form elements are accessible through the form element in the DOM via the `elements` property. A form element named `"email"` would be reachable from a form submit handler through `evt.target.elements.email`.

5. All controlled inputs must always have the `value` and the `onChange` properties defined.

Summary

- Handling form data is a first-class priority in React, and forms and inputs are very easy to work with.
- Form input elements can be either controlled or uncontrolled.
- The recommended approach is to use controlled inputs, which give you the option to validate, modify, and filter input on the fly.
- To use a controlled input, you must specify the value and onChange properties on the input element in JSX and "confirm" every change by updating the value property.
- The alternative is to use uncontrolled inputs, which reduce your options of modifying data but also reduce the amount of code you need to work with for forms that require little data control.
- Uncontrolled inputs can specify the initial value using defaultValue, but must not set the value property.
- You can use all types of HTML inputs in React, including but not limited to, text inputs, number inputs, calendar and time inputs, password inputs, check boxes, radio buttons, drop-downs, range meters, and text areas.
- Some input types have some slight variations in the API, for example, reading the state of check boxes, radio buttons, and multiselect boxes.
- File inputs can only ever be uncontrolled, as you can't control the value of a file input in JavaScript.

Advanced React hooks for scaling

This chapter covers

- Structuring data flow with React Context
- Managing complex state with reducers
- Creating custom hooks for code reuse

So far, you've learned all you need to know to build small, simple React applications by yourself. You have all the knowledge and tools required to create stateful, interactive, and relevant React widgets with a few interconnected components—but only as long as you're working on fairly small projects.

In the real world, your React applications will most likely be a lot bigger and more complex than any of the examples we've examined thus far. You could create small widgets (e.g., a BMI calculator) for a website that have just a couple of components and still do a good job, but those are few and far between and mostly relevant to the hobby developer.

As a professional React engineer, you'll more likely either be developing a larger application on your own or an even larger application as part of a team. As applications grow larger, component interfaces grow more complex, and working on the codebase requires more finesse.

A couple of things might start to become a problem if you develop your applications without structure or procedure:

1 Complex data flow can lead to an abundance of properties on all the components to transfer all the data required.
2 Intricate state flows can result in invalid states if attention is not paid carefully to synchronization of related state values.
3 Duplicated code can sometimes be hard to generalize if you only try to generalize whole components and not also parts of components.

All of these problems will arise regardless of whether you're working on your own or in a larger team. These are scaling problems. What works at a small scale, doesn't necessarily work at a large scale.

We saw similar scaling problems when we created more complex forms in chapter 9. When you have just 1 or 2 inputs, using a state value for each is fine. But if you have 5 or 10 inputs, having a separate state value for each is a nuisance and, frankly, bad software design. When concepts are applied to larger items, they are often tweaked to allow for better scaling.

In this chapter, we'll discuss tools that can greatly help you organize and structure your React application and React project as a whole to create better software and better developer experiences.

The solutions to the preceding three scaling problems will be covered in this chapter:

1 You can make values available to components regardless of depth using React Context, which is a great way to organize complex data flow. We'll cover this in section 10.1.
2 When you have multivalue state that is interdependent, you can perform state updates using a reducer, which is an idea borrowed from functional programming. We'll cover this in section 10.2.
3 Custom hooks are a great way to generalize both small and large chunks of business logic, and we'll cover that in section 10.3. Custom hooks are quickly becoming the main way of providing reusable functionality both internally in projects and also as open source libraries available on GitHub and/or npm.

NOTE The source code for the examples in this chapter is available at https://rq2e.com/ch10. But as you learned in chapter 2, you can instantiate all the examples directly from the command line using a single command.

10.1   *Resolving values across components*

Let's once again build an application that solves a real-world problem. This time, we'll use a user dashboard, which is the screen you see after you log into some application. This dashboard shows a message that welcomes you by name, as well as a button in the top-left corner that displays your name and links to your settings page. The trick here is that the name is dynamic and will be returned to us by some backend. The end result is supposed to look like figure 10.1.

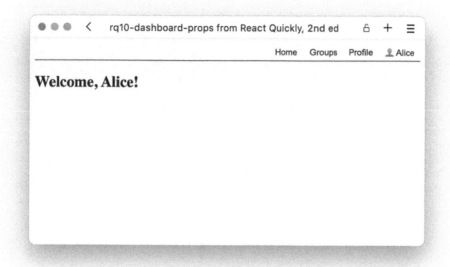

Figure 10.1   The desired end result for our user dashboard. The user's name is displayed twice in this screenshot, which is the core of the problem here.

Let's break this down into components. We want the top menu to be part of a header. The central welcome page is just one of many pages that can be displayed by our application. We know we'll add more stuff in the future, so let's add some extra layers in expectation of that. We'll use a component approach as laid out in figure 10.2.

However, as you can see in figure 10.2, we didn't display how we got the name from the very top of the component tree, where it's passed into the dashboard component all the way down to the two smaller components at the end that need to display it.

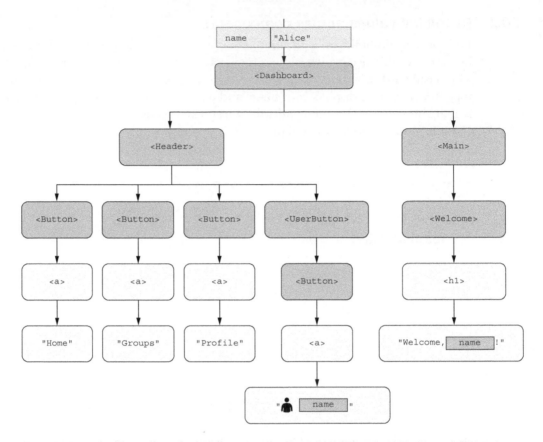

Figure 10.2   Our component structure with the necessary placeholders needed for the name. Note how the `"name"` property is used twice, but still not passed along as a property anywhere.

Using what we've done so far, we would need to pass the property through every component on its way to the component that needs it. If we did so, it would look like figure 10.3.

But note, in this component tree, we're passing the name property to both the Header and the Main component. Neither of those components needs this property by itself. The only reason why we have to pass this property to these two components is so that they can forward the property to yet another component. Nevertheless, this works and can be implemented, as shown in listing 10.1.

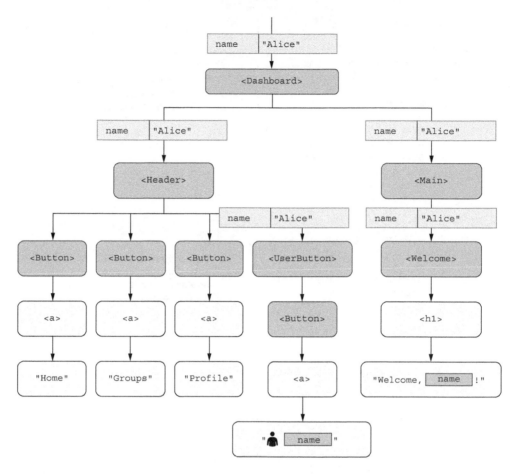

Figure 10.3 Our component structure if we pass the name to every component that needs to pass it on. Five components need the name property, but only two of them display it.

Listing 10.1 Dashboard with a lot of `name` properties

```
const BUTTON_STYLE = {
  display: "inline-block",
  padding: "4px 10px",
  background: "transparent",
  border: "0",
};
const HEADER_STYLE = {
  display: "flex",
  justifyContent: "flex-end",
  borderBottom: "1px solid",
};
function Button({ children }) {
  return (
    <button style={BUTTON_STYLE}>
      {children}
```

```
        </button>
      );
    }
    function UserButton({ name }) {
      return <Button>👤 {name}</Button>;
    }
    function Header({ name }) {
      return (
        <header style={HEADER_STYLE}>
          <Button>Home</Button>
          <Button>Groups</Button>
          <Button>Profile</Button>
          <UserButton name={name} />
        </header>
      );
    }
    function Welcome({ name }) {
      return (
        <section>
          <h1>Welcome, {name}!</h1>
        </section>
      );
    }
    function Main({ name }) {
      return (
        <main>
          <Welcome name={name} />
        </main>
      );
    }
    function Dashboard({ name }) {
      return (
        <>
          <Header name={name} />
          <Main name={name} />
        </>
      );
    }
    function App() {
      return <Dashboard name="Alice" />;
    }
    export default App;
```

Did you know you can use emojis directly in React? You can!

The component is only passed the property to be able to pass it on to another component.

Passes a name property to a component that doesn't actually need to use the property itself

Repository: rq10-dashboard-props

This example can be seen in repository `rq10-dashboard-props`. You can use that repository by creating a new app based on the associated template:

```
$ npx create-react-app rq10-dashboard-props --template rq10-dashboard-props
```

Alternatively, you can go to this website to browse the code, see the application in action directly in your browser, or download the source code as a zip file:

https://rq2e.com/rq10-dashboard-props

This is a reasonable approach, and it works. If you open this up in the browser, you see exactly what we wanted in figure 10.1.

10.1.1 React Context

Those properties being passed to components, only for them to be passed on to another component, doesn't look like good software design. There must be a better way. What if we could have a storage object encapsulating a number of components that could feed data to all its child components when they asked for it without having any extra properties passed around?

Congratulations, we've just invented React Context. A context does exactly that—it wraps a number of components with a value that all descendant components can access without going through properties at all.

Prop drilling

The practice of adding properties to a component with the sole purpose of allowing that component to pass those properties on to other components, which might in turn only be necessary to allow those components to pass those properties on to yet another layer of components, is called *prop drilling*. You *drill* your *property* through many layers of components because you need to get it from the outside to the inside.

Prop drilling can very quickly become a problem in large codebases, and React Context is one of the best tools to combat this. Without proper design patterns such as using context providers, you might end up with dozens of properties on some components, only added because they are needed further down the component tree.

This is obviously bad software design and one of the reasons React Context is so popular.

A context in React consists of two parts. It needs a provider that contains the value you want to pass to any descendant component, and it needs a consumer that you use in each descendant component that wants access to the provided value.

The context provider is a pretty simple React component. The consumer can most easily be created as a `useContext` hook. In essence, using a context looks something like figure 10.4.

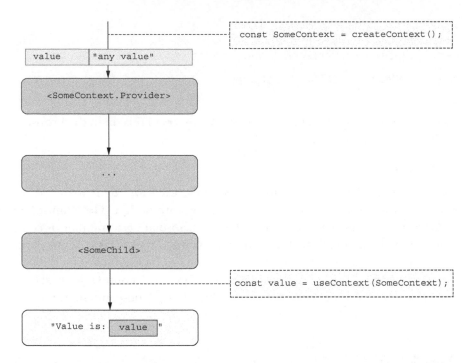

Figure 10.4   Passing a value from a provider to a consumer using the `useContext` hook

We need two pieces of the React Context API here. First, we need `createContext` to define the context, which we store in a variable. This variable is created outside any component and lives in the same places as other components, so it can be referenced just like any other component. Second, we need the `useContext` hook. This hook takes a reference to the context and returns the current context value. Let's add a `NameContext` to our dashboard application from earlier to the component tree, as shown in figure 10.5.

That's literally all it takes. We can implement this as shown in the following listing. We get the same result as before, but with a much nicer flow of data.

Listing 10.2   Dashboard with context

```
import { createContext, useContext } from "react";      ⇠──┐ Imports the two
const BUTTON_STYLE = {                                        functions from the
  display: "inline-block",                                    React package
  padding: "4px 10px",
  background: "transparent",
  border: "0",
};
const HEADER_STYLE = {
  display: "flex",
  justifyContent: "flex-end",
  borderBottom: "1px solid",
};
```

```
const NameContext = createContext();
function Button({ children }) {
  return <button style={BUTTON_STYLE}>{children}</button>;
}
function UserButton() {
  const name = useContext(NameContext);
  return <Button>👤 {name}</Button>;
}
function Header() {
  return (
    <header style={HEADER_STYLE}>
      <Button>Home</Button>
      <Button>Groups</Button>
      <Button>Profile</Button>
      <UserButton />
    </header>
  );
}
function Welcome() {
  const name = useContext(NameContext);
  return (
    <section>
      <h1>Welcome, {name}!</h1>
    </section>
  );
}
function Main() {
  return (
    <main>
      <Welcome />
    </main>
  );
}
function Dashboard({ name }) {
  return (
    <NameContext.Provider value={name}>
      <Header />
      <Main />
    </NameContext.Provider>
  );
}
function App() {
  return <Dashboard name="Alice" />;
}
export default App;
```

The context is created in the global scope, so we can access it from anywhere.

The two components that need access to the name can do so by hooking into the context using useContext.

In the dashboard component, we make sure to wrap the entire tree in a context provider with the name as the context value.

In the main application component, we initialize the entire dashboard with the name "Alice".

A lot of our components don't take any properties at all anymore.

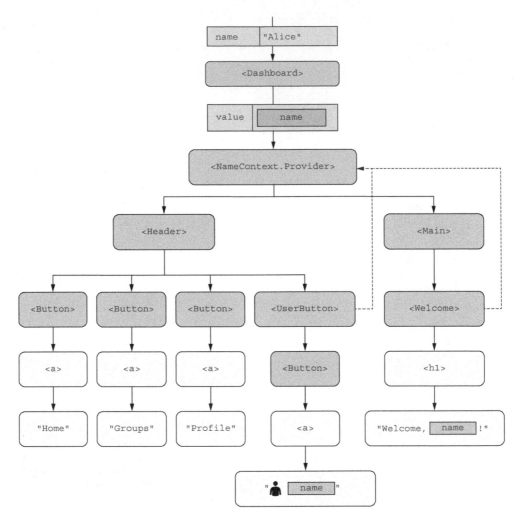

Figure 10.5 The dashboard application component tree with a context surrounding it all. The dash arrows show components that use the context and refer back to the current value as defined by the context provider.

Repository: rq10-dashboard-context

This example can be seen in repository `rq10-dashboard-context`. You can use that repository by creating a new app based on the associated template:

```
$ npx create-react-app rq10-dashboard-ctx --template rq10-dashboard-context
```

Alternatively, you can go to this website to browse the code, see the application in action directly in your browser, or download the source code as a zip file:

https://rq2e.com/rq10-dashboard-context

10.1.2 Context states

Using a context to store a static value that is used throughout an application is definitely nice, but what's even nicer is that we can store dynamic information there as well. The useContext hook is stateful, so if the context value changes, the useContext hook will cause the component using it to re-render automatically.

Let's imagine that same dashboard, but this time you're an administrator who wants to be able to see what the dashboard looks like for any user in the database. As an administrator, you have a drop-down of users that you can see the dashboard for. We'll implement this like figure 10.6, where the dashboard component is the same component as before (we just don't show all of its child components to save space).

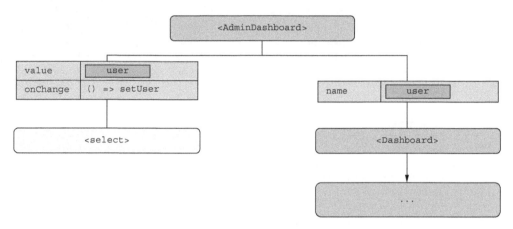

Figure 10.6   The admin dashboard allows the user to choose which user to see the dashboard for. The admin dashboard includes a select box and the regular user dashboard.

We'll use a simple select element to allow the user to select between the three users in the system: Alice, Bob, and Carol. We can use a simple useState for remembering the selected user and pass that on to the components as needed. Let's extend the previous example with this new administrator dashboard.

Listing 10.3   Administrator dashboard

```
import {
  useState,               ◁——    We need to import
  createContext,                  the useState hook
  useContext,                     as well.
} from "react";
const BUTTON_STYLE = {
  display: "inline-block",
  padding: "4px 10px",
  background: "transparent",
  border: "0",
};
```

```
const HEADER_STYLE = {
  display: "flex",
  justifyContent: "flex-end",
  borderBottom: "1px solid",
};
const NameContext = createContext();
function Button({ children }) {
  return <button style={BUTTON_STYLE}>{children}</button>;
}
function UserButton() {
  const name = useContext(NameContext);
  return <Button>👤 {name}</Button>;
}
function Header() {
  return (
    <header style={HEADER_STYLE}>
      <Button>Home</Button>
      <Button>Groups</Button>
      <Button>Profile</Button>
      <UserButton />
    </header>
  );
}
function Welcome() {
  const name = useContext(NameContext);
  return (
    <section>
      <h1>Welcome, {name}!</h1>
    </section>
  );
}
function Main() {
  return (
    <main>
      <Welcome />
    </main>
  );
}
function Dashboard({ name }) {
  return (
    <NameContext.Provider value={name}>
      <Header />
      <Main />
    </NameContext.Provider>
  );
}
function AdminDashboard() {
  const [user, setUser] = useState("Alice");
  return (
    <>
      <select
        value={user}
        onChange={(evt) => setUser(evt.target.value)}
      >
        <option>Alice</option>
```

Everything inside the dashboard component is exactly as before.

Creates a simple state, defaulting to Alice

Uses a controlled select element to choose a user

```
        <option>Bob</option>
        <option>Carol</option>
      </select>
      <Dashboard name={user} />                    ◁────   Passes the currently
    </>                                                     selected user to the
  );                                                        dashboard component
}
function App() {
  return <AdminDashboard />;
}
export default App;
```

If we try this in the browser, it looks like figure 10.7. Go ahead and select a different name from the drop-down, and see the name correctly update in the dashboard in both the menu and the headline.

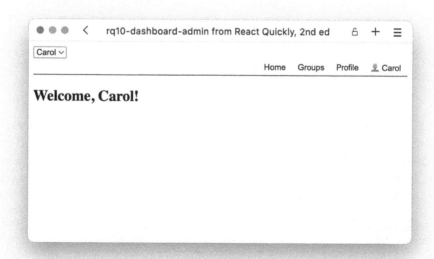

Figure 10.7 The admin dashboard displaying the user dashboard for Carol, as we've selected her name in the admin drop-down in the top left

10.1.3 React Context deconstructed

At this point, let's take a step back and look more at React Context in detail. As mentioned, to use React Context, you need to create a provider and a consumer. You can create consumers in two different ways: either as a hook or by using a *render prop*. But before you can do any of this, you need to create the context itself by using the function createContext, which exists in the React package:

```
import { createContext } from 'react';
const MyContext = createContext(defaultValue);
```

There are two things to note here:

- It's common to name the context variable with an uppercase letter as it kind of serves the purpose of a React component (or at least the properties on it do).
- createContext takes a single argument, which is the default value. We'll get back to how that plays out in just a little bit.

CONSUMING A CONTEXT

When you have a context variable, for example, MyContext in the preceding snippet, it has two properties, which are what we care about: MyContext.Provider and MyContext.Consumer. We've already explained how you can consume a context using the useContext hook. You can do a similar thing with the MyContext.Consumer property, but it's a bit trickier.

Let's say we want to display a paragraph with the name provided by the nearest name context in a component named DisplayName. We can do that using the useContext hook:

```
function DisplayName() {
  const name = useContext(NameContext);
  return <p>{name}</p>
}
```

This is pretty simple. We invoke the hook and get the current value back as a variable, which we can directly use in the component.

If we try to do the same thing using the Consumer component, we have to invoke the consumer component with a function as the first and only child, and that function will be invoked with the value of the context:

```
function DisplayName() {
  return (
    <p>
      <NameContext.Consumer>
        {(name) => name}
      </NameContext.Consumer>
```

```
      </p>
  );
}
```

Passing a function that returns JSX as a child to a component is a render prop (as mentioned earlier) because it's a property that can render JSX when invoked. You can probably see how this is a lot more work to type, and if we need to do some calculations or logic with the returned value, we have to restructure our component quite a bit.

Using the `Consumer` component is quite rare in functional codebases. It's mainly used in older class-based projects.

CONTEXT COMPOSITION

The provider is used to create a context that can be consumed. The consumer is used to consume the nearest provided context. Note that you can provide the same context many times throughout your application, and you can even provide the same context nested. You can also use the same context many times, even outside any provider.

When you consume a context, you'll get the value provided by the nearest provider going up the JSX document tree. If no provider exists above the consumer, you'll get the default value as defined when the context was created. All of this is illustrated in figure 10.8.

Following are a few things to note in figure 10.8:

- If you consume a context that doesn't have a provider above it, as in `Top-Component`, you'll get the default value from the definition of the context (`0` in this case).
- If you consume a context that has multiple providers above it, as in `Bottom-Component`, you'll get the value from the nearest provider looking up through the document tree (e.g., `17` rather than `2` in this case).

NESTED CONTEXT EXAMPLE

You can imagine a use case for nested contexts for UI variables, such as an app where we have buttons with different border widths throughout the application. Our web application is a web shop with different items for purchase and pages about the business. We have some buttons in the header and another in the footer. We also have buttons to open the shopping cart in both the header and the footer.

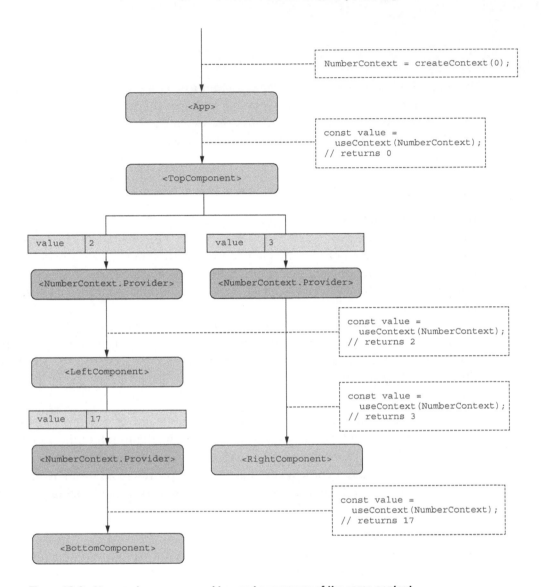

Figure 10.8 You can have many providers and consumers of the same context.

By default, all buttons have a border width of 1 pixel, but all buttons have a border width of 2 pixels in the footer. Furthermore, every button that leads to the shopping cart must always have a border width of 5 pixels because it's an important button. Let's sketch this system first, as shown in figure 10.9.

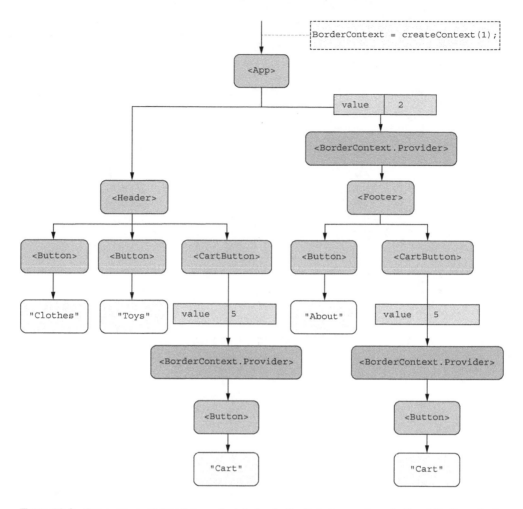

Figure 10.9   Our component tree for our shopping website. Note how we have both a default context value and several context providers throughout.

Now, every button component will look up the component tree to find the nearest border context provider and use the border width taken from there. If no provider is found up the tree, the button will use the default value as defined in the original context creation. Let's annotate the tree with all these lookups for the nearest provider in figure 10.10.

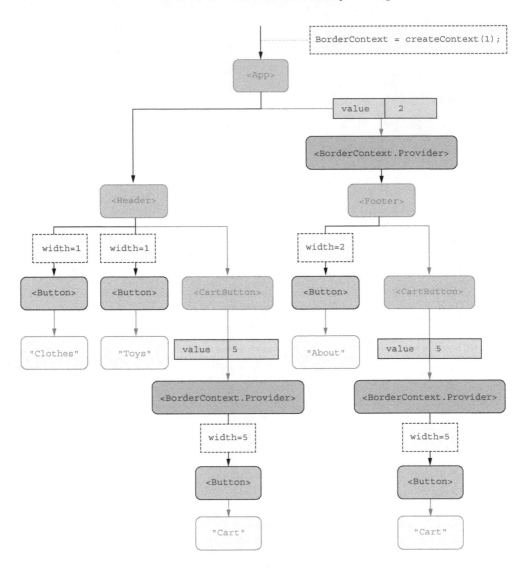

Figure 10.10 **The component tree with the nearest provider (or the root) is marked with a heavier arrow for every button component, and the border width is resolved for that component.**

Now that we have all the information we need, let's implement this, as shown in listing 10.4. Once we open this in the browser, we're treated with figure 10.11.

Figure 10.11   Our shop website shows all the buttons with the correct widths exactly as designed. It doesn't look good, but it's what the client wanted for some reason!

Listing 10.4   Border width by context

```
import { useContext, createContext } from "react";
const BorderContext = createContext(1);
function Button({ children }) {

  const borderWidth = useContext(BorderContext);
  const style = {
    border: `${borderWidth}px solid black`,
    background: "transparent",
  };
  return <button style={style}>{children}</button>;
}
function CartButton() {
  return (
    <BorderContext.Provider value={5}>
      <Button>Cart</Button>
    </BorderContext.Provider>
  );
}
function Header() {
  const style = {
    padding: "5px",
    borderBottom: "1px solid black",
    marginBottom: "10px",
    display: "flex",
    gap: "5px",
    justifyContent: "flex-end",
  };
```

Creates the initial context with a default value of 1

In the button component, we consume whatever value is provided by the nearest provider and use that as the border width property in CSS.

Adds a border width provider around the button inside the cart button to provide this button with exactly 5 px

```
  return (
    <header style={style}>
      <Button>Clothes</Button>
      <Button>Toys</Button>
      <CartButton />
    </header>
  );
}
function Footer() {
  const style = {
    padding: "5px",
    borderTop: "1px solid black",
    marginTop: "10px",
    display: "flex",
    justifyContent: "space-between",
  };
  return (
    <footer style={style}>
      <Button>About</Button>
      <Button>Jobs</Button>
      <CartButton />
    </footer>
  );
}
function App() {
  return (
    <main>
      <Header />
      <h1>Welcome to the shop!</h1>
      <BorderContext.Provider value={2}>      ⟵  We surround the footer with a
        <Footer />                                provider that makes sure all the
      </BorderContext.Provider>                   buttons inside by default will have
    </main>                                       2 px borders, unless another, more
  );                                              specific provider tells them otherwise.
}
export default App;
```

Repository: rq10-border-context

This example can be seen in repository `rq10-border-context`. You can use that repository by creating a new app based on the associated template:

```
$ npx create-react-app rq10-border-context --template rq10-border-context
```

Alternatively, you can go to this website to browse the code, see the application in action directly in your browser, or download the source code as a zip file:

https://rq2e.com/rq10-border-context

10.2 How to handle complex state

Let's go back to our favorite example of all time: the counter with increment *and* decrement buttons! This time, we'll use a different approach. Instead of using a regular useState hook to hold and manage the state value, we'll use a reducer and the useReducer hook.

We'll give you a quick introduction to how the useReducer hook works now just to get started on the example, but you'll get more details in the following subsections.

The useReducer API looks like this:

```
const [state, dispatch] = useReducer(reducer, initialState);
```

These four elements go together somewhat, as shown in figure 10.12.

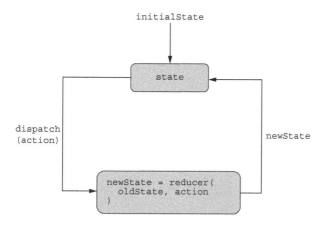

Figure 10.12 **The flow of data in a** useReducer **hook is somewhat similar to a regular** useState **hook, in that it starts with an initial value and then updates as the application progresses. But the way you update the internal state is more complex, in that you "reduce" the new state from the old one using functions and actions.**

There are four separate parts to this. The state and initialState work just like they do for useState(). So, for our counter, the initial state will be 0, and the state will be whatever our counter has reached at that moment.

The two new things in this single piece of code are the dispatch function and the reducer function. dispatch works as our enhanced setter function, which allows us to not set the value directly, but rather instruct the reducer function on how to set the value. The reducer function is hence a function that takes the current state and a dispatched action and returns a new state based on them. You invoke dispatch with an *action* object, which is then passed to the reducer along with the old state, and the reducer is expected to return the new state. For now, let's implement this for our up-and-down counter.

Listing 10.5 Counter component with reducer

```
import { useReducer } from "react";
function reducer(state, { type }) {
  switch (type) {
```

Creates a reducer function that takes the old state (the current value) and the action object, which has a type

```
      case "INCREMENT":                      Returns the old value plus
        return state + 1;                    or minus 1, depending on
      case "DECREMENT":                      the type
        return state - 1;
      default:
        return state;
    }
  }
function Counter() {                                      Initializes the hook
  const [counter, dispatch] = useReducer(reducer, 0);    with the reducer
  return (                                                function and the
    <section>                                             initial value, 0
      <h1>Counter: {counter}</h1>
      <div>
        <button onClick={
          () => dispatch({ type: "INCREMENT" })
        }>
          Increment                          Invokes the dispatch
        </button>                            function with the
        <button onClick={                    relevant action objects
          () => dispatch({ type: "DECREMENT" })
        }>
          Decrement
        </button>
      </div>
    </section>
  );
}
function App() {
  return <Counter />;
}
export default App;
```

Repository: rq10-counter-reducer

This example can be seen in repository `rq10-counter-reducer`. You can use that repository by creating a new app based on the associated template:

`$ npx create-react-app rq10-counter-reducer --template rq10-counter-reducer`

Alternatively, you can go to this website to browse the code, see the application in action directly in your browser, or download the source code as a zip file:

https://rq2e.com/rq10-counter-reducer

É voilà! We have once again re-implemented the counter. We did it in a much more complex and elaborate way, but this reducer concept can be utilized for more complex state scenarios, as you'll see in the next subsection.

10.2.1 *Interdependent state*

Another problem that can come up as your application grows more complex is interdependent state. This happens when you have different values in state that are related, but aren't just copies of each other. For instance, let's imagine a simple component for loading some external content and displaying the content once loaded. Because this is external content, the load might fail. If so, we need to show an error message.

The simple way to construct such a component is to have three different state values. One value represents the loading progress (is it loading, did loading succeed, did loading fail), another holds the result object if the loading succeeded, and the last state holds the error message if the load failed. We can picture this simple state flow in figure 10.13.

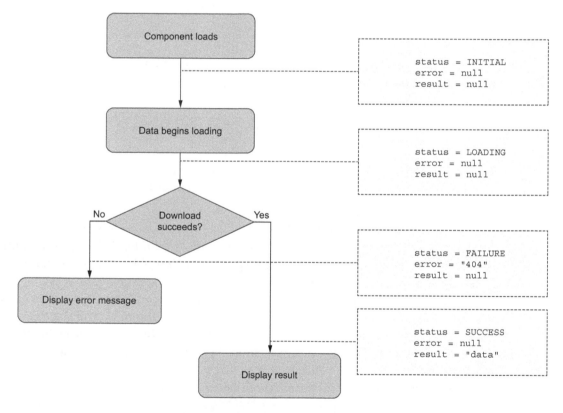

Figure 10.13 **The state flow in a simple loading component. The dashed boxes indicate the desired state at the given point in the program execution.**

We have three different values that are interdependent, which means we only have semantic meaning for certain combinations of values. For instance, if the status is LOADING, it makes no sense for the error or result to be anything but null because we haven't downloaded anything (or failed to do so) yet. Likewise, if the status is FAIL-URE, the result state can't have a value because it just can't.

As a developer, however, you must keep this relationship between the values in mind. We can't directly code this relationship with simple state values when using useState(). We have to remember to clear the error and result states when reloading the external resource because, if we don't, it can lead to the component being in an invalid state and not knowing what it's supposed to show.

A better solution here is to create a single function that allows us to move between the different semantic states of the system rather than just the individual variables. For example, imagine what happens when loading fails if we have three separate variables and need to set two of them:

```
fetch(...).catch(() => {
  setStatus(FAILURE);
  setError("Loading failed");
});
```

If we adopted the recommended approach of calling a single function that changed the semantic state, we would instead do the following:

```
fetch(...).catch(() => {
  failureHappenedAndThisIsTheErrorMessage("Loading failed");
});
```

The difference here is pretty big. The former syntax has a lot of room for error, whereas the latter is a much cleaner API with very little room to misinterpret what to do.

USEREDUCER TO THE RESCUE

All of this is to say that this is exactly where useReducer comes into the picture. But instead of having a single primitive value as our state, we can hold an object of multiple values of state. We can then also use dispatched action objects to manipulate this entire object of state values as we need to.

So, let's go back to our state flow diagram and look at which action objects we need to advance the state and what payload arguments they require to update the state values as needed (see figure 10.14). Now we just need to define the reducer function, which takes the existing state and an action object and then generates a new state based on that.

The overall structure of a reducer is commonly organized as follows:

```
function reducer(state, { type, payload }) {
  switch (type) {
    case "TYPE_A":
      // return new state based on TYPE_A
    case "TYPE_B":
      // return new state based on TYPE_B
  }
}
```

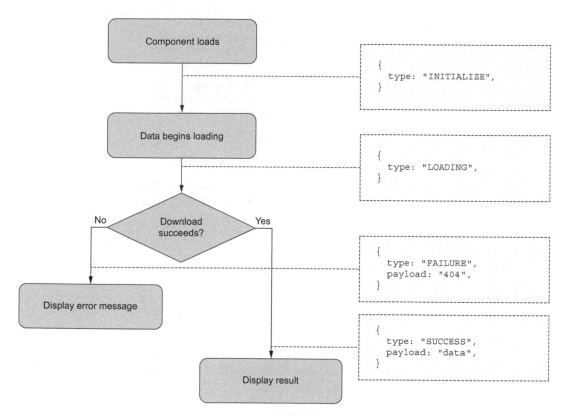

Figure 10.14 The state flow with the desired action API. In this diagram, the dashed boxes indicate the action object that we'll dispatch to the reducer to have the reducer update the internal state as desired.

So, for our particular use case, the action types are already defined as `"INITIALIZE"`, `"LOADING"`, `"ERROR"`, and `"SUCCESS"`. The following states result from each of these actions:

- When initializing, set the status to `"INITIALIZE"`, and all other variables to `null`, regardless of their existing value.
- When loading, set the status to `"LOADING"`, and keep everything else as is.
- When loading fails, set the status to `"FAILURE"`, and set the error to the passed payload.
- When loading succeeds, set the status to `"SUCCESS"`, and set the result to the passed payload.

Now, let's implement that in the preceding reducer structure:

```
function reducer(state, { type, payload }) {
  switch (type) {
    case "INITIALIZE":
      return {
```

```
            status: "INITIALIZE",
            result: null,
            error: null,
          };
        case "LOADING":
          return {
            ...state,
            status: "LOADING",
          };
        case "FAILURE":
          return {
            ...state,
            status: "FAILURE",
            error: payload,
          };
        case "SUCCESS":
          return {
            ...state,
            status: "SUCCESS",
            result: payload,
          };
      }
    }
```

When we initialize, we clear everything regardless of what the state was before.

When loading happens, we only change the status and nothing else.

When an error happens, we change the status and set the error.

When loading succeeds, we change the status and set the result.

Alright, let's get back to the original purpose. We need a component that can load some data and display status along the way. We'll use a reducer as defined previously to handle the state, but we'll also change a few things.

Listing 10.6   Loading component with reducer

```
import { useReducer, useEffect } from "react";
const URL = "//swapi.dev/api/films";
const INITIAL_STATE = {
  status: "INITIALIZE",
  result: null,
  error: null,
};
function reducer(state, { type, payload }) {
  switch (type) {
    case "LOADING":
      return { ...state, status: "LOADING" };
    case "FAILURE":
      return { ...state, status: "FAILURE", error: payload };
    case "SUCCESS":
      return { ...state, status: "SUCCESS", result: payload };
    default:
      return state;
  }
}
function Loader() {
  const [state, dispatch] =
    useReducer(reducer, INITIAL_STATE);
  useEffect(() => {
```

We've extracted the initial state to a variable rather than one of the options inside the reducer.

We now only expect actions of type LOADING, FAILURE, and SUCCESS.

We've added a default case to the switch to handle the case where some unknown nonsense is dispatched.

When the loading succeeds, we change the status and set the result.

```
    dispatch({ type: "LOADING" });
    fetch(URL)
      .then((res) => res.json())
      .then(
        ({ results }) =>
          dispatch({
            type: "SUCCESS",
            payload: results,
          })
      )
      .catch(
        ({ message }) =>
          dispatch({
            type: "FAILURE",
            payload: message,
          })
      );
  }, []);
  const { status, error, result } = state;
  if (status === "INITIALIZE") {
    return <h1>Initializing...</h1>;
  }
  if (status === "LOADING") {
    return <h1>Loading...</h1>;
  }
  if (status === "FAILURE") {
    return <h1>Error occurred: {error}</h1>;
  }
  return (
    <>
      <h1>Results are in</h1>
      <ul>
        {result.map(({ title }) => (
          <li key={title}>{title}</li>
        ))}
      </ul>
    </>
  );
}
function App() {
  return <Loader />;
}
export default App;
```

In an effect hook, we start by setting the status to **LOADING** by dispatching the proper action.

If the results are returned, we set them in the state by dispatching the **SUCCESS** action.

If some error occurs along the way, we dispatch an **ERROR** action with a message.

With all of this out of the way, we can now destructure the state into the three variables we know it contains.

Finally, we display the proper message depending on the status variable using the values of error and result where necessary.

Repository: rq10-reducer-load

This example can be seen in repository `rq10-reducer-load`. You can use that repository by creating a new app based on the associated template:

```
$ npx create-react-app rq10-reducer-load --template rq10-reducer-load
```

Alternatively, you can go to this website to browse the code, see the application in action directly in your browser, or download the source code as a zip file:

https://rq2e.com/rq10-reducer-load

If we spin this up in the browser, it works! Check out figure 10.15.

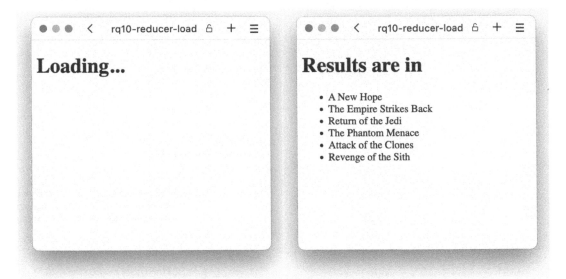

Figure 10.15   Our loading component in action—first in the loading state and second in the success state

If we change the URL to something that doesn't exist, for example, if we change it as follows:

```
const URL = '//swapi.dev.invalid/api/films';
```

our load will fail and we'll instead see the error message shown in figure 10.16.

Figure 10.16   If the load fails, an error message is displayed.

One of the nice things about this reducer we've created is that it's completely generalized. It doesn't care what we're loading or how we're loading it. The reducer only manages the state around things that can be loaded and potentially fail to load. Those things can be data, images, videos, fonts, baby otters, or anything else.

> **What is a reducer?**
>
> The term *reducer* comes from the software engineering model *MapReduce*, which is a way to think about data models and data streams regarding how to update your data models on the fly based on records in a data stream.
>
> Reducers are generally thought to be pure, simple, and side-effect-free functions that are deterministic and defined solely by their parameters. A reducer generally takes the current state of the world and some new record/action and updates the state of the world based on that.
>
> In large-scale computing and data analysis, reducers are used to quickly and efficiently traverse complex data structures.
>
> In React, *reducer* refers to the function or set of functions that converts the current state into a new state based on a given action. In React, we expect reducers to be pure, deterministic, and free of side effects as well.

10.3   Custom hooks

Let's go back to the dashboard example earlier in this book. We had this bit of code in multiple locations:

```
const name = useContext(NameContext);
```

Even though this piece of code is quite simple, it does require you to combine the two pieces, `useContext` and `NameContext`, correctly. Instead, we can make it a bit easier by moving this functionality to a new function and replacing the preceding code with this:

```
const name = useName();
```

Can we do this? Yes, of course, we can! We just create a custom function that does this work behind the scenes. So, this function uses the `useContext` hook to extract the current value from the `NameContext` context:

```
function useName() {
  return useContext(NameContext);
}
```

That's it—simply generalizing functionality by moving the duplicated part of the code to a common function.

But there's a twist here in that we're generalizing functionality *based on a React hook* and there are *rules* for how we can use React hooks. First, we can't use React hooks outside of functional components. Second, we can only use React hooks if we always use the same hooks in the same order.

This new function that we've created here, `useName`, also has to obey those rules. This function is now also a hook. It's a custom hook, and you've just created the very first one in this book! Note that this hook is very simple and doesn't take any arguments, but custom hooks can take arguments if they need to. You'll see some custom hooks in the next subsection. Now let's explore exactly what makes a function a custom hook, how you decide when and where to use custom hooks, and where you can find more of them.

10.3.1 *When is something a custom hook?*

A custom hook is a function that uses a hook. A hook can be any built-in hook or a custom hook, so it almost seems like a self-referential definition, but it's not. The whole thing starts with the 10 built-in hooks that we laid out earlier. If you create a function using any of those 10 hooks, then you've created a custom hook. If you create a function using any of those 10 hooks or using a custom hook that has used one of those 10 hooks, you've also created a custom hook, and so on. Thus, you do need to have one or more built-in hooks in there somewhere down the line for a function to be a custom hook. Some examples of this are shown in figure 10.17.

Note the naming of the functions here. It's a common practice to name all custom hooks as `use*` and name nothing else like that. However, there is no special magic associated with the naming itself. It's up to you as a developer to make sure that your

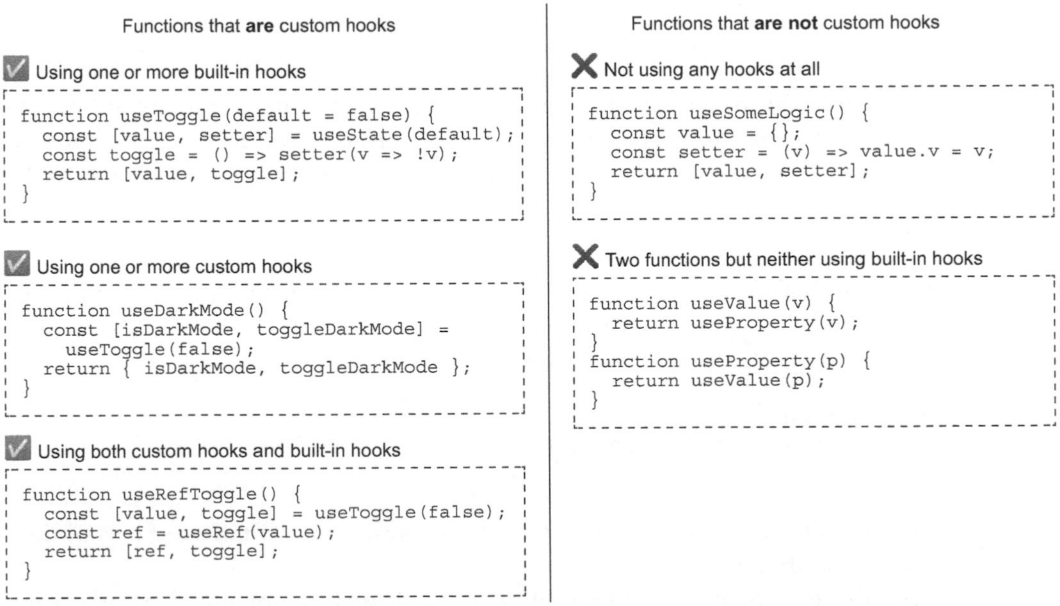

Functions that **are** custom hooks

✅ Using one or more built-in hooks

```
function useToggle(default = false) {
  const [value, setter] = useState(default);
  const toggle = () => setter(v => !v);
  return [value, toggle];
}
```

✅ Using one or more custom hooks

```
function useDarkMode() {
  const [isDarkMode, toggleDarkMode] =
    useToggle(false);
  return { isDarkMode, toggleDarkMode };
}
```

✅ Using both custom hooks and built-in hooks

```
function useRefToggle() {
  const [value, toggle] = useToggle(false);
  const ref = useRef(value);
  return [ref, toggle];
}
```

Functions that **are not** custom hooks

❌ Not using any hooks at all

```
function useSomeLogic() {
  const value = {};
  const setter = (v) => value.v = v;
  return [value, setter];
}
```

❌ Two functions but neither using built-in hooks

```
function useValue(v) {
  return useProperty(v);
}
function useProperty(p) {
  return useValue(p);
}
```

Figure 10.17   Examples of what a custom hook is and is not

custom hook is named use*. Likewise, you must check that something named use* is
in fact a custom hook.

10.3.2 *When should I use a custom hook?*

You should use a custom hook whenever you see the need for it. You can almost
never make your code too streamlined and compact. Well, you can, but that limit is
pretty far off.

You'll often find that your custom hooks take one of two forms:

- You're creating a custom hook for functionality that you're going to need in
  multiple places.
- You're moving functionality to a custom hook to clean up a component and
  make it simpler to read.

Both of these goals are completely valid and you'll often see developers using them
both. The difference between the two is often found in the naming of the hooks. If
the hook has a generic-sounding name, it's probably a reusable functionality. If it has
a very specific name, it's probably just an extraction of complex logic to an external
file to make the overview easier. Let's get started with some examples from previous
applications we've built in this book.

USETOGGLE

Let's look at one of our earlier components from chapter 6, where we had this excerpt
of code in the interactive countdown:

```
function Countdown({ from }) {
  ...
  const [isRunning, setRunning] = useState(false);
  ...
  onClick={() => setRunning((v) => !v)}
  ...
}
```

This functionality of creating a Boolean flag in state and having a toggle function that
allows the flag to alternate seems like a pretty general procedure.

Let's generalize that into a hook that kind of looks like the regular useState hook,
except that instead of a setter function, it returns a toggle function. Only Boolean values are allowed as state values:

```
function useToggle(default = false) {
  const [value, setter] = useState(Boolean(default));
  const toggle = () => setter(v => !v);
  return [value, toggle];
}
```

Note how this hook returns an array of a value and a function as the normal useState
hook. This is a common pattern in custom hooks too, as it makes the custom hook
familiar to work with. The value returned from the useToggle hook can be used in the

same way as the value returned from the `useState` hook, but the function is different. Where the `setter` function returned by the `useState` hook can be used to set the value to any value, the `toggle` function returned by the `useToggle` hook can only be used to invert the current Boolean value—the `toggle` function doesn't take an argument.

That's all it takes. This is a nice generic toggle. We can apply it to our interactive countdown like this:

```
function Countdown({ from }) {
  ...
  const [isRunning, toggleRunning] = useToggle();
  ...
  onClick={toggleRunning}
  ...
}
```

We didn't save a lot of characters, but it looks a lot simpler now without the extra function in there. We also can use this hook elsewhere, if we need a stateful toggle for something else.

USEFORM

You might remember from chapter 9 that we had this functionality in our form component:

```
function Address() {
  const [data, setData] = useState({
    address1: "",
    address2: "",
    zip: "",
    city: "",
    state: "",
    country: "",
  });
  const onChange = (evt) => {
    const key = evt.target.name;
    const value = evt.target.value;
    setData(oldData => ({ ...oldData, [key]: value }));
  };
  ...
}
```

We can also generalize this functionality into a custom hook that can be used, not just for this form with its six specific inputs, but for any form with any number of inputs:

```
function useForm(initialValues) {
  const [data, setData] = useState(initialValues);
  const onChange = (evt) => {
    const key = evt.target.name;
    const value = evt.target.value;
    setData(oldData => ({ ...oldData, [key]: value }));
  };
  return [data, onChange];
}
```

We can use that in our specific form as follows:

```
function Address() {
  const [data, onChange] = useForm({
    address1: "",
    address2: "",
    zip: "",
    city: "",
    state: "",
    country: "",
  });
  ...
}
```

That definitely looks nice and reusable.

USELOADER

Remember the reducer that we created earlier in this chapter? It was a generic hook for loading content of any type that allowed the component to specify whether loading was underway, successful, or failed. However, we didn't actually make the reducer generic, but just kept it inside our component. The component looked like this before:

```
import { useEffect, useReducer } from "react";
function reducer(state, { type, payload }) {
  switch (type) {
    case "LOADING":
      return { ...state, status: "LOADING" };
    case "FAILURE":
      return { ...state, status: "FAILURE", error: payload };
    case "SUCCESS":
      return { ...state, status: "SUCCESS", result: payload };
    default:
      return state;
  }
}
const INITIAL_STATE = { status: "INITIALIZE", result: null, error: null }
function Loader() {
  const [state, dispatch] = useReducer(reducer, INITIAL_STATE);
  useEffect(() => {
    dispatch({ type: "LOADING" });
    fetch(URL)
      .then((res) => res.json())
      .then(
        ({ results }) => dispatch({ type: "SUCCESS", payload: results })
      )
      .catch(
        ({ message }) => dispatch({ type: "FAILURE", payload: message })
      );
  }, []);
  ...
}
```

We can again extract the generic parts of the logic to an external hook and use that in the component. The hook would become the following:

```
import { useReducer } from "react";
function reducer(state, { type, payload }) {
  switch (type) {
    case "LOADING":
      return { ...state, status: "LOADING" };
    case "FAILURE":
      return { ...state, status: "FAILURE", error: payload };
    case "SUCCESS":
      return { ...state, status: "SUCCESS", result: payload };
    default:
      return state;
  }
};
function useLoader(initialState) {
  return useReducer(reducer, initialState);
}
export default useLoader;
```

If we save the preceding snippet to the file useLoader.js located next to the original component, our component will be simplified to just this:

```
import { useEffect } from "react";
import useLoader from "./useLoader";
const INITIAL_STATE = { status: "INITIALIZE", result: null, error: null };
function Loader() {
  const [state, dispatch] = useLoader(INITIAL_STATE);
  useEffect(() => {
    dispatch({ type: "LOADING" });
    fetch(URL)
      .then((res) => res.json())
      .then(
        ({ results }) => dispatch({ type: "SUCCESS", payload: results })
      )
      .catch(
        ({ message }) => dispatch({ type: "FAILURE", payload: message })
      );
  }, [actions]);
  ...
}
```

This separation of logic into two separate units makes both parts read a lot more clearly.

USECOUNTER

In this example, we extract our business logic inside a component to an external one just to make the original component easier to get an overview of without seeking to create generic functionality. Let's take our counter component from earlier with increment and decrement buttons. We don't need to use this specific functionality elsewhere; we're seeking to make our component less cluttered.

Before, the component looked like this:

```
function StyledCounter() {
  const [counter, setCounter] = useState(0);
  const update = (d) => setCounter((v) => v + d)
  const handleIncrement = () => update(1);
  const handleDecrement = () => update(-1);
  return (
    <section>
      <h1>Counter: {counter}</h1>
      <div>
        <Button handleClick={handleIncrement} label="Increment" />
        <Button handleClick={handleDecrement} label="Decrement" />
      </div>
    </section>
  );
}
```

If we extract the following part into a custom hook like

```
import { useState } from "react";
function useCounter() {
  const [counter, setCounter] = useState(0);
  const update = (d) => setCounter((v) => v + d);
  const handleIncrement = () => update(1);
  const handleDecrement = () => update(-1);
  return {counter, handleIncrement, handleDecrement};
}
export default useCounter;
```

and save the preceding snippet to the file useCounter.js located next to the original component, our component then becomes just this:

```
import useCounter from "./useCounter";
function StyledCounter() {
  const {counter, handleIncrement, handleDecrement} = useCounter();
  return (
    <section>
      <h1>Counter: {counter}</h1>
      <div>
        <Button handleClick={handleIncrement} label="Increment" />
        <Button handleClick={handleDecrement} label="Decrement" />
      </div>
    </section>
  );
}
```

Now that's a clean component! Just a single hook up top creates all the state values and callbacks needed to fulfill the responsibility, and the rest of the code in the component is the JSX.

10.3.3   *Where can I find custom hooks?*

You can find custom hooks everywhere! Custom hooks are one of the best ways to expose complex logic rules, and you'll find that many libraries and online utilities come in the form of custom hooks. Hooks are much more versatile than components because they don't come with implicit ideas about semantics, UIs, or HTML elements. Custom hooks are pure functionality that you can apply in whatever way fits your application. Here's an inexhaustive list of excellent custom hooks you can use directly in your application:

- *useHooks* (https://usehooks.com)—A collection of various general-purpose hooks for everyday work.
- *Collection of React Hooks* (https://nikgraf.github.io/react-hooks)—A huge library of more than 400 user-submitted hooks for all sorts of purposes.
- *React Aria* (https://react-spectrum.adobe.com/react-aria)—An open source library of accessibility-specific hooks providing proper keyboard and pointer bindings for many different more or less complex widgets developed and maintained by Adobe
- *awesome-react-hooks* (https://github.com/rehooks/awesome-react-hooks)—A curated list of React hooks sorted by category with a short description for each

10.4   *Quiz*

1 Which of the following is the correct way to create a context provider for a context named `StyleContext` with the value `style`?

   a ```
      <StyleProvider value={style}>
        ...
      </StyleProvider>
      ```

   b  ```
      <StyleContext.Provider value={style}>
        ...
      </StyleContext.Provider>
      ```

   c ```
      <StyleProvider style={style}>
        ...
      </StyleProvider>
      ```

   d  ```
      <StyleContext.Provider style={style}>
        ...
      </StyleContext.Provider>
      ```

2 If you use the `useContext` hook with a context that does not have an associated provider above the component in question in the JSX document tree, the hook throws an error. *True* or *false*?

3 The `useState` hook is superior to the `useReducer` hook in every way, and anything you can do with the latter, you can do better with the `useState` hook. *True* or *false*?

4 If you define a custom hook, you have to register it as an *official* custom hook using a specific React function. *True* or *false*?

5 Custom hooks are a great way to generalize functionality in your applications and make components simpler to read and use. *True* or *false*?

Quiz answers

1
```
<StyleContext.Provider value={style}>
  ...
</StyleContext.Provider>
```

You always provide a context through the context's `.Provider` property and you always provide the context value using the `value` property.

2 *False.* The `useContext` hook will return the default value provided to `create-Context`, if no associated provider is found.

3 Mostly *false*, however, there are definitely situations where you want to use a `useState` hook over a `useReducer` hook. These two hooks serve slightly different purposes and are rarely in direct competition with each other.

4 *False.* Any function you define that makes use of another hook automatically becomes a custom hook. You don't have to do anything else to make it work as a hook.

5 *True.* Custom hooks are one of the primary ways to share complex business logic between components in an application, and even between different applications. Many React libraries expose their functionality in the form of custom hooks.

Summary

- React Context and the `useContext` hook are extremely versatile and useful tools in your React developer toolbox.
- React Context is the perfect tool to avoid prop drilling—the practice of passing properties to a component with the sole purpose of having the component pass the property on to the next component down the line. This is bad software design, and React Context helps you avoid this.
- A React Context consumer (either through the `.Consumer` property or via the `useContext` hook) will get the current context value from the nearest React Context provider of the same type when looking up the component tree—or the default value if no provider is found.
- The `useContext` hook is recommended for any functional codebase over the `.Consumer` component property.
- React Context can be used for very complex data management in large applications with great success.
- Reducer hooks are ideal for managing complex state in your applications. They're a great tool to handle interdependent variables and ensure that invalid state configurations aren't possible.
- Reducers are functions that reduce state to a new state based on a given action.
- Reducers are pure and free of side effects in their nature.
- You can create custom hooks to generalize functionality.
- Custom hooks are often a lot easier to generalize than whole components and are often the primary way to share business logic between parts of your application.
- You can find a ton of custom hooks online in packages or for simple copy-paste.

Project: Website menu

We've reached a milestone. With the completion of chapter 10, you now know all you need to know about React itself to start building some pretty complex web applications. This and the next two chapters are all project chapters. These projects are much larger examples that guide you through the first steps of creating a full-featured web application and set you up for creating more advanced variants of those same applications.

The project in this chapter is a website menu. It's a top-bar menu component that you can directly use in a website. We'll create this project in five steps, as outlined in figure 11.1.

The scaffold is where you start out building this application. Each additional step of the application adds more advanced features to the menu while utilizing new parts of the React API. We'll set up step 1 first in this chapter, and then we'll

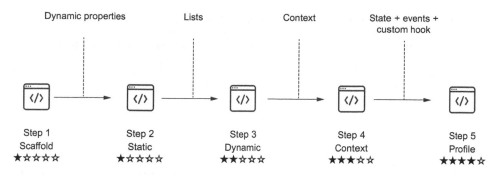

Figure 11.1 We start this project with a scaffold, and through the steps in this chapter, we'll build a fully fledged dynamic menu with an optional link to a profile page.

solve step 2 together. From then on, we'll introduce the subsequent steps to you, but then you have to solve them yourself.

Of course, we'll provide a reference solution to all the steps, including steps 3 to 5, but we won't tell you how we got there. Your solution to steps 3 to 5 will most definitely not be identical to ours because there are so many different ways to do things. If you're ever stuck, feel free to peek at our solutions to the latter steps, but please first try to solve them yourself.

Table 11.1 outlines exactly what happens at each step in terms of what functionality we're creating as well as which parts of the React API we're utilizing.

Table 11.1 The five steps of the menu project

Step	Feature	Additional React API used	Difficulty
Step 1: Scaffold	Create the basic component structure for a website with an empty menu.	Chapters 1–4: Functional components using JSX	★☆☆☆☆
Step 2: Static menu	Add a static JSX menu using a custom menu item component with dynamic properties.	Chapters 3–4: Using JSX with dynamic properties	★☆☆☆☆
Step 3: Dynamic menu from a list of links	Render the menu from a list of objects describing the menu items. Note: This is homework. You have to create this step *yourself!*	Chapters 3–4: Rendering lists of JSX elements	★★☆☆☆
Step 4: Retrieving links from context	Retrieve the list of menu items from a context provided around the entire application. Note: This is homework. You have to create this step *yourself!*	Chapter 10: Context	★★★☆☆

Table 11.1   The five steps of the menu project *(continued)*

Step	Feature	Additional React API used	Difficulty
Step 5: Adding an optional link	Add a login/logout button that will dynamically add and remove a profile link to/from the menu. Note: This is homework. You have to create this step *yourself!*	Chapter 5: State Chapter 8: Events Chapter 10: Complex context and custom hooks	★★★★☆

Before we get started, let's take a look at what we're building. It's a minimalist website with a top bar with menu links. Take a look at figure 11.2 for a screenshot of the menu in action.

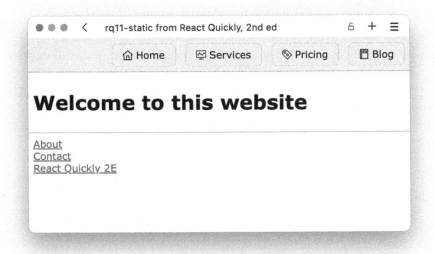

Figure 11.2   This is the website we'll build. The menu at the top—Home, Services, Pricing, and Blog—is the main focus. In the first iteration, the menu items are statically defined.

For a little flair, we'll also add some UX, including a slight hover effect when you move your pointer over one of the menu items. Figure 11.3 shows what this looks like. With the design and end goal out of the way, let's get started!

> **NOTE**   The source code for the scaffolding and suggested solutions to all the sections in this chapter are available at https://rq2e.com/ch11. But as you learned in chapter 2, you can instantiate all the examples and solutions directly from the command line using a single command.

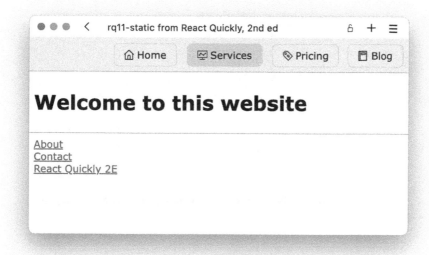

Figure 11.3 When the user hovers over a menu item, the background turns a slightly darker gray to highlight what the user is interacting with.

11.1 Scaffolding for the menu

Okay, here we go. Our first "real" React project is on the line. To do this, we need a plan. We'll think this through as if it was a real project that we had to solve for a client, an employer, or your uncle's lawn mowing and babysitting business, aka Laps & Naps Inc.

Starting with the desired result as illustrated in figures 11.2 and 11.3, we'll go through these steps:

1 Define the HTML output that will render the desired result.
2 Create a number of React components that will render JSX to achieve the desired HTML.
3 Place static images in the public folder that we can load at runtime.
4 Create a stylesheet.
5 Implement the components that we need to get the necessary functionality.

Let's get cracking!

11.1.1 HTML output

In this project, we're starting out by building a static HTML page with React and JSX. In general, you neither would nor should use React for this, but because it's only the first step, and we'll be adding dynamic functionality on top of that later, it makes sense to start out with static output. The desired output HTML for the scaffolding looks like figure 11.4.

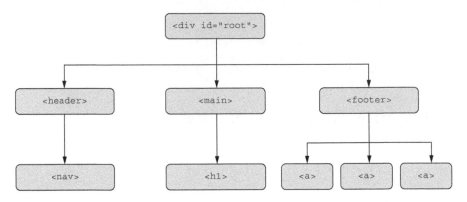

Figure 11.4   The HTML node tree for the scaffold of the menu application consists of just these elements.

11.1.2 *Component hierarchy*

To render the desired HTML tree, we need a React application that renders a similar set of JSX nodes. We could use any number of React components to implement this. We could create a component for every HTML node if we wanted to, or we could create a single component that renders the entire thing. This is where the developer's judgment comes into play.

You've seen us devise the desired React component structure for all the examples so far in this book. But soon (later in this chapter), this will be on you. You have to be in charge. You have to come up with a component tree for a given desired output.

Figuring out how to cut the cake and split a given desired output into components is a task central to being a React developer. In figure 11.5, you can see two different approaches to how to create components that render the desired output.

There's more than one way to skin a component tree, and no one way is the right one. When deciding how to structure your components, you should aim for a balance between complexity and responsibility. In this case, we could easily implement the whole application in a single component as in the left-most case in figure 11.5; but knowing we'll add extra functionality inside the <nav> element in the header, we'll encapsulate that as its own component. It will be a very small component for now, but we'll expand it later.

11.1.3 *Icons*

As you might have noticed in the original screenshot in figure 11.2, we have some icons in the menu. Let's take a closer look at those in figure 11.6.

There are many ways to render icons in React, but we're using the simplest one for now. We'll render scalable vector graphics (SVG) images loaded from an external file.

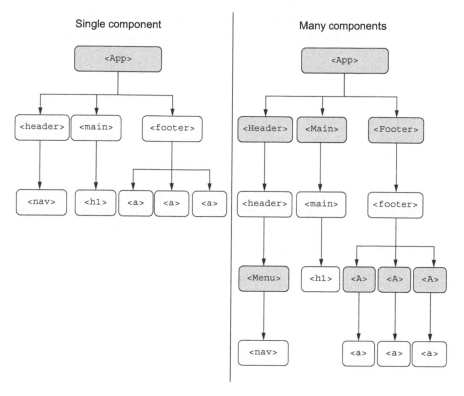

Figure 11.5   Two different approaches to creating components for a desired output. We're actually going to go for neither, but rather a medium approach between the two because we're focusing on the menu only.

Figure 11.6   A close-up of the icons in the menu

We can do that by placing files inside the public folder in the React application folder like so:

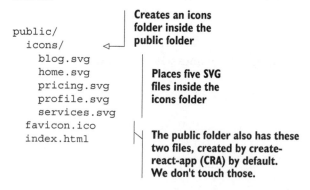

```
public/
  icons/
    blog.svg
    home.svg
    pricing.svg
    profile.svg
    services.svg
  favicon.ico
  index.html
```

Creates an icons folder inside the public folder

Places five SVG files inside the icons folder

The public folder also has these two files, created by create-react-app (CRA) by default. We don't touch those.

When these files are inside the public folder, we can load them wherever via the path "/icons/blog.svg". For example, we can render the blog icon as an `<img>` tag:

```
<img src="/icons/blog.svg" alt="" />
```

Note that we also have a `profile.svg` image in the `icons` folder. We don't need that for the first versions of the menu, but we'll need it later, so it's already there if you keep working on the same application. All the icons are public domain and completely free to use in whatever context you desire.

11.1.4 CSS

Finally, we'll need quite a bit of CSS for this application. So far, we've used inline styles via the style attribute on JSX elements. This has worked okay because we only had very limited styling to apply. In this application, however, we need a lot of styles, and we need hover styling. Rendering a lot of styles is possible using inline styles, though it's not optimal. But hover styling is impossible using inline styles, so we'll need a proper stylesheet.

React and CRA, fortunately, make this incredibly simple. We haven't discussed this much, but in a React file, you can import a stylesheet directly, and the React compiler will convert it to a regular stylesheet inserted in the HTML when needed.

The pros and cons of loading styles inline or using stylesheets is outside the scope of this book, so, for now, we'll use this approach because it's simple and it works well for smaller applications:

1 Create a stylesheet, `style.css`, inside the `src` folder.
2 Load the stylesheet inside the main `App.js` file where the root application is defined.
3 Apply class names to JSX elements and have them render using the rules defined in the stylesheet.

And that's it!

Loading a stylesheet in JavaScript means importing the file. You don't import it *as* something, like you do for components, you simply import the file like this:

```
import "./style.css";
```

That's all it takes. You can now apply class names where relevant.

11.1.5 Template

We've created this whole scaffold as a template for you to start your work on.

> **Repository: rq11-scaffold**
>
> This example can be seen in repository `rq11-scaffold`. You can use that repository by creating a new app based on the associated template:
>
> ```
> $ npx create-react-app rq11-scaffold --template rq11-scaffold
> ```
>
> Alternatively, you can go to this website to browse the code, see the application in action directly in your browser, or download the source code as a zip file:
>
> https://rq2e.com/rq11-scaffold

This template comes with the following files relevant for your application:

```
public/
  icons/
    blog.svg
    home.svg          Icons used
    pricing.svg       to render the
    profile.svg       menu items
    services.svg
  favicon.ico
  index.html          Default files included in
src/                  a CRA minimal project
  App.js              untouched by us
  index.js
  Menu.js
  style.css     ◁     A complete
                      stylesheet with all
  Custom              the rules required to
  components with     complete this project
  the basic scaffold
```

However, if you want to start from scratch, you can do so. You can use the following template that only contains the icons and stylesheet, but no custom components. The src folder is completely standard based on the regular minimal template except for the stylesheet needed:

```
npx create-react-app web-menu --template rq11-minimal
```

If you do use this latter approach, you'll have to start editing src/App.js. Remember to import the stylesheet as well. This minimal template contains these files:

```
public/
  icons/
    blog.svg
    home.svg          Icons used
    pricing.svg       to render the
    profile.svg       menu items
    services.svg
  favicon.ico
  index.html          Default files included in
src/                  a CRA minimal project
  App.js              untouched by us
  index.js
  style.css           A complete stylesheet with
                      all the rules required to
                      complete this project
```

11.1.6 Source code

The source code for the scaffolding application, defined in src/App.js, follows.

> **Listing 11.1**   src/App.js **in the scaffolding**

```
import Menu from "./Menu";              The menu is defined
import "./style.css";                   in an external file and
function App() {                        imported at the top.
  return (
    <>                                  Defines the CSS
      <header>                          externally in a file
        <Menu />                        named style.css
      </header>
      <main>
        <h1>Welcome to this website</h1>
      </main>
      <footer>
        <a href="/about">About</a>
        <a href="/contact">Contact</a>
        <a href="//reactquickly.dev">React Quickly 2E</a>
      </footer>
    </>
  );
}
export default App;
```

Renders the menu component in the header at the relevant place

The source code for the CSS file, src/style.css, is defined in the next listing.

> **Listing 11.2**   src/style.css **in the scaffolding**

```
html,
body {
  margin: 0;
  font-family: Verdana;
}
```

```css
main,
header,
footer {
  padding: 8px;
}

header {
  border-bottom: 1px solid darkgray;
  background: #eee;
}
footer {
  border-top: 1px solid darkgray;
  display: flex;
  flex-direction: column;
}
.menu {
  display: flex;
  gap: 16px;
  padding: 0;
  margin: 0;
  list-style: none;
  justify-content: flex-end;
}
.menu-link {
  text-decoration: none;
  color: inherit;
  display: flex;
  align-items: center;
  gap: 5px;
  padding: 8px 16px;
  border: 1px solid lightgray;
  border-radius: 8px;
}
.menu-link:hover {
  background: lightgray;
}
```

The source code for the menu, defined in `src/Menu.js`, follows.

Listing 11.3   `src/Menu.js` in the scaffolding

```js
function Menu() {
  return <nav></nav>;              ⟵───  The menu only renders an empty
}                                         <nav> element for now.
export default Menu;
```

11.1.7 *In the browser*

If we run this in the browser, we get a nice website with an empty menu, as shown in figure 11.7.

Figure 11.7   A website with a temporarily empty menu that we'll soon fill with some great links

11.2   *Rendering a static menu*

In this step of the project, we'll take the current state of affairs after completing the first part of the exercise and add the required functionality to render a static menu with a fixed list of menu items.

You can start the project by either implementing the scaffolding yourself based on the information given in the previous section or starting from the application defined in the `rq11-scaffold` template. The result of this step is the application defined in the following repository.

Repository: rq11-static

This example can be seen in repository `rq11-static`. You can use that repository by creating a new app based on the associated template:

```
$ npx create-react-app rq11-static --template rq11-static
```

Alternatively, you can go to this website to browse the code, see the application in action directly in your browser, or download the source code as a zip file:

https://rq2e.com/rq11-static

11.2.1 The goal of this exercise

The goal of this exercise is to populate the empty menu in the previous step. The menu component was just this—a completely empty element with no menu items:

```
function Menu() {
  return <nav></nav>;
}
```

Before we get started, we first need to define the desired HTML output, then decide on a component tree that best creates this output, and, finally, implement these components.

11.2.2 Desired HTML output

We're focusing on the HTML output inside the <nav> component only. To render a list of links in a menu, the HTML tree visualized in figure 11.8 renders the desired outcome.

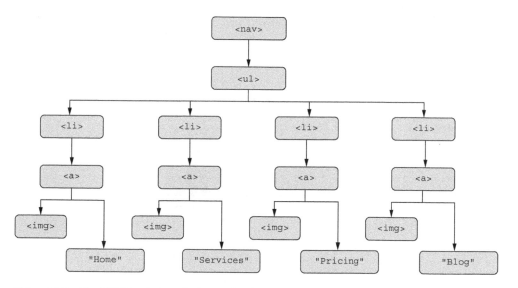

Figure 11.8 The HTML node tree for the navigation element is an unordered list of links.

11.2.3 Component tree

The component tree for this one kind of writes itself. We want to create a component that encapsulates the duplicated HTML in the HTML tree in figure 11.8. We can call that a MenuItem component, which takes three properties:

- href—The actual target URL that the link will point to
- icon—The name of the SVG file to load as an icon
- children—The text that goes inside the link

We can illustrate this as a component tree in figure 11.9.

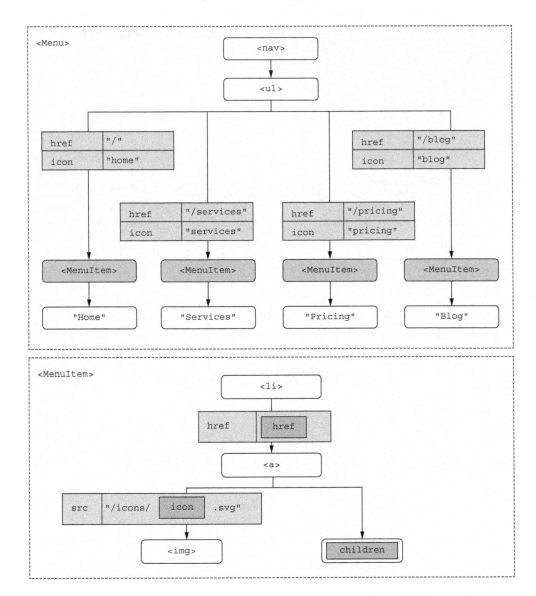

**Figure 11.9 Along with having two components, we pass two properties and children to the
MenuItem component.**

With that out of the way, we can now implement the required changes in the relevant
components.

11.2.4 Source code

First, we implement the updated `Menu.js` component in the next listing. As illustrated in figure 11.7, we need to render a list of four `MenuItem` instances.

Listing 11.4 `src/Menu.js` **for a static menu**

```
import MenuItem from "./MenuItem";
function Menu() {
  return (
    <nav>
      <ul className="menu">
        <MenuItem href="/" icon="home">
          Home
        </MenuItem>
        <MenuItem href="/services" icon="services">
          Services
        </MenuItem>
        <MenuItem href="/pricing" icon="pricing">
          Pricing
        </MenuItem>
        <MenuItem href="/blog" icon="blog">
          Blog
        </MenuItem>
      </ul>
    </nav>
  );
}
export default Menu;
```

Four instances of our MenuItem component, each with slightly different properties

Second, we implement the new component, `MenuItem.js`.

Listing 11.5 `src/MenuItem.js` **for a static menu**

The MenuItem component takes three properties, of which one is the special children property.

Defines the icon source based on the known location of the icon files as well as the passed icon property

```
function MenuItem({ href, icon, children }) {
  const iconSrc = `/icons/${icon}.svg`;
  return (
    <li>
      <a href={href} className="menu-link">
        <img src={iconSrc} width="16" alt="" />
        {children}
      </a>
    </li>
  );
}
export default MenuItem;
```

The anchor element needs an href, which we take from the properties.

The image element needs a source, which we've calculated in a variable.

Renders the children property next to the image as the link text

11.2.5   *In the browser*

If we run this in the browser, we get exactly what we wanted as originally illustrated in figure 11.2, but repeated here in figure 11.10 for comparison.

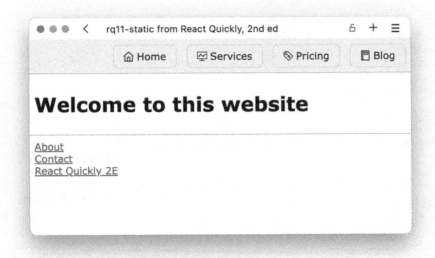

Figure 11.10   Our static menu works! Try hovering the menu items in your browser to see the slight hover effect achieved by the stylesheet rules.

11.3   *Homework: A dynamic menu*

After step 2, we have a nice static menu, so you might now be wondering why we would want to do that differently. Well, the thing is, the menu items will be dynamic in a later stage of this project (management told us some time ago), so we might as well prepare ourselves for that.

Dynamic menu items mean that the number of items as well as the text, icon, and perhaps `href` of the individual menu items might be updated as the user interacts with the site. Imagine that you log into the website as a customer, and suddenly some of the menu items are removed and others are added. Different customers might see different menu items once logged in. So, while the current approach works, it's not ideal for a dynamic menu, where we have to update the menu items depending on state and external data.

11.3.1   *Goal for this step*

The goal for this step is to prepare the project for dynamic rendering by switching to a list of objects to be rendered as menu items, rather than manually typing all the menu items out in JSX. The structure of the project will be the same as you'll probably have the same number of components, but a bit more data will be passed between components.

However, it's a requirement that the list of menu items is defined in the App component (because some senior architect says so, and who are we to question seniority?). Because we'll use this list in the Menu component, we need to pass this list as a property.

11.3.2 Hints for solving this step

The central points of this step require answering these two questions:

1   How will the list items be structured to capture all the information we need to render the menu items?
2   How will we render the menu items based on a list of objects?

We'll give you a hint for each of these questions.

DEFINING LIST ITEMS

The list items need to contain information about where the menu item link points to (the href), which icon is going to be displayed, and what text is going to be displayed. This can be captured in an object like this:

```
{ title: "Home", href: "/", icon: "home" }
```

Naming properties is completely up to you, and you might do it differently than this if you want to.

RENDERING LIST ITEMS

To render JSX nodes based on a list of items, think back to section 3.2.8 on rendering a list of JSX objects. This generally takes the following structure:

```
<parent>
  {list.map((object) => (          ←——| Maps the list of objects
    <node                              | to a list of JSX nodes
      key={object.id}            ←——
      otherProp={object.other}   ←——| Adds a unique
      ...                            | key for each node
    />          Adds any other relevant
  ))}             properties from the
</parent>        mapped list element
```

Importantly, remember to define a unique key on each node in the mapped response.

11.3.3 Component hierarchy

The number of components doesn't change, but we use them a bit differently. Where we previously had a static list of four MenuItem component instances inside the Menu component, we now have a dynamic list of MenuItem instances based on the length of the array of links. We need to pass this list of links from the App component to the Menu component. The only unchanged component is the MenuItem component, as it was already dynamic and capable of displaying dynamic content.

Our recommendation for a component hierarchy is displayed in figure 11.11, but you're free to come up with your own structure, if you so desire. There is no single correct solution to this.

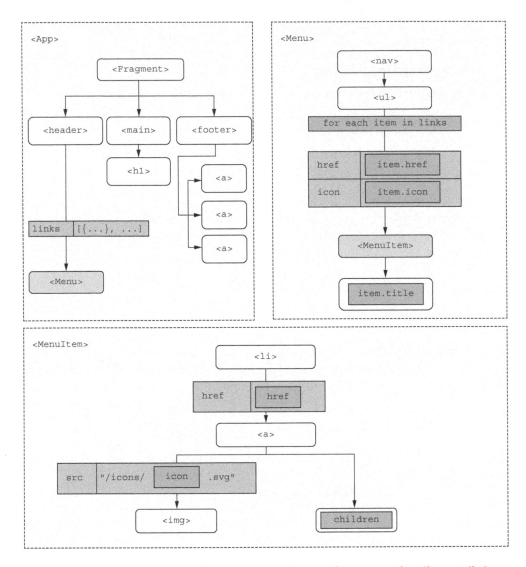

Figure 11.11   We now pass a property to the `Menu` component from `App`, and we then use that property to generate a dynamic number of `MenuItem` instances.

11.3.4 *What now?*

We strongly recommend that you have a go at this yourself. If you followed in step 2 implementing the static list yourself, we recommend that you just keep going from there. But if you want to start from a clean slate, you can also start with our implementation of step 2 from the `rq11-static` repository.

After completing this exercise, you might want to compare your solution to our version, not to see if you got it 100% identical (because odds are small that you did), but just to see if we had a different approach.

> **Repository: rq11-dynamic**
>
> This example can be seen in repository `rq11-dynamic`. You can use that repository by creating a new app based on the associated template:
>
> ```
> $ npx create-react-app rq11-dynamic --template rq11-dynamic
> ```
>
> Alternatively, you can go to this website to browse the code, see the application in action directly in your browser, or download the source code as a zip file:
>
> https://rq2e.com/rq11-dynamic

If you enjoyed this step, we recommend that you try the next two steps in this project, though they do get a little bit harder.

11.4   Homework: Retrieving items from context

We've made the menu dynamic now, which is a great first step. But to make it truly dynamic, we need to be able to manipulate the list of menu items from throughout the application. Passing lists of links around to a lot of components would be annoying, so we would rather move the list of links to a context that surrounds the entire application. This will ensure that we have access to the list easily from anywhere.

11.4.1   Goal for this step

In this step, we'll take the abstraction up another level. Rather than pass the list of links around as a property between components, we'll move it to a context. For now, this context will only contain our list of links, which is used inside the `Menu` component. To prepare for the next step, where the context will need to also be accessible from the rest of the application, we recommend wrapping the context around the entire application.

11.4.2   Hints for solving this step

To load the links from a context, we need to do three things:

1 Define a React context in a variable that is accessible from multiple components.
2 Create a context provider around the relevant part of the application.
3 Apply the `useContext` hook where we need access to the context variable.

DEFINING A CONTEXT

To define a React context, you simply invoke the `createContext()` function from the React package. To make sure this variable is accessible from multiple components, you can create it in a separate file and export it. This is the shortest way to achieve this goal:

```
import { createContext } from 'react';
const Context = createContext([]);      ⟵┤ The default argument is an
export default Context;                         empty array in this instance.
```

Note how we supply an empty array as the default context value. If, for some reason, we tried to access the context where it isn't defined, we would get an empty list of links as the value.

CREATING A CONTEXT PROVIDER

To create a context provider, wrap the relevant components inside a `Context.Provider` component. This component instance should be supplied with a `value` property, which will contain the current context value.

If you have the context in a variable named `MenuContext` and a list of links in a variable named `links`, you can provide a context for a set of components, A, B, and C, like this:

```
return (
  <MenuContext.Provider value={links}>
    <A />
    <B />
    <C />
  </MenuContext.Provider>
);
```

ACCESSING THE CONTEXT VALUE

To access the context value, you use the `useContext` hook inside a component that exists somewhere inside the context provider. If the context in question is named `MenuContext`, you can access the current value like this:

```
import { useContext } from 'react';
function SomeComponent() {
  const value = useContext(MenuContext);
  ...
}
```

11.4.3 Component hierarchy

Once again, you can do this in many ways. We've outlined our suggestion for how to accomplish this in figure 11.12, but it's just one such tree diagram. Many other solutions are possible.

11.4.4 What now?

We recommend that you have a go at this yourself. If you've completed step 3, we recommend that you keep going from there. But if you don't like your result or for some other reason want to start from a fresh slate, you can start with our implementation of step 3 in the `rq11-dynamic` repository. When complete, you'll probably want to compare your solution to ours for educational purposes.

Now that you've come this far, we suggest that you also try the next step. It's a bit harder, but most likely worth it, as you'll really see how things start to work together.

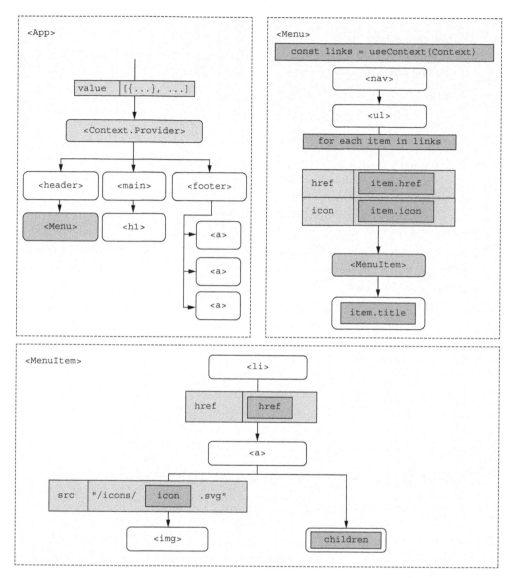

Figure 11.12 The whole application is wrapped in a context provider, and we use the same context to retrieve the context value inside the menu component.

Repository: rq11-context

This example can be seen in repository `rq11-context`. You can use that repository by creating a new app based on the associated template:

```
$ npx create-react-app rq11-context --template rq11-context
```

(continued)

Alternatively, you can go to this website to browse the code, see the application in action directly in your browser, or download the source code as a zip file:

https://rq2e.com/rq11-context

11.5   *Homework: Optional link*

We've reached the last step of this project. We'll now add some very simple authentication mechanics, and, once authenticated, the user will be presented with an additional link in the menu.

How basic of an authentication scheme, you ask? Trust-based. If you click the Log In button, you're logged in. If you then click the Log Out button, you're logged out. This isn't useful for any real authentication, of course, but for demonstration purposes, it will serve us fine. The flowchart for this application is incredibly simple, as you can see in figure 11.13.

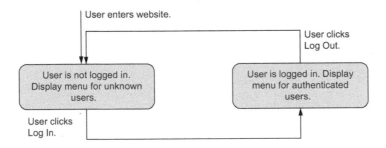

Figure 11.13   A user will either be logged in or not, and the menu will reflect that.

To achieve this, we'll add a very simple Log In button to the main section of the page below the headline. You can see what the website should look like in this state in figure 11.14.

If you click the button, you're considered logged in and can see the new profile link in the menu. You can see what this should look like in figure 11.15.

11.5.1   *Goal for this step*

The goal for this step is to extend the context provider with the extra properties required to know the state and to manipulate it. We also need to store the state somewhere in an updatable way.

While doing this work, feel free to reorganize components as you see fit. You might want to add extra components if that seems like the right thing to do. As mentioned earlier, that is a judgment call for the developer to make.

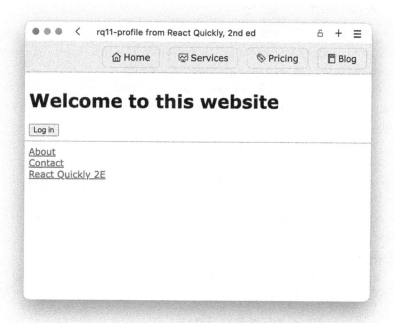

Figure 11.14 When the user is unknown, the main section of the website contains a Log In button, and the menu still has four menu items like before.

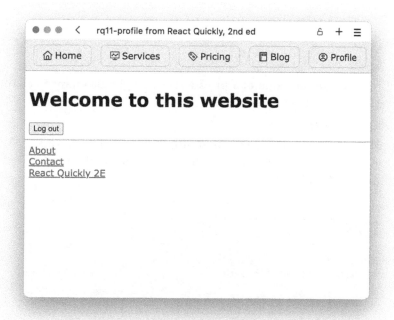

Figure 11.15 When the user is authenticated, the main section of the website now contains a Log Out button, and the menu has an extra, fifth, menu item.

11.5.2 *Hints for solving this step*

Here are some hints that might help you solve this:

- In step 4, the context value was only a list of links. You now need the context to hold more than one value, so you probably want to use an object.
- You can create a custom hook to more easily access the value of a context.
- To keep track of the Boolean state of whether the user is authenticated or not, you probably need a stateful hook.
- Moving the context provider to a dedicated component might make the application easier to understand.
- Because the main section of the application now has more logic, it could benefit from becoming its own component.
- Remember that you can use the special property `children` to pass components "through" another component.

OBJECT AS A CONTEXT VALUE

While we did not directly address this in chapter 10, you can store multiple values in a context. You do so by using an object:

```
const value = {              We can have as many values as
  someValue,          ⭠      we want in a provider object.
  someFunction,       ⭠
);                              We can even put
return (                        functions in there.
  <Context.Provider value={value}>
    ...
  </Context.Provider>
);
```

Remember, if you change the value of a provider, you might also want to change the initial default value passed to `createContext`.

CUSTOM HOOK FOR CONTEXT ACCESS

If you have a context that you want to use in multiple places—let's say it's an API context for access to some general API functionality—you can use the `useContext` hook directly in multiple places like so:

```
// In Component.js
import { useContext } from 'react';
import APIContext from './API';
...
function Component() {
  const value = useContext(APIContext);
  ...
}
```

But to make life simpler for yourself (and perhaps your fellow team members), you can create a custom hook that does this for you. Then, you only have to import a single thing:

```
// In API.js
...
export function useAPI() {
  return useContext(APIContext);
};
// In Component.js
import { useAPI } from './API';
...
function Component() {
  const value = useAPI();
  ...
}
```

Creating tiny custom hooks like that might look a bit silly, but it's actually helpful and a very common practice.

STATEFUL BOOLEAN

If you need a simple value to be stateful in React, the easiest way is to apply the use-State hook, as explained in chapter 5:

```
import { useState } from 'react';
const [isVisible, setVisible] = useState(false);  ⟵
```

The return value from useState can be deconstructed into the value and the setter function.

Remember that you don't have to expose the state setter directly. You can create your own functions to make it easier to work with:

```
const [isVisible, setVisible] = useState(false);
const show = () => setVisible(true);
const hide = () => setVisible(false);
```

These are just general examples, of course; you have to modify them for the application in question.

In addition, remember to actually use this stateful variable in your application. In this application in particular, you want to vary the value of the links variable depending on the stateful Boolean.

DEDICATED CONTEXT PROVIDER COMPONENT

When we add more logic and more values to our context, it often makes sense to move it to a dedicated component. So rather than

```
function App() {
  ...
  const value = { a, b, c };
  return (
    <Context.Provider value={value}>
      ...
    </Context.Provider>
  );
}
```

we can instead create two components, `App` and `ValueProvider`, and split them up like this:

```
function ValueProvider() {
  const value = { a, b, c };
  return (
    <Context.Provider value={value}>
      ...
    </Context.Provider>
  );
}
function App() {
  ...
  return (
    <ValueProvider>
      ...
    </ValueProvider>
  );
}
```

CONVERTING PART OF A COMPONENT TO A SEPARATE COMPONENT

If a component grows too complex, it can make sense to split a part of it out. Let's say we have a component with several different sections, and we're adding complexity to one of them:

```
// In App.js
function App() {
  const onClickButton = () => { ... };        ◄── This variable is
  return (                                          only used inside
    <>                                              the main section.
      <header>
        ...
      </header>
      <main>
        <p>This is main</p>                        The main section here is
        <button onClick={onClickButton}>           growing a bit large and
          ...                                        can be refactored into a
        </button>                                    new component.
      </main>
      <aside>
        ...
      </aside>
    </>
  );
}
```

At some point, you might feel that the main section of the application grows a bit large and it should become its own component. If you want to do so, you take the relevant JSX (and associated variables) of the component and move it to a new component:

```
                                    We created a new component
                                    (in a new file) with only part of
// In Main.js                       the previous component.
function Main() {              ◄──
```

```
      const onClickButton = () => { ... };
      return (
        <main>
          <p>This is main</p>
          <button onClick={onClickButton}>
            ...
          </button>
        </main>
      );
    }
    // In App.js
    function App() {
      return (
        <>
          <header>
            ...
          </header>
          <Main />
          <aside>
            ...
          </aside>
        </>
      );
    }
```

> **We can now safely replace the entire main section from before with our new component.**

Both components are now much simpler, and it's easier to understand their purpose.

THE CHILDREN PROPERTY

Sometimes you might create a new component, but you don't want to make it too specific. You still want to be able to populate it with different content in different circumstances. Let's say that you have an application with multiple identically styled sections, but the contents are different:

```
function App() {
  return (
    <main>
      <section className="section section-fancy">
        <A />
      </section>
      <section className="section section-fancy">
        <B />
      </section>
      <section className="section section-fancy">
        <C />
      </section>
    </main>
  );
}
```

> **But the contents are different.**

> **We have the same class on all the sections.**

Here, it can make sense to create a component for the sections that still allow you to pass in arbitrary children. You can do just that with the `children` property:

```
function Section({ children }) {
  return (
    <section className="section section-fancy">
      {children}
    </section>
  );
}
function App() {
  return (
    <main>
      <Section>
        <A />
      </Section>
      <Section>
        <B />
      </Section>
      <Section>
        <C />
      </Section>
    </main>
  );
}
```

This is a new component with the generic section markup.

Remember to render the children property where you want the children to appear.

We can now replace the sections with our new component, which makes the app look a lot neater without the repeated logic.

Why do we mention that in this step? Well, this is often used for dedicated provider components, so you can do something like this:

```
function App() {
  ...
  return (
    <ValueProvider>
      <h1>Some title in here</h1>
    </ValueProvider>
  );
}
```

11.5.3 *Component hierarchy*

You have a lot more choices to make in this last step, so we're not going to try to influence you too much. However, figure 11.16 shows a high-level overview of how we might see the components laid out in the final application.

11.5.4 *What now?*

If you want to have a go at this yourself, and we really think you should, you can keep working on your application from the previous step. If you want to start from our application as completed after step 4, you can start with the rq11-context repository. When complete, you probably want to compare your solution to ours for educational purposes.

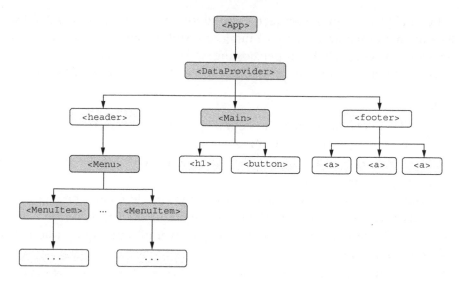

Figure 11.16 A high-level overview of how the components could be laid out in the application in this final step

Repository: rq11-profile

This example can be seen in repository `rq11-profile`. You can use that repository by creating a new app based on the associated template:

```
$ npx create-react-app rq11-profile --template rq11-profile
```

Alternatively, you can go to this website to browse the code, see the application in action directly in your browser, or download the source code as a zip file:

https://rq2e.com/rq11-profile

And that's it. That's the end of the project for now. But feel free to expand this to add more functionality and play around with just how powerful contexts are for data control. You can add a different login button that would log you in as an administrator, which might render even more menu items—or maybe a completely different menu.

11.6 Final thoughts

This first project had a lot of handholding, and we went through the steps very slowly with lots of rather detailed hints on how to complete them. In the next two projects, there will be less handholding and fewer verbose hints. But don't hesitate to refer back to this project to see which steps you might want to go through to complete an exercise.

The final product in this project is a solid foundation for building a website with a dynamic menu. However, a lot of things are still missing to make this useful in a real website. These include proper hosting, server-side rendering, backend authentication, and much more, but those topics are beyond the scope of this book.

Summary

- In this project, we learned the steps that you would go through in a real project when working with React on a regular basis.
- Start the process with the desired result, and try to create the HTML that would render the desired output.
- From there, devise the component tree that would create the equivalent JSX. You can make it completely static and stateless in the first iteration.
- Then, slowly add more and more complexity until you end up where you want your application to be.
- Becoming more experienced as a React developer, you'll gain the confidence to skip more steps in this process and perhaps jump directly to the last step because you're already very familiar with how to best use contexts, lists of JSX objects, stateful variables, and all the other things required.

Project: Timer

Welcome to this next project, where we're going to build a countdown timer. It's just like the timer app on your phone, only you build this one yourself! We'll also get a bit more ambitious on your behalf in this exercise, so, compared to chapter 11, there will be less so, and guidance from us and more development work to figure out on your own. But don't worry, you have our full trust and confidence—we know you can do it!

We'll set up the foundations for the project for you, so you don't have to mess too much with design or semantics. For that purpose, we've set up a scaffold for you in step 1, which contains the static HTML and semantics required for step 2, but also all the images, icons, and styles that you need for the whole project. See figure 12.1 for the high-level overview of this project.

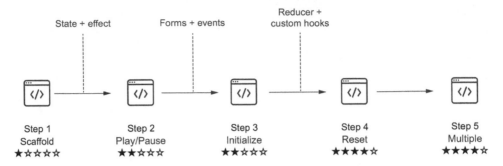

Figure 12.1   When you're completing the timer project, you'll go through these five steps to end up with a fairly advanced timer.

In step 2, together we'll convert the static output from step 1 to a working, albeit functionally limited, timer with a fixed duration, by adding statefulness. In step 3, we'll add an initialization step so you can set the timer to an arbitrary number and also dismiss a running timer. This requires adding form and event handling. When we add the extra option of resetting the timer in step 4, we'll also refactor how the state is being kept by moving to a reducer and a custom hook. Finally, in step 5, we'll add the option of having multiple timers running independently of each other.

As mentioned, we're getting more ambitious on your behalf in this project, so the last two steps are fairly complicated. You can see a more detailed overview of the process and the technologies involved in table 12.1.

Table 12.1   The five steps of the timer project

Step	Feature	Additional React API used	Difficulty
Step 1: Scaffold	Create the basic component structure for a time display and buttons.	Chapters 1–4: Functional components using JSX	★☆☆☆
Step 2: Play/Pause	Implement a stateful component that will count down when started until paused or done.	Chapter 5: State Chapter 6: Effect hook	★★☆☆
Step 3: Initialize	Initialize the timer at a custom time defined by the user through a form with inputs. Note: This is homework. You have to create this step *yourself*!	Chapter 8: Listening for events Chapter 10: Handling user input in forms	★★☆☆
Step 4: Reset	Convert the state logic to a reducer, and add more logic to handle resetting the timer as well. Note: This is homework. You have to create this step *yourself*!	Chapter 10: Reducer and custom hook	★★★★☆

Table 12.1 The five steps of the timer project *(continued)*

Step	Feature	Additional React API used	Difficulty
Step 5: Multiple timers	Allow the user to define multiple timers that will run independently of each other. Note: This is homework. You have to create this step *yourself!*		★★★★☆

As a further enticement before we get going, we'll present some screenshots of the final product. Note that although the book is printed in grayscale, the actual timer comes with a pleasing purple gradient as background. The initial result of step 1 is displayed in figure 12.2, whereas the final multi-timer is displayed in figure 12.3.

Figure 12.2 Step 1 sets up the project structure and styles required to render a static timer like this one. The button doesn't do anything at this point, and the time doesn't tick down.

Alright, let's start the countdown!

> **NOTE** The source code for the scaffolding and suggested solutions to all the sections in this chapter are available at https://rq2e.com/ch12. But as you learned in chapter 2, you can instantiate all the examples and solutions directly from the command line using a single command.

Figure 12.3   After you've completed step 5, you'll have created this monster of an application, where you can have as many independently running timers as you want. Just imagine how many differently sized eggs you can boil simultaneously!

12.1   *Scaffolding for the timer*

To help you focus on implementing React code and not fiddling with HTML and CSS, we'll provide all the required styles and semantics for you. We'll also set it all up here in the scaffolding for the application. As in the previous project (and really any web development project), we'll go through these steps to complete the project:

1 Define the HTML output that will render the desired result.
2 Create a number of React components that will render JSX to achieve the desired HTML.

  3 Place static images in the public folder that we can load at runtime.
  4 Create a stylesheet.
  5 Implement the components that we need to get the necessary functionality.

The last point is the interesting bit, and we'll solve that in steps 2–5 in this project. Step 1 will complete the first four points in the preceding list.

12.1.1 HTML output

For the HTML output for this project, we'll go over one part at a time and detail how we'll model it using HTML. We'll then add some appropriate CSS classes to each node, which we can target in our stylesheet in the next part. When we have all the individual parts, we can start putting them together to form the whole project. The parts of this project are highlighted in the graphic in figure 12.4.

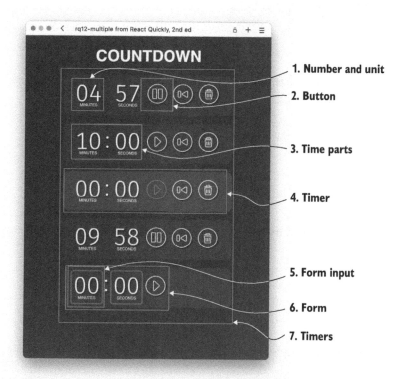

Figure 12.4   The seven parts that make up the complete timer application. Starting from the innermost, we have a number and unit, a button, a collection of two numbers with a colon between them, a complete timer, a form input, a form with multiple inputs and a button, and, finally, the whole list of timers.

Let's go over each of these parts and detail the associated HTML structure.

NUMBER AND UNIT

Each number in the time display has an associated unit below it. The number and unit text fields are combined in the list item. This list item will be used in the time display as a whole. Therefore, each individual number and unit is a list item with paragraphs inside:

```
<li class="part">
  <p class="number">05</p>
  <p class="unit">minutes</p>
</li>
```

BUTTON

A button is, of course, a button, but with an icon that matches the title:

```
<button title="Play" class="toggle">
  <img src="/icons/play.svg" alt="Play" />
</button>
```

TIME PARTS

The time display is a list of parts, namely, a number and unit, then a colon, and then another number and unit:

```
<ul class="parts">
  <!-- number + unit -->
  <li class="colon">:</li>
  <!-- number + unit -->
</ul>
```

TIMER

The timer is a section that consists of a list of time parts followed by one or more buttons:

```
<section class="timer">
  <!-- time parts -->
  <!-- button(s) -->
</section>
```

While the timer is running, add a class `timer-ticking` to make the colon in the time display blink:

```
<section class="timer timer-ticking">
  <!-- time parts -->
  <!-- button(s) -->
</section>"
```

If the timer has reached 0 and should start blinking to indicate that the time has run out, it can be marked by adding the class `timer-ringing`:

```
<section class="timer timer-ringing">
  <!-- time parts -->
  <!-- button(s) -->
</section>
```

FORM INPUT

The input is a number and unit, but instead of the two elements being two para-graphs, they are an input and a label. They still form a part, which is an element in a list:

```
<li class="part">
  <input class="number" type="number" name="seconds" id="seconds" />
  <label class="unit" for="seconds">Seconds</label>
</li>
```

FORM

The inputs make up the form along with a button. Because a button automatically serves as a Submit button when inside a form, we don't need to do anything special to get the form to work:

```
<form class="timer timer-new">
  <ul class="parts">
    <!-- input -->
    <li class="colon">:</li>
    <!-- input -->
  </ul>
  <!-- button -->
</form>
```

TIMERS

The list of timers is just an element surrounding all the timers and potentially the form to add a new one at the end:

```
<div class="timers">
  <!-- timer(s) -->
  <!-- optional form -->
</div>
```

If the timer list has a plus button at the end to start a new timer, it can be added as a button with classes `timer` and `timer-add`:

```
<div class="timers">
  <!-- timer(s) -->
  <button class="timer timer-add">+</button>
</div>
```

12.1.2 Component hierarchy

The previous section lists some parts of the application that might very well translate directly to the React components that we need to render the application. However, for the scaffold, we'll have far fewer components, and only once we start adding function-ality in step 2 will we start splitting the components up into all the parts. For this scaf-fold, we'll only have three components, as you can see in figure 12.5.

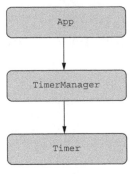

Figure 12.5 This might be our simplest component tree in a very long time. Note that we only display the React components here and not all the plain JSX nodes that we're also rendering.

Once we get to future steps, we'll start adding more functionality and logic, which will inherently increase the complexity of the component tree.

12.1.3 Project structure

For this project, we'll need some icons. We need four different types of buttons to complete the whole project. You can see them all displayed in figure 12.6.

Figure 12.6 The four types of buttons we need include a play, pause, reset, and trash.

Just like in chapter 11, we'll place these icon files in the public folder inside a separate `icons` folder. Besides that, we'll need the three components that we laid out in the previous section in the component tree, and then, of course, we need a stylesheet. This leads us to the following list of files in the scaffold:

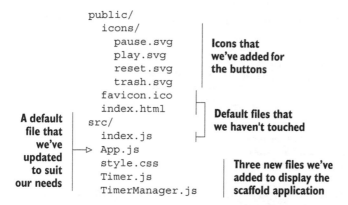

From there, you're ready to go. Keep reading this section (12.1) for some extra details about the source in the scaffold, but if you like what you see, you can also skip ahead to section 12.2, where we start implementing the simplest version of the timer.

12.1.4 *Source code*

This section includes the source code for the base components included in the scaffolding. You don't have to copy it from here, though, as these sources are ready to go in the previously mentioned template.

STYLESHEET

We aren't listing the whole stylesheet because it's just a lot of simple CSS rules, but there are a few things we want to highlight. First, we're loading a font from the Google Fonts API, named Fira Sans, which has some nice numbers that we want to use for the actual clock display. This font also supports a feature called *tabular numbers*. We want our numbers to be displayed in a fixed-width format; that is, we don't want the numbers to change width when the clock ticks down from 10 to 09. But in many fonts, the 1 and the 0 don't have the same width, and this would cause our numbers to jump a bit unless we put each number in a separate box.

Some font families have a feature in which you can request your numbers to be displayed as fixed-width characters so that they all take the same number of pixels in width at the same font size. We load the font and trigger this tabular variant for numbers in CSS by using this declaration:

```
@import url("https://fonts.googleapis.com/css2
   ?family=Fira+Sans:wght@300&display=swap");
.number, .colon {
  font-family: "Fira Sans", sans-serif;
  font-variant-numeric: tabular-nums;
}
```

Instructs these classes to use the loaded font

Triggers the font to use the font variant "tabular-nums" to ensure the use of fixed-width numbers

Not all fonts support this font variant, so if you want to use a different font for your numbers, check that it supports this for the most visually pleasing result.

Secondly, if you look through the stylesheet, you might note that we do most of the layouts in the stylesheet using Flexbox. It's just a very handy tool for aligning elements in an application like this.

MAIN APPLICATION

The main application component is the starting point for the application. It remains completely identical to this first version (listing 12.1) throughout the exercise, as it contains only a headline and the `TimerManager` component. All the logic of the timers will go inside there, so there will be no global state in this application.

Note that we also load the CSS stylesheet in this root component. We only need to load it once, so it makes sense to load it in the root. You can see the file `src/App.js` in the following listing.

Listing 12.1   `src/App.js` in the scaffolding

```
import "./style.css";
import TimerManager from "./TimerManager";
function App() {
  return (
    <main className="wrapper">
      <h1 className="title">Countdown</h1>
      <TimerManager />
    </main>
  );
}
export default App;
```

Imports the stylesheet so we can use the styles from the start

Loads the timer manager component

Renders it where needed

THE TIMER MANAGER

The timer manager is the container that will hold one or more timers as well as contain the logic for initializing or adding new timers. This component won't be in charge of actually managing the individual timers (e.g., ticking time ahead), but rather will manage the different timers and the starting times.

In the scaffold, the timer manager contains a single timer instance with no properties. This file, `src/TimerManager.js`, is displayed next.

Listing 12.2   `src/TimerManager.js` in the scaffolding

```
import Timer from "./Timer";
function TimerManager() {
  return (
    <div className="timers">
      <Timer />
    </div>
  );
}
export default TimerManager;
```

The timer manager imports the timer component to display an instance of it.

Renders the instance without any properties or other logic

THE INDIVIDUAL TIMER

The timer component is where most of the future work will take place. In this initial scaffold, it's a purely static component with a fixed JSX response that displays 05 minutes and 00 seconds and a Play button. None of it's functional for now, though.

Note that this contains some duplicated JSX that can be optimized later by turning it into individual components, including the number and unit display. The button is also ripe for *componentization*, as it will be used in multiple places later. This file, `src/Timer.js`, is shown in the next listing.

Listing 12.3   `src/Timer.js` in the scaffolding

```
function Timer() {
  return (
    <section className="timer">
      <ul className="parts">
        <li className="part">
          <p className="number">05</p>
          <p className="unit">minutes</p>
        </li>
        <li className="colon">:</li>
        <li className="part">
          <p className="number">00</p>
          <p className="unit">seconds</p>
        </li>
      </ul>
      <button title="Play" className="toggle">
        <img src="/icons/play.svg" alt="Play" />
      </button>
    </section>
  );
}
export default Timer;
```

We've hardcoded a remaining time of 05 minutes and 00 seconds for now.

12.1.5 *Running the application*

If we spin this application up in the browser, we see what we displayed in the beginning in figure 12.2, repeated here in 12.7. This application doesn't do anything, but it looks pretty nice, no?

Figure 12.7   The scaffold for the timer doesn't do anything—yet.

12.2   *Adding a simple play/pause timer*

The previous step resulted in a nice but very boring application because it didn't do anything. We're going to change that now. First, we'll make this simplest of countdown timers work by making the play button play the countdown. You can also pause the countdown, if the explosion looms close—or the egg is almost done cooking.

12.2.1 *The goal of this exercise*

The goal of this exercise is to create the required functionality to make a working countdown. To achieve this goal, we recommend going about it in these steps, but they're definitely not the only or even necessarily best way to do it. It's just our way:

1. Identify parts of the timer to componentize to make the timer simpler to work with.
2. Create state in the timer component to record the progression of the countdown as well as the Boolean state of whether the countdown is running or not.
3. Add an effect to the timer to decrease the remaining time every second.
4. Display a play button that starts the countdown if the timer is paused, and a pause button that pauses it if the timer is running.

PRECISION

Note that timing precision is *not* a goal of this exercise. We're fine with doing the countdown in a setInterval, even though the precision of setInterval is notoriously untrustworthy. This will result in a countdown that's probably a few hundredths up to a tenth of a second off on every tick of the countdown. When a full 5 minutes have passed on the countdown in the app, this offset could account for about half a minute extra in "real time."

If you're using this timer for anything requiring actual precision, this isn't the way to do it. But precision timing isn't the goal of this exercise, so we'll use this approach for the entire project.

Feel free to improve the precision of the actual countdown by the end, if you feel so inclined. Look into performance.now() for precision timing (down to the microsecond, if the OS supports it).

12.2.2 *Component hierarchy*

As mentioned, the first goal of this exercise is to componentize the timer parts into relevant atoms that can be combined into a whole as appropriate. For this purpose, we'll refer back to the initial list of HTML parts and split the component along the lines divided there. Thus:

- Timer—A timer consists of a time display and one or more buttons.
- TimeDisplay—A time display is a list of a number and unit, followed by a colon, followed by a number and unit.
- Number—A number and unit is just that, with the proper class names to elicit the desired styling.
- Button—A button has a label for accessibility and an icon for visual recognition.

These four components now make up a timer and are connected as you see in figure 12.8. You can also see that we'll pass in the starting time to the timer directly from the timer manager.

The timer will only have a single button, but the button icon, label, and click handler will vary depending on whether the timer is currently running or not. In addition, note that the time display will only get a single time as input, which is the remaining seconds to display. The time display component then has to split that into minutes and seconds to pass to the two number components.

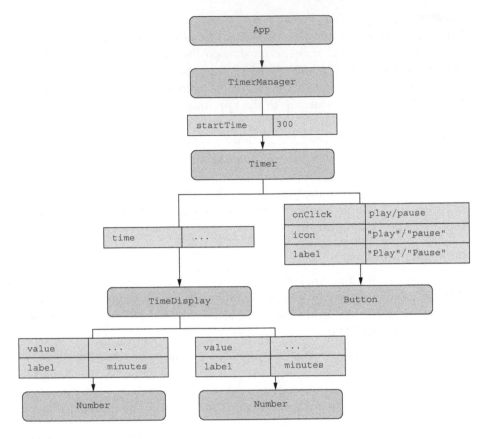

Figure 12.8 The component tree for our single timer application consists of a few instances of three new components: time display, number, and button.

12.2.3 *Updated project structure*

In this step of the project, we're adding some new components as well as updating others. This leads to the following updated file structure after completing this step:

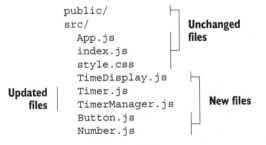

```
public/                     ┐
src/                        │  Unchanged
  App.js                    │  files
  index.js                  │
  style.css                 ┘
  TimeDisplay.js            ┐
  Timer.js                  │
  TimerManager.js           │  New files
  Button.js                 │
  Number.js                 ┘
```

Updated files

We recommend that you try to implement this step yourself, and you can do so either by starting from your own implementation of the scaffolding in step 1 of this project or from our implementation in the `rq12-scaffold` repository. Once completed, feel free to compare your solution to ours.

Repository: rq12-playpause

This example can be seen in repository `rq12-playpause`. You can use that repository by creating a new app based on the associated template:

```
$ npx create-react-app rq12-playpause --template rq12-playpause
```

Alternatively, you can go to this website to browse the code, see the application in action directly in your browser, or download the source code as a zip file:

https://rq2e.com/rq12-playpause

12.2.4 Source code

In this section, we'll provide the full source code for all the updated and new files added in this step along with some implementation details that will be relevant for understanding our choices.

THE TIMER MANAGER

The timer manager still doesn't really do anything. The only thing changed here is that we explicitly set the default time for the timer. Feel free to change that to something else to test it out. See the full contents of `src/TimerManager.js` next.

Listing 12.4 `src/TimerManager.js` in the simple timer

```
import Timer from "./Timer";
function TimerManager() {
  return (
    <div className="timers">
      <Timer startTime={300} />      ◄── Adds a property
    </div>                                with the default
  );                                      start time
}
export default TimerManager;
```

A GENERIC BUTTON COMPONENT

We need a new button component. It's very simple and renders a button element with an appropriate title and an icon inside. If we pass extra properties to the button component, we forward them to the button element. See the following listing for the full contents of `src/Button.js`.

Listing 12.5 `src/Button.js` in the simple timer

```
function Button({ icon, label, ...rest }) {      ◄── We need to pass an icon and a label,
  return (                                            but we can also pass any other button
                                                      properties to this component.
```

```
    <button title={label} className="toggle" {...rest}>
      <img src={`/icons/${icon}.svg`} alt={label} />
    </button>
  );
}
export default Button;
```

All the extra properties will be added to the button element. This is where things like onClick should be added.

THE NUMBER AND UNIT DISPLAY

The number and unit display just displays properties. The number has to be formatted to always be two digits, though, so we convert it to a string and add leading zeros if required, as shown in the following listing.

Listing 12.6 `src/Number.js` **in the simple timer**

```
function Number({ value, label }) {
  return (
    <li className="part">
      <p className="number">
        {String(value).padStart(2, "0")}
      </p>
      <p className="unit">{label}</p>
    </li>
  );
}
export default Number;
```

We display the number here, but we make sure it's always two characters long by converting it to a string and padding it with leading zeros. This causes a number like 7 to be displayed as 07.

The label is displayed as is—we later use CSS to make it uppercase for visual appeal.

THE TIME DISPLAY COMPONENT

This component takes in the time to display, splits it into minutes and seconds (using division, flooring, and modulo), and then passes those values on to two number component instances. You can see the source for `src/TimeDisplay.js` next.

Listing 12.7 `src/TimeDisplay.js` **in the simple timer**

```
import Number from "./Number";
function TimeDisplay({ time }) {
  const minutes = Math.floor(time / 60);
  const seconds = time % 60;
  return (
    <ul className="parts">
      <Number value={minutes} label="minutes" />
      <li className="colon">:</li>
      <Number value={seconds} label="seconds" />
    </ul>
  );
}
export default TimeDisplay;
```

The number of minutes remaining is the time remaining divided by 60 rounded down.

The number of seconds remaining is the remainder after division by 60.

THE TIMER COMPONENT

This is where it all comes together. We've illustrated the flow of logic in the timer component in a state diagram in figure 12.9.

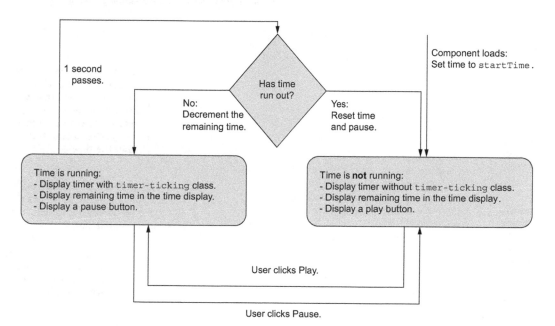

Figure 12.9   The state chart for the simple timer component—time is either running or not, which determines what is displayed and which effects are running.

Remember that the timer now takes a single property, `startTime`, which determines what the timer will start at. From that, we can initialize the local state with the remaining seconds that we can tick down, as well as a separate state that contains a Boolean about whether the timer is even ticking at all.

Then, we do different things depending on whether time is running or not. If running, we run an effect hook decrementing (until it reaches zero, then we reset everything). We also display a pause button if running.

If time isn't running, we don't run any effect hook (or we do, because we have to, but we don't do anything inside the hook), and we display a play button. The full file, `src/Timer.js`, is displayed in the following listing.

Listing 12.8   `src/Timer.js` in the simple timer

```
import { useState, useEffect } from "react";
import Button from "./Button";
import TimeDisplay from "./TimeDisplay";
function Timer({ startTime }) {
  const [remaining, setRemaining] =
    useState(startTime);
```

To have a timer, we need two stateful values. First, we need to know how many seconds are remaining.

Second, we need to know whether the timer is currently running or not.

Always clean up after yourself.

Passes the remaining time to the time display component

Displays a different button depending on whether the time is running or not

```
const [isRunning, setRunning] = useState(false);
useEffect(() => {
  if (!isRunning) {
    return;
  }
  function tick() {
    setRemaining((oldValue) => {
      const value = oldValue - 1;
      if (value <= 0) {
        setRunning(false);
        return startTime;
      }
      return value;
    });
  }
  const interval = setInterval(tick, 1000);
  return () => clearInterval(interval);
}, [isRunning, startTime]);
const play = () => setRunning(true);
const pause = () => setRunning(false);
return (
  <section className={
    `timer ${isRunning ? "timer-ticking" : ""}`
  }>
    <TimeDisplay time={remaining} />
    {isRunning ? (
      <Button
        icon="pause"
        label="Pause"
        onClick={pause}
      />
    ) : (
      <Button
        icon="play"
        label="Play"
        onClick={play}
      />
    )}
  </section>
);
}
export default Timer;
```

We implement the eternal progress of time toward the eventual heat death of the universe as an effect hook. The hook only does something if the timer is actually running, though.

If the timer is running, we schedule an interval to be run every second that will decrement the remaining seconds or stop the timer if it reaches 0 (and then reset the timer).

This hook depends on whether the timer is running or not as well as the start time (as we need it to reset the timer upon completion).

Adds a conditional class to the timer section to display the ticking colon when running

If running, we display a pause button that pauses the timer. If not running, we do the opposite.

12.2.5 *Running the application*

If you spin this application up in the browser, you'll see the web app in figure 12.10.

Figure 12.10   The timer can be running or paused. While running, the colon flashes as time ticks down. The button changes appearance and behavior depending on the play state.

12.3   Homework: Initializing the timer to a custom time

The goal for this step is to initialize the timer at a custom time defined by the user through a form with inputs. Here are a few hints to complete this objective:

1 Create a new component to handle adding a new timer. See the stylesheet for some classes that will help you out in styling this form and its inputs.

2 Decide between making the new timer form controlled or not. Both are valid options for this component.

3 Remember that adding a button to a form will make it a Submit button, even if it doesn't have a click handler.

4 Make the timer manager stateful, and remember whether you have a timer set or not and what the starting time of that timer is.

5 Add a Trash button (with the trash icon) to the timer component.

6 The timer component wants a new property, that is, a callback to invoke when the timer has either run out or been discarded. This callback should reset the timer manager so you can use the new timer form again.

We, of course, want you to work from your existing application that you developed in the previous step, but if you want to start from our solution to that step, you can do so by checking out the `rq12-playpause` repository. Once completed, feel free to compare your solution to ours.

> ### Repository: rq12-initialize
>
> This example can be seen in repository `rq12-initialize`. You can use that repository by creating a new app based on the associated template:
>
> ```
> $ npx create-react-app rq12-initialize --template rq12-initialize
> ```
>
> Alternatively, you can go to this website to browse the code, see the application in action directly in your browser, or download the source code as a zip file:
>
> https://rq2e.com/rq12-initialize

12.4   *Homework: Resetting timers*

The goal for this step is to convert the state logic to a reducer and add more logic to handle resetting the timer as well. Here are a few hints to complete this objective:

1   Convert the state in the timer to a reducer.

2   Add a new Reset button to the timer, and allow a timer to be restarted by invoking the proper action on the reducer. Think carefully about what should happen to both values in the reducer on reset.

3   Finally, you might want to change what happens when a timer completes. So rather than just deleting it, you could leave it in place until actively deleted.

We, of course, want you to work from your existing application that you developed in the previous step, but if you want to start from our solution, you can do so by checking out the `rq12-initialize` repository. Once completed, feel free to compare your solution to ours.

> ### Repository: rq12-reset
>
> This example can be seen in repository `rq12-reset`. You can use that repository by creating a new app based on the associated template:
>
> ```
> $ npx create-react-app rq12-reset --template rq12-reset
> ```
>
> Alternatively, you can go to this website to browse the code, see the application in action directly in your browser, or download the source code as a zip file:
>
> https://rq2e.com/rq12-reset

12.5   *Homework: Multiple timers*

The goal for this step is to allow the user to define multiple timers that will run independently of each other. Here are a few hints to complete this objective:

1   Update the state kept in the timer manager to allow multiple managers to be running at the same time (with different starting times).

2 Make sure to still support deleting timers at any point.

3 Allow a timer to display completion by flashing (there's a class in the stylesheet for that), so that the user can either reset or discard the timer at this point.

4 In the timer manager, allow the user to press a button to add a new timer, but don't display the new timer form until the Add button is pressed. When a new timer is added, reset to the Add button again.

We, of course, want you to work from your existing application that you developed in the previous step, but if you want to start from our solution to that step, you can do so by checking out the `rq12-reset` repository. Once completed, feel free to compare your solution to ours.

> **Repository: rq12-multiple**
>
> This example can be seen in repository `rq12-multiple`. You can use that repository by creating a new app based on the associated template:
>
> ```
> $ npx create-react-app rq12-multiple --template rq12-multiple
> ```
>
> Alternatively, you can go to this website to browse the code, see the application in action directly in your browser, or download the source code as a zip file:
>
> https://rq2e.com/rq12-multiple

Summary

- In this project, we take on a more complex application that has some real-world usage possibilities.

- We once again go over the steps that you would be going through if taking on such a project in a professional setting—whether working alone or in a team.

- Remember to study your designs and your subject matter up front, as this will often give you a good idea about how to structure your final application. In this project, we were able to deduce which components we needed directly from the design alone and keep that separation of logic throughout.

- Also think about the internal state of components, and remember that you can have state in many different layers at the same time. In this project, we have state in three different layers that work independently of each other, though they have an interface between themselves as they interact.

- The list of timers has just that—a list of timers. It knows what each timer is started at, but doesn't actually know which ones are running, if they have expired, or if they're just ticking away.

- The individual timer runs on its own until it's deleted. When that happens, it invokes a callback provided from its parent without actually caring what happens afterward.

- The form to add a new timer remembers the state of the form and calls a call-back once submitted. It has no idea what happens after the form has been submitted.
- If you're building real-world applications, think about proper semantics (not everything should be a `<div>`), and pay attention to accessibility (add proper roles and labels to elements where applicable).

Project: Task manager

This chapter covers

- Creating the necessary scaffolding for a task manager
- Implementing a simple list of tasks
- Homework: Adding advanced features to the task manager

Welcome to the third and final project for this book. You'll now have to wield all the magic and spells that you've learned so far as well as some extra knowledge about JavaScript and HTML that you've hopefully picked up elsewhere—however, that's only required for the very advanced homework at the end of this chapter.

In this project, we'll build a task manager. By *task manager*, we mean a slightly more complex variant of a to-do list. The task manager at first consists of a simple to-do list implemented as cards that can be started and completed. We then add in substeps to each task, so the user can add some finer details to their tasks at hand. Next, we add in the option of changing the order of the steps in each task, first only using buttons, but then also using drag and drop. It's that last bit in step 5, the drag and drop part, that's going to be tricky to complete. You can see this development in figure 13.1, where we'll use advanced events to get to the final step 5.

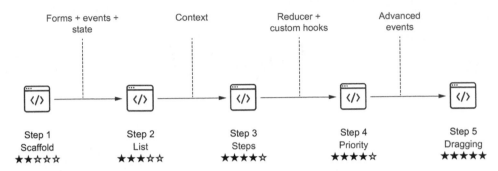

Figure 13.1   As you implement the task manager, you'll go through these five steps to add more and more functionality and complexity to the application.

Once again, we'll set up the foundations for the project in the first step so you don't have to mess around too much with HTML, icons, and CSS to get the basics to work. However, the foundation created in step 1 will be completely inert and won't do anything. To add functionality, you'll have to go through the steps to increase the complexity of the project as we go along.

We've also listed the steps in table 13.1 with some more detail about what you'll be doing and which chapters you'll be referring to when completing the exercises.

Table 13.1   The five steps of the task manager project

Step	Feature	Additional React API used	Difficulty
Step 1: Scaffold	Create the basic component structure for a list of tasks and a form for adding new tasks.	Chapters 1–4: Functional components using JSX	★☆☆☆
Step 2: List	Convert static structure to a dynamic list of tasks stored in state, with options for editing and deleting tasks as well.	Chapter 5: State Chapter 8: Events Chapter 9: Forms	★★★☆☆
Step 3: Steps	Add steps and progress to each task, including the option of deleting and completing steps. The task list also works as an accordion, where only one is expanded at a time. Note: This is homework. You have to create this step *yourself*!	Chapter 10: Context	★★★★☆

Table 13.1 The five steps of the task manager project *(continued)*

Step	Feature	Additional React API used	Difficulty
Step 4: Priority	Add the option to prioritize the steps of a task by reordering items. This is made simpler by converting the state to a reducer. Note: This is homework. You have to create this step *yourself*!	Chapter 10: Reducer and custom hook	★★★★☆
Step 5: Dragging	Allow the user to drag the steps around to change the prioritization, rather than only use the arrows to move one step up and down. Note: This is homework. You have to create this step *yourself*!	Chapter 8: Event handlers	★★★★★

The first iteration of this exercise, which you'll reach after completing step 2, is a very simple task manager, as shown in figure 13.2.

Figure 13.2 The first iteration of the task manager simply has a list where you can add, delete, and edit the tasks.

However, when you complete this project all the way through step 5, you'll have a much more advanced application, as you can see in figure 13.3, with a lot more options.

Figure 13.3   Now each task has a list of steps, and you can add, complete, edit, delete, and reprioritize these steps inside the task.

You can even drag the steps around inside each task, as you can see in figure 13.4.

Figure 13.4   You can drag steps in the list for easier reprioritization.

With all that to get through, let's get started with this final project of the last chapter of the book.

> **NOTE** The source code for the scaffolding as well as suggested solutions to all the steps in this chapter is available at https://rq2e.com/ch13. But as you learned in chapter 2, you can instantiate all the examples and solutions directly from the command line using a single command.

13.1 Scaffolding for the task manager

Once again, we're going to get you started with a basic scaffold for this application. We're going to create the HTML output for a static task manager and provide all the styles necessary as well. It won't be dynamic nor even functional, but it'll look like the finished thing; it just needs some React magic to get going.

We're also going to provide you with some icons that you'll need for some icon buttons through the solution.

13.1.1 Component hierarchy

In this step for this project, we're going to cheat a bit. We're creating the entire (static) application in a single component. We could split things up, but we feel that this allows you to decide better how to split things up into components yourself.

With a single component returning all the JSX for the entire application in a static, fixed setup, you can see exactly how the whole thing is created and how best to move forward from here. That leaves a trivially simple component diagram for this application, as you can see in figure 13.5.

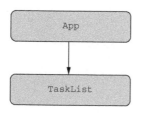

Figure 13.5 Although we mentioned that the component tree in figure 12.5 was our simplest yet, we think we have it beat with this one!

13.1.2 Project structure

With such a simple component hierarchy in this step, there's not much to say about the source folder. We have a main application file and a CSS file as usual, along with our single application-specific component, `TaskList`.

We do, however, also have some icons for this project, and we've added eight different SVGs in the public folder that we'll need throughout the project. That leaves us with the following file structure:

```
public/
  icons/
    caret.svg
```

```
        check.svg
        down.svg
        drag.svg
        pencil.svg
        plus.svg
        trash.svg
        up.svg
      favicon.ico
      index.html
  src/
    App.js
    index.js
    style.css
    TaskList.js
```

> ### Repository: rq13-scaffold
>
> This example can be seen in repository `rq13-scaffold`. You can use that repository by creating a new app based on the associated template:
>
> ```
> $ npx create-react-app rq13-scaffold --template rq13-scaffold
> ```
>
> Alternatively, you can go to this website to browse the code, see the application in action directly in your browser, or download the source code as a zip file:
>
> https://rq2e.com/rq13-scaffold

13.1.3 Source code

There are only two source files of significance to list in this step. We have the main application file, which is almost identical to all the other ones we've been using, and then the application-specific task list.

THE MAIN APPLICATION

The main application is included in `src/App.js`, and it should look very familiar to you by now. The file is shown in the following listing.

Listing 13.1 `src/App.js` **in the scaffolding**

```
import "./style.css";              ◁              Loads the
import TaskList from "./TaskList";  ◁             CSS file
function App() {
  return (
    <main>                                        Loads the top-
      <h1>Task Manager</h1>                       level component
      <TaskList />         ◁                      of the application
    </main>
  );                        Renders that
}                           component in the
export default App;         relevant JSX tree
```

THE TASK LIST

The file src/TaskList.js is displayed in listing 13.2. It contains all the JSX to render a list of two tasks as well as a form for adding a new task at the bottom. All of it is completely inactive though, so nothing (interesting) happens when you click the buttons.

Listing 13.2 src/TaskList.js **in the scaffolding**

```
function TaskList() {
  return (
    <ol className="lane">                    The lane of tasks
                                             is an ordered list.
      <li className="card">
        <header className="card-header">      A task has a header
          <p className="card-title">This is a task</p>   with a title.
        </header>
        <ul className="card-controls">
          <li>
            <button className="card-control">Edit</button>
          </li>
          <li>
            <button className="card-control">Delete</button>
          </li>
        </ul>
      </li>
      <li className="card">                    A task has a
        <header className="card-header">        header with
          <p className="card-title">This is another task</p>   a title.
        </header>
        <ul className="card-controls">
          <li>
            <button className="card-control">Edit</button>
          </li>
          <li>
            <button className="card-control">Delete</button>
          </li>
        </ul>
      </li>
      <li className="card">
        <header
          className="card-header card-header-new"
        >
          <form className="card-title-form">
            <input
              className="card-title card-title-input"
              placeholder="Add new task"
              name="title"
            />
            <button className="icon-button">
              <img src="icons/plus.svg" alt="Add task" />
            </button>
          </form>
        </header>
      </li>
    </ol>
  );
```

Each task is a list item.

Below the task title is an unordered list of buttons.

The last task in the list is slightly different, as it contains a form to add a new task using an input and an icon button

```
}
export default TaskList;
```

13.1.4 Running the application

The scaffold results in a nice-looking but otherwise completely useless application with a static list of tasks and a form at the bottom, as you can see in figure 13.6.

Figure 13.6   If only the buttons actually worked, this would be a somewhat useful application.

13.2 A simple list of tasks

Now that we have all the basics out of the way—that is, we have the JSX, styles, and icons all under control—we go to the next step of creating the actual task manager application. What we have so far is "just" regular web development, and all that work required skills mostly outside the scope of this book. What comes now is React development, and this is where we have to apply all the skills we've learned so far in this book.

13.2.1 The goal of this exercise

In this step of the project, we'll add the actual functionality to the structure that was outlined in the scaffold. After completing this step, we want to have a simple task manager that can do the following:

- Show a list of tasks
- Allow the user to add a new task by writing the task title
- Allow the user to delete a task
- Allow the user to rename a task

We'll do this in two steps:

1 Split the single big component into multiple smaller components that make sense in terms of component size, responsibility, and visual representation.
2 Make the application stateful, so it starts with a predefined list, and users can then append, delete, and update tasks as they see fit.

13.2.2 Component hierarchy

While we only had a single component, `TaskList`, related to the actual task manager in the scaffold, we'll extend that to multiple components in this step. You can see the breakdown in figure 13.7.

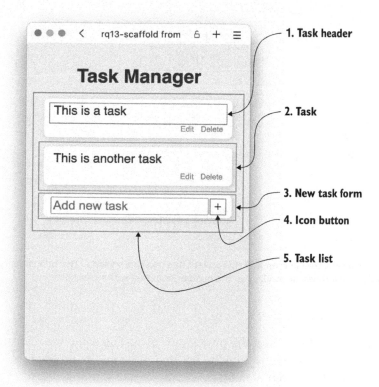

Figure 13.7 The task manager in this step breaks down neatly into five different components: the task header with the title or input to edit the title; the task, including the header and some controls; the form to add new tasks; an icon button; and, finally, the full task list.

To start at the innermost level, the title of a task can be a large paragraph or an input where you can edit the title and click to submit that new title. We'll create that as our first component, `TaskHeader`. Building on top of this, each task is then an individual component, `Task`, which handles the state of a task, namely, whether the title is being edited or not.

At the bottom of the task list, we'll create a new component for adding a new task. That's where our third new component, TaskAdd, will be, which contains a form and will invoke a callback once submitted.

Finally, we need to add an icon button for this project, so we might as well add that now. Let's be super inventive and call this component Button. We'll only need the icon button inside the new task form, but we have many future uses for it in the next steps. This all comes together as you can see in figure 13.8, where the component tree is laid out.

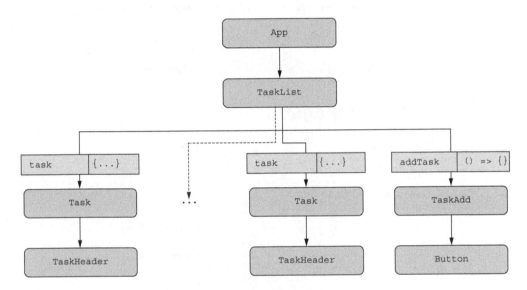

Figure 13.8   The component tree of step 2 of this project has five components. The task component in particular is used several times depending on the number of actual tasks to display.

13.2.3   *Updated project structure*

As mentioned earlier, in this step of the project, we're adding some new components as well as updating others. As a new thing, we're also adding a plain JavaScript file for setting up the initial value of our stateful task array. We're naming this file fixture .js, as *fixture* is often used as the term for "fixed" data that you want to populate your application with.

Finally, as another new improvement, we'll use a nested file structure. We aren't adding a lot of components yet, but we're expecting more components to be added later, so we'll encapsulate the four components related to tasks specifically, to go in their own folder. To make these easier to import, we're adding an index file to this folder as well that will export only the necessary components from this folder.

This leads to the following updated file structure after completing this step:

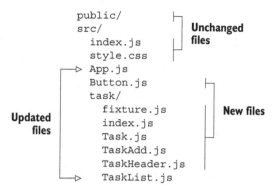

We recommend that you try to implement this step yourself, and you can do so either by starting from your own implementation of the scaffolding in step 1 of this project or from our implementation in `rq13-scaffold`. Once completed, feel free to compare your solution to ours.

> **Repository: rq13-list**
>
> This example can be seen in repository `rq13-list`. You can use that repository by creating a new app based on the associated template:
>
> `$ npx create-react-app rq13-list --template rq13-list`
>
> Alternatively, you can go to this website to browse the code, see the application in action directly in your browser, or download the source code as a zip file:
>
> https://rq2e.com/rq13-list

13.2.4 *Source code*

In this section, we'll provide the full source code for all the updated and new files added in this step along with some implementation details that will be relevant for understanding our choices.

THE MAIN APPLICATION FILE

The only change to the main application component is the location of the imported task list. Instead of importing the task list as a default import from a file named `Task-List`, we instead import it as a named import from the folder named `task`. You can see this change in the next listing.

Listing 13.3 `src/App.js` in the simple task list

```
import "./style.css";
import { TaskList } from "./task";       ◁─┐  The only change here is
function App() {                              the location and import
  return (                                    style of the task list
    <main>                                     component.
```

```
      <h1>Task Manager</h1>
      <TaskList />
    </main>
  );
}
export default App;
```

THE ICON BUTTON

We create a very simple icon button in the file `src/Button.js`.

Listing 13.4   `src/Button.js` in the simple task list

**We can pass in a number of named
properties and then any other properties
that can go on a link.**

```
function Button({ className = "", icon, label, ...rest }) {
  return (
    <button className={`icon-button ${className}`} {...rest}>
      <img draggable={false} src={`icons/${icon}.svg`} alt={label} />
    </button>
  );
}
export default Button;
```

**The only thing that's a bit special here is the draggable
attribute on the image. This is done in preparation for
the last step, where we don't want our icon buttons
to drag independently of the entire step.**

THE PUBLIC INTERFACE FOR THE TASK FOLDER

We use the `task` folder as a kind of separated module, in which we use a number of components internally as we see fit, but to the outside world we only expose the task list component as the "public" component. This isn't a technical limitation, though, as you could import any component from the `task` folder, but it's a first step toward a packaged project structure. This leaves `src/task/index.js` as a very simple index file, as you can see in the following listing.

Listing 13.5   `src/task/index.js` in the simple task list

```
export { default as TaskList } from "./TaskList";
```

**We only expose the task list component from this
folder, and we do so as a named export.**

THE FIXTURE WITH DEFAULT TASKS

We store the task list in local storage in the browser, but the first time you visit the application, you won't have a task list to restore, so we need some default content for the application to function. We could use an empty list, but you'll often see apps populate an application with some sample data to inspire you.

While our sample data might not be all that inspiring, we've definitely set you up for a quick start. You can see the file `src/task/fixture.js` in the next listing.

Listing 13.6 `src/task/fixture.js` **in the simple task list**

```
const initialState = [
  { id: 1, title: "Make task manager" },
  { id: 2, title: "Now add some more tasks" },
];
export default initialState;
```

THE TASK HEADER

The task header seems simple because it's just the title. However, the title can be edited, and if it's editable, the header changes to a form with a checkmark icon as a Submit button. You can see src/task/TaskHeader.js implemented next.

Listing 13.7 `src/task/TaskHeader.js` **in the simple task list**

```
function TaskHeader({
  task,                    │ This component accepts        When the edit form is
  isEditable,              │ some properties necessary     submitted, we prevent the
  setEditable,             │ to make the header            default action (i.e., reload the
  editTask,                │ editable.                     page), update the current task
}) {                                                       with the new value, and, finally,
  const { title } = task;                                  set the header to be not
  const handleEditTask = (evt) => {    ◄──────────         editable again.
    evt.preventDefault();
    editTask(task.id, evt.target.title.value);
    setEditable(false);
  };
  if (isEditable) {          ◄──│ If the header is editable,
    return (                     │ we return one set of JSX.
      <header className="card-header">
        <form
          className="card-title-form"         This JSX includes a form
          onSubmit={handleEditTask}           with our submit handler
        >                                     defined earlier.
          <input
            className="card-title card-title-input"
            defaultValue={title}
            name="title"
          />
          <button className="icon-button">
            <img src="/icons/check.svg" alt="Edit step" />
          </button>
        </form>
      </header>
    );                                            If the header isn't
  }                                               editable, we simply
  return (                                        return some static JSX
    <header className="card-header">   ◄──│       with the current header.
      <p className="card-title">{title}</p>
    </header>
  );
}
export default TaskHeader;
```

THE ENTIRE TASK

The preceding task header is included inside each task. A task can be edited and deleted. When a task is edited, the header is updated with the relevant properties, including the callback to update the task as passed from the parent component. When a task is deleted, we simply invoke the delete callback directly. All of this is implemented in src/task/Task.js.

> Listing 13.8   `src/task/Task.js` **in the simple task list**

The task takes all the information about the current task to display, as well as two callbacks to edit and delete a task, respectively.

Keeps a local state inside each task capturing whether the user is currently trying to edit the task title or not

```
import { useState } from "react";
import TaskHeader from "./TaskHeader";
function Task({ task, editTask, deleteTask }) {
  const [isEditable, setEditable] = useState(false);
  return (
    <li className="card">
      <TaskHeader
        task={task}
        isEditable={isEditable}
        setEditable={setEditable}
        editTask={editTask}
      />
      <ul className="card-controls">
        {!isEditable && (
          <li>
            <button
              className="card-control"
              onClick={() => setEditable(true)}
            >
              Edit
            </button>
          </li>
        )}
        <li>
          <button
            className="card-control"
            onClick={() => deleteTask(task.id)}
          >
            Delete
          </button>
        </li>
      </ul>
    </li>
  );
}
export default Task;
```

Renders the previously defined task header component with all relevant properties at the top of the component

Below the header we have two buttons; the first toggles the local editable flag to true.

The second button invokes the delete callback.

THE NEW TASK FORM

When we want to add a new task, we do so in a form with a single uncontrolled input for the task title and a Submit button in the form of an icon button. See file `src/task/TaskAdd.js` in the following listing.

> **Listing 13.9** `src/task/TaskAdd.js` in the simple task list

The task form component takes a single property, which is the callback to invoke with the new task to be added.

When the task form is submitted, we do three things: cancel the default action, invoke the callback, and reset the form so it's ready for a new task to be added.

```
import Button from "../Button";
function TaskAdd({ addTask }) {
  const handleAddTask = (evt) => {
    evt.preventDefault();
    addTask(evt.target.title.value);
    evt.target.reset();
  };
  return (
    <li className="card">
      <header className="card-header card-header-new">
        <form
          className="card-title-form"
          onSubmit={handleAddTask}
        >
          <input
            className="card-title card-title-input"
            placeholder="Add new task"
            name="title"
          />
          <Button icon="plus" label="Add task" />
        </form>
      </header>
    </li>
  );
}
export default TaskAdd;
```

This submit handler is added to the form node.

THE COMPLETE AND STATEFUL LIST OF TASKS

The last component in this step—the task list—is both the most important one and the one with the most responsibilities. It takes care of three different things:

1. Manages the state of all the tasks and provides callbacks to add, edit, and delete tasks
2. Initializes the task list either from local storage or from the fixture
3. Displays all the tasks in a list, followed by the new task form

This is a lot of responsibility for a single component, and it could make sense to move a part of it (especially items 1 and 2) to a custom hook to simplify the overview of this component. However, we'll keep it as a single file for now, but this is one of the things that we recommend you change in future steps in this project. The file `src/task/TaskList.js` is implemented in the next listing.

Listing 13.10 `src/task/TaskList.js` in the simple task list

We use this function that returns the initial state as
an argument for the stateful hook. Remember that this
function will then only be invoked on the first render of
this component and not on subsequent re-renders.

```
import { useState, useEffect } from "react";
import Task from "./Task";
import TaskAdd from "./TaskAdd";
import initialState from "./fixture";
function getInitialState() {
  return (
    JSON.parse(localStorage.getItem("task-manager-items-list")) ||
      initialState
  );
}
function TaskList() {
  const [tasks, setTasks] = useState(getInitialState);
  useEffect(() => {
    localStorage.setItem(
      "task-manager-items-list",
      JSON.stringify(tasks)
    );
  }, [tasks]);
  const addTask = (title) =>
    setTasks((ts) => ts.concat(
      [{ id: Math.random() * 1000000, title }]
    ));
  const editTask = (id, title) =>
    setTasks((ts) => ts.map(
      (task) =>
        (task.id === id ? { ...task, title } : task)
    ));
  const deleteTask = (id) => setTasks(
    (ts) => ts.filter((task) => task.id !== id)
  );
  return (
    <ol className="lane">
      {tasks.map((task) => (
        <Task
          key={task.id}
          task={task}
          editTask={editTask}
          deleteTask={deleteTask}
        />
      ))}
      <TaskAdd addTask={addTask} />
    </ol>
  );
}
export default TaskList;
```

The initial state of the task list is a
parsed value from local storage if it
exists or the initial state as
returned by the fixture.

Adds an effect to store
the task list in local
storage every time the
task list changes

First, the first of three callbacks is
the function to add a new task. It
appends the argument to the task
list using the update function.

Second, the callback to edit a task
maps the entire task list to a new
array and updates the relevant
task as it loops over all the items.

Third, the callback to delete a
task filters the existing task list to
remove the now-irrelevant task.

Two callbacks are passed
to a task component for
each task in the list of
all tasks.

Finally, the new task
form is added at the
end of the list.

13.2.5 *Running the application*

Let's see this in action in figure 13.9 and then start creating some tasks that we can delete later.

Figure 13.9 **The first iteration of our application that actually works. We can create, delete, and edit tasks.**

13.3 *Homework: Task steps and progress*

The goal for this step is to complete the following:

- Add an ordered list of *"completable"* steps inside each task.
- At the bottom of the list, always include an input field to allow the user to add a new item to the end of the list.
- For each step in the list, add a checkbox to mark the step as completed or not, as well as a button to delete the step.
- Allow the user to hide and show the steps of a task (hidden by default).
- Summarize the completion of the task with a progress bar that shows the ratio of the steps in the task that have been completed. This progress bar should be visible even if the list of steps is hidden.

Here are a few hints to help you complete this objective:

1 While we could get away with keeping the state as a simple array maintained by a useState hook, we need more fine-grained control of the state now, so

convert the state to a reducer, and add actions for the different updates necessary, for example: `addTask`, `editTask`, `deleteTask`, `addStep`, `editStep`, and `deleteStep`.

2 You might also want to wrap the task list in a context provider to make access to the preceding actions easier inside nested components.

3 To add a progress bar, use the `<progress />` HTML element. It's simple to use and already styled in the existing CSS file in the scaffold.

4 To display a list of steps with a checkbox, use the proper semantic HTML elements for all of those things (`<ol />`, `<li />`, `<label />`, and `<input type="checkbox" />` would be a good start).

5 Adding a new step requires a form with an input and a button. That should be pretty straightforward at this point.

Of course, we want you to work from your existing application that you developed in the previous step, but if you want to start from our solution to that step, you can do so by checking out this application in `rq13-list`. Once completed, feel free to compare your solution to ours.

Repository: rq13-steps

This example can be seen in repository `rq13-steps`. You can use that repository by creating a new app based on the associated template:

```
$ npx create-react-app rq13-steps --template rq13-steps
```

Alternatively, you can go to this website to browse the code, see the application in action directly in your browser, or download the source code as a zip file:

https://rq2e.com/rq13-steps

13.4 *Homework: Prioritization of steps*

The goal for this step is to complete the following:

- Add a button to rename a step inside a task.
- Add buttons to reprioritize the steps inside each task.

Here are a few hints to help you complete this objective:

1 If you didn't already convert the data structure to a reducer rather than a simple state array in the previous step, you definitely want to do so now. Moving elements in an array isn't too complex, but remember that you have to create a new array every time; you can never mutate the existing one. That's why it can be nice to centralize and organize the functionality in a reducer function.

2 Allowing a step to be renamed works exactly as allowing the overall task to be renamed—set a local state value that the text should be replaced with, and input and update the data using the provider once the input form is submitted.

3 Other than that, adding the three extra buttons next to each step and calling the right functions in the reducer should be a piece of cake at this point.

4 For added bonus and ease of development, consider this: All the functions to be invoked inside a single task (e.g., adding steps, moving steps, deleting steps, etc.) need the ID of the task to be able to reference the correct object in the overall task object. You might be able to use an additional provider around each single task that abstracts this task ID away from the individual calls inside the task itself.

Of course, we want you to work from your existing application that you developed in the previous step, but if you want to start from our solution to that step, you can do so by checking out this application in `rq13-steps`. Once completed, feel free to compare your solution to ours.

Repository: rq13-priority

This example can be seen in repository `rq13-priority`. You can use that repository by creating a new app based on the associated template:

```
$ npx create-react-app rq13-priority --template rq13-priority
```

Alternatively, you can go to this website to browse the code, see the application in action directly in your browser, or download the source code as a zip file:

https://rq2e.com/rq13-priority

13.5 Homework: Drag and drop

The goal for this step is to make the steps draggable inside each task. Here are a few hints to help you complete this objective:

1 Drag and drop can be implemented in two ways in HTML. You can either use the built-in functionality in HTML5 with the `draggable` attribute and the `dragstart`, `dragover`, `dragenter`, `dragleave`, and `drop` events (all of which are supported in React), or you can roll your own functionality using pure mouse events, for example, `mousedown`, `mousemove`, and `mouseup`.

2 Whichever way you go, this won't be an easy task to complete. There are many things to consider. For instance: If you start dragging element number 3 in a list, you have to be able to drop it into any other position in the list, including before the first item and after the last item. You must make sure that your application supports this correctly.

3   You also have to update your reducer to allow moving a step to an arbitrary position inside the list of steps for the given task. A possible interface could be `moveStepTo({ taskId, step, position })`. In addition, consider the difference between moving a step to an earlier position in the list versus to a later position.

4   In the `rq13-dragging` application repository, we've used the HTML5 native drag-and-drop functionality. To have a place to drop an item when dragging a step around, we display new elements between all the existing steps in the list with an `onDrop` handler attached, so the user is able to drop the items there. Note that you also have to attach `onDragEnter`, `onDragLeave`, and `onDragOver` event handlers (where you prevent the default action, which is to not allow dropping) for an element to be considered a valid drop target.

5   Don't worry if you find this to be a difficult exercise. It is! Our implementation isn't particularly clean either, but it works and looks okay.

Of course, we want you to work from your existing application that you developed in the previous step, but if you want to start from our solution to that step, you can do so by checking out this application in `rq13-priority`. Once completed, feel free to compare your solution to ours.

Repository: rq13-dragging

This example can be seen in repository `rq13-dragging`. You can use that repository by creating a new app based on the associated template:

```
$ npx create-react-app rq13-dragging --template rq13-dragging
```

Alternatively, you can go to this website to browse the code, see the application in action directly in your browser, or download the source code as a zip file:

https://rq2e.com/rq13-dragging

13.6   *Conclusion*

This third project in the book is the most challenging yet. We gave you a solid foundation, but you still had to do a lot of engineering and apply a lot of common sense as well as computer science intuition to solve the steps.

This project is an example of a real-world project situation, including the iterated increase in complexity as well as utilizing useful and transferable React coding patterns. For this final project, you were definitely thrown into the deep end of the pool if you tried to go all the way and complete step 5. Sometimes, we need a push to go that extra mile—we might be mixing metaphors here, though.

Summary

- Breaking a design down into visual parts and then converting each part to a separate React component is a great practice that will come in handy often.
- Choosing between `useState` and `useReducer` can be difficult at times because the line between them is blurry, and it comes down to personal preference. In this project, we started out with `useState`, but moved to a reducer as things got more complex for convenience, even though we didn't strictly have to.
- The provider pattern is so versatile that we managed to use it again for this project, but in a slightly different way than earlier. Try to remember this pattern because it will often prove useful.
- Writing state updates can be tricky when you need to remember to keep objects and arrays immutable. Array manipulation can be especially tricky, moving elements around by copying all the elements to a new array in the correct order.
- Single events are easy to work with in React, but complex event patterns, such as drag and drop, are still annoyingly difficult to manage even in a nice system like React. This might become easier in the future, but for now, it's a lot of work.

index

A

\<a> tag 73
abstractions 7
Accessible Rich Internet Applications (ARIA)
  properties 131
action object 333
App component 55, 58, 67, 105, 109, 290, 365, 374
application data, storing in state 141–142
App root 55
App structure 68
ARIA (Accessible Rich Internet Applications)
  properties 131
autoplay attribute 94

B

Barklund, Morten 223
\<body> element 17
\<body> node 35
Booleans
  attribute values 95–96
  properties 95–96
  stateful 373
branching, in JSX 76–83
  early return 76–77
  extra components for complex branching 79–83
  logical operators 77–78
  switching 78–79
  ternary operator 77
build command 28

buttons
  form submission vs. button click 294–295
  radio buttons 297–298
  task manager project 412
  timer project
    generic button component 393
    HTML output 384

C

\<Captcha /> component 2
Cascading Style Sheets (CSS) 107, 200, 356
CBA (component-based architecture) 5–7, 42
checkboxes 297–298
checked property 297, 311
children property
  in JSX 74–75
  overview of 52–55
  website menu project 375–376
class attribute 94
class-based components
  conversion to functional components 121–134
  complexity and 133–134
  using constructor 131–133
  using render method 122–125
  using secondary method as utility only 125–128
  using secondary method with class access 128–131

life cycle of 210–212
  converting life cycle methods to hooks 211–212
  legacy life cycle methods 211
  life cycle methods 210–211
state 176–180
  differences from functional component process 179–180
  similarities with functional component process 178
classes
  class-based codebase 120
  implementation using 105–107
  libraries requiring class-based components 120–121
className attribute 94
colon-blinking class 384
comments, in JSX 83–84
community 9–10
component-based architecture (CBA) 5–7, 42
componentDidCatch method 120
componentDidUnmount() method 211
component effects 222
components
  class-based
    conversion to functional components 121–134
    life cycle of 210–212
    state 176–180

components *(continued)*
  custom
    in JSX 67–68
    in React 42–45
    with Boolean
      properties 95–96
  functional 103–135
    conversion from class-based
      components to 121–134
    menu example
      application 105–108
    state 143–176
    types of 116–119
    when not to use 119–121
  running effects in 183–201
    and cleanup on some
      renders 195–198
    on mount 185–187
    on mount, and cleanup on
      unmount 187–190
    on some renders 192–194
    on unmount 190–191
    synchronously 198–201
  state 215–222
    creating complex state 216
    low-priority state
      updates 221–222
    multicomponent state
      220–221
    remembering value without
      re-rendering 216–220
    simple state values 216
  task manager project 405,
      409–410
  timer project
    component hierarchy
      385–386, 391
    generic button component
      393
    time display component 394
    timer component 395
  website menu project
    dynamic menu 365
    optional link 374–376
    retrieving items from
      context 368
    scaffolding for 354
    static menu 361–362
Consumer component 326–327
Context.Provider
  component 368
controlled form inputs 275–303
  checkboxes 297–298
  extra properties 302–303
  filtered input 277–280

form submission 289–295
  many similar inputs 282–289
  masked input 280–282
  multiline inputs 301–302
  numeric inputs 296–297
  radio buttons 297–298
  select boxes 299–301
  uncontrolled vs. 274–275
Countdown component 76
CRA (create-react-app) tool
  24–32, 66, 107, 355
  file structure 29
  project commands 27–29
  pros and cons of 31–32
  templates 30
createContext() function 326,
  367
createElement() parameter 41
CSS (Cascading Style
  Sheets) 107, 200, 356
.current property 218
custom components
  in JSX 67–68
  in React 42–45
  with Boolean properties
    95–96
custom hooks 225, 341–348

D

dangerouslySetInnerHTML
  property 91
data- attributes 100
<datalist> element 303
data- prefix 100
<DatePicker /> component 2
DateTimeNow component 70
debugging hooks 224
declarative style 4–5
default actions 251–255
  default event action 252–253
  other default events 255
  preventing 253–254
default values 111–113
dispatch function 333
DisplayName component 326
<div> container 17
<div> node 17
<div h1> container 40
div HTML element 41
document events 260–263
DOM diffing 6
DOM (Document Object
  Model) 3, 33, 85
  creating stable identifiers 223

event handling 228–270
  combining React and DOM
    event handling 265–269
  listening to DOM events
    manually 260–269
  nonbubbling DOM
    events 251
  manipulating elements
    directly 207
  references to elements 220
dragenter event 419
dragleave event 419
dragover event 419
dragstart event 419
drop event 419
Dynamic SSR (server-rendered
  React) 14

E

early return 76–77
ecosystem of React 9–10
effect hook 183
effects 182–213
  life cycle methods 210–212
    converting to hooks
      211–212
    legacy 211
    overview of 210–211
  rendering 201–210
    inside functions 207–210
    on mount 202–203
    on parent render 203–205
    on state update 205–207
  running before
    rendering 225
  running in components
    183–201
    and cleanup on some
      renders 195–198
    on mount 185–187
    on mount, and cleanup on
      unmount 187–190
    on some renders 192–194
    on unmount 190–191
    synchronously 198–201
eject command 29
elements
  creating in JSX 66–67
  manipulating directly 207
  nesting 33–41
  references to 220
  self-closing 90
.elements collection 304
elements property 311

em element 36
EmptyMenu component 109
error boundaries 119–120
event handling 228–270
    default actions 251–255
        default event action
            252–253
        other default events 255
        preventing 253–254
    defining event handlers
        236–237
    event handler functions from
        properties 256–259
    event handler
        generators 259–260
    event objects 255
        access to native events 241
        consistency 240
        overview of 237–239
        performance 240
        synthetic event API 241
        synthetic event object
            persistence 241–243
    event phases and
        propagation 243–251
        handling event phases 250
        in browsers 247–250
        nonbubbling DOM
            events 251
        unusual event
            propagation 250
    events supported by
        React 234
    listening to DOM events
        manually 260–269
        combining React and
            DOM event handling
            265–269
        unsupported HTML
            events 263–265
        window and document
            events 260–263
    overview of 230–234
event objects 255
    access to native events 241
    consistency 240
    overview of 237–239
    performance 240
    synthetic event API 241
    synthetic event object
        persistence 241–243
event phases and propagation
    243–251
    handling event phases 250
    in browsers 247–250

nonbubbling DOM
    events 251
unusual event
    propagation 250
evt.target.valueAsNumber
    property 296

F

falsy values 78, 92
file inputs 310
file structure 29
filtered input 277–280
focus() method 224
for attribute 94
forms 272–311
    controlled inputs 275–303
        checkboxes 297–298
        extra properties 302–303
        filtered input 277–280
        form submission 289–295
        many similar inputs
            282–289
        masked input 280–282
        multiline inputs 301–302
        numeric inputs 296–297
        radio buttons 297–298
        select boxes 299–301
        uncontrolled vs. 274–275
    storing data in state 142
    timer project 385
    uncontrolled inputs 303–310
        controlled vs. 274–275
        file inputs 310
        opportunities for
            using 307–310
form submission
    button click vs. 294–295
    overview of 289–294
Fragment element 38, 86–87
fragments, in JSX 86–88
functional components
    103–135
    conversion from class-based
        components to 121–134
    complexity and 133–134
    using constructor
        131–133
    using render method
        122–125
    using secondary method as
        utility only 125–128
    using secondary method
        with class access
        128–131

menu example
    application 105–108
    default values 111–113
    destructuring properties
        109–111
    implementation using
        classes 105–107
    implementation using
        functions 107–108
    pass-through properties
        113–116
    rest syntax 114–116
state 143–176
    destructuring state value
        and setter 154–155
    importing and using
        hooks 146–148
    initializing state 148–154
    multiple states 169–171
    rules of hooks 146–148
    setting state 158–169
    state scope 172–176
    using state value 156–158
types of 116–119
    benefits of 117
    choosing 118–119
    disadvantages of 118
    nonfactors between 118
when not to use 119–121
    class-based codebase 120
    error boundaries 119–120
    libraries requiring class-
        based components
        120–121
    snapshots before updating
        121
functions
    event handler functions from
        properties 256–259
    implementation using
        107–108
    initializing state to 153–154
    memoizing 223
    rendering effects inside
        207–210
    setting state to 160–162

G

generatePassword() function
    152–153
getDerivedStateFromError
    method 119
getSnapshotBeforeUpdate built-
    in function 121

H

<h1> node 35–36, 67, 98
Header component 316
Hello World app 15–21
    going to local website 20–21
    installing and running web
        server 19
    output 16
    writing 16–19
hooks 214–226
    complex component
        libraries 225
    creating component
        APIs 223–224
    debugging hooks 224
    running effects before
        rendering 225
    synchronizing non-React
        data 224
    converting life cycle methods
        to 211–212
    custom hooks 341–348
        context access 372–373
        finding 348
        overview of 342–343
        when to use 343–347
    importing and using
        146–148
    key principles of 225
    minimizing re-rendering
        creating stable DOM
            identifiers 223
        memoizing functions 223
        memoizing values 223
    rules of 146–148
    scaling 313–349
    stateful components 215
        creating complex state 216
        low-priority state
            updates 221–222
        multicomponent state
            220–221
        remembering value with-
            out re-rendering
            216–220
        simple state values 216
href property 72, 114–115
HTML
    JavaScript and 64–66
    timer project 383–385
        button 384
        form 385
        form input 385
        number and unit 384

time parts 384
timer 384
timers 385
unsupported HTML
    events 263–265
website menu project 353,
    361
<html> node 35

I

icons
    task manager project 412
    website menu project 354–356
<img> nodes 35–36, 125
imperative style 4–5
initializer function 152–153
<input> element 297
internal state 5
isActive flag 185
isError Boolean flag 96
isMenuVisible 150
isRunning flag 198
isVisible property 147

J

JavaScript
    component-based
        architecture 5–7
    HTML and 64–66
Job-Ready React (Barklund) 223
JSON (JavaScript Object
    Notation) 287
JSX (JavaScript XML) 7, 31, 62–
    101, 108, 137, 182, 275, 382,
    405
    branching 76–83
        early return 76–77
        extra components for com-
            plex branching 79–83
        logical operators 77–78
        switching 78–79
        ternary operator 77
    comments 83–84
    creating elements 66–67
    custom components 67–68
    edge cases and oddities 89–
        100
        Boolean attribute
            values 95–96
        data- attributes 100
        multiword attributes 94–95
        reserved names 94
        self-closing elements 90

special characters 90–91
        string conversion 91–93
        style attribute 93–94
        whitespace 97–100
    fragments 86–88
    lists of objects 84–86
    multiline objects 69–70
    outputting variables 70–72
    properties 72–75
    reasons for using 63–66
    transpiling 89
JSX ref property 220

K

key property 85–87
KISS (keep it simple, stupid)
    principle 3

L

label property 72, 114–115
layout effect hook 199
life cycle methods 210–211
    converting to hooks 211–212
    legacy 211
Link component 43, 55, 58–59,
    72
links variable 368, 373
Link type 46
list items
    defining 365
    rendering 365
lists
    in JSX 84–86
    task manager project 407–417
        complete and stateful list of
            tasks 415
        component hierarchy
            409–410
        entire task 414
        fixture with default tasks 412
        goal of exercise 408–409
        icon button 412
        in action 417
        main application file 411
        new task form 415
        public interface for task
            folder 412
        source code 411–415
        task header 413
        updated project
            structure 410–411
logical and expression 92
logical operators, in JSX 77–78

M

\<main\> element 70, 98
Main component 316
main HTML element 41
many similar inputs 282–289
MapReduce software engineering model 341
masked input 280–282
max property 296
memoizing
functions 223
values 223
Menu component 105, 365, 367
MenuContext variable 368
menu example application 105–108
default values 111–113
destructuring properties 109–111
implementation using classes 105–107
implementation using functions 107–108
pass-through properties 113–116
rest syntax 114
in practice 114–115
property ordering and 116
MenuItem component 114, 361, 365
MenuItem instances 363, 365–366
MenuItem.js component 363
Menu.js component 363
min property 296
multiline inputs 301–302
multiline objects, in JSX 69–70
multiword attributes 94–95
MVC (Model-View-Controller) 5
MyContext.Consumer property 210, 326
MyContext.Provider property 326

N

NameContext context 341
name property 286–289
NaN (Not a Number) 92, 154
\<nav\> component 361
nested context 327–330
nesting elements 33–41
node hierarchy 35–36
siblings 38–41
simple nesting 36–38

node hierarchy 35–36
Not a Number (NaN) 92, 154
npm (Node Package Manager) alternatives 26
npm start command 26
npx (node package runner) tool 25
numeric inputs 296–297

O

Object.isFrozen() method 46
onChange event handler 278, 311
onChange property 276–277, 311
onClick event 7
onDragEnter event handler 420
onDragLeave event handler 420
onDragOver event handler 420
onDrop handler 420
onSubmit callback 302
\<option\> element 84, 300

P

\<p\> node 9, 35–36
package.json 29
partially server-rendered web applications 11
passive state 217
pass-through properties 113–116
pnpm package manager 26
\<pre\> element 287
ProfileLink dynamic component 72
prop drilling 319
properties 45–55
children property
in JSX 74–75
overview of 52–55
website menu project 375–376
destructuring 109–111
event handler functions from 256–259
in JSX 72–75
multiple 48–52
name property 286–289
ordering 112–113
pass-through properties 113–116
single 46–48
props object 109

R

radio buttons 297–298
React 1–61
advantages of 2–10
ecosystem and community 9–10
simplicity 3–8
speed and testability 8–9
application structure 55–60
create-react-app tool 24–32
file structure 29
project commands 27–29
pros and cons of 31–32
templates 30
custom components 42–45
disadvantages of 10
effects 182–213
forms 272–311
functional components 103–135
Hello World app 15–21
going to local website 20–21
installing and running web server 19
output 16
writing 16–19
hooks 214–226
nesting elements 33–41
node hierarchy 35–36
siblings 38–41
simple nesting 36–38
project examples in book 32–33
properties 45–55
children property 52–55
multiple 48–52
single 46–48
scaling 313–349
single-page applications 10–13
stack 13–15
state 136–181
React API 320, 350
React boilerplate 30
React.Component class 43
React Context API 210, 319–320, 326–330
composition 327
consuming 326–327
nested 327–330
states 323–325

React Context API *(continued)*
  website menu project 367–368
    accessing context value 368
    creating context
        provider 368
    custom hook for context
        access 372–373
    dedicated context
        provider 373–374
    defining context 367–368
    object as context value 372
React.createElement()
    statements 65
React Developer Tools 164
ReactDOM.createRoot()
    method 18
ReactDOM.createRoot().ren-
    der() method 38
React.Fragment component 40
React Quickly 32
readOnly Boolean attribute 95
reconciliation of state and
    view 6
reducer function 333
reducing state 216
RemoteDropdown
    component 202
render() method 43, 45
render props 202, 209, 326
reserved names 94
rest syntax
    in practice 114–115
    overview of 114
    property ordering and 116
rest variable 115
root ID 17
root.render() method 18
rq02-custom-links repository 45
rq02-link-props repository 50
rq02-links-app-alt repository 59
rq02-links-app repository 57
rq02-links-children
    repository 54
rq02-nesting-italic repository 37
rq02-nesting repository 32, 34
rq02-siblings-div repository 39
rq02-siblings-fragment
    repository 40
rq03-alert repository 96
rq03-bad-whitespace
    repository 97
rq03-cart-multi repository 82
rq03-cart-single repository 81
rq03-children repository 75
rq03-correct-select repository 86

rq03-dog-breeds repository 88
rq03-good-whitespace
    repository 100
rq03-jsx-links repository 69
rq03-naive-select repository 85
rq04-gallery-class-v1 repository
    123
rq04-gallery-class-v2 repository
    126
rq04-gallery-class-v3 repository
    129
rq04-gallery-class-v4 repository
    132
rq04-gallery-function-v1
    repository 124
rq04-gallery-function-v2
    repository 127
rq04-gallery-function-v3
    repository 130
rq04-gallery-function-v4
    repository 133
rq04-menu-class repository 107
rq04-menu-default repository
    112
rq04-menu-destruct repository
    110
rq04-menu-function repository
    108
rq04-menu-rest repository 115
rq05-accordion repository 159
rq05-bad-todo repository 167
rq05-calculator repository 162
rq05-filter-todo repository 171
rq05-functional-counter
    repository 145
rq05-nice-todo repository 175
rq05-proper-todo repository 169
rq05-reset-counter repository
    163
rq05-triple-counter repository
    150
rq06-blog-title repository 193
rq06-countdown repository 198
rq06-dice-roller repository 205
rq06-email-input repository 194
rq06-push-button2
    repository 209
rq06-push-button repository 208
rq06-remote-dropdown
    repository 186
rq06-stopwatch repository 189
rq07-double-counter
    repository 220
rq09-address repository 285
rq09-color repository 279

rq09-controlled-sum repository
    276
rq09-natural-sum repository 305
rq09-smart-address
    repository 289
rq09-ticket-no repository 282
rq09-todo repository 294, 296
rq10-border-context
    repository 332
rq10-counter-reducer
    repository 334
rq10-dashboard-admin
    repository 325
rq10-dashboard-context
    repository 322
rq10-dashboard-props
    repository 318
rq10-reducer-load
    repository 339
rq11-context repository 369,
    376
rq11-dynamic repository 367–368
rq11-profile repository 377
rq11-scaffold repository 357
rq11-static repository 360, 366
rq12-initialize repository 398
rq12-multiple repository 399
rq12-playpause repository 393,
    397
rq12-reset repository 398–399
rq12-scaffold repository 387,
    393
rq13-dragging repository 420
rq13-list repository 411
rq13-priority repository 419
rq13-scaffold repository 406
rq13-steps repository 418

S

scalable vector graphics
    (SVGs) 94, 354, 405
scaling 313–349
    complex state 333–341
    custom hooks 341–348
        finding 348
        overview of 342–343
        when to use 343–347
    interdependent state 335–341
    React context 319–320,
        326–330
        composition 327
        consuming 326–327
        nested 327–330
        states 323–325

<script> element 17–18
<section> node 35–36
section HTML element 41
<select> element 84
select boxes 299–301
Select component 84
self-closing elements 90
SEO (search engine
    optimization) 8
set* prefix 155
setCounter function 143
setSeconds variable 189
setState method 180
setter function 158–169, 344
sibling elements 38–41
simplicity of React 3–8
    abstractions 7–8
    component-based architec-
        ture 5–7
    declarative vs. imperative
        style 4–5
snapshots 121
SPAs (single-page applications)
    10–13
special characters 90–91
speed of React 8–9
src property 125
SSG (Static site generators) 14
stack 13–15
start command 28
startTime property 395
state 136–181, 215–222
    class-based components
        176–180
        differences from functional
            component process
            179–180
        similarities with functional
            component process
            178
    complex state
        creating 216
        scaling 333–341
    functional components
        143–176
        destructuring state value
            and setter 154–155
        importing and using
            hooks 146–148
        initializing state 148–154
        multiple states 169–171
        rules of hooks 146–148
        setting state 158–169
        state scope 172–176
        using state value 156–158

information to avoid storing
    in 142
information to store in
    141–142
    application data 141–142
    form data 142
    UI state 142
interdependent state 335–341
low-priority state updates
    221–222
multicomponent state 220–221
overview of 139
React context 323–325
reconciliation of 6
reducing 216
remembering value without
    re-rendering 216–220
    passive state values 217–220
    references to DOM
        elements 220
    rendering effects on state
        update 205–207
    manipulating DOM ele-
        ments directly 207
    storing higher-level
        information 206
    simple state values 216
    where to put 139–140
stateful components 137–138
stateless components 137–138
state value
    destructuring 154–155
    passive 217–220
    using 156–158
static value, setting state to
    158–159
step property 296
string conversion 91–93
style attribute 93–94
StyleContext context 348
SVGs (scalable vector
    graphics) 94, 354, 405
switching, in JSX 78–79
switch statement 79
synchronizing non-React
    data 224
syntactic sugar 7, 63
synthetic events
    API 241
    object persistence 241–243

T

tabular numbers 387
TaskAdd component 410

Task component 409
TaskHeader component 409
Task instances 173
TaskList component 405, 409
task manager project 401–421
    component hierarchy 405
    drag and drop 419–420
    list of tasks 408–417
        component hierarchy
            409–410
        goal of exercise 408–409
        in action 417
        source code 411–415
        updated project
            structure 410–411
    prioritization of steps
        418–419
    project structure 405
    running app 408
    source code 406–407
        main application 406
        task list 407
    task steps and progress
        417–418
templates
    overview of 30
    website menu project 357
ternary operator, in JSX 77
testability of React 8–9
test command 28
thick clients 12
this.props object 46
this.state class member 178
TimerManager component
    388
timer project 379–400
    adding play/pause
        timer 390–396
        component hierarchy 391
        generic button
            component 393
        goal of exercise 390–391
        in browser 396
        number and unit
            display 394
        precision 391
        source code 393–395
        time display
            component 394
        timer component 395
        timer manager 393
        updated project
            structure 392–393
    component hierarchy
        385–386

timer project *(continued)*
 HTML output 383–385
  button 384
  form 385
  form input 385
  number and unit 384
  time parts 384
  timer 384
  timers 385
 initializing timer to custom
   time 397
 multiple timers 398–399
 project structure 386–387
 resetting timers 398
 source code 387–389
  in browser 390
  individual timer 389
  main application 388
  stylesheet 387–388
  timer manager 388–389
title property 72
TodoApplication
   component 172, 176
toggle function 344
transpiling, in JSX 89
truthy value 78

U

UI state 142
UIs (user interfaces) 42, 64, 191
uncontrolled form inputs
   303–310
 controlled vs. 274–275
 file inputs 310
 opportunities for using
   307–310
updaters, setting state 160
url property 48, 72
use* hook 146
useCallback hook 223
useContext hook 210, 220–221,
   319–320, 323, 326, 341,
   367–368, 372
useCounter hook 146, 346–347
useDebugValue hook 224

useDeferredValue hook 221–222
useEffect hook 152, 183–184,
   191, 199, 201, 211–213
useForm hook 344–345
useId hook 223
useImperativeHandle
   hook 223–224
useInsertionEffect hook 225
useLayoutEffect hook 199, 201
useLoader hook 345–346
useMemo hook 133, 223
useName hook 342
useReducer API 333
useReducer hook
 interdependent state 336–341
 overview of 216
useRef hook 216–220
useState hook 137, 146–147,
   154–155, 157, 169, 179, 181,
   189, 216–217, 333, 343–344,
   349, 373, 417
useState React package 143
useState setter 221
useSyncExternalStore hook 224
useToggle hook 343–344
useTransition hook 221–222

V

valueAsNumber property 296
value property 74, 276–277, 311,
   349, 368
ValueProvider component 374
variables, outputting in JSX
   70–72
view, reconciliation of 6
virtual DOM 6

W

website menu project 350–378
 dynamic menu 364–367
  component hierarchy 365
  defining list items 365
  goal for step 364–365
  rendering list items 365

optional link 370–377
 children property 375–376
 component hierarchy 376
 converting part of component to separate
   component 374–375
 custom hook for context
   access 372–373
 dedicated context
   provider 373–374
 goal for step 370
 object as context value 372
 stateful Boolean 373
 retrieving items from
   context 367–368
  accessing context value 368
  component hierarchy 368
  creating context
    provider 368
  defining context 367–368
  goal for step 367
 scaffolding for 353–359
  component hierarchy 354
  CSS 356
  HTML output 353
  icons 354–356
  in browser 359
  source code 358–359
  template 357
 static menu 360–364
  component tree 361–362
  desired HTML output 361
  goal of exercise 361
  in browser 364
  source code 363
whitespace 97–100
widgets 11
window events 260–263
window.ReactDOM global
   object 17
window.React global object 17

Y

yarn command 26
Yarn package manager 26